POLICE EXAM PREP

SEVENTH EDITION

Our 80 years' expertise = Your competitive advantage

4 PRACTICE TESTS + PROVEN STRATEGIES

The FrontLine National™ Test for Law Enforcement is a product of Ergometrics and the National Testing Network.

Published by Kaplan Publishing, a division of Kaplan, Inc.
1515 W Cypress Creek Road
Fort Lauderdale, FL 33309

ISBN: 978-1-5062-7648-9
10 9 8 7 6 5 4 3 2 1

PART ONE: INTRODUCTION

PART TWO: SKILLS

Introduction

CHAPTER 1

Police Careers

Congratulations! You have taken the first steps toward securing a career in law enforcement. By purchasing this book, you have demonstrated a commitment to stand alongside thousands of others who have entered this challenging and rewarding field. By choosing Kaplan's *Police Exams Prep,* you have guaranteed yourself tough, effective preparation that will guide you to success on your exam.

A career in law enforcement has become more complex in recent years as new and varied threats to the safety of our communities arise. However, the core of police work remains the same. Police agencies are always looking for men and women who can effectively serve their fellow citizens. Service to one's community is an honorable calling—the term "public servant" is interchangeable with police officer. In the past, "customer service" was not always stressed as much as it is today. Now, agencies are increasingly looking for those who can communicate effectively and provide their clients with exceptional service.

Read on to find out more about the exciting and ever-changing career that awaits you!

HIERARCHY OF DUTIES

First, let's go into the levels of responsibility a typical police officer faces on the job. No matter what state or county you reside in, the following will apply to you and your team.

First: Help anyone in danger

When it comes to policing, the first priority is to protect the lives of citizens. As a police officer, always keep at the forefront of your mind that your primary duty is to protect life—no matter who you are helping and what situation you encounter. All officers have an obligation and must swear to protect the lives of victims, bystanders, suspects, and offenders—and of course their own lives as well as the lives of fellow officers.

Second: Secure public order

Police officers are also responsible for preserving the peace and maintaining public order on a daily basis. Officers must also maintain the peace during special events such as parades, sports, political events, and other community functions. When a law enforcement team secures public order and preserves the peace, demonstrations and rallies then remain orderly and lawful and a sense of safety and security is maintained. If a riot threatens, officers need to do everything they can to defuse the situation. Any acts of aggression or destruction must be stopped, without inciting further action.

Third: Uphold the law

To uphold the law and prevent crime is of course a main function for police officers. Understanding the law and how to apply it to difficult situations may not always be easy. At any given time, an officer must be trained in how to assess the situation, determining what laws may apply. Protecting crime scenes is also a crucial part of upholding the law: officers must know how to preserve evidence in order to assist in the investigation that will lead to an arrest, prosecution, and conviction of a guilty party. However, the crime scene should only be protected once it is deemed safe and clear by the officers at the scene.

Fourth: Customer service—help those needing assistance

A healthy percentage of a police officer's calls may be service related. These types of calls are usually not crime related, and the public is looking for the officer to help them in whatever situation arises. These calls could range from medical assistance, traffic accidents with or without injuries, a lost child, mediation between neighbors, and even directions to tourists. You will also be required to respond appropriately to people who can't adequately care for themselves and require your help. These can include the elderly, children, the mentally or physically disabled, the homeless, and others in similar situations.

Social service calls play a huge role in law enforcement, and the responding police officer must be prepared to serve as the "face" of the department.

Fifth: Tend to your beat or patrol area

As any police officer will tell you, the job isn't as well plotted as a TV series. In real life, you don't get a weekly jolt of heart-stopping drama. Most of your job consists of keeping an eye on your little piece of the world. This is especially true now, as community policing becomes more and more widespread. The beat or patrol officer should act as a liaison between the community and the department. Enforcing quality of life (QOL) issues not only helps build trust between the officer and the community, but can also help reduce or prevent criminal behavior.

Getting to know the people within an officer's community is crucial. This will help the flow and exchange of information that is needed for the officer to properly do his or her job. The officer can quickly learn what "normal" looks like, and can spot anything that's out of place. Is there anyone around who looks like he or she doesn't belong? A light on in a store at a time when the owner's not usually there? If you want to know about what's going on in the neighborhood, who do you go to?

Sixth: Maintain a sense of ethics

As a police officer, your day-to-day interactions with people of all races, nationalities, and diverse beliefs reflect not only on you, but your agency and all other police officers as well. Ethical issues aren't easy to prioritize, but keep some of the basics in mind as you make decisions.

Remember your oath to serve

You have made a commitment to perform certain duties; you are expected to respond, as an officer of the law, in any situation that requires law enforcement assistance. Police officers work under the motto "To Serve and Protect," and this concept of helping and serving the public should not be taken lightly and should never be lost in your moral compass as a police officer.

Avoid even the appearance of corruption

This is one of the hot-button areas of law enforcement. Police corruption, or the suspicion of it, has set off more investigations and ruined more careers than any other single issue. Don't put yourself in the neighborhood of this accusation. Follow your conscience and remember your oath of service; this should help you navigate through those tough decisions.

Don't play favorites

As you work a beat, you will inevitably develop opinions and attitudes about the people you see regularly. It's just human nature. You are going to like some of these folks, and others are going to drive you up a wall. You can't help that, but you also can't let your personal feelings influence your responses. All people are entitled to equal treatment under the law—even really irritating people.

Remember, police officers must learn how to use a lot of discretion and use it wisely. Your ability to do so will result in strengthening your own personal judgment and adherence to the laws and rules that you must follow. As an officer, you must encounter the public for all different reasons. Ultimately, try to remember that you are representing your department at all times, and that the purpose of every encounter is to protect the public.

CAREER OPPORTUNITIES

The most demanding and probably the most rewarding job in a police agency is the police officer. This role is extremely important because it is a "front-line" position. As a front-line officer you are the most crucial in affecting people's lives and responding to their needs. The vast majority of the time, you will be a decision maker responsible for choices that influence the lives and welfare

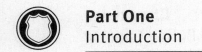
of the citizens you serve. These decisions may be life-changing for all involved, and you will be expected to make them without the benefit of counsel from others. Such a great amount of responsibility makes this career very demanding and rewarding. It is also why those who make law enforcement a career tend to stay for a long time and feel a great sense of accomplishment.

The career descriptions that follow are fairly general; the specific details for the department you are interested in will vary depending on your location.

General police patrol

Whether riding in a patrol car or walking a post (beat) in an urban setting, you are the first responder for those who need assistance. This is where you gain the most diverse experience in dealing with a wide variety of people in an endless array of circumstances and incidents. General patrol work can also include enforcing vehicle and traffic laws.

Besides general patrol, there are many types of patrol that can be particularly challenging and rewarding. These types of patrols can also be highly sought after by officers within the department. For instance, one of the most popular types of patrol is bicycle patrol—these positions are not only extremely effective, but also one of the most growing and popular patrols that police departments across the country use.

Mounted and K-9 patrols are also being deployed throughout the country. Even small departments realize the importance and advantages of K-9 patrol and its effectiveness at investigating narcotics, bombs, evidence, and search and rescue efforts. Mounted police can also be found in various departments, including city police departments. Horses are great for crowd control as well as parks, rough terrain, and mountainous regions.

Other types of patrol include harbor and aviation. Police departments deploy all sorts of patrols that are beneficial to them and the communities they serve.

Investigators, detectives, and plainclothes officers

Police officers who work as investigators, detectives, and plainclothes officers are considered the "next level" in a police department's organizational chain. In some departments, these positions are considered a promotion. In other departments, they are considered a reassignment or lateral transfer from the uniform function. In this second case, the assignment may only be temporary before you are returned to uniform patrol. This position sometimes involves the investigation of higher-grade crimes or the follow-up work needed to solve crimes or resolve incidents. Duties include conducting preliminary and follow-up investigations, preparing the required investigative reports, identifying and apprehending the suspect, and preparing a case for a successful prosecution.

A relatively new area of responsibility for detectives is counter-terrorism investigation. Detectives may be responsible not just for investigating potential terrorist threats, but also for conducting threat assessments and providing input on how to secure locations from potential terrorist attack. Detectives also may have to coordinate local efforts with federal personnel who specialize in counter-terrorism.

Management positions

Usually the first step into management is the first-line supervisor position, which may be a sergeant, a corporal, or a senior patrol officer. These are vital leaders who ensure that jobs are getting done. They also provide valuable training and guidance for patrol officers. There also may be further advancement opportunities, depending on the size of the department. Middle-management positions can include the ranks of lieutenant and captain. The scope widens at this level with more responsibilities that may include managing more personnel at the scene of more serious crimes and incidents, as well as facility management and budgeting.

On the Beat

"The patrolman should walk with purpose, energetically and on the alert, avoiding the appearance of one who has nothing to do but put in time. His movement should be unhurried, even while apprehending a criminal unless there is something definite to be gained by speed; a running policeman will attract a crowd quickly. The patrolman should ordinarily patrol to the left, that is, with his shield to the curb. This is done for the reason that superior officers patrol to the right and, therefore, can more readily find the patrolman.

"Patrolling should never under any circumstances be reduced to a habit so that the patrolman is ordinarily at a given spot at a given time; the patrol should be irregular. The competent beat patrolman stops occasionally and casually looks back to observe what is going on. He cuts through alleys, yards, and private passageways; he retraces his steps. At night, he occasionally stands in dark spots in order to scrutinize closely all passersby. Patrolling after dark is ordinarily done along the property line in order to try more readily doors and windows. The patrolman keeps on the outside in patrolling a crowded thoroughfare so that he may be seen. That is the reason the patrolman wears a uniform; its presence distinctly acts as a deterrent to crime …

"Patrolling a beat properly is both a science and an art. Improper and incompetent patrolling is a nuisance to the public and a cause of unhappiness and dissatisfaction to the beat patrolman.

"The outstanding patrolman knows almost every person on his beat and has their unqualified confidence. They know him, they respect him, and they bring their troubles to him. Consequently, they admire him and look up to him. No reward is as rich in the esteem of one's fellow men. The work of the beat patrolman can bring that and, therefore, be full of happiness. The beat patrolman has the opportunity to reap rewards far beyond his monetary salary."

—from *Basic Police Procedure*, published by the Pennsylvania Chiefs of Police Association, 1940

Upper-management positions can include deputy chief, deputy superintendent, or deputy commissioner. Responsibilities may include department-wide planning, hiring, and larger-scale operations. Upper management also is responsible for creating and writing department policies and procedures. These upper-management positions report directly to the head of the agency (chief, commissioner, superintendent, or sheriff). The agency head is the person who must answer to criticism when things go wrong (such as a controversial police shooting) and the person who can take credit for all the positive accomplishments (such as a reduction in the crime rate).

Besides upper management, there is also a rank structure that can be found in most police departments, which consists of captain, lieutenant, and sergeant. Sergeants are usually known as front-line supervisors, where they help manage police officers and the daily patrol operations.

CHOOSING A LOCATION

As you go through the process of choosing the agency you want to work for, remember you most likely will be spending your entire career in that one department. Most police careers range from 20 to 25 years! There are many types of police departments and agencies to choose from, and deciding upon which agency fits you the best may not be an easy decision to make. There are many factors that go into this decision-making process when choosing the proper agency.

The larger the agency, the greater the number of opportunities that are available. Agencies such as the New York City Police Department, California Highway Patrol, and Chicago Police Department serve large populations over vast amounts of geography. These large agencies have crime labs; SWAT teams; K-9, aviation, and marine units; and computer crime specialists. Their resources and missions are usually more diverse and greater than those of the small-town 10-member police departments. Or perhaps you are looking for a smaller department to increase local community interaction and have a closer personal relationship with the people in town, which you might not get in larger cities. All police agencies, regardless of size, provide a highly valued service to society and need to employ consummate, dedicated police professionals.

You also need to ask yourself: What are your interests and goals? Does the agency you want to work for offer different assignments and opportunities for promotion? Then there are the specialized agencies and departments that may fit your personality or interest.

If you live in an area geographically surrounded by woods, mountains, hunting facilities, or parks, then perhaps being a conservation or parks police officer may interest you. If you live near the ocean, maybe beach patrol or a harbor unit is something for you to think about. There are transit police for trains and transportation hubs, as well as sanitation police enforcing the laws for illegal dumping and protecting the environment.

Take a look at the following examples of two different police departments in the same state: one in Saratoga Springs, New York, and the other in New York City.

> **Saratoga Springs Police Department**
>
> The Saratoga Springs Police Department has 72 full-time officers who protect a population of more than 28,000 in a 28-square-mile area. The department has one captain and four lieutenants. There are 11 investigators who perform detective functions. To learn more about the Saratoga Springs Police Department, visit their website at **www.saratogapolice.org**.

> **New York City Police Department**
>
> The New York City Police Department employs 34,000 sworn members who protect a population of more than 8.5 million residents in a 322-square-mile area. The department has over 400 members of the elite Emergency Services Unit, which includes such specialties as SWAT and K-9. The Harbor Unit includes a Scuba Team of 30 divers and also deploys 27 marine vessels. There are approximately 750 captains and more than 1,500 lieutenants. To learn more about the NYPD, visit their website at **www.nyc.gov/nypd**.

Note that this is not meant to compare the value of the work in these two departments. The officers in Saratoga Springs do important work and so do the folks in the NYPD. But if your fondest dream is to fly a police helicopter, Saratoga Springs may not be the place for you. Decide what you want out of your career and take that into consideration when deciding where to pursue your police work.

PREPARE YOURSELF

You have already taken a big step toward becoming a police officer: you've been proactive, seeking out this book to make yourself a better candidate. This book is unique among all the police exam prep books out there because we recognize the basic fact that police exams differ from city to city. A prep book that focuses only on the New York City test will not be the best preparation for a candidate seeking work in Seattle, and vice versa. Seems obvious, right? But most police prep books focus on only one test.

A serious candidate needs serious, rigorous preparation for whatever may appear on the test he or she faces. That's why we rolled up our sleeves and really dug into the released sample tests from multiple major police forces. We examined exactly what types of questions were asked and compared the exams against each other. Then we created practice tests and materials for you that provide coverage of the toughest questions you are likely to face. Once you finish working with this book, you will be well prepared for any police exam.

To learn more about how to find employment opportunities with police departments throughout the United States, as well as what the application process is like, turn to chapter 2.

CHAPTER 2

The Application Process

This chapter reviews in detail all the steps of the application process. It's important to know that the application process is not the same as being hired. You will usually have to pass each step before you can proceed and have the job you want. Remember, this is a general guide; you should always review the process specific to the police department to which you are applying. You may consider applying to numerous departments.

FINDING JOB OPENINGS

Before you can apply for a job, you have to know that one is available. Fortunately, most police departments have websites. With access to the Internet, you also have access to all the recruitment postings and job openings available within the department you are interested in. If you don't know the website address for the department you are interested in, use any search engine and type in "[city's name] police department." Once at the website, you should look for keywords such as *jobs*, *careers*, *employment*, and *recruitment*.

If you do not have access to the Internet, you should call your local police department (you will find the number in the government pages of the phone book), go to your local library, or check your local newspaper or community bulletin board for job openings. In larger cities, such as New York, you may even see billboards and posters for upcoming recruitment drives. Today, many departments will also set up recruitment drives at shopping malls and on college campuses.

Because police tests are extremely competitive, it is recommended that you take as many police exams as possible. Some of the bigger departments that hire on a regular basis may give the test more frequently throughout the year. However, other agencies, such as smaller departments and specialized agencies, may only offer the test once every few years or so.

This is where you need to explore and decide on different agencies that may interest you.

- What will you do if you find out the department you really want to join doesn't offer another test for 2 or even 4 years?

- What if your preferred agency institutes a hiring freeze before you can complete the application process?

That is why we recommend you find other agencies and jurisdictions that interest you and take as many tests as you possibly can.

- First, see what departments are hiring when you want to start—you want to get your police career off the ground, and waiting a few years to get hired can be stressful.

- If you get hired by a department that's not your first choice, you can still take other exams and transfer to the department you want. Depending on the department, you may be able to transfer your seniority, retirement package, and investments like 401(k) plans. Even if you cannot transfer to your preferred department right away, at least you will gain police experience and skills that will make you a more appealing prospect for other departments in the future.

- Even if you are working for a department that was not your initial choice, you may grow to love the department and want to stay. Once you form a bond with your colleagues, you might realize that your initial impression of the department was inaccurate. By staying in the same department, you might also find yourself a few steps closer to opportunities for specialty units and promotions.

Many police agencies have walk-in examinations. The New York City Police Department (NYPD) offers a walk-in exam in some locations, such as on college campuses. It is usually limited to "first come, first served" candidates. The San Francisco Police Department gives an exam every month. All you need for these walk-ins is some form of valid identification and/or a driver's license. Check the announcements on the respective department websites for details.

MINIMUM REQUIREMENTS

Minimum requirements vary depending on the department in which you hope to work. Some possible types of requirements are:

- **Citizenship.** Most departments require applicants to be citizens of the United States by the time of hiring.

- **Age.** Age requirements for prospective applicants can vary. The age requirement for taking the test can be lower than the age for hiring. The New York City Police Department applicants can file for the exam at 17.5 years old. Most agencies require applicants to be 21 years old at the time of actual hiring. The upper limit can also vary. The NYPD upper limit is 35 years old. There may be further allowance for military experience. Some police departments have abandoned this upper limit.

- **Education.** In most cases, a high school diploma or GED is required. Many agencies now require college credits (60 hours for the NYPD and the New York State Police [NYSP]). Some agencies will accept military experience in lieu of college credits.

- **Licensure.** A current, valid driver's license is usually required.

- **Convictions.** Applicants should *not* have any felony convictions or dishonorable discharges from the military. You should also take into account that your driving record may come under scrutiny as well, even though it probably will not disqualify you. You will be asked how many violations you have, whether they were paid, and whether your license was ever suspended as part of your background check.

- **Vision/health.** Generally, applicants are required to have good or correctable vision, to have a reasonable height/weight ratio, and to not take illegal drugs.

You should also expect to be subjected to a background check and drug test. The specifics of these screenings depend upon the jurisdiction where you are applying. However, you should expect the department to access your school records and any criminal records related to you. The department might also interview your family members and friends. And if you have any social media accounts, be aware of this: departments are now checking your social media accounts and analyzing your behavior and posts to get a better sense of your character. Putting up certain posts and pictures may be fun and get some laughs, but depending on the content, they may also hurt you in the long run. Exercise caution and good judgment every time you present yourself to the world, because that is what you'll be required to do as a police officer.

FILLING OUT THE APPLICATION

Whether filling out an application online or submitting a written version, make sure it is *accurate, complete, legible*, and *free from spelling and grammar errors*! This application is actually the beginning of your background investigation. It is the first impression the agency will have of you!

We really can't say it enough: do not forget to proofread the whole application. Check your spelling and grammar. If you are not sure about something, look it up. Have someone else read what you have written to make sure it makes sense.

Something you should always strive for regardless of the type of application you complete is honesty. *Don't try to hide anything on your application.* Tell the truth. If there is a gap in your work record because you took three months off to hike the Appalachian Trail, that's fine. Or what if you dropped out of high school and drifted for a while before you got back on track and went back for your GED? Recruiters know they are dealing with human beings with different life situations.

You should try to build a relationship or rapport with your recruiter (sometimes known as your investigator). An investigator assigned to you will understand that people go through different stages in life. As long as you are a decent person without any prior convictions, he or she will help you through the process. The investigator may instruct you on certain information to provide, such as previous and present employment and college or military transcripts and documents.

Your relationship with your investigator should be on a professional level—keep it friendly and not confrontational. The investigator may need to call you back in several times for clarification on certain matters or gaps in dates, but do not see this as a negative sign. This is part of the job to get you processed to be hired. Remember, this is not an ordinary job—your background and character count.

Once you have submitted your application, you just have to wait. Most departments will notify you when they receive your application. Even if they don't, have patience! Some agencies process thousands of applicants. The application itself should state what you will hear and when.

PHYSICAL TEST/PRELIMINARY MEDICAL REVIEW

Many departments will conduct a preliminary medical review, which includes vision and hearing tests and height/weight ratios, when you show up for the physical agility testing segment of the application process. (If you successfully complete all the steps of the entire hiring process, you may undergo a more extensive medical examination prior to being offered a job, and usually there is a pre- and post-examination.) During your medical examination, you may be put on hold for further review.

If you are not physically fit during these examinations or do not meet the physical standards, you may be disqualified at this point in the hiring phase. If you don't already have some sort of physical fitness routine, start one immediately. Law enforcement agencies want people who have adopted a lifestyle of fitness; fit officers are more productive and have fewer injuries.

Your primary task is usually to pass a specific physical test. You should start immediately by researching what your specific test will entail and then training for those specific events. Agencies will require you to adhere strictly to the test protocols. If you are required to do 40 sit-ups in one minute, being able to do 100 crunches is meaningless unless you can do the 40 sit-ups.

The specific test you will have to pass will depend on the program, but almost all of them include most or all of the following:

- **Distance run.** You will have to run a certain distance. Many programs use the 40th or 50th percentile of the Cooper Institute for Aerobics Research Standards as the minimum standard to complete a 1.5-mile run. The requirements may be age- and gender-normed.

- **Obstacle course.** This involves a kind of rapid scramble over and through different kinds of barriers—fences, barrels, low monkey bars, whatever the department has set up.

- **Dummy drag.** You will have to drag a certain amount of dead weight, usually 150 pounds, for a specific distance. Even if you are strong and fit, this is harder than it sounds; it requires you to use muscles not often called upon. Definitely try to practice beforehand.

- **Weight lifting.** Usually, this involves basic bench presses, squats, and curls. How much you have to lift and how many reps depends on your size and gender.

- **Sit-ups, push-ups, and pull-ups.** Find out the specific number of repetitions required; if it's more than you can comfortably do now, slowly work up to it.

Keep in mind, your performance on Test Day could suffer because of nervousness. Train to a level that will give you a cushion of 20% or more; however, don't overtrain just before the physical test. You might consider taking a day or two off before the event. If you haven't done your homework before this, cramming your workouts in at the last minute may only hurt you. It is always recommended that before starting any fitness plan, you consult with a physician first.

It is worth noting that some programs have dropped these strict physical fitness tests in favor of more job-specific testing. Such a test might mimic a foot chase, or a similar high-intensity, police-related scenario. These newer types of tests are meant to focus on job-specific skills rather than brute strength, which may be inherently biased against certain otherwise skilled candidates, particularly women.

In general, being physically fit will help you handle stress (always a big part of any law enforcement job). Fitness increases your stamina and really does help you think more clearly. It will also, when combined with the training you will receive, give you confidence in yourself. There is a physical component to being a police officer that sometimes gets overlooked. Emergency calls happen in seconds, which may require you to jump into action unexpectedly and do anything, including running, lifting objects, climbing fences, or confronting a suspect that you are trying to apprehend.

Remember, always check with the department you are applying to. They will give you specifics about their standards. Some of the larger forces even have scheduled training programs to help applicants get up to the required fitness level.

THE PSYCHOLOGICAL EXAM

In general, people tend to get nervous at the mention of "psychological" anything, but there's really no point in getting wound up about this portion of the application process.

Actually, this might be one of the easiest parts of the whole process—you can't study for this test and you can't outguess it, so there is really nothing to do to prepare. Here is some information about what the psychological test entails.

The written test

Almost all departments give applicants a standardized multiple-choice test—either one they have designed themselves or one that is commonly used in psychological settings.

The most common test is the Minnesota Multiphasic Psychological Inventory (MMPI). Updated versions of the test include the MMPI-2 and the MMPI-2RF. These tests are comprised of over 500 true-false statements, which you read and respond to. Just to give you some idea of what it's like, the statements range from things like "I prefer romance novels to mysteries," to "My father is a good man," to "I am an important person." You mark your answers, depending on whether the statement never applies to you, sometimes applies to you, often applies to you, or always applies to you. And that's it. Another commonly used self-reporting instrument is the California Psychological Inventory. This instrument is comprised of over 400 similar questions.

Other tests may ask you to complete sentences or to react to specific phrases, such as "When I'm at home" or "My mother's favorite." Don't obsess over your answers. Answer honestly, but think about what you are writing. "My mother's favorite color is purple" will probably send a better message than "My mother's favorite was always my worthless brother." However, do not waste a lot of time trying to come up with the "right" or the "best" answers. You are better off just answering honestly. The MMPI and all psychological tests are specifically designed to pick up inconsistencies that indicate someone is manipulating the answers. You don't gain anything by being dishonest in your responses.

The psychological interview

In some departments, you will have an interview with a psychologist, usually sometime after you complete the written test. The psychologist will probably ask you some follow-up questions about the results of your written test, and he or she may also ask other questions to find out a little more about what kind of person you are.

Don't worry too much about this. Anything you say is private, and you are not going to leave the testing room in a straitjacket. You may be asked questions no one's ever asked you before—things like "What's the worst thing you've ever done?" or "Do you have a happy marriage?" Don't say, "None of your business"—although that will probably be your first impulse.

THE POLYGRAPH TEST

Many police departments require polygraphs. If you have never taken one before, the idea can be intimidating. You may be asking yourself the following: How does it work? What are they going to ask about? What if I'm nervous during the test?

The polygraph measures several involuntary physiological responses to stress—specifically, the stress involved in lying. When you are actually "hooked up," you will be seated in a chair near the polygraph. Three sensors will be attached:

1. Blood pressure cuff, to measure heart rate

2. Convoluted rubber tubes, attached around the abdomen and chest, to measure respiratory activity

3. Two small metal plates, attached to the fingers, to measure sweat gland activity

Before you are hooked up to the polygraph, the examiner will ask you several questions. There are the baseline questions—"Is your name Jane Doe? Were you born in Peoria, Illinois?" Then there are the real questions, such as "Have you ever manufactured, transported, or sold illegal drugs?" You are not going to lie about your name or where you were born; even if your heart is beating faster than it normally would because you are nervous, that elevated heart rate is going to register as the baseline for the test.

The pretest may ask you questions outside of the application, like "Did you ever steal candy when you were younger?" or "Did you lie as a child?" For the most part, we have all done something like that. Remember: no one is perfect, and the examiner doesn't expect anyone to be. But what the examiner *will* expect is honesty.

After you are hooked up to the polygraph, the examiner will go through the questions again. There will also be follow-up questions that aim to catch you off guard and elicit an immediate, uncontrollable response. For example, an examiner might ask, "Did you lie when you told me you haven't manufactured, transported, or sold illegal drugs?" The examiner might also drill down on certain topics that seem to provoke an unusual physiological response.

POLYGRAPH TIPS

As you can see, taking a polygraph test can be nerve-wracking, and it will likely create some anxiety or stress. There are a few things you can do to eliminate some of the stress you may be feeling that day.

First, do not be late. Being late to any type of job interview can cause stress or anxiety. Because the polygraph is part of the hiring phase, being on time is also part of the process. Remember, the test measures stress and nervousness. Give yourself plenty of time to get there and keep yourself relaxed. Stay away from caffeine that day; drink water instead. Also try to relax your breathing.

Dress appropriately and professionally. This is no ordinary job interview. You need to act and dress professionally at all stages of the application process, including this one.

Finally, during the test, do not give evasive answers. Try to keep your answers to a simple "yes" or "no" if at all possible. Also make sure that any information you provide during the polygraph matches the information you provided elsewhere during your application.

THE INTERVIEW

For most people, this is the most stressful part of the application process. Don't worry. Just prepare yourself ahead of time, and you will do fine.

Before the interview

Do your homework. Find out about the interview process. If it's a small local department, they may want to ask you about your knowledge and interest in the community and the department. You may be directly interviewed by the chief. How many officers are on the force you are applying to? What is the major crime problem in the community? Have there been any big changes in policy or focus recently? Are there any cases or investigations that have been widely covered in the news? Who is the police chief? How long has he or she been there? Did he or she come in from outside or was he or she promoted from within? How does he or she get along with the mayor? You can get information like this from local newspapers or from the department itself; work it into your answers where appropriate, and you will impress your interviewers.

For example, if a question refers to gang graffiti, you can say something like, "Well, the gang problem is the main target of the new Street Shield unit, and they have been having some success—gang activity is down 12% since last year. In light of that, I would coordinate my efforts with the unit to build on their success."

Of course, you won't impress anyone if your information is wrong or doesn't really connect with what you are saying. Think about the information you are going to use; don't just blurt things out.

There are agencies in which the interviews are designed as a specific part of the background investigation. You will most likely be asked about your personal history in conjunction with certain results of the psychological exam and/or polygraph. Sometimes these types of questions are asked just for clarification purposes.

There are those departments that have a much more formal, structured interview process. These questions may be competency-based, can be more complex, and can revolve around a scenario you are given, with accompanying laws or regulations. You would then be given questions regarding what issues or problems you may see and how you would respond. The questions are designed to elicit responses that indicate if the candidate has the abilities the department has determined are essential in good job performance. The line of questioning may also be more behavior-based. This means you may be asked about your past experiences and how you demonstrated competent behavior. An example might be how you exhibited good communication skills. Usually, such departments offer a more detailed preparatory guide for these interviews.

Anticipate the questions. All interviewers want to know if you can deal with conflict, get along with other people, and learn from mistakes. To get at that information, they will ask you for details about your previous experience and education. To further probe for these qualities, they will sometimes give you a hypothetical situation and ask for your response. This also tests your ability to make good decisions and think on your feet. Here are some general ways you can prepare yourself:

- Look at the interview process and your own application, and put yourself in the interviewers' shoes. They are going to push to find out if you have got what it takes to be a good, responsible police officer. Come up with your own questions and honest answers.

  Here is an example: "I see you left your job at Kasper Dry Cleaning after only three months. Why is that?" Do not say: "I had to quit because the manager was a pushy jerk, and he kept trying to make me do stuff that wasn't in my job description." That makes you sound like someone who is always looking for a scapegoat.

  Instead, put it like this: "I had a personality conflict with the manager that we just weren't able to resolve. That was one of my first jobs out of school, and since then I've really worked on my people skills. In fact, at my current job, I was able to negotiate with the boss to get a better scheduling system set up for all the employees."

This shows that you are able to learn from your mistakes and that you have developed the ability to work with others—both important aspects of being a good police officer.

This is an important step in your preparation, so take your time. Ask a friend to help you if you are having trouble coming up with difficult questions. You really can't overprepare; even if the interviewers don't ask exactly the same questions you come up with, they will probably be similar. It will also mean there is less chance you will be caught off guard.

- Imagine some difficult situations a police officer might face and come up with your responses. You will need to have some practice at making good decisions quickly. These are the kinds of things you might be asked:

"You are on patrol, and you see a car being driven erratically. You pull it over, and the driver is the police chief's 16-year-old daughter. There are empty beer bottles in the front seat, and her eyes are red. She says they were left by her boyfriend, whom she just dropped off, and her eyes are red because they had a fight and she was crying. What do you do?"

"You are working on a narcotics case, and you make a big bust. Another police officer, your partner's brother-in-law, pockets some of the cash before it's booked into evidence. You tell your partner, and he just shrugs and says that the guy's a bum, but his sister loves him. What do you do?"

"The station gets an anonymous call about child abuse at a certain address. You are sent to check it out. When you get there, the man who answers the door says there is no problem. You hear a kid screaming in the background. When you ask to come in and take a look, the man tells you to come back with a warrant. What do you do?"

When you are in the interview, the officers will keep adding complications to the original situation. Don't rush into an answer, and don't change your answer once you have given it. Most of the time, there is no black-and-white answer they are looking for; they just want to see how you react to stress and whether you are able to make reasonable decisions under pressure. The only time you should take back your answer is if you realize that there really is a better solution than the one you first gave. Whatever you do, do not change any answer more than once.

Practice with a friend. Get someone you trust to do some role-playing with you. Ideally, this will be a friend who is a police officer and who has been through the interview process. But whoever it is, make sure it is someone who can give you honest feedback.

Give that person the questions and situations you have come up with, along with your application. Ask him or her to write out some more questions and then put you through an interview. This might seem weird at first, and neither one of you may want to take it seriously, but keep at it. This is the best way to prepare yourself, so you can walk into that interview room feeling confident.

Take notes while you are practicing, and ask your friend to do the same. What do you need to work on? What are your strengths? Keep thinking about how to improve your performance, and incorporate those ideas into your notes.

Prepare a closer. At the end of the interview, you will almost always be asked, "Do you have any questions?" Have your answer prepared. If you have a couple of good questions, ask them. Don't ask about retirement benefits or how soon you can be promoted to detective. That really sends the wrong signal—that you are assuming you are going to be hired and that you are focused a bit too much on your own personal goals. *Simple questions about the application process can show interest and initiative as well.* If you can't think of any questions, just say something like, "I don't have any questions, but I would like to say that becoming a police officer has been a lifelong goal, and I believe my skills would make me an asset to this department."

Make sure you know how to get to the interview site. Do not assume it is at the police station. Check your notification form. Even if you have been to the station, or the courthouse, or wherever it is you are supposed to go, make another trip. If you can, go at the same time of day you will be heading in for your interview. Time the trip, then add a safety margin for traffic jams, subway delays, flat tires, or any other transportation disaster.

The night before the interview

Check your transportation. If you are driving, do you have enough gas in the tank? Have you been having problems with your car? If so, arrange a backup—get a friend to stand by in case you need a ride, or make sure you have enough money for cab fare and the number of a good company. If you are using mass transit, make sure you have a ticket or money to pay for one.

Check your clothes. For some people, this is second nature, but others may need a little prompting here. Men should wear a suit or a sport coat and tie. Women should wear a dress or suit. Lay out every single thing you are going to wear to the interview, including your underwear. Make sure it is all clean, matching, with no buttons missing or seams ripped. If you haven't worn those clothes for a while, try them on now while there is still time to find an alternative in case they don't fit. You want to minimize any nasty surprises in the morning.

Go over your notes. Read through your application so it is fresh in your mind. The interviewers will have read it and will probably have it in front of them, and you won't want to just repeat what you have already told them. Read the notes from your mock interview. Think about the positive aspects about yourself that you want to get across.

Get a good night's sleep. This is not the time to go out for a drink with your friends. Have a good dinner, and do something relaxing like watching TV or reading a book.

The day of the interview

Make sure you get up early. You do not want to be rushed, so give yourself plenty of time to get ready. If you are a sound sleeper, set two alarms and have a friend call you.

Eat breakfast, but don't overdo the caffeine. You want to give yourself some fuel, but you don't want to be hyped up on caffeine. Have a sensible breakfast like cereal and fruit or eggs and toast.

Leave early. You want to be in the waiting room 15 minutes before your appointment—regardless of traffic or a slow bus. Believe me, people notice promptness, and it makes a good impression. Bring your notes, and you can use the waiting time for a little last-minute reviewing. If you are starting to get stressed out, take a few really deep breaths. Don't start worrying about all the things that could go wrong; instead, focus on doing well and making a good impression. That should be the image you carry into the room.

In the interview

Acknowledge everyone. Someone will take the lead and introduce himself or herself and the other interviewers. This person may or may not be the chief decision maker in this situation, so you need to acknowledge and address all the interviewers—now and throughout the interview.

When you are introduced, smile, shake hands, and greet each of the interviewers. When you answer questions, make eye contact with everyone. I'm not saying you should sit there with your eyes darting from person to person, but you do need to acknowledge that you are addressing more than one interviewer.

Listen to the questions. One of the biggest mistakes people make is answering the question they think they have heard, instead of the question that has been asked. If you are in any doubt, ask for clarification.

Don't blurt out your answer right away. You don't get extra points for speed. Give yourself a second or two to gather your thoughts and focus on the best answer to the question. You don't want to have to retract your answer later.

Identify the "bad cop." If one of the interviewers begins to play the heavy, the one who challenges your answers and tries to get you to back down, don't be aggressive with this person, but don't let him or her bully you either. Address this person directly; don't get thrown by the questions or by his or her tone. And don't take it personally. This person is not out to get you—the point is to see how you react to stress and confrontation.

Thank the interviewers. When you get up to leave, shake hands again with each of the interviewers and thank them for the opportunity to speak with them.

CHAPTER 3

About the Police Examinations

Your police entrance exam is one of the first major hurdles you will have to overcome on your path toward a career in law enforcement. No matter what academy you hope to join, you will be required to take a written test of some kind. There are a few things to know.

- **There is no one standard police exam nationwide.**

  ◦ Some states have a standardized test (often a civil service test) unique to their state; applicants to all municipal police departments throughout the state take the same standardized test, and each city sets its own passing score.

  ◦ However, some cities—especially large ones—use their own tests.

- The **FrontLine National™ Test for Law Enforcement** (copyright Ergometrics) is also frequently used, at times in combination with another written exam.

Whatever the questions look like, however, most police exams test similar topics.

That's where this book comes in. It includes review for all the content that will appear on your exam, whichever it is. The staff of Kaplan analyzed recent police exams from major cities and identified the most frequently tested topics. The review chapters in this book are taken directly from that research.

LAW ENFORCEMENT AS A CAREER IN THE UNITED STATES

Law enforcement in the United States is a unique profession, encompassing a wide variety of hiring processes and requirements across all agencies. In other words, there is no one standard process. In particular, application and testing processes vary depending on location. Naturally, this state of affairs is very challenging for the applicants.

Consider this example:

> Carlo is 23 years old and was recently honorably discharged from the Marine Corps after serving for 4 years. He plans to pursue a career in law enforcement. To this end, Carlo moves back to his hometown of Riverside, California, and begins to look at agencies. His uncle, Tomas, who has been a police officer for the Los Angeles Police Department for 30 years, advised Carlo to apply to multiple agencies to increase his chances of getting hired.
>
> As Carlo researches different police departments, he is surprised to learn that they all have different hiring processes—even those that are only a few miles apart. Carlo expresses his frustration to his uncle. "There's a lot of information to organize. Why isn't there one standard hiring process for all police officers nationwide?"

While concerns like Carlo's are understandable, there is an explanation for the lack of standardization in law enforcement hiring.

- Under the U.S. Constitution, states are able to make most of their own decisions. Thus, each state has the right to determine what minimum standards it wants to establish for its law enforcement officers.

- All 50 states have basic requirements for police officers. However, each state establishes its own minimum requirement.

- Complicating matters, police agencies must use *both* the state-mandated minimum requirements and any other criteria unique to that agency. For example, the state of Wisconsin may require a high school diploma for all police officer applicants throughout the state, but a police agency in Madison could also require education beyond a high school diploma.

- As a result, neighboring agencies may have very different hiring practices, potentially causing confusion or anxiety for applicants.

POLICE EXAMS IN GENERAL

Pay attention to the information provided by the program to which you are applying. When you register for the exam, review all the materials about what will be tested, so that nothing is a surprise on Test Day. As with any standardized test, preparation is the key to success.

- However your written exam is designed, it almost always takes the form of a standardized multiple-choice test with around 100 questions.

- Once the exam starts, you will read and follow all the directions precisely. For example, the directions may indicate that the section is timed and tell you when you can advance to the next page, or there may be particular instructions on how to answer certain topics or sections. Whatever the exam directions are, you must follow them.

- Police work is in part about following directions and paying attention to details. Doing well on your exam is not only about choosing the correct answer, but also doing what is asked of you and paying attention to detail.

Content

While the questions on your police exam may be police related, they will not ask about police procedures. **Everything you need to answer the questions will be provided on the exam.** Your police exam will test your aptitude in several general categories, as follows.

- **English language skills, reading comprehension, and verbal expression** (especially language used in law enforcement)

  ○ Recognize the correctly spelled word within a group of similar words.

  ○ Select the best vocabulary word to complete a sentence or choose the best definition of a selected word.

  ○ Select a sentence out of a group that is correctly or incorrectly punctuated.

  ○ Read a passage and answer questions about identifying details and making inferences from what you are given

  ○ Interpret a police report.

  ○ Understand law enforcement vocabulary and identify where it is used correctly.

- **Mathematics and logic** (basic math and possibly basic geometry and algebra, often presented as a word problem; logic questions that test your ability to interpret given information)

  ○ Read a set of laws and an action taken by an officer, and determine whether the officer acted correctly or incorrectly.

  ○ Read a report about locations and times of crimes committed in a certain area, and choose the best time to patrol selected areas.

  ○ Interpret information given in tables, charts, and graphs.

  ○ Define a crime committed using the appropriate statute.

  ○ Select the most relevant details from a given report.

- **Spatial orientation, visualization, and memorization** (skills of observation, visual logic, map reading, and ability to remember what you see)

  ○ Observe a street scene, then answer questions about it after it is taken away.

  ○ Find efficient routes based on a map or paragraph description of directions.

  ○ Identify differences and similarities in faces.

  ○ Decipher complex patterns of rotated or shifted shapes.

  ○ Identify visual depictions of traffic incident descriptions.

- **Information management and problem sensitivity** (job-related information and making common-sense decisions)

   ° Place a scrambled witness statement into a proper, logical order.

   ° Select the best police response to a given scenario.

   ° Identify the most and least important details when given a description of a scenario or a crime scene.

Remember, everyone knows you are *not* yet a police officer! These questions are testing your common sense and logic skills.

Scoring

Bear in mind that any academy or training program, large or small, can accept only so many people. While a bigger department needs more personnel than a smaller one, that doesn't necessarily translate to an easier acceptance process: there may be thousands of people taking the test every year. No matter what program you are aiming for, the exam is the one standardized part of the evaluation process that programs use to keep or eliminate unqualified applicants.

The average passing score is 70% of all questions answered correctly.

- For the practice exams in this book, aim for at least 70%; anything less than that means a program might not consider your application.

- Although 70% is passing, a minimum passing score may not guarantee that you will be selected. As with any test, the higher you score, the better.

- Aim for 85% or higher just to be in contention for admittance (each school/program is different).

Before taking any exam, try to find out how the program to which you are applying approaches scoring. Certain qualifications might confer additional exam points that increase an applicant's chances of being accepted—for example, applicants with military experience or applicants who reside in a certain geographic area.

- If you have military experience when you file for the test, let the program know you are an honorably discharged veteran. Depending on the program, veteran status might earn you up to 5 bonus points.

- If you have preferred residency, you might be able to earn up to 5 extra points. This is helpful if you are seeking a job in a given metropolitan area.

These extra points can be very beneficial—say you score 85% on the test; adding another 5 points bumps you up to 90%, which will improve your chances of acceptance.

FRONTLINE NATIONAL TEST

The FrontLine National test is an attempt by the law enforcement profession to standardize the application process throughout the country. which helps departments to identify appropriate candidates for employment.

What the FrontLine test is:

- Psychometric—that is, designed to measure a person's abilities or knowledge
- Designed to measure communication, observation skills, decision-making ability, and judgment

What the FrontLine test is not:

- A personality test; rather, it is a test designed to assess skills required and the examinee's potential for success in a law enforcement career
- A test exclusively for candidates with a background in policing or criminal justice; rather, it is a test designed to assess skills in anyone, and no prior training or knowledge of police policy is required

Specifically, the FrontLine evaluates the examinee's potential to do the following:

- Observe situations
- Take responsibility
- Determine courses of action
- Display a level of maturity required to enforce the law
- Communicate effectively with diverse populations
- Display ethical behavior

The FrontLine does not test knowledge about specific policies or laws. Instead, it provides general scenarios that might be encountered while on police duty. Applicants are asked to determine a best course of action or response. In addition to police officer, it is used to identify candidates for deputy sheriff trainee, reserve police officer, corrections deputy, and park ranger.

At press time, approximately 280 agencies in 14 states used the FrontLine in the hiring process.

- **Eastern United States:** Florida, Illinois, Maryland, Michigan, Minnesota, Ohio
- **Western United States:** Arizona, California, Colorado, Idaho, Nevada, New Mexico, Oregon, Washington
- Washington D.C. and U.S. Virgin Islands

Scheduling the FrontLine National Test

The FrontLine test is administered through Ergometrics and the National Testing Network, an independent company that contracts with public safety departments nationwide. When you apply to a law enforcement agency that uses the FrontLine National, you will receive specific instructions about when to take the test.

To schedule the test, go to **nationaltestingnetwork.com**, create a profile, and pay the exam fee. Then choose your preferred testing location. As of this printing, there were testing centers in 30 states and Washington, D.C. The accessibility of the testing centers varies by state.

- During the registration process, you will be asked to select the law enforcement department(s) where you'd like your score sent. This cannot be changed later, so be certain of your choices.

- Before you select your test date and location, make sure you can allow 4–5 hours of your time on Test Day.

Taking the FrontLine National Test

There are 3 components to the test: human relations (video-based test), writing (writing a report), and reading. Testing takes 2–3 hours.

- **Situational Judgment and Human Relations Test**
  - You will watch videotaped scenarios simulating those a law enforcement professional might experience.
  - You will then be given a set of multiple-choice questions, with a limit of 10 seconds to respond to each question.
  - Questions typically focus on the appropriate response or next step that should be taken in the scenario. The idea is to assess your decision-making skills and judgment—vital attributes for a police officer. As a police officer, you will need to exercise mature and logical decision-making and be able to articulate the reasons behind your decisions and choices.
  - After you choose the *best* course of action, you will be asked to choose what would be the *worst* course of action.
  - See the Logic and Reasoning chapter of this book to practice similar questions.
- **Written Report Writing Test**
  - You will read a well-written police report and then watch a short video that displays a police incident, e.g., police officers responding to a complaint of property damage by a homeowner.
  - You will be shown the video twice (with time in between to take notes). After your second viewing, you will have 10 minutes to write a brief report on the incident.

- º Finally, you answer a set of multiple-choice questions about the incident.

- º See the Verbal Expression chapter of this book to review tips for preparing a clear and concise report. (These recommendations include preparing an outline first, taking a short break between drafting the report and submitting the final version, and avoiding vague words.

- º See the Verbal Expression chapter of this book to practice report writing.

- **Reading Test**

- º You will be tested on your ability to read, write, and speak English fluently, as it is needed in your role as a police officer.

- º You will have 15 minutes to read a technical passage and identify which words are missing.

  - *Context* refers to information within the sentence that provides surrounding details and illustrates a broader meaning. Context is important in reading comprehension, especially if you do not recognize a specific word.

  - Consider the statement *"I have never seen my aunt cry so much."* Without context, it is hard to know the circumstances surrounding the aunt's crying. See how the entire meaning changes when a small detail is added to provide context. Compare the difference in meaning that additional context gives this statement: *"The comedian was so funny we were crying; I have never seen my aunt cry so much."* Versus: *"My uncle's funeral was so sad; I have never seen my aunt cry so much."*

  - Context also helps to illustrate the meaning of words you don't recognize. Assume you don't know what "vivacious" means, but a friend says, *"She is so vivacious; she was laughing and dancing the entire night, and it seemed like she was having so much fun."* Based on the context, the word "vivacious" is probably related to *laughing* and *dancing*, so it speaks to someone's behavior or state of being.

  - See the Reading Comprehension and Verbal Expression chapters for more practice with context and reading comprehension.

PRACTICE QUESTIONS

Familiarize yourself with each question type by answering the following sample question for each section.

Situational Judgment and Human Relations Practice Questions

1. You are a uniformed police officer assigned to work at the front desk of the police department. At 10:30 p.m., a 19-year-old woman named Beatriz enters the department and approaches the front desk. When you ask how you can help, Beatriz asks if she can speak to a police officer. You advise Beatriz that you are a police officer and are willing to assist her. Beatriz tells you that last night she was interviewed by a detective at your agency because she was a witness to a fatal vehicle hit-and-run that occurred last night during a street festival. Beatriz tells you that she has more information to provide about the incident that she did not tell the detective last night because she felt the detective she spoke with was rude to her and did not take her seriously. What is the most appropriate response?

   (A) Tell Beatriz that you are sorry the detective was rude and she should come back tomorrow morning to speak to another detective.

   (B) Thank Beatriz for coming into the department, advise her you are happy to help her tonight, and ask if she would be willing to provide the additional information to you.

   (C) Provide Beatriz a brochure on how to file a complaint against an officer with Internal Affairs.

   (D) Tell Beatriz she should have provided all her information last night and she is now subject to arrest for obstruction.

2. You are a new officer in field training, and you are riding in the passenger seat of a marked squad car while your training officer, Officer Young, is driving. As you and Officer Young drive down a residential street, you observe a light-colored 4-door sedan run through a stop sign, speed away from the intersection, and cross the center median line several times before pulling into the driveway of a residence. When you suggest following up with the driver, Officer Young says, "Are you kidding? We get off shift in an hour, and I have plans after work. If we pull over this drunk, we'll be doing at least 2 hours of paperwork. The car is off the road now anyway." What is the most appropriate response?

   (A) "You're right. What are these after-work plans you've got?"

   (B) "Let me drive the squad car, and I'll decide what work we both will do."

   (C) "Stop at the residence. I'm worried that the driver is intoxicated or having a medical emergency. I'll do all the paperwork."

   (D) Radio the shift commander, "My field training officer won't follow up on a problem driver, and I'd like you to intervene."

3. You are a uniformed police officer on duty, and you are dispatched to a local grocery store in response to a report of theft. At the store, employees from loss prevention state that a male and female wheeled a shopping cart full of food and other items through the front door and loaded it, cart and all, into the back of a truck, then drove away. They tell you that it will take some time before they can access video of the incident recorded by surveillance cameras in the store, but one of the store's cashiers, Jason, saw the entire incident. "That's Jason right there," one says, pointing toward a male in the driver's seat of a vehicle in the parking lot. Jason rolls down his window as you approach the vehicle and introduce yourself. "I know why you are here," Jason interrupts, "but I can't stay and talk to you. I have to be at my child's school in 10 minutes to pick them up, so I'm leaving. You can watch the surveillance video of the theft." What is the most appropriate response?

(A) Reach inside the vehicle, turn off the ignition, and remove the keys to ensure Jason cannot leave before talking to you.

(B) Tell Jason he can leave, and you will use the surveillance footage for evidence.

(C) Tell Jason you understand, obtain his contact information, and set up a time and place to interview him after he picks up his child.

(D) Ask Jason what school his child attends and tell him you will send another officer to pick up his child so Jason can stay and talk to you.

4. You are a uniformed police officer on duty, and you are dispatched to assist with crowd control at a crime scene on a busy street. When you arrive at the scene, you observe that the entire street and sidewalk are visibly closed with crime scene tape. Over 100 civilians are standing near the crime scene tape, along with media vans and news reporters. The officer in charge of the scene, Detective Adebayo, tells you that they are investigating a homicide that occurred in the street in front of a residence on this block and asks you to provide perimeter security by standing near the crime scene tape and ensuring nobody crosses it. After approximately an hour, you observe an adult female known to you as a resident in the neighborhood approaching the crime scene tape approximately 40 feet away and lifting it up, apparently intending to enter the crime scene. What is the most appropriate response?

(A) Approach the female, introduce yourself, and ask her to step back behind the crime scene tape.

(B) Shout to the female that she must step back or be arrested.

(C) Shout and motion to other civilians near the female that they should grab her and pull her back from the tape.

(D) Let the female enter the scene, and radio Detective Adebayo to report what is happening.

5. You are a police officer in uniform, but off duty, and you stop at a local convenience store to pick up dinner on your way home. While waiting for the cashier, you observe an adult female with 2 small children in line ahead of you. One of the children picks up a pack of chewing gum, asks the female if he can have it, and is told, "Put that back. I'm not buying it." Then you see the child turn toward the display and put the gum in their front pants pocket. What is the most appropriate response?

    (A) Ignore it. You are off duty, the offense is trivial, and the offender is too young to be of concern.

    (B) Tell the child loudly, "I am a police officer. Put the gum back, or you'll be in trouble for stealing."

    (C) Wait until the woman and children go through the line, then tell the cashier what happened and offer to pay for the gum the child took.

    (D) Tap the woman on the shoulder, quietly tell her what is happening, and ask if you can assist her in any way.

6. You are a uniformed police officer on duty, and you are dispatched with your partner and other officers to a physical disturbance call. Neighbors next to a residence called 911 to report 2 adult males physically fighting each other in the front yard of a residence. When you and the other officers arrive at the residence, the men are no longer physically fighting but are yelling at each other and appear very agitated; both have injuries, including bloody noses. As you and your partner approach them, one of the men walks toward a vehicle in the driveway and attempts to get in the car. What is the most appropriate response?

    (A) Along with your partner, approach the male before he enters the vehicle, introduce yourselves, and ask to talk to him.

    (B) Wait for the man to get into the vehicle, then get into your squad car to conduct a traffic stop.

    (C) Let the man leave. The men are no longer fighting, so this is not a police matter.

    (D) Call out to the man, "Stop. If you try to leave now, we will arrest you."

7. You are a uniformed police officer on duty today but on your break. While waiting in line to order at a local coffee shop, you overhear 2 teenage boys in front of you laughing and talking about how much they dislike the police. One looks at you, then says to his friend, "Must be nice to get paid to order coffee and be as useless as every other cop in this city." They laugh louder, and the other boy says, "I hope the cop behind us gets fired. One less cop is a good thing." What is the most appropriate response?

    (A) Politely ask the teenage boys to stop talking about you.

    (B) Ignore the teenagers; they are not causing a disturbance or inciting violence, and they have a right to express their opinion.

    (C) Ask both teenagers to show their identification, and tell them they are being rude and need to change their attitudes.

    (D) Ask the manager of the coffee shop to remove the teenage boys.

8. You are a uniformed police officer on duty and in a marked police squad car. You are dispatched in response to a reported robbery that just occurred at a small bodega. Dispatch describes the suspect as a Hispanic male, 20–25 years old, with dark hair, a mustache, and a tattoo on his neck, wearing jeans and a blue-and-yellow striped shirt. As you drive to the scene, you observe a man matching that description standing at a bus stop 2 blocks from the bodega; the man then sees you and begins to run. When he begins crossing backyards to get away, you park and pursue him on foot. After about 4 blocks, you catch up and are only a few feet behind him when he turns his ankle and falls to the ground. The man puts his hands up quickly while on the ground and says, "I give up, I give up." Which is the most appropriate response?

(A) Approach the man and place handcuffs on him while he is on the ground.

(B) Tell the man to stand up, and order him to walk back to your squad car with you.

(C) Stay a short distance away, order the man to stay on the ground with his hands visible, and wait for backup officers to arrive.

(D) Ask the man if he was the one who robbed the bodega and where he is holding the money he stole.

9. While on duty and in uniform, you finish a response to a property damage complaint at a downtown business and begin walking back to your squad car. On a side street, you observe a middle-aged woman in an electric wheelchair in the roadway. She is next to the curb in an empty but marked parking space in front of some local small businesses. You approach the woman and ask if she is okay. She states that her wheelchair battery has died but that she does not want your help. "I hate the police," she tells you. "I'm scared of you people. None of you have ever helped me before, you just make things worse." Which is the most appropriate response?

(A) Explain to the woman that she should not turn down help from the police; she should be grateful that you want to help her.

(B) Leave her alone. She is not in trouble, and she refused your help.

(C) Introduce yourself, tell the woman you understand she may have had bad experiences before, and explain that you want to help get her out of the street so she does not get hurt or cause a traffic incident.

(D) Enter the business beside the parking space and ask the personnel there to keep an eye on the woman to make sure she is okay.

10. You are a uniformed police officer on duty and in a marked police squad car when you observe a minivan going 15 miles per hour over the posted speed limit on a residential street. You follow and also observe failure to use signals several times, swerving over the center line a few times, and failure to stop completely at a stop sign. You then activate your lights and siren to conduct a traffic stop. When you approach the vehicle, you observe a female driver, another adult female in the passenger seat, and 4 children. The driver provides her driver's license, registration, and insurance paperwork. She is cooperative, apologizing for her driving and saying she was trying to get home quickly because all her children need lunch, and one of them also needs medication soon. When you provide her information to dispatch, you are advised that the female driver has 2 active warrants for forgery and burglary. Which is the most appropriate response?

(A) Instruct the driver to step outside because she is under arrest for her warrants.

(B) Ask the driver to step outside so you can speak privately, tell her there are warrants for her arrest, and ask if she is comfortable with the other adult taking the children home.

(C) Approach the passenger of the vehicle, tell the adult passenger that you are going to arrest the driver, and instruct her to take the car keys and drive the children home.

(D) Inform the driver that she has warrants she needs to take care of, but you will let her go home today so she can care for her children.

Written Report Writing Practice Questions

Read the following police reports and answer the questions that follow.

Questions 11–20

Officer Gutierrez was dispatched to the residence at 1711 N. 5th Street for a report of a burglary. Upon arrival on scene, the officer spoke with the homeowner, Thomas Chu. Mr. Chu stated that he left his residence at approximately 7:00 a.m. this morning to go to work and that he is confident all the doors and windows in the home were closed and locked. Mr. Chu stated that he returned home from work at 3:45 p.m., and when he pulled into his driveway, he observed his front door standing open. Officer Gutierrez asked if anyone else lived in the residence, and Mr. Chu stated that he and his wife live in the residence, but his wife has been out of town for work for the past week and will not return home for another 4 days. Mr. Chu denied anyone else having a key to the house or permission to enter. Mr. Chu stated that he entered the house and found no one inside but that items are missing. Officer Gutierrez accompanied Mr. Chu into the home and observed damage to the front door, including tool marks on the lock and wooden splinters on the floor inside the door. Mr. Chu reported that the missing items from his residence are a brand-new video game console (Serial # 450393590459), 2 new video games entitled "First Person Shooter" and "Operation: Password," 2 console controllers, a television soundbar speaker (serial #3KLDHD331), and an electronic tablet (serial #M7D903759). Mr. Chu estimated that the total cost of the missing items exceeds $2,200, he has no suspects in mind, and he does not know of anyone who would break into his home or steal these items.

Officer Gutierrez conducted a neighborhood canvass of residences located near Mr. Chu's residence and did not find evidence of any other potential break-ins. Samantha Williams, a neighbor residing at 1708 N. 5th Street, was home and spoke with Officer Gutierrez. Her residence is directly across the street from Mr. Chu's. Ms. Williams stated that she was home all day and that at approximately 11:15 a.m., she observed a dark-colored, older model Chevrolet Silverado pickup truck parked in Mr. Chu's driveway. Ms. Williams stated that she wrote down the license plate on the truck because she had never seen the vehicle in the neighborhood before and she knows that Mr. Chu works during the day. Ms. Williams gave Officer Gutierrez a photograph of the truck that she took on her cell phone, which shows a blue Chevrolet Silverado pickup truck with an Illinois license plate of 159 SXN. Ms. Williams stated that she did not have a description of the driver in the pickup truck.

11. According to Mr. Chu, the estimated total value of all missing items is:

   (A) $220

   (B) $2,200

   (C) $12,200

   (D) $22,000

12. The neighbor that provides information to the investigating officer is named:

   (A) Sarah Williams

   (B) Samantha Gutierrez

   (C) Samantha Williams

   (D) Sarah Gutierrez

13. The address where the burglary occurred is:

   (A) 1711 N. 5th Street

   (B) 1171 N. 5th Street

   (C) 1711 S. 5th Street

   (D) 1711 N. 15th Street

14. The address of the witness is:

   (A) 1708 N. 5th Street

   (B) 1708 S. 5th Street

   (C) 1708 N. 15th Street

   (D) 1708 S. 15th Street

15. Mr. Chu reported that he arrived home from work at:

    (A) 3:15 a.m.

    (B) 3:15 p.m.

    (C) 3:45 a.m.

    (D) 3:45 p.m.

16. The total number of items reported as stolen is:

    (A)   5

    (B)   7

    (C)   9

    (D) 11

17. The color of the vehicle observed by the witness is:

    (A) Green

    (B) Blue

    (C) Black

    (D) Unknown

18. The make and model of the vehicle observed by the witness is:

    (A) Chevrolet Silverado

    (B) Chevrolet Suburban

    (C) Ford F150

    (D) GMC Yukon

19. Mr. Chu stated that the only other person with a key to the residence is:

    (A) His parents

    (B) His gardener

    (C) His wife

    (D) His best friend

20. The witness reported that they observed a vehicle in the driveway at:

(A) 11:15 a.m.

(B) 11:15 p.m.

(C) 11:45 a.m.

(D) 11:45 p.m.

Questions 21–30

On Sunday, June 23, 2019, at 3:15 a.m., Officers Mark Matuszak and Stephanie Murphy were riding together in a marked squad car and were dispatched to a 911 call from 933 W. Highland Avenue. Dispatch reported that a female caller on 911 provided this address and possibly said there was a physical disturbance; the female caller was difficult to understand, was yelling loudly and slurring her words, and would not respond to questions asked by the call taker but continued to request that police be sent. Dispatch also advised that this address had had multiple prior calls, most for physical disturbances between 2 adult sisters living in the home.

Officers Matuszak and Murphy arrived at the call address at approximately 3:19 a.m., and they observed 4 people standing in the front yard of the residence and 2 people standing in the middle of the street; it appeared to the officers that all parties were yelling at each other. Upon exiting their squad car, the officers heard an adult female who was standing in the middle of the street yell, "I told you I called the cops! They're here to arrest you all!" Officer Matuszak then approached the 2 parties in the street and asked them to step onto the sidewalk across the street from the other parties, and Officer Murphy went to talk to the 4 parties in the yard.

The 2 women who had been standing in the street were identified as Lisa Pulcher and Tammy Swanson. Ms. Swanson, a 45-year-old female, told Officer Matuszak that she was the person who had called 911 and that she lived at the call address with her roommate, Ms. Pulcher. Officer Matuszak observed that Ms. Swanson appeared to be intoxicated. Ms. Swanson stated that about an hour earlier, she and her roommate were drinking beer on the front porch of their residence when her sister, Marilyn Swanson, walked up the sidewalk toward her home accompanied by 3 people that Ms. Swanson denied knowing. Ms. Swanson told Officer Matuszak that her sister, Marilyn Swanson, used to live with her but moved out over 3 months ago because of their frequent fights over shared boyfriends and money problems. Ms. Swanson stated that tonight, Marilyn Swanson approached her uninvited and demanded $600 owed to her. Ms. Swanson also stated that the last time the police were called, she was told she would be arrested and charged with domestic violence if she fought with her sister, so tonight she walked across the street with her roommate and called the police. Ms. Swanson demanded that the officers remove her sister and the 3 unknown individuals, stating that Marilyn Swanson was trespassing as she no longer lived at the residence.

21. What time were Officers Matuszak and Murphy dispatched?

    (A) 3:15 p.m.

    (B) 5:15 p.m.

    (C) 3:15 a.m.

    (D) 5:15 a.m.

22. Officer Matuszak's partner is:

    (A) Officer Stephanie Morgan

    (B) Officer Stephanie Murray

    (C) Officer Stephanie Matuszak

    (D) Officer Stephanie Murphy

23. How was dispatch contacted by the reporting party?

    (A) A 911 phone call

    (B) A non-emergency phone call

    (C) In person at the police department

    (D) An emergency text message

24. When Officers Matuszak and Murphy arrive at the call address, how many people were present on scene?

    (A) 2

    (B) 5

    (C) 6

    (D) 8

25. The address that the officers were dispatched to is:

    (A) 913 W. Highland Avenue

    (B) 933 W. Highland Avenue

    (C) 933 E. Highland Avenue

    (D) 933 N. Highland Avenue

26. The name of the 911 caller is:

    (A) Lisa Pulcher

    (B) Tammy Swanson

    (C) Marilyn Swanson

    (D) Ron Swanson

27. The name of Tammy Swanson's roommate is:

    (A) Marilyn Swanson

    (B) Lisa Pulcher

    (C) Stephanie Murphy

    (D) Morgan Swanson

28. How did Marilyn reportedly arrive at the call address?

    (A) She drove her vehicle to the residence.

    (B) She drove her sister's vehicle to the residence.

    (C) She walked up to the residence.

    (D) She took public transportation to the residence.

29. How many people reportedly accompanied Marilyn to the call address?

    (A) 2

    (B) 3

    (C) 5

    (D) 7

30. What information does Lisa Pulcher provide to officers?

    (A) She provides the time Marilyn arrived at the house.

    (B) She confirms that Tammy and Marilyn used to be roommates.

    (C) She does not provide any information.

    (D) She confirms that Tammy was the caller to 911.

Reading Practice Questions

Read the following statements and choose the most appropriate word to fill in the blanks.

Questions 31–34

It is important for police officers to be aware of (1) _____ strategies that can improve their interactions with victims of violent crime. Patrol officers are often the (2) _____ point of contact for victims and frequently have the responsibility to obtain the initial information from the victim about what occurred. Knowledge of trauma-informed communication strategies can (3) _____ patrol officers in obtaining the necessary information from a victim without causing further trauma or harm to the (4) _____.

31. For blank #1, choose the best word offered:

    (A) Tactical

    (B) Administrative

    (C) Communication

    (D) Legal

32. For blank #2, choose the best word offered:

    (A) First

    (B) Last

    (C) Worst

    (D) Best

33. For blank #3, choose the best word offered:

    (A) Harm

    (B) Help

    (C) Hinder

    (D) Limit

34. For blank #4, choose the best word offered:

    (A) Officer

    (B) Victim

    (C) Supervisor

    (D) Offender

Questions 35–38

The Fourth Amendment to the Constitution of the (1) _____ is a very important amendment for professional law enforcement officers to understand. Ratified in 1791, the Fourth Amendment provides for the (2) _____ of the people to be secure in their persons, houses, papers, and effects, against unreasonable searches and seizures. Further, the Fourth Amendment also requires that any warrant be supported with probable cause and an oath or affirmation. For law enforcement officers, (3) _____ of the Fourth Amendment allows them to function legally within their duties and responsibilities. All searches and seizures that law enforcement officers may undertake must be supported with (4) _____ cause.

35. For blank #1, choose the best word offered:

   (A) Netherlands

   (B) United States

   (C) Philippines

   (D) Caribbean

36. For blank #2, choose the best word offered:

   (A) Right

   (B) Privilege

   (C) Benefit

   (D) Reward

37. For blank #3, choose the best word offered:

   (A) Assumption

   (B) Guess

   (C) Inference

   (D) Knowledge

38. For blank #4, choose the best word offered:

   (A) Probable

   (B) Reasonable

   (C) Suggestive

   (D) Just

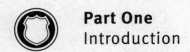

ANSWERS

1.	B	11.	B	21.	C	31.	C
2.	C	12.	C	22.	D	32.	A
3.	C	13.	A	23.	A	33.	B
4.	A	14.	A	24.	C	34.	B
5.	D	15.	D	25.	B	35.	B
6.	A	16.	B	26.	B	36.	A
7.	B	17.	B	27.	B	37.	D
8.	C	18.	A	28.	C	38.	A
9.	C	19.	C	29.	B		
10.	B	20.	A	30.	C		

Scoring

After completing the FrontLine National test, you must go into your online profile to view your score. Your score is not sent by mail.

- Your score is sent within a few days to the agency/agencies you selected when you registered.
- If you do not get a passing score, you can retake the test after 3 months.

CHAPTER 4

Test-Taking Strategies

CREATE A STUDY PLAN

No matter what is on your police exam, in order to do well you'll need to:

- Familiarize yourself with the question types that are common to all police exams
- Answer sample questions to assess your strengths and weaknesses
- Review the strategies you'll need in order to answer questions confidently and correctly
- Assess your progress with more practice questions
- Take full-length practice exams so you get a sense of timing, structure, and how to pace yourself on Test Day

The good news is that this review book has everything you'll need in order to prep for Test Day—it's a complete, comprehensive guide to all the major components that you will see on the day of your exam.

- Chapters 5–11 contain a thorough review of the question types common to police exams.
- Practice Tests 1–4 are 100-question exams that look like the one you will take on Test Day.

Before you dive in, we suggest drawing up (and sticking to) a study schedule that will guide your preparation.

Three levels of study

Perhaps you are already pretty good at most of the topics featured on the test, but you need to brush up on specific skills or quickly review all of the skills before Test Day. Or perhaps you feel moderately confident about some topics, but you need some significant review on others. Or perhaps, like many people, you have forgotten much of what you learned in high school, are not familiar with police scenarios, and need a comprehensive review.

The chart below outlines the different approaches you might take depending on your needs. Of course, your individual situation may vary; these are simply broad guidelines.

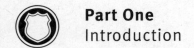
If you need a quick brushup or a light overall review ...	If you need a moderate review of some or all topics ...	If you need to learn or relearn many of the skills from scratch ...
Start by devoting two study sessions of review to each chapter covering a topic you'd like to review in more detail. During those study sessions, read the appropriate chapter and do the practice items at the beginning and end.	Take one practice exam and carefully review which questions you got right and which questions you got wrong. Use the results to identify your areas of greatest need. Start by devoting 2–3 study sessions to each chapter you need to review in more detail. During each of those study sessions, read the appropriate chapter and do the practice items at the beginning and end.	Give yourself plenty of time to work through this book, chapter by chapter. Periodically review the earlier chapters so that those skills do not rust.
After you've completed your comprehensive review, take one full-length test in the book. If you haven't seen significant improvement, continue to work on the areas you find most challenging. Take another full-length test every week or two, depending on your test date.	After you've done so, take another full-length test to gauge your progress. Continue to study and take a full-length test every week or two, depending on your test date. In the last few weeks before your test date, give several days to each of the content areas in which you were already strong.	Don't take many full-length tests until you've reviewed most of the subject tests. In the last few weeks before Test Day, take a full-length practice test once a week or once every two weeks, depending on your test date.

Most importantly, aim to complete all four practice exams in this book before your test date. The more practice tests you do (and review after you have finished), the more it will increase your chances to earn a high score.

MANAGE YOUR STRESS

You have a lot riding on your police exam. You're also doing the work you need to do to reach your goals. Unfortunately, though, simply knowing that you're working hard won't make your test anxiety go away. Thus, here are some stress-management tips from our long experience of helping students prepare for standardized tests.

Clock in and out

Once you've set up a study schedule for yourself, treat it like a job. That is, imagine clocking yourself in and out of police exam studies according to that schedule. Do your best to stick to your schedule, and when you're not "clocked in," don't let yourself stress out about your upcoming exam. That will help you release your stress about the test in between study sessions.

Know when it's time for a break

If you get tired, overwhelmed, or discouraged when studying, don't respond by pushing yourself harder. Rather, step away and engage in a relaxing activity like going for a walk, watching a movie, or playing with your cat or dog. Then, when you're ready, return to your studies with fresh eyes.

Set small, manageable goals

Each week, set manageable goals related to your police exam progress, and reward yourself when you've achieved them. Examples of small goals might be:

- One week, memorize and practice question types that fall under the umbrella of Spatial Orientation, Visualization, and Memorization until you're confident about what you will have to do if you see these question types on your exam.

- One week, take a practice exam under test-like conditions: time yourself and find a quiet room with no distractions. Allot time to review all answer explanations and make a note next to the question types that are giving you the most trouble. Review the chapters that cover the material giving you the most trouble.

- One week, review all Information Management and Problem Sensitivity question types until you can identify each question's type and its appropriate strategy.

Keep yourself healthy

Poor health, fatigue, and isolation make it harder to cope with stress and anxiety. Get on a regular sleep schedule as much as possible during your studies, eat well, continue to exercise, and spend time with those you care about. Also, don't fuel your studies with caffeine and sugar. Those substances may make you feel alert, but they can also damage focus.

Keep the right mindset

Most importantly, keep telling yourself that you can do this. Don't fall into the trap of thinking that you're not "allowed" to feel confident yet. That's a self-punishing attitude that will only hurt you. Remember that confidence breeds success. Let yourself be confident about your abilities. You're obviously ambitious and have a solid career goal in mind, so walk into your exam knowing that about yourself.

If you get discouraged about your goals, stop what you're doing and make a list of everything you're good at. List every specific skill that you are bringing to the police exam. Post that list in a place where you'll see it every day and add to it as you continue to study.

We at Kaplan recommend this because many people focus too heavily on their weaknesses while preparing for a standardized test. But if you only focus on your weaknesses, you aren't seeing an objective picture. There are skills on the exam that you're good at. Keep that in mind, and focus on building on those strengths.

FINAL PREPARATIONS FOR TEST DAY

In the last few weeks before Test Day, do a comprehensive review of all police exam topics. Take a full-length practice test at least once a week, and use the results to guide your final review.

Also, contact the program administering your exam to find out what you should bring to the testing center, what you should *not* bring to the testing center, and when you can expect to receive your score.

Your activities in the last week before Test Day should include:

- **Rest:** Make sure you're on a regular sleep schedule.

- **Rehearse:** Find out where your testing center is located and drive or commute there a few days beforehand to get an idea of the trip.

- **Review:** Do a very brief, high-level review, i.e., flip through the lessons and rework a few practice problems to reinforce the good habits you have developed. (Redoing practice problems you've already done is fine: you can actually learn a lot that way about how to approach those types of questions more efficiently in the future.)

- **Stop:** Two days before the test, stop studying. It's important to walk into the test feeling rested.

- **Relax:** The evening before the test, do something fun but not tiring. Make sure to go to bed at your usual time.

On Test Day itself

On the day of the test, be sure to follow the guidance below:

- **Warm up:** Before you take the test, briefly awaken your brain. You probably can't take any practice materials into the testing center, but you can do a few easy practice problems at home or in the car before you go into the testing center.

- **Don't let nerves derail you:** If you feel nervous while taking the test, remember to breathe deeply into your stomach. Take a few deep breaths and focus your eyes on something other than the computer screen or test booklet for a moment.

- **Keep moving:** Don't let yourself get bogged down on any one question. If the test you are taking allows you to skip questions and come back later, do so when they're slowing you down. If the test you are taking is computerized and doesn't allow you to come back to questions later, you may have to make a guess if a question is threatening to take too much time.

- **Don't assess yourself:** This is very important. Taking a standardized test hardly ever feels good. Your own impressions of how it's going are totally unreliable. So, instead of focusing on that, remind yourself that you're prepared and that you are going to succeed, even if you feel discouraged as the test is underway.

GOOD LUCK!

PART TWO

Skills

CHAPTER 5

Spelling and Grammar

Depending on where you are applying, you may or may not run into specific questions that test spelling and grammar on the police exam. If you need to brush up on these basics, this chapter contains the information most likely to show up on an exam. Remember, even if your program's test doesn't include specific grammar or spelling questions, both good grammar and accurate spelling are required for clear and effective writing—another skill that may be tested. No matter what the actual exam covers, it won't be a waste of your time to review this chapter and to complete the practice questions that follow. After all, as a police officer, you will be expected to write reports, and the skills you learn here can make the difference between a clearly worded report and a confusing one.

LEARNING OBJECTIVES

In this chapter, you will review how to:

- ☐ Avoid common spelling errors
- ☐ Select the correct verb tense
- ☐ Check for subject-verb agreement
- ☐ Select the correct pronoun
- ☐ Place modifiers in the right spot
- ☐ Use commas correctly
- ☐ Avoid double negatives
- ☐ Check for parallelism

TEST WHAT YOU KNOW

Directions: Choose the ONE best answer for each question.

1. An officer is preparing a report after a car theft. He reviews the rough draft of his report, which contains the following two sentences:

   1. At 8:00 p.m., Lansky's Market on Second Avenue was burgled.

   2. There were no witnesses at the scene of the crime.

   Which of the following best describes the above sentences?

   (A) Only sentence #1 is grammatically correct.

   (B) Only sentence #2 is grammatically correct.

   (C) Neither sentence #1 nor sentence #2 is grammatically correct.

   (D) Both sentence #1 and sentence #2 are grammatically correct.

2. The suspect ran down the alley at _____ speed.

   (A) breakneck

   (B) brakeneck

   (C) breaknek

   (D) brakenek

3. Officer Unger must _____ when deciding which incident to pursue first.

   (A) prioratize

   (B) prioritize

   (C) prioretize

   (D) prioritise

4. An officer is preparing a report about a burglary. She reviews the rough draft of her report, which contains the following two sentences:

    1. Mrs. Lang heard a suspicious noise in the driveway and decided to find out who it was.

    2. Mrs. Lang then saw her car pull out of the driveway and he then drove away.

    Which of the following best describes the above sentences?

    (A) Only sentence #1 is grammatically correct.

    (B) Only sentence #2 is grammatically correct.

    (C) Neither sentence #1 nor sentence #2 is grammatically correct.

    (D) Both sentence #1 and sentence #2 are grammatically correct.

5. An officer is preparing a report about a burglary. He reviews the rough draft of his report, which contains the following two sentences:

    1. Ms. Evers, a resident of 621 Humbolt Avenue, finally provide a valuable detail about the burglary.

    2. Before that, Officer Prince, who had gone next door to interview Ms. Evers's neighbor, return with new information.

    Which of the following best describes the above sentences?

    (A) Only sentence #1 is grammatically correct.

    (B) Only sentence #2 is grammatically correct.

    (C) Neither sentence #1 nor sentence #2 is grammatically correct.

    (D) Both sentence #1 and sentence #2 are grammatically correct.

6. An officer is preparing a report about a bank robbery. She reviews the rough draft of her report, which contains the following two sentences:

    1. The bank robbery take place at 4:40 p.m. on August 1st.

    2. Although the thieves were armed, no one was injured.

    Which of the following best describes the above sentences?

    (A) Only sentence #1 is grammatically correct.

    (B) Only sentence #2 is grammatically correct.

    (C) Neither sentence #1 nor sentence #2 is grammatically correct.

    (D) Both sentence #1 and sentence #2 are grammatically correct.

7. An officer is preparing a missing persons report. He reviews the rough draft of his report, which contains the following two sentences:

   1. The child is Mrs. and Mr. Skals.

   2. She was last seen at Riverside Park.

   Which of the following best describes the above sentences?

   (A) Only sentence #1 is grammatically correct.

   (B) Only sentence #2 is grammatically correct.

   (C) Neither sentence #1 nor sentence #2 is grammatically correct.

   (D) Both sentence #1 and sentence #2 are grammatically correct.

8. An officer is preparing a missing persons report. She reviews the rough draft of her report, which contains the following two sentences:

   1. Mr. Campeon was last seen at his home on January 21st.

   2. Mrs. Campeon waded 24 hours before filing a missing persons report.

   Which of the following best describes the above sentences?

   (A) Only sentence #1 is grammatically correct.

   (B) Only sentence #2 is grammatically correct.

   (C) Neither sentence #1 nor sentence #2 is grammatically correct.

   (D) Both sentence #1 and sentence #2 are grammatically correct.

9. An officer is preparing an accident report. He reviews the rough draft of his report, which contains the following two sentences:

   1. Mr. Curtiz had been taking barbiturates, drinking alcohol, and smokes marijuana prior to getting into his car.

   2. Mr. Curtiz collided into a tree on Maplewood Dr.

   Which of the following best describes the above sentences?

   (A) Only sentence #1 is grammatically correct.

   (B) Only sentence #2 is grammatically correct.

   (C) Neither sentence #1 nor sentence #2 is grammatically correct.

   (D) Both sentence #1 and sentence #2 are grammatically correct.

For the following items, please choose the line that contains the error by choosing the line number. Only one of the lines will contain an error.

10. I.   Officer Davies interviewed Mrs. Patrick for a half hour before concluding that she

 II.   had no information about her assailant who'd attacked her from behind.

 III.   The officer proceeded to the store, in front of which Mrs. Patrick

 IV.   was assaulted, to ask if any employees could describe the assailant.

(A) Line I

(B) Line II

(C) Line III

(D) Line IV

11. I.   The man became very belligerent after ranting about all of the

 II.   "un-American" people in his office. The officers managed to calm down the man,

 III.   who then appeared to regret his behavior. He then seemed rational

 IV.   enough to return to work, and the officer exited the premeses.

(A) Line I

(B) Line II

(C) Line III

(D) Line IV

12. I.   Mr. Woolery and Mr. Harvis explained to the officer

 II.   that numerous items had been stolen from their shop

 III.   during the break-in. He then listed all of the stolen items:

 IV.   12 cases of beer, $500, and 12 packs of batteries.

(A) Line I

(B) Line II

(C) Line III

(D) Line IV

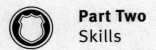

13. I.   The police officer recognized the suspect, who was running east on

    II.   Flatbush Street, by the scar on his neck and his dirty gray overcoat.

   III.   The officer then knew there was hardly no way the suspect could get away

   IV.   from him on foot, because the street led to a dead end.

   (A) Line I

   (B) Line II

   (C) Line III

   (D) Line IV

ANSWERS AND EXPLANATIONS

1.   D

Learning Objective: Select the correct verb tense

Both of these sentences are grammatically correct. They are properly spelled, complete sentences that follow all rules of grammar and common usage. Therefore, Choice (D) is correct. Choices (A), (B), and (C) can be eliminated because they each indicate that there is at least one error in either sentence.

2.   A

Learning Objective: Avoid common spelling errors

"Breakneck" is the correctly spelled option.

3.   B

Learning Objective: Avoid common spelling errors

"Prioritize" is the correctly spelled option.

4.   C

Learning Objective: Select the correct pronoun

Both of these sentences suffer from ambiguous pronoun use. It is unclear to whom the pronoun "who" refers in sentence 1 since it appears to refer to the noun "noise," which is not a person. It is unclear to whom the pronoun "he" refers in sentence 2 since "he" seems to refer to the noun "car," which is not a person either. Therefore, any answer choice indicating that sentence 1 or sentence 2 is correct is wrong, which eliminates Choices (A), (B), and (D).

5.   C

Learning Objective: Check for subject-verb agreement

Both sentences contain grammatical errors. Sentence 1 uses the plural verb "provide" with the singular subject "Ms. Evers." Sentence 2 commits a similar error, matching the plural verb "return" with the singular subject "Officer Prince." Therefore, Choices (A), (B), and (D) can be eliminated.

6.   B

Learning Objective: Select the correct verb tense

The report is describing events that happened in the past. Therefore, all verbs should be in the past tense. "Take," in the first sentence, is a verb in the present tense. The verb should be "took." There is no error in the second sentence, and so Choice (B) is correct.

7.   B

Learning Objective: Avoid common spelling errors

The child belongs to the Skals, so there should be an apostrophe to show possession. The sentence should read, "The child is Mrs. and Mr. Skal's." Sentence 2 is correct, which eliminates Choices (A), (C), and (D).

8.   A

Learning Objective: Avoid common spelling errors

Sentence 2 contains a spelling error ("waded" instead of "waited"), and any answer choice that fails to indicate that it is wrong while sentence 1 is right. This eliminates Choices (B), (C), and (D).

9.   B

Learning Objective: Check for parallelism

The first sentence is incorrect because it contains an error in parallelism, combining the past-perfect progressive tenses of "take" and "drink" with the present-tense form of "smoke." Therefore, Choices (A), (C), and (D) cannot be correct.

10.   B

Learning Objective: Use commas correctly

Line II contains an error because it is missing a comma to offset the phrase "who'd attacked her from behind" from the rest of the sentence. Lines I, III, and IV contain no errors.

11. D

Learning Objective: Avoid common spelling errors

Line IV contains a spelling error. The correct spelling of the word is "premises," not "premeses."

12. C

Learning Objective: Select the correct pronoun

Line III contains the pronoun "he," but it is unclear to whom "he" refers. Is it Mr. Woolery, Mr. Harvis, or the officer? If you use a pronoun, it must have a clear antecedent, which is the noun that it replaces.

13. C

Learning Objective: Avoid double negatives

"Hardly no way" is a double negative that actually means there *is* a way. Remove the word "hardly" and the sentence makes sense: "The officer then knew there was no way the suspect could get away…."

AVOID COMMON SPELLING ERRORS

In some languages, words are spelled pretty much the way they sound—not in English. Take a look at *through* and *rough*. Or *through* and *threw*. There aren't many shortcuts here. Other than the old standby, I before E except after C or when it sounds like A, as in "neighbor" and "weigh"—which has many, many exceptions ("What a weird society!") to the point of being more misleading than helpful—there aren't many helpful hints for remembering how to spell. You'll just have to memorize the words you have trouble with.

Here is a list of some of the most commonly misspelled words.

Incorrect	Correct
athelete	athlete
calender	calendar
definately	definitely
docter	doctor
eleminate	eliminate
excelerate	accelerate
oppertunity	opportunity
persued	pursued
seperate	separate

Do any of these words pose problems for you? Make a list of the words that you consistently have trouble spelling. Make a note in your phone, or write them on index cards and carry the cards around with you. Anytime you have a few minutes, take a look. Make yourself as familiar as possible with them, so you will be more likely to spot the correct spelling right away.

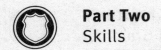

There are also some commonly misspelled words that tend to come up more often in law enforcement scenarios. You should familiarize yourself with these words, since they often appear in police reports.

Commonly Misspelled Words Related to Law Enforcement	
accessory	adjacent
affidavit	aggravated
allegation	arraign
belligerent	caliber
conscious	contusion
corroborate	counterfeit
delinquent	erratically
felony	forfeiture
harassment	illicit
indicted	interrogate
laceration	malicious
misdemeanor	necessary
noticeable	obstruction
occurrence	ordinance
possessions	resuscitate
statutory	subpoena

Then there are the cases when people confuse words that sound similar but mean totally different things. This confusion often arises when it comes to words with an apostrophe. So let's take a little punctuation detour, shall we?

The apostrophe

This bit of punctuation can indicate two totally separate ideas: possession or a contraction.

For instance, when you write *That locker is Tammy's*, the apostrophe tells readers you are talking about a locker that belongs to Tammy, not a locker built out of several people named Tammy. And while we are on the topic of possessives—what if you are talking about something belonging to several people named Tammy? In other words, you want the plural possessive. In that case, you add the apostrophe after the *s* indicating the plural: *It turned out that all three of the Tammys' dates were named Todd.*

Then there is the other meaning of the apostrophe. If you write *That locker can't be Tammy's*, the apostrophe in *can't* signals a contraction—a shortened combination of two words, with the apostrophe marking the place of the missing letter or letters.

The real confusion arises when words sound identical but are spelled differently. Take a look and see if any of these present problems for you.

their/there/they're

- **Their** indicates possession by more than one person, not including the speaker—*That's their car.*

- **There** indicates distance from the speaker—*That's their car over there.*

- **They're** is a contraction for *they are*—*That's their car over there; they're sitting inside it.*

your/you're

- **Your** indicates possession by someone the speaker is talking to—*Your golf game has improved.*

- **You're** is another contraction, meaning *you are*—*Your golf game has improved a lot. You're just about to break par.* (Note that "a lot" is two words, not one.)

its/it's

- **Its** is the possessive form of *it*—*The department has really raised its standards.*

- **It's** is a contraction of *it is*—*The department has really raised its standards, and it's a great morale booster.*

Soundalike words

Of course, the apostrophe isn't responsible for all sources of confusion. Certain words are close to others in sound and meaning, but different in spelling; it is important to know the difference so you can express yourself accurately.

lay/lie

- **Lay** is a transitive verb, one that indicates an action done to something or someone. Transitive verbs are incomplete without an object—*I'm going to lay tile in the new family room.*

- **Lie** is a regular verb, one that indicates an action done by something or someone—*I'm going to lay tile in the new family room, and then I'm going to lie down for a nap.*

raise/rise

This difference is similar to that between *lay* and *lie*.

- **Raise** is done to someone or something—*The candidate is going to have to raise a lot of money.*

- **Rise** is done by someone or something—*The candidate is going to have to raise a lot of money before he can rise in the political structure.*

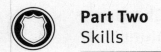

accept/except

- **Accept** means taking possession or acknowledging ownership of something—*The professor said he wouldn't accept late papers.*

- **Except** indicates a special case—*The professor said he wouldn't accept late papers, except in situations involving medical or family emergencies.*

effect/affect

- **Effect** is a noun, a result of some action—*The effect of the earthquake is devastating.*

- **Affect** is a verb, resulting in an effect—*The effect of the earthquake is devastating; nothing this disastrous has ever affected the region before.*

site/sight

- **Site** indicates a location—*The site of the outdoor music festival was a pasture south of town.*

- **Sight** is related to vision, either the sense itself or something that is seen—*The site of the outdoor music festival was a pasture south of town. After three days of crowds and rain, the area was quite a sight.*

persecute/prosecute

- **Persecute** means inflicting some kind of torment on someone—*I don't know why he keeps persecuting his assistant with unkind comments.*

- **Prosecute** involves bringing legal action—*I don't know why he keeps persecuting his assistant with unkind comments. If he doesn't watch it, she might try to have him prosecuted for harassment.*

precede/proceed

- **Precede** means to come before—*A Secret Service team always precedes the president as he travels.*

- **Proceed** means to continue—*A Secret Service team always precedes the president as he travels. If the security team doesn't feel a site is secure, the event will not proceed.*

SELECT THE CORRECT VERB TENSE

Grammar is the structure of language—how words fit together to form meaningful sentences. Most of the grammatical mistakes people make can be avoided by reviewing this chapter. Identify your weak spots and focus on those.

Here are some important terms and concepts to review before you read this section:

Verb: A word that expresses an action or a state of being.

Verbal: A word that is formed from a verb but is not functioning as a verb. There are three kinds of verbals: participles, gerunds, and infinitives.

It is important to realize that a verbal is not a verb, because a sentence must contain a verb, and a verbal won't do. A group of words containing a verbal but lacking a verb is not a sentence.

Participle: Usually ends in *-ing* or *-ed*. It is used as an adjective in a sentence.

- Let *sleeping* dogs lie.
- It is difficult to calm a *frightened* child.
- *Peering* into his microscope, Robert Koch saw the tuberculosis bacilli.

Gerund: Always ends in *-ing*. It is used in a sentence as a noun.

- *Skiing* can be dangerous.
- *Raising* a family is a serious task.
- I was surprised at his *acting* like such a coward.

Note from the third sentence that a noun or pronoun that comes before a gerund is in the possessive form: *his*, not *him*.

Infinitive: The basic form of a verb, generally preceded by *to*. It is usually used as a noun but may be used as an adjective or an adverb.

- Winston Churchill liked *to paint*. (infinitive used as a noun)
- The will *to conquer* is crucial. (infinitive used as an adjective—modifies "the will")
- Students in imperial China studied the Confucian classics *to excel* on civil service exams. (infinitive used as an adverb—modifies "studied")

Verb tense

You need to be familiar with both the way each tense is used individually and the ways the tenses are used together.

Present tense

Use the present tense to describe a state or action occurring in the present.

Congress is debating about health policy this session.

Use the present tense to describe habitual action.

Many Americans jog every day.

Use the present tense to describe "general truths"—things that are always true.

The earth is round and rotates on its axis.

Past tense

Use the past tense to describe an event or state that took place at a specific time in the past and is now over and done with.

Hundreds of people died when the Titanic *sank.*

Few people bought new cars last year.

Future tense

Use the future tense for intended actions or actions expected in the future.

The 22nd century will begin in the year 2101.

We often express future actions with the expression *going to*.

I am going to move to another apartment as soon as possible.

The present tense is also used to speak of future events. This is called the anticipatory future. We often use the anticipatory future with verbs of motion such as *come, go, arrive, depart,* and *leave*.

The senator is leaving for Europe tomorrow.

We also use the anticipatory future in two-clause sentences when one verb is in the regular future tense.

The disputants will announce the new truce as soon as they agree on its terms.

Present perfect tense

Use the present perfect tense for actions and states that started in the past and continue up to and into the present time.

Hawaii has been a state since 1959.

Use the present perfect for actions and states that happened a number of times in the past and may happen again in the future.

Italy has had many changes in government since World War II.

Use the present perfect for something that happened at an unspecified time in the past. Notice the difference in meaning between the following two sample sentences:

Present perfect: *Susan Sontag has written a critical essay about Leni Riefenstahl.* (We have no idea when—we just know she wrote it.)

Past: *Susan Sontag wrote a critical essay about Leni Riefenstahl in 1974.* (We use the simple past because we're specifying when Sontag wrote the essay.)

Past perfect tense

The past perfect tense is used to represent past actions or states that were completed before other past states or actions. The more recent past event is expressed in the past, and the earlier past event is expressed in the past perfect.

After he came to America, Vladimir Nabokov translated novels that he had written in Russian while he was living in Europe.

Note the difference in meaning between these two sentences:

The Civil War had ended when Lincoln was shot. = The war was over by the time of Lincoln's death.

The Civil War ended when Lincoln was shot. = The war ended when Lincoln died.

The first sentence is historically accurate.

Future perfect tense

Use the future perfect tense for a future state or event that will take place before another future event.

By the time the next election is held, the candidates will have debated at least once. (Note that the present tense form [anticipatory future] is used in the first clause.)

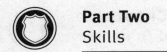

CHECK FOR SUBJECT-VERB AGREEMENT

We have talked about what a sentence has to have—a subject and verb. But they can't be just any subject and verb; they have to match in person and number. So, what does that mean?

Person indicates whom the speaker or writer is talking about or talking to. *First person* means the speaker is referring to or describing himself or herself—*I am*. *Second person* means the sentence is addressed to or describing the audience—*you are*. *Third person* means the sentence describes or refers to someone or something that is neither the speaker nor the audience—*he/she/it is*.

Then there is *number*—singular or plural. The previous examples are all singular in number. *We are, you are, they are*—that's first person plural, second person plural, and third person plural.

All the given examples match in person and number. You wouldn't say *I are a good student*. That's a pretty easy mistake to spot, but it can get trickier. Here are some of the easy-to-miss situations.

Subject separated from the verb

Do not get distracted by phrases that come between the subject and verb. Take a look at this sentence and see if you can tell which verb is correct:

Officer Prince, who spends many days off jumping with an elite group of skydivers, remain/remains *calm under the most stressful circumstances.*

The right answer is the singular form, *remains*. Even though there is a plural noun right before the verb, the subject of the sentence is *Officer Prince*, a singular noun. Everything between the commas just gives you more information about the singular subject.

Compound subjects

Another tricky situation occurs when you have a sentence in which the subject is a list of some kind.

The applicant told the interviewers that his drive, determination, and intelligence makes/make *him an ideal recruit.*

The correct answer is *make*—that list of three singular nouns combined with the word *and* adds up to one compound subject, which requires a plural verb.

Compound impostors

As if compound subjects weren't difficult enough, there are some sentences that seem to have compound subjects when they really don't. Watch out for phrases containing or beginning with *neither/nor, either/or, along with, as well as,* or *in addition to.* These are the compound impostors.

Neither the rookie nor the old-timer knows/know *how to handle the situation.*

Here, the right answer is the singular verb—*knows*—even though this looks like a list of two nouns. To make it clearer, rewrite the sentence as *Neither one knows how to handle the situation.* That is the implied meaning of *either/or* and *neither/nor.*

However, what if you had rookies and old-timers?

Neither the rookies nor the old-timers knows/know *how to handle the situation.*

Here the sentence takes a plural verb, *know.* That is because you are dealing with plural subjects.

Officer Tremblay, along with half of the 9th Precinct, was/were *a rabid softball player.*

The sentence takes a singular verb, *was. Officer Tremblay* is the real subject of the sentence. The phrase along with *half of the 9th Precinct* is just a kind of detour; grammatically, it doesn't become part of the subject.

SELECT THE CORRECT PRONOUN

Pronouns stand in for other nouns in a sentence. Take a look at the following table listing the different kinds of pronouns.

Type of Pronoun	Purpose	Examples	Sample Sentence
Personal Pronouns	Stand in for people or things	I, me, you, he, she, him, her, it, we, us, they, them, one	*John and Latisha have been friends for years; they went to kindergarten together.*
Relative Pronouns	Used in clauses relating to someone or something	who, whom, which, that, where, whose	*The suspect, who had been arrested many times before, seemed quite comfortable with the processing routine.*
Possessive Pronouns	Refer to things belonging to some individual or group	mine, yours, his, hers, theirs, ours, its	*Enriqué did well on the screening test, but Sally did even better; in fact, hers was the highest score in the state.*

Pronouns are used most often to eliminate repetitiveness. Here's an example:

The department offers a wide range of benefits for the department's employees.

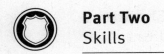
Using a pronoun, this sentence becomes: *The department offers a wide range of benefits for its employees.*

The original noun (*department*) is called the antecedent. You should always make sure that there is no confusion about which noun is the antecedent of a pronoun. This grammatical error is called ambiguous pronoun reference.

Here are a couple of examples:

I've always been interested in forensic psychology, so I've decided to be one.

One what? No one can be a forensic psychology. Here is one way to make the sentence clearer:

I've always been interested in forensic psychology, so I've decided to make that my specialty.

Officers Smith and Jones jumped into their cruiser and, hitting the siren, raced to the scene. It was brand new.

What is new—the scene, the siren, or the cruiser? The way the sentence is written, it's impossible to tell. Here's a possible fix:

Officers Smith and Jones jumped into their brand-new cruiser and, hitting the siren, raced to the scene.

PLACE MODIFIERS IN THE RIGHT SPOT

Modifying phrases can help describe something more precisely or explain something more fully.

Misplaced modifiers

If modifiers are not clearly linked to the noun they are modifying, these phrases can also make a sentence confusing. For example:

With its contents spilling onto the highway, Lieutenant Stanley ran toward the overturned tanker truck.

The way this is written, it seems as though the contents of Lieutenant Stanley are spilling; it is actually the tanker truck's contents. To make this sentence clear and grammatically correct, it should be rewritten like this:

Lieutenant Stanley ran toward the overturned tanker truck, which was spilling its contents onto the highway.

Dangling modifiers

A modifying phrase or clause should clearly refer to a particular word in the sentence. A modifying phrase or clause that does not sensibly refer to any word in the sentence is called a dangling modifier. The most common sort of dangler is an introductory modifying phrase that's followed by a word it can't logically refer to.

Wrong: *Desiring to free his readers from superstition, the theories of Epicurus are expounded in Lucretius's poem "De rerum natura."*

The problem with this sentence is that the phrase that begins the sentence seems to modify the noun following it: *theories*. In fact, there is really nowhere the modifier can be put to make it work properly and no noun to which it can reasonably refer (*Lucretius's*, the possessive, is functioning as an adjective modifying *poem*). Get rid of dangling constructions by clarifying the modification relationship or by making the dangler into a subordinate clause.

Correct: *Desiring to free his readers from superstition, Lucretius expounded the theories of Epicurus in his poem "De rerum natura."*

Now the phrase *desiring to free his readers from superstition* clearly refers to the proper noun *Lucretius*.

USE COMMAS CORRECTLY

When using commas, follow these rules:

A. Use commas to separate items in a series. If more than two items are listed in a series, they should be separated by commas; the final comma—the one that precedes the word *and*—is optional. Never use a comma after the word *and*.

Wrong: *My recipe for buttermilk biscuits contains flour, baking soda, salt, shortening, and, buttermilk.*

Correct: *My recipe for buttermilk biscuits contains flour, baking soda, salt, shortening, and buttermilk.*

B. Do not place commas before the first element of a series or after the last element.

Wrong: *My investment advisor recommended that I construct a portfolio of, stocks, bonds, commodities futures, and precious metals, to succeed.*

Correct: *My investment advisor recommended that I construct a portfolio of stocks, bonds, commodities futures, and precious metals to succeed.*

C. Use commas to separate two or more adjectives before a noun; do not use a comma after the last adjective in the series.

Wrong: *I can't believe you sat through that long, dull, uninspired, movie three times.*

Correct: *I can't believe you sat through that long, dull, uninspired movie three times.*

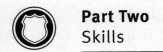

D. Use commas to set off parenthetical clauses and phrases. (A parenthetical expression is one that is not necessary to the main idea of the sentence.)

Correct: *Gordon, a writer by profession, bakes an excellent cheesecake.*

The main idea is that Gordon bakes an excellent cheesecake. The intervening clause merely serves to identify Gordon; thus, it should be set off with commas.

Correct: *The newspaper that has the most insipid editorials is* The Daily Times.

Correct: *The newspaper, which has the most insipid editorials of any I have read, won numerous awards last week.*

In the first of these examples, the clause beginning with *that* defines which paper the author is discussing—it is necessary to the sentence and should not be set off by commas. In the second example, the main point is that the newspaper won numerous awards, and the intervening clause beginning with *which* gives additional information.

E. Use commas after introductory participial or prepositional phrases.

Correct: *Having watered his petunias every day during the drought, Harold was very disappointed when his garden was destroyed by insects.*

Correct: *After the banquet, Harold and Martha went dancing.*

F. Use commas to separate independent clauses (clauses that could stand alone as complete sentences) connected by coordinate conjunctions *and, but, not, yet, for, or,* and *so*. Make sure the comma separates two independent clauses, joined by a conjunction. It is incorrect to use a comma to separate the two parts of a compound verb.

Correct: *Susan's old car has been belching blue smoke from the tailpipe for two weeks, but it has not broken down yet.*

Wrong: *Barbara went to the grocery store, and bought two quarts of milk.*

AVOID DOUBLE NEGATIVES

In English, if a sentence contains two negatives—words such as *not* or *without*—the words cancel each other out. Sometimes people intentionally use double negatives, especially when they are trying to sound sophisticated. Saying that the little bistro was not without charm means it was a cute place. But it takes a second to figure that out. It is better to avoid double negatives altogether.

Watch out for the less obvious negatives—*hardly, barely, scarcely, cannot*. They do count as negatives.

Here are some examples of double negatives and ways to fix them:

> *The suspect said that she didn't commit no burglaries.*

If you want to be clear and correct, you shouldn't write this way. *Didn't* is a contraction for *did not*—that is one negative. Combined with *no*, you have a double negative. Here are two ways to fix it:

> *The suspect said she didn't commit any burglaries.*

> OR

> *The suspect said she committed no burglaries.*

Here's another example:

> *Recruit Smith hasn't hardly any worries about how he will do on the running portion of the test.*

Hasn't is a contraction for *has not*, and *hardly* is one of those tricky negatives. You have one negative too many. Here are two ways to fix it:

> *Recruit Smith has hardly any worries about how he will do on the running portion of the test.*

> OR

> *Recruit Smith hasn't any worries about how he will do on the running portion of the test.*

One last example:

> *With the new computerized databases, it doesn't take scarcely any time to run a license check.*

Try one of these instead:

> *With the new computerized databases, it doesn't take any time to run a license check.*

> OR

> *With the new computerized databases, it takes scarcely any time to run a license check.*

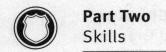
CHECK FOR PARALLELISM

Remember, when you express a number of ideas of equal importance and function in the same sentence, you should always be careful to make them all the same grammatical form (that is, all nouns, all adjectives, all gerunds, all clauses, or whatever). That's called parallel structure, or parallelism.

Coordinate ideas

Coordinate ideas occur in pairs or in series, and they are linked by conjunctions such as *and*, *but*, *or*, and *nor* or, in certain instances, by linking verbs such as *is*.

Wrong: *To earn credits, an American college student can take up folk dancing, ballet, or study belly dancing.*

Correct: *To earn credits, an American college student can take up folk dancing, ballet, or belly dancing.*

Note that once you begin repeating a word in a series like the following, you must follow through:

Wrong: *A wage earner might invest her money in stocks, in bonds, or real estate.*

Correct: *A wage earner might invest her money in stocks, in bonds, or in real estate.*

Also correct: *A wage earner might invest her money in stocks, bonds, or real estate.*

This principle applies equally to prepositions (*in, on, by, with,* etc.), articles (*the, a, an*), helping verbs (*had, has, would,* etc.), and possessive pronouns (*his, her,* etc.). You must either repeat the preposition, article, helping verb, or possessive pronoun in front of each element in the series or include it in front of only the first item in the series.

Correlative constructions

There is a group of words in English called correlative conjunctions. They are used to relate two ideas in some way. Here's a list of them:

both … and

either … or

neither … nor

not only … but also

You should always be careful to place correlative conjunctions immediately before the terms they're coordinating.

Wrong: *Isaac Newton not only studied physics, but also theology.*

The problem here is that the author intends to coordinate the two nouns *physics* and *theology* but makes the mistake of putting the verb of the sentence (*studied*) after the first element of the construction (*not only*), which destroys the parallelism. Note that the solution to an error like this is usually to move one of the conjunctions.

Correct: *Isaac Newton studied not only physics, but also theology.*

Compared or contrasted ideas

Frequently, two or more ideas are compared or contrasted within the same sentence. Compared or contrasted ideas should be presented in the same grammatical form.

Certain phrases should clue you in that the sentence contains ideas that should be presented in parallel form. These phrases include *as … as* and *more (or less) x than y*.

Wrong: *Skiing is as strenuous as to run.*

Correct: *Skiing is as strenuous as running.*

Wrong: *Skiing is less dangerous than to rappel down a cliff.*

Correct: *To ski is less dangerous than to rappel down a cliff.*

To be

In certain cases, sentences with forms of *to be* must be expressed in parallel form.

Wrong: *To drive while intoxicated is risking grave injury and criminal charges.*

When an infinitive is the subject of *to be*, don't use a gerund after the verb, and vice versa. Pair infinitives with infinitives and gerunds with gerunds.

Correct: *To drive while intoxicated is to risk grave injury and criminal charges.*

Note that we wouldn't change both words to gerunds in this sentence because it wouldn't sound idiomatic in its current form. However, you could use gerunds if you changed the verb to something like this:

Correct: *Driving while intoxicated means risking grave injury and criminal charges.*

Now that you have reviewed these basic grammar and spelling rules, see if you can answer the following practice questions. These questions are an excellent way to find out your strengths and weaknesses in these subjects. Questions on the police exam you take may be a little different than these but are likely to cover the same basic principles.

TEST WHAT YOU LEARNED

> **Directions:** Choose the ONE best answer for each question.

1. An officer is preparing a missing persons report. She reviews the rough draft of her report, which contains the following two sentences:

   1. Denise Blackwell were reported missing on March 17th, 2019.

   2. By that point, she had been missing for 2 days.

   Which of the following best describes the above sentences?

   (A) Only sentence #1 is grammatically correct.

   (B) Only sentence #2 is grammatically correct.

   (C) Neither sentence #1 nor sentence #2 is grammatically correct.

   (D) Both sentence #1 and sentence #2 are grammatically correct.

2. The 16-year-old boy was intoxicated and _____, so it took 2 officers to subdue him.

   (A) inraged

   (B) enraged

   (C) enrajed

   (D) ennraged

3. An officer is preparing a report about a burglary. He reviews the rough draft of his report, which contains the following two sentences:

   1. The alarm sounded at 6:09 p.m. on July 2nd.

   2. Officer Cristo and me responded to the alarm immediately.

   Which of the following best describes the above sentences?

   (A) Only sentence #1 is grammatically correct.

   (B) Only sentence #2 is grammatically correct.

   (C) Neither sentence #1 nor sentence #2 is grammatically correct.

   (D) Both sentence #1 and sentence #2 are grammatically correct.

4. Police officers must be trained to assist citizens in _____ situations.

    (A) sensitive

    (B) sensative

    (C) sensetive

    (D) sensiteve

5. An officer is preparing a missing persons report. She reviews the rough draft of her report, which contains the following two sentences:

    1. On September 30th, 2018, Mr. Richard Fetter, a teacher and basketball coach at Oakdale High School, were last seen.

    2. Mrs. Anna Wilson, a science teacher at the school, were the last person to see Mr. Fetter.

    Which of the following best describes the above sentences?

    (A) Only sentence #1 is grammatically correct.

    (B) Only sentence #2 is grammatically correct.

    (C) Neither sentence #1 nor sentence #2 is grammatically correct.

    (D) Both sentence #1 and sentence #2 are grammatically correct.

6. An officer is preparing a burglary report. He reviews the rough draft of his report, which contains the following two sentences:

    1. The forensics team noted that the suspect did not leave no fingerprints at the crime scene.

    2. However, the team also discovered several fibers that may provide clues to the suspect's identity.

    Which of the following best describes the above sentences?

    (A) Only sentence #1 is grammatically correct.

    (B) Only sentence #2 is grammatically correct.

    (C) Neither sentence #1 nor sentence #2 is grammatically correct.

    (D) Both sentence #1 and sentence #2 are grammatically correct.

7. An officer is preparing an auto theft report. She reviews the rough draft of her report, which contains the following two sentences:

   1. A witness said that she saw a six-foot man at the scene of the crime.

   2. However, the footprints near the stolen car were too small to be a six-foot mans'.

   Which of the following best describes the above sentences?

   (A) Only sentence #1 is correct.

   (B) Only sentence #2 is correct.

   (C) Neither sentence #1 nor sentence #2 is correct.

   (D) Both sentence #1 and sentence #2 are correct.

8. An officer is preparing a report after a murder. He reviews the rough draft of his report, which contains the following two sentences:

   1. We found the victim laying on the sidewalk in front of 101 Bergman Avenue.

   2. The knife protruding from the victim's sternum and it's handle failed to turn up any fingerprints.

   Which of the following best describes the above sentences?

   (A) Only sentence #1 is grammatically correct.

   (B) Only sentence #2 is grammatically correct.

   (C) Neither sentence #1 nor sentence #2 is grammatically correct.

   (D) Both sentence #1 and sentence #2 are grammatically correct.

9. An officer is preparing a drunk and disorderly behavior report. She reviews the rough draft of her report, which contains the following two sentences:

   1. The man became extremely belligerent.

   2. The officer handcuffed the intoxicates man.

   Which of the following best describes the above sentences?

   (A) Only sentence #1 is grammatically correct.

   (B) Only sentence #2 is grammatically correct.

   (C) Neither sentence #1 nor sentence #2 is grammatically correct.

   (D) Both sentence #1 and sentence #2 are grammatically correct.

10. An officer is preparing a stolen goods report. He reviews the rough draft of his report, which contains the following two sentences:

    1. Ms. Tomlin reported that several items had been stolen from her office.

    2. These items were taken from her desk drawer, the cubbyhole above her desk, and taken from the cloak room.

    Which of the following best describes the above sentences?

    (A) Only sentence #1 is grammatically correct.

    (B) Only sentence #2 is grammatically correct.

    (C) Neither sentence #1 nor sentence #2 is grammatically correct.

    (D) Both sentence #1 and sentence #2 are grammatically correct.

For the following items, please choose the line that contains the misspelled word, grammatical error, or punctuation error by choosing the line number. Only one of the lines will contain an error.

11. I.   On her first day in the police department, Officer Cady patrolled Brooker Avenue,

    II.   wrote three parking tickets, and, asked a man loitering in front of a bank

    III. to move to another location. It was an uneventful but positive first day on the job.

    IV.   She knew that every day would not go so smoothly.

    (A) Line I

    (B) Line II

    (C) Line III

    (D) Line IV

12. I.   The officer approached Mr. Bradley, who was asleep on the sidewalk

    II.   in front of Murray's Pub. The officer asked him to move along, but he was

    III. very slow to respond. Eventuly he sat up to explain himself,

    IV.   but his speech was difficult to understand; he was clearly very intoxicated.

    (A) Line I

    (B) Line II

    (C) Line III

    (D) Line IV

13. I.   Going way over the speed limit, 23 people were injured when the

    II.   bus careened off Oakdale Drive. The officers attended to the injured parties

    III. as best as they could while waiting for backup. Additional officers arrived at

    IV.   3:30 p.m. Several ambulances arrived to tend to the injured people.

    (A) Line I

    (B) Line II

    (C) Line III

    (D) Line IV

14. I.   As Lucy Witt exited the store, the alarm sounded. Officer Aimee Shuk then

    II.   arrived to interview her. She took a quick break to take a phone call.

    III. The officer then viewed the security camera recording, which clearly

    IV.   showed Witt shoplifting the sweater.

    (A) Line I

    (B) Line II

    (C) Line III

    (D) Line IV

ANSWERS AND EXPLANATIONS

1. B

Learning Objective: Check for subject-verb agreement

Sentence 1 contains an error in subject-verb agreement since "Denise Blackwell" is a singular subject and "were" is a plural verb. Sentence 2 contains no errors, so any choice that suggests sentence 1 is correct or sentence 2 is incorrect can be eliminated. Therefore, Choices (A), (C), and (D) can all be eliminated.

2. B

Learning Objective: Avoid common spelling errors

"Enraged" is the correctly spelled option.

3. A

Learning Objective: Select the correct pronoun

Sentence 2 uses the incorrect pronoun "me" when "I" is required. Sentence 1 is correctly written. Therefore, any answer choice suggesting that sentence 1 is incorrect or sentence 2 is correct can be eliminated. This eliminates Choices (B), (C), and (D).

4. A

Learning Objective: Avoid common spelling errors

"Sensitive" is the correctly spelled option.

5. C

Learning Objective: Check for subject-verb agreement

Both sentences match singular subjects with the plural verb "were." "Was" is the correct singular verb to use in both cases. Therefore, Choice (C) is correct, and Choices (A), (B), and (D) can be eliminated.

6. B

Learning Objective: Avoid double negatives

Sentence 1 contains a double negative—"did not leave no"—which is grammatically incorrect. Sentence 2 contains no errors. Therefore, Choice (B) is the best answer.

7. A

Learning Objective: Avoid common spelling errors

Sentence 2 is constructed to show that the footprints belong to a six-foot man, but the sentence fails to show possession correctly. The apostrophe belongs between "man" and the letter "s." Only sentence 1 is correct, so Choice (A) is correct and the other answer choices can be eliminated.

8. C

Learning Objective: Avoid common spelling errors

Both sentences contain errors. Sentence 1 requires the regular verb "lying," not the transitive verb "laying." Sentence 2 requires the possessive noun "its," not "it's," a contraction of "it" and "is." Therefore, any answer choice indicating that either sentence 1 or sentence 2 is correctly written can be eliminated. This eliminates Choices (A), (B), and (D).

9. A

Learning Objective: Select the correct verb tense

Sentence 2 requires a verbal called a participle, which is a verb used as an adjective. Participles usually end in -ing or -ed, so "intoxicated" would be a better word to use than "intoxicates." Sentence 1 contains no errors, so Choices (B), (C), and (D) can be eliminated.

10. A

Learning Objective: Check for parallelism

The second sentence is incorrect because it contains an error in parallelism, failing to coordinate its ideas by using the same construction for all three items in the list of places where Ms. Tomlin's items were stolen. Therefore, Choices (B), (C), and (D) cannot be correct.

11. B

Learning Objective: Use commas correctly

Line II contains an error because it contains an unnecessary comma after the conjunction "and." Lines I, III, and IV contain no errors.

12. C

Learning Objective: Avoid common spelling errors

There is a spelling error in Line III. "Eventuly" is incorrect; the correct spelling is "eventually."

13. A

Learning Objective: Place modifiers in the right spot

The modifying phrase "going way over the speed limit" should be placed just before or after "the bus." Its placement in Line I makes the phrase technically modify "23 people," which is incorrect.

14. B

Learning Objective: Select the correct pronoun

Line II is incorrect because it is unclear to whom the pronoun "she" is referring. Is it Lucy or Aimee? If you use a pronoun, its antecedent—or the word it is replacing—must be clear.

SELF-REFLECTION

In this chapter, you learned the skills necessary to both perform well on the spelling and grammar sections of the exam. This will help you write clear and effective reports during your career as an officer. You learned how to work your way through such tricky situations as soundalike words and subjects separated from their verbs. You learned how to avoid such common errors as double negatives, fragments, misplaced modifiers, and ambiguous pronouns. You also learned the importance of using apostrophes correctly and ensuring that singular and compound subjects agree with their accompanying verbs. Keep practicing and you'll be able to put these skills to their optimum use on Test Day and beyond!

Test What You Know score: _____/13 correct

Test What You Learned score: _____/14 correct

After working through the practice problems in this chapter, which of the Learning Objectives have you mastered? Place a check mark next to those objectives to keep track of your progress.

- ☐ Avoid common spelling errors
- ☐ Select the correct verb tense
- ☐ Check for subject-verb agreement
- ☐ Select the correct pronoun
- ☐ Place modifiers in the right spot
- ☐ Use commas correctly
- ☐ Avoid double negatives
- ☐ Check for parallelism

CHAPTER 6

Reading Comprehension

As with grammar and spelling, you may or may not have a test section specifically covering reading comprehension. However, the entire police exam will require you to read and apply skills encompassed in reading comprehension. This chapter includes strategies for effective comprehension and offers practice questions to help you hone your skills.

LEARNING OBJECTIVES

In this chapter, you will review how to:

- [ ] Apply active reading strategies
- [ ] Identify main ideas
- [ ] Identify keywords to determine meaning

TEST WHAT YOU KNOW

> **Directions:** Choose the ONE best answer for each question.

Please use the following passage to answer questions 1–2.

Police officers Leah Grossman and Jessica Dukes were patrolling the 72nd Precinct on foot at 5:35 p.m. on July 31, 2019. They came upon the scene of a hit-and-run accident at the corner of 1st Street and 6th Avenue, which occurred six minutes earlier. A Hispanic man, approximately 22 years old, 5 feet 7 inches, 156 lb, with black hair and brown eyes, was lying unconscious in the street. He was wearing a blue T-shirt, black shorts, and white Nike sneakers. The man was bleeding from his forehead and it appeared that his left leg was broken. A witness named Mr. Chris Reese told Officer Dukes that a black Chevrolet Camaro came careening down 1st Street, hit the man—who had been crossing the street—and sped off without stopping. Mr. Reese then called an ambulance on his cell phone. Mr. Reese did not take notice of the Camaro's license plate number.

As the ambulance arrived to take the injured man, identified as Walter Guzman, to St. Peter's Hospital on 8th Avenue, Officer Grossman interviewed another witness, named Ms. Petra Brida. Ms. Brida did note the Camaro's license plate number: MW5-P87. Officer Grossman traced the license to Mr. Lon Price, a 17-year-old Caucasian male living at 67 12th Avenue. Upon arriving at the residence, Officer Grossman found Mr. Price's mother. She explained that her son was not at home, but he had left his driver's license behind. Officer Grossman asked to examine the license, issued in the state of New Jersey with the identification number 291 796 783. The expiration date was August 1, 2020. The officer asked Mrs. Price how her son was dressed that day, to help identify him, and Mrs. Price explained that her son was wearing a green T-shirt and white shorts.

Officers Grossman and Dukes took Mr. Price into custody at 6:12 p.m. They then filled out a crime report. The report number is 09373889357.

1. According to the passage, how many witnesses saw the hit-and-run accident?

    (A) Zero

    (B) One

    (C) Two

    (D) Three

2. According to the passage, at what time did the accident occur?

   (A) 5:35 p.m.

   (B) 5:29 p.m.

   (C) 5:41 p.m.

   (D) 6:12 p.m.

Please use the following passage to answer questions 3–5.

Police officers Diana Garrido and Andy Wong are dispatched to 7 Acme Avenue, Apt. 3, at 9:23 a.m. on June 16, 2017, in response to a domestic disturbance reported by a Mr. Dinsmore. They arrive at the apartment at 9:42 a.m., ring the third-floor buzzer, and are greeted by Ms. Jennifer Lilya. Ms. Lilya tells the officer that she'd returned from her overnight shift at the 7-11 convenience store at 9:30 a.m. Mr. Dennis Hayes then emerges from the bathroom and informs the officers that his wife, Ms. Lilya, had been home since 9:00 a.m. when she became agitated because he was still in bed and had yet to leave for his morning shift at the Central Blvd. Elementary School, where he works as a janitor. Mr. Hayes then claims that Ms. Lilya began screaming at him and threw a glass flower vase against their bedroom wall. Ms. Lilya then claims that her husband is lying and that she only arrived from work at 9:30 a.m.

While Officer Wong begins to fill out a crime report, Officer Garrido enters the bedroom with the consent of Mr. Hayes. On the bedroom carpet, she finds a broken vase, scattered flowers, and a puddle of spilled water. Ms. Lilya then claims that she accidentally bumped into the vase upon returning home because she was tired from working all night.

The officers let Ms. Lilya off with a warning and let her know that they will have to take her to the station if they receive another similar complaint lodged against her in the future. The officers complete their investigation, exit the premises at 9:47 a.m., and fill out their report back at the station at 9:55 a.m.

3. The passage is mainly about:

   (A) a domestic disturbance at the Lilya/Hayes residence

   (B) a woman who is physically abusive toward her husband

   (C) a man who works as a janitor at an elementary school

   (D) a flower vase that is mysteriously destroyed

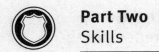
4. At what time did Ms. Lilya claim to have returned home from work on June 16, 2017?

    (A) 9:00 a.m.

    (B) 9:23 a.m.

    (C) 9:30 a.m.

    (D) 9:47 a.m.

5. Which of the following is the best summary of the first paragraph of the passage?

    (A) Officer Garrido finds a broken vase in the bedroom of Ms. Lilya, who claims she bumped into the vase.

    (B) Ms. Lilya becomes agitated because her husband is still in bed when he is supposed to be at work.

    (C) Ms. Lilya screams at Mr. Hayes and throws a glass flower vase against their bedroom wall.

    (D) Mr. Hayes and Ms. Lilya disagree about the details regarding the domestic disturbance at their residence.

Answer questions 6–8 solely on the basis of the following passage.

Police officers Elizabeth Nussbaum and Philip Ryan are dispatched to 55 East End Drive at 7:52 p.m., on February 1, 2017, in response to a burglary reported by a Mr. Nesmith. They arrive at the house at 8:02 p.m., ring the doorbell, and are greeted by Mr. David Nesmith. Mr. Nesmith tells the officers that he drove home from John F. Kennedy Airport at approximately 7:30 p.m. Mr. Nesmith states that he had just returned home from a week-long trip to Orlando, Florida. Upon entering his home, he immediately noticed that his television was missing. He then entered his bedroom to find his computer was missing. Mr. Nesmith then called the police at 7:52 p.m. While he waited for the police to arrive, Mr. Nesmith checked the bottom drawer of his armoire and discovered that a baseball card collection valued at $2,000 was also missing.

While Officer Nussbaum begins to fill out a crime report, Officer Ryan exits 55 East End Drive and goes across the street to interview neighbors who may have information related to the burglary.

Mrs. Thorkelson, age 62, who lives at 56 East End Drive located directly across the street from Mr. Nesmith's residence, tells Officer Nussbaum that she happened to be looking out of her window at approximately 10:00 p.m. on January 29, 2017, when she saw a man on the front lawn of 55 East End Drive. Believing the man to be Mr. Nesmith, she paid him no mind and had no additional details about him.

Officer Ryan then goes to 57 East End Drive and interviews the neighbor who lives there, Mr. Samuel Jones, age 48. Mr. Jones tells the officer that he too took notice of a man on Mr. Nesmith's property on January 29. Mr. Jones describes the man as Caucasian, about 30 years old, 5 feet 4 inches, 130 lb, with blond hair, and carrying what looked like a small bag. Officer Ryan then contacts other neighbors on East End Drive, but none report similar sightings of a man on the Nesmith property on January 29.

While Officer Ryan interviews neighbors, Office Nussbaum acquires additional information from Mr. Nesmith. Nesmith reveals that he kept his baseball card collection in a small bag. He also states that he is 42 years old. His telephone number at work is (212) 564-8679, and his work address is 655 Commercial Parkway. Mr. Nesmith does not have a home telephone number, but he does have a cell phone, and its number is (212) 456-9383.

Officers Nussbaum and Ryan finish their investigation and complete the crime report.

6. According to the passage, where was Mr. Nesmith on January 29, 2017?

   (A) 55 East End Drive

   (B) John F. Kennedy Airport

   (C) Orlando, Florida

   (D) 655 Commercial Parkway

7. What is the age of the victim of the theft?

   (A) 42 years old

   (B) 62 years old

   (C) 30 years old

   (D) 48 years old

Read this sentence from the passage:

They arrive at the house at 8:02 p.m., ring the doorbell, and are greeted by Mr. David Nesmith.

8. How long did it take police to respond to Mr. Nesmith's house?

   (A) 7 minutes

   (B) 10 minutes

   (C) 22 minutes

   (D) 32 minutes

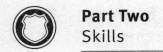
ANSWERS AND EXPLANATIONS

1. C

Learning Objective: Apply active reading strategies

The passage notes two different people who witnessed the accident, Chris Reese and Petra Brida. Note that the victim could have also seen the accident as it happened, but that information is not included in the passage because the victim was unconscious and could not provide a statement.

2. B

Learning Objective: Apply active reading strategies

The passage states that the officers arrived on the scene at 5:35 p.m., but that the accident had occurred six minutes earlier.

3. A

Learning Objective: Identify main ideas

As a whole, the passage is about a domestic disturbance at the home of Jennifer Lilya and Dennis Hayes. There is no proof that Lilya is actually abusive toward her husband in the passage, so Choice (B) does not describe its main idea accurately. The fact that Hayes is a janitor at an elementary school is a minor detail in the passage and hardly sums up its main idea, so Choice (C) is not the best answer. The destruction of the vase is an important detail in the passage, but it is still only a detail and hardly the passage's main idea, so Choice (D) is not the best answer either.

4. C

Learning Objective: Apply active reading strategies

According to the passage, Ms. Lilya claimed to have returned home from work at 9:30 a.m. on June 16, 2017. Choice (A) is the time that Mr. Hayes said Ms. Lilya arrived home, not the time Ms. Lilya claimed. Choice (B) is the time the officers were dispatched to the Lilya/Hayes residence. Choice (D) is the time that the officers arrived at the residence.

5. D

Learning Objective: Identify main ideas

Choice (D) is an accurate summary of the most important points in the first paragraph of the passage. Choice (A) is a summary of the passage's second paragraph, not its first one. Choices (B) and (C) are details in the first paragraph and fail to summarize the most important ideas in the paragraph as a whole.

6. C

Learning Objective: Apply active reading strategies

Mr. Nesmith states on February 1 that he has just returned home from a week-long trip to Orlando, Florida, which means he must have been in Orlando on January 29.

7. A

Learning Objective: Apply active reading strategies

The final paragraph notes that the theft victim, Mr. Nesmith, is 42 years old.

8. B

Learning Objective: Apply active reading strategies

According to the passage, Officers Nussbaum and Ryan are dispatched at 7:52 p.m., and they arrive at 8:02 p.m. It took 10 minutes for police to get to Mr. Nesmith's house.

APPLY ACTIVE READING STRATEGIES

Here are some basic tips for focusing on the important aspects of a written passage. As you prepare for your test, try applying these techniques to everything you read—from the morning paper, to your sports magazine, to the novel you are reading.

Pre-reading

You can often get a pretty good idea of what a story or article is about by quickly glancing over it. Before you read the entire thing, put it through a quick pre-reading survey:

- Is there a title? If so, what does it tell you about the article?

- Are there pictures, charts, or illustrations? What information do they give you?

- What does the first sentence say?

- What can you tell about the source of the information?

- Does the article present fact, opinion, or both?

Based on your pre-reading, you can often make an accurate prediction about the content of the text.

Active reading

It's probably been drilled into your head that you shouldn't write in books. Although this is the respectful choice if the book doesn't belong to you, you can mark up your own books, magazines, and newspapers. And you should mark them up. That's part of active reading, which will help you focus on the meaning of the text. Mark words that are repeated. Write down any questions you have as you read, or circle words you don't understand. Underline the sentence, or sentences, that introduce or sum up the author's main point, as well as the details that support that main point.

After reading

Before you move on, think about what you have just read and make sure you fully understand it:

- **Identify the key points.** What are the most important statements the author made? List them.

- **Separate fact from opinion.** Note which statements are supported by facts and which statements represent the author's opinion.

- **Summarize.** Try to shrink these statements down to one or two sentences.

- **Any questions?** If you wrote down questions that remain unanswered when you finish reading, take another look. Focus on the specific sentences or passages that prompted the questions.

Summarizing

Being able to sum up the material you have read is an important aspect of reading comprehension. It demonstrates that you have understood the argument well enough to state the author's main idea in your own words. Here is a sample paragraph of information to be summarized:

Hollywood movies and television series tend to show criminal profiling as a mysterious, supernatural talent, something like mind-reading or predicting the future. In fact, criminal profiling consists of close analysis of crime scene evidence, using a large body of information gathered from other offenders to make reasonable assumptions about the offender in a particular case. Like any other human activity, some people have more of a knack for profiling than others, but anyone can learn the basic principles and techniques of criminal profiling.

An accurate summary of the paragraph's topic would be something like this:

Criminal profiling is not a mysterious talent, but a set of principles and techniques that can be taught.

This sentence sums up the author's argument; everything else in the paragraph provides details. If you get stuck thinking of a summary, or have any other trouble with a passage, keep reading to learn ways to move past your problems.

IDENTIFY MAIN IDEAS

Why did the author write the material you are reading? To inform you? To persuade you? To motivate you? What particular issue does the text cover? In the margin, write down what you think the author's purpose is. It will be related to, but not exactly the same as, the main idea.

The main idea is a specific idea that supports the author's broader purpose. Often, the first sentence clues you in to the main idea, or topic; sometimes, the first sentence is a straightforward statement of the topic. However, don't count on that. A writer may choose to leave the main idea unstated, expecting you to draw your own conclusions from the evidence and arguments assembled in the passage.

Think of the main idea as the spine of the passage; it is the long line that holds everything together.

Look for a statement of the main idea; if you find it, underline it. If there doesn't seem to be a sentence that sums up the topic, write your own statement of the main idea in the margin.

Paragraph topics

If the main idea is the spine of the passage, the paragraph topics are the bones; they provide the underlying structure. Each paragraph adds something slightly different to the author's argument; the supporting element contained in a paragraph is the paragraph topic. As with the main idea, paragraph topics may or may not be directly stated.

After you finish each paragraph, look for its topic sentence and underline it. If you can't find a topic sentence, write your own statement in the margin.

Identify the key points

So far, we have the skeleton of a passage, with the basic substructure of main idea and paragraph topics in place. But it is still a bit flimsy. That's why the author adds key points or details. The key points are the muscles attached to that skeleton, making it stronger and more stable. These key points can be examples or logical arguments, but they have to be directly connected to the paragraph topic they flesh out.

The key points are always directly stated; otherwise, they wouldn't be very useful. Number the key points the author gives to build up the paragraph topics. You will always have more key points than anything else. After all, there can be only one main idea per passage, and one paragraph topic per paragraph. But within a single paragraph, the author may provide several supporting points.

IDENTIFY KEYWORDS TO DETERMINE MEANING

Okay, now we have a fairly functional organism here: a stable structure made up of the main idea and the paragraph topics fleshed out with key points. We can complete things with keywords, which will keep everything working together.

Keywords link the sentences within and between paragraphs; they also guide the reader through the author's argument. There are six types of keywords, each with a different function in the paragraph.

Type of Keyword	Purpose	Examples	Sample Sentence
continuation keywords	These tell you that you are getting more of the same kind of information. The new detail builds on the earlier one.	and, also, moreover, furthermore	The U.S. team won the gold medal in the 400-meter relay. Furthermore, it established a new world record.
illustration keywords	These let you know that the author is about to give you an example of an idea or concept.	for example, for instance	Psychology has many practical uses. For example, it is used regularly in advertising research.
contrast keywords	These tell you that the author is about to change direction in his or her argument or mention an opposing idea.	but, however, although, otherwise, nevertheless, by contrast	Yesterday was rainy and cold. However, today it's sunny and warm.
conclusion keywords	These let you know that the author is about to summarize or restate an important idea. Conclusion keywords often signal that the author is wrapping up the argument. Pay attention to conclusion keywords because they often relate directly to the main idea.	therefore, thus, in conclusion, consequently, hence	The score was tied after nine innings. Therefore, the game went into extended innings.
evidence keywords	These tell you that the author is going to offer a piece of evidence that supports an idea that was just stated. Often, the evidence has a cause-and-effect relationship with the idea it supports.	because, since	In today's job market, it is a good idea to know a second language because many employers demand bilingual skills.
importance keywords	These let you know that the author thinks a particular idea or fact is very important.	especially, above all, most of all, primarily, particularly	It is important to make eye contact during a job interview; most of all, you should always thank your interviewer.

TEST WHAT YOU LEARNED

> **Directions:** Choose the ONE best answer for each question.

Please use the following passage to answer questions 1–3.

The police are contacted by Elliott Wedren at 11:03 a.m. on Saturday, March 4, 2017, and Mr. Wedren reports that his car has been stolen. Officers Kenny Daniels and Anthony Baker are dispatched to Mr. Wedren's residence at 62 Cherry Tree Drive. They arrive at 11:16 a.m. Mr. Wedren explains that he stepped out of his home that morning with the intention of driving to the Piggly Wiggly Supermarket to do his weekly food shopping when he discovered that his 2014 Mini Cooper Countryman was missing from his driveway. He had parked it there after returning from his job at Wegman's Hardware Store at approximately 5:20 p.m. on March 3, 2017.

Officer Baker asks if any other member of Mr. Wedren's family has keys to the Mini Cooper. Mr. Wedren explains that his wife, Ethyl, does, but she has been in Martha's Vineyard visiting her sick aunt since February 28 and is not expected to return home until March 11. A call placed to Ethyl Wedren confirms that she is still in Martha's Vineyard. Mr. Wedren explains that he and his wife do not have any children and no member of his extended family has keys to the Mini Cooper.

Officer Daniels visits the neighbors at 61 Cherry Tree Drive, located directly across the street from Mr. Wedren's house. Mrs. Veronica Townshend, age 47, answers the door, but she explains that she did not notice any suspicious activity outside the Wedren residence the previous night or the current morning.

Officer Daniels then visits Mr. Wedren's next-door neighbor living at 60 Cherry Tree Drive, Mr. Leland Kurtz. Mr. Kurtz explains that he did notice someone outside the Wedren residence after Mr. Kurtz stepped outside to water his lawn at 7:10 a.m. on March 4. Mr. Kurtz describes the individual as an Asian male, approximately 30 years old, 5 feet 8 inches, 170 lb, and bald. While Mr. Kurtz noticed the man on the Wedrens' property, he did not actually witness the man stealing the car.

Officer Daniels then returns to the Wedrens' residence. During his absence, Officer Baker learned that Mr. Wedren is 35 years old while his wife, Ethyl, is 43. Their home telephone number is 376-0978. Mr. Wedren's cell phone number is 645-4556. Mrs. Wedren's cell phone number is 756-4444. Officer Daniels fills out a complete crime report.

1. Based on the information in the passage, which of the following is most likely true?
   (A) Mr. Wedren last saw his car at 5:20 p.m. on March 3.
   (B) Mr. Wedren and his wife are separated.
   (C) Mrs. Townshend is trying to cover for the thief.
   (D) Mr. Wedren is an assistant manager at Wegman's Hardware Store.

2. Why was Mr. Kurtz outside on the morning of March 4?

   (A) He saw someone suspicious in his neighbor's yard.

   (B) He came outside to talk to Mr. Wedren.

   (C) He was watering his lawn.

   (D) He was concerned about his neighbor, Mrs. Townshend.

3. The passage is mainly about:

   (A) the fact that Mr. Elliott Wedren drives a 2014 Mini Cooper Countryman

   (B) the apparent theft of Mr. Elliott Wedren's car

   (C) the location of Mrs. Ethyl Wedren

   (D) the fact that a bald Asian man stole Mr. Elliott Wedren's car

Please use the following passage to answer questions 4–5.

On Thursday, May 11, 2017, at 5:03 p.m., Michael Coklyat calls 911 to report that his 9-year-old daughter, Ana, has gone missing. Mr. Coklyat explains that his daughter was expected home at 3:00 p.m. that day after being released from Jimmy Carter Elementary School at 2:50 p.m. Officers Hester Derden and Janely Rodriguez are dispatched to the Coklyat residence at 376 Jackson Avenue, Apt. B, to fill out a missing persons report. They arrive at 5:09 p.m. Mr. Coklyat describes his daughter as 4 feet 2 inches, 100 lb, with black hair and brown eyes. She has a small scar on her left cheek, which resulted from a fall from a tree when Ana was 5 years old.

Officer Derden inquires about Ana's mother. Mr. Coklyat explains that his wife, Zelda, died when Ana was 2 years old, and he has not remarried. He has sole custody of Ana.

The officers inquire about the route Ana takes home from school, and Mr. Coklyat explains that his daughter usually walks down Crescent Avenue, where Jimmy Carter Elementary is located, before making a left onto 4th Avenue, before turning right onto Jackson Avenue where his residence is located. However, on Thursdays, Ana normally goes to piano lessons at the home of Mrs. Agatha Krieg, who lives at 121 Murray Street. Mrs. Krieg had called on the afternoon of May 10 to explain that she had to cancel this week's lesson for personal reasons.

Officer Rodriguez then leaves Mr. Coklyat's residence in the patrol car to visit Mrs. Krieg. There, Officer Rodriguez discovers Ana Coklyat, who had forgotten that her piano lesson had been canceled. Upon Ana's arrival, Mrs. Krieg decided to proceed with the piano lesson, explaining that she'd originally canceled the lesson because of a scheduled doctor's appointment. When Mrs. Krieg returned home after getting out of the appointment earlier than expected, she found Ana waiting on her door-step. At 5:18 p.m., Officer Rodriguez places a call to her partner, and Officer Derden explains to Mr. Coklyat that his daughter has been found.

4. On what day did Mrs. Krieg call Mr. Coklyat to cancel Ana's piano lesson?

(A) Wednesday

(B) Thursday

(C) Tuesday

(D) Monday

5. On which street is Jimmy Carter Elementary School located?

(A) Jackson Avenue

(B) 4th Avenue

(C) Crescent Avenue

(D) Murray Street

Use the following passage to answer questions 6–8.

Police officers Dale Horne and Audrey Cooper are dispatched to 21 Sparkwood Avenue, Apt. 403, at 9:01 p.m. on May 22, 2018, in response to a burglary reported by Mr. Will Frost. They arrive at the apartment at 9:10 p.m., ring the doorbell, and Mrs. Eileen Frost and Mr. Will Frost greet them. Mr. Frost tells the officers that he left his job at Deer Meadow Hospital, where he works as an orderly, at 7:00 p.m. After work, he met his wife, Eileen, for dinner at Mary's Diner on 21st Street, where the two dined until approximately 8:30 p.m. Upon returning home at approximately 8:41 p.m., Mr. and Mrs. Frost noticed that the lock on their front door was broken. After entering their home, they discovered that both of their wedding rings, each valued at $3,000, were missing from the top of their dresser in the bedroom. Mr. Frost explains that he always removed his wedding ring before going to work at the hospital because he was afraid to lose it. Mrs. Frost did the same before going to work at the Fine Arts art studio because she did not want to get paint on her ring. Mrs. Frost then discovered that the rest of her jewelry collection, valued at an additional $8,000, was also missing from a box above the bathroom medicine chest.

While Officer Horne fills out a crime report, Officer Cooper goes to other apartments on the Frosts' floor to interview neighbors who may have any information related to the burglary.

Mrs. Hayward, age 27, a computer programmer who lives in apt. 404, tells Officer Cooper that she heard a banging sound in the hallway at approximately 6:45 p.m. She assumed it was the superintendent repairing a piece of molding in the hallway that had been broken for the past two weeks and paid the noise no mind.

Officer Cooper then knocks on the door of apt. 401. A Mr. Truman, age 81, answers the door. He confirms the noise at 6:45 p.m. and explains that he opened his door to see a woman crouched at the door of apt. 403. The woman claimed to be a locksmith replacing a broken lock. Mr. Truman describes the woman as approximately 25 years old, 5 feet 11 inches, 150 lb, with short red hair, green eyes, and dental braces. Officer Cooper then knocks on the doors of apartments 402 and 405, but no other residents answer their doors.

Officer Cooper then returns to apartment 403 to tell her partner what she has learned. In the meantime, Mrs. Frost explains to Officer Horne that Mrs. Frost's niece, who has a criminal record for shoplifting and drug offenses, often admired her jewelry collection. The niece, Ms. Sheryl Palmer, is described as 24 years old, 6 feet tall, thin, with short, strawberry-blonde hair, green eyes, and braces on her teeth. The Frosts do not know Ms. Palmer's current address, because she has been "crashing with friends" due to conflicts with her parents, according to Mrs. Frost.

Officer Horne is also told that Mr. Frost is 54 years old, and Mrs. Frost is 52 years old. Her telephone number at work is 475-8676, and her work address is 3 Peaks Lane. The Frosts' home telephone number is 657-7546.

Officers Cooper and Horne finish their investigation and complete their crime report.

6. According to the passage, where did the Frosts keep their wedding rings while working?

   (A) With Mrs. Frost's jewelry collection

   (B) On their fingers

   (C) Above the bathroom medicine chest

   (D) On top of the bedroom dresser

7. According to the passage, who lives in apartment 401?

   (A) Mr. and Mrs. Frost

   (B) Mrs. Hayward

   (C) Ms. Palmer

   (D) Mr. Truman

8. Based on the passage, which of the following is most likely true?

   (A) Sheryl Palmer should be taken in for questioning.

   (B) Sheryl Palmer sold the jewelry to buy drugs.

   (C) Sheryl Palmer works as a locksmith.

   (D) Sheryl Palmer is an extremely rude person.

ANSWERS AND EXPLANATIONS

1.   A

Learning Objective: Apply active reading strategies

Although the passage does not explicitly state that Mr. Wedren last saw his car at 5:20 p.m. when he parked in his driveway, you can infer that this is true because he would have told the police if he had seen the car, still in the driveway, at a later time. While any of the other answer choices *could* be true, there is not enough information in the passage to make those inferences.

2.   C

Learning Objective: Apply active reading strategies

Although Mr. Kurtz ended up seeing a suspicious person on Mr. Wedren's property, he originally went outside to water his lawn.

3.   B

Learning Objective: Identify main ideas

The main idea of the passage as a whole is that Mr. Elliott Wedren's car has apparently been stolen. Choices (A) and (B) describe important details in the passage, but they are still only details and fail to capture the most important idea in the passage as a whole. Choice (D) draws a conclusion about the main idea that is reasonable but not specifically reached in the passage, so it cannot express the passage's main idea.

4.   A

Learning Objective: Apply active reading strategies

According to the passage, May 11, 2017, is a Thursday, and Mrs. Krieg called on May 10 to cancel the lesson. Therefore, May 10 must be a Wednesday.

5.   C

Learning Objective: Apply active reading strategies

The passage states that Jimmy Carter Elementary is located on Crescent Avenue.

6.   D

Learning Objective: Apply active reading strategies

The passage states that the rings were "missing from the top of their dresser in the bedroom."

7.   D

Learning Objective: Apply active reading strategies

When Officer Cooper knocks on the door of apt. 401, Mr. Truman answers.

8.   A

Learning Objective: Apply active reading strategies

Based on information in the passage, Sheryl Palmer is the most promising suspect in the theft, so it is reasonable to conclude that the police should take her in for questioning. While Choice (B) is not an unreasonable conclusion based on the evidence, it is not as clear a conclusion as the one in Choice (A), so it is not the very best answer. Based on evidence in the passage, Sheryl Palmer most likely lied about being a locksmith to cover up her crime, so Choice (C) is not the best answer. While the likelihood that she committed a crime indicates that Sheryl Palmer might not be the most upstanding person in the world, Choice (D) reaches a conclusion about her personality that evidence in this passage does not really support.

 **SELF-REFLECTION**

As you can see, there are a lot of things to keep in mind when writing and reading police reports. Pre-reading, reading actively, identifying main ideas, understanding keywords, summarizing, and asking questions are strong techniques for comprehending information in any piece of writing. Effective police officers also rely on their abilities to observe and memorize key details to solve problems. These are the kinds of essential skills that will be tested in the kinds of reading comprehension exams you can expect to take on your way to becoming a police officer. Good luck!

Test What You Know score: _____ /8 correct

Test What You Learned score: _____ /8 correct

After working through the practice problems in this chapter, which of the Learning Objectives have you mastered? Place a check mark next to those objectives to keep track of your progress.

- [ ] Apply active reading strategies
- [ ] Identify main ideas
- [ ] Identify keywords to determine meaning

CHAPTER 7

Verbal Expression

You might not have to write any essays on your police exam, but you will still need a firm grasp on writing concepts to answer questions about effective writing, grammar, and usage. This chapter will tell you all you'll need to know about handling those kinds of multiple-choice questions on Test Day.

LEARNING OBJECTIVES

In this chapter, you will learn how to:

- [ ] Master writing techniques
- [ ] Write clear, concise reports
- [ ] Use strong language
- [ ] Create clear sentences
- [ ] Use context to determine the meaning of a word
- [ ] Identify the clearest and most accurate report of an incident

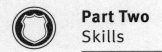

TEST WHAT YOU KNOW

Directions: Choose the ONE best answer for each question.

In each of the following sentences, choose the word or phrase that most nearly has the same meaning as the underlined word. Mark on your answer sheet the letter that identifies the correct choice.

1. The attacker delivered a <u>lethal</u> blow to the victim.

   (A) destructive

   (B) excessive

   (C) repeated

   (D) fatal

2. The officer <u>assessed</u> the damage to the car and concluded that it was minor.

   (A) repaired

   (B) mitigated

   (C) evaluated

   (D) corroborated

Officer Smith responds to a report of a larceny and gathers the following information:

Location: 980 First Street

Time: 11:45 p.m.

Victim: Mr. Clay Vale

Crime: larceny

Suspect: black male, approx. 5 feet 5 inches, wearing overalls

Location of Suspect: unknown

Item Stolen: red 1965 Ford Mustang

3. Officer Flanagan is writing his report. Which of the following expresses the information most clearly and accurately?

(A) Mr. Clay Vale, of 980 First Street, reported that his red 1965 Ford Mustang was stolen at 11:45 p.m. by a suspect he describes as a black male, approximately 5 feet 5 inches, wearing overalls. The suspect's location is unknown.

(B) Mr. Clay Vale's prized vintage 1965 Ford Mustang, which is red, was stolen at 11:45 p.m. from his house at 980 First Street by a black male who Mr. Vale, the victim, describes as about 5 feet 5 inches tall. The suspect is wearing overalls.

(C) A black man, approx. 5 feet 5 inches tall, wearing overalls, is suspected of stealing a red Ford Mustang at 11:45 p.m. from 980 First Street. The whereabouts of the suspect and the vehicle are unknown. The vehicle is owned by Mr. Clay Vale of the aforementioned address, and is a red 1965 Ford Mustang.

(D) At 11:45 p.m., a red Ford Mustang was stolen from Mr. Clay Vale at 980 First Street. The car was manufactured in 1965. The suspect's location is unknown, as is the vehicle's. The suspect is described as a black male, 5 feet 5 inches tall.

Responding to the report of an assault at a local elementary school, Officer Shawn gathers the following information:

Location: Eubanks Elementary School

Time: 4:45 p.m.

Crime: assault

Victim: Mrs. Lebotnik, a teacher

Suspect: Evan Meredith, a fourth-grade student

Injury: Mrs. Lebotnik is unconscious and has a concussion.

Weapon: a soccer trophy

Action Taken: Mrs. Lebotnik was taken to the hospital by an ambulance.

Status of Suspect: Evan Meredith confessed and was taken to the precinct, where he is awaiting a visit from a juvenile court service worker.

4. Officer Shawn is filling out his report on the incident. Which of the following expresses the information most clearly and accurately?

(A) Mrs. Lebotnik, a teacher at Eubanks Elementary School, stated that she was assaulted by Evan Meredith, a student at the school, at 4:45 p.m. at Eubanks Elementary School and suffered a concussion. Evan Meredith confessed and is waiting for a court service worker from juvenile court to talk to him at the precinct, where he is.

(B) Evan Meredith, a student at Eubanks Elementary School, assaulted Mrs. Lebotnik, a teacher at Eubanks Elementary School, with a soccer trophy. She has a concussion and is unconscious and at the hospital. He is at the precinct awaiting a visit from juvenile court. Evan Meredith confessed to assaulting Mrs. Lebotnik at 4:45 p.m., at which time the assault took place on school grounds.

(C) Mrs. Lebotnik, a teacher at Eubanks Elementary School, was assaulted with a soccer trophy at 4:45 p.m. at the school by a fourth-grade student named Evan Meredith. Mrs. Lebotnik suffered a concussion and remains unconscious at the hospital, where she was taken by ambulance. Evan Meredith confessed to the assault and is at the precinct, where he awaits a visit from a juvenile court service worker.

(D) Mrs. Lebotnik was assaulted with a soccer trophy by a student, Evan Meredith, who assaulted Mrs. Lebotnik at the school where he went and she worked, Eubanks Elementary School. Evan Meredith confessed to the assault, and Mrs. Lebotnik was taken by ambulance to the hospital, where she is unconscious and has a concussion. Evan Meredith is at the precinct.

ANSWERS AND EXPLANATIONS

1. D

Learning Objective: Use context to determine the meaning of a word

Choice (D) is correct because both "lethal" and "fatal" describe something that causes death. While something destructive (Choice A) causes harm, and "excessive" (Choice B) is too much, neither one causes death. "Repeated" (Choice C) simply means "more than once."

2. C

Learning Objective: Use context to determine the meaning of a word

Choice (C) is correct because both "assess" and "evaluate" mean "to determine." Choice (A) is incorrect because "repair" means "to fix." To mitigate, Choice (B), is to lessen harm or damage. Finally, Choice (D) is incorrect because "corroborate" means "to support with evidence."

3. A

Learning Objective: Identify the clearest and most accurate report of an incident

Choice (A) best presents the information completely, clearly, and accurately, without redundant, unclear, or missing information. Choice (B) is a confusing, repetitive, and disorganized run-on sentence. Choice (C) is not concise, as it repeats the color and make of the car twice. Finally, Choice (D) includes an unnecessary sentence about the car's year of manufacture.

4. C

Learning Objective: Identify the clearest and most accurate report of an incident

Choice (C) best presents the information completely, clearly, and accurately, without redundant, unclear, or missing information. Choice (A) is incorrect because Mrs. Lebotnik is unconscious and therefore unable to give a statement. Choices (B) and (D) present the information in a disorganized manner and are confusing to read.

MASTER WRITING TECHNIQUES

Let's start with some essay-writing strategies you can apply to those multiple-choice questions. First of all, to write an effective essay, you need to do three things:

1. Be concise

2. Be forceful

3. Be correct

An effective essay is concise: it wastes no words. An effective essay is forceful: it makes its point. And an effective essay is correct: it conforms to the generally accepted rules of grammar and form.

The following pages break down the three broad objectives of concision, forcefulness, and correctness into a series of specific principles. Don't panic! Many of them will already be familiar to you.

Be concise

The first principles of good writing relate to the goal of expressing your points clearly in as few words as possible. Each principle represents a specific way to tighten your writing.

Avoid wordiness

Do not use several words when one will do. Wordy phrases are like junk food: they add only fat, not muscle. Many people make the mistake of writing phrases (such as *at the present time* or *at this point in time* instead of the simpler *now* or *take into consideration* instead of simply *consider*) in an attempt to make their prose seem more scholarly or more formal. It does not work. Instead, their prose ends up seeming inflated and pretentious. Don't waste your words or your time.

Wordy: *I am of the opinion that the aforementioned managers should be advised that they will be evaluated with regard to the utilization of responsive organizational software for the purpose of devising a responsive network of customers.*

Concise: *We should tell the managers that we will evaluate their use of flexible computerized databases to develop a customer network.*

Don't be redundant

Redundancy means that the writer needlessly repeats an idea. It's redundant to speak of "a beginner lacking experience." The word *beginner* implies lack of experience by itself. You can eliminate redundant words or phrases without changing the meaning of the sentence. Watch out for words that add nothing to the sentence.

Here are some common redundancies:

Redundant	Concise
refer back	refer
few in number	few
small-sized	small
grouped together	grouped
end result	result

Redundancy often results from carelessness, but you can easily eliminate redundant elements when proofreading.

Avoid needless qualification

Because the objective of an essay is to convince a reader of a particular opinion or point, a writer will want to adopt a reasonable tone. Occasional use of such qualifiers as *fairly, rather, somewhat,* and *relatively* and of such expressions as *seems to be, a little,* and *a certain amount of* will let a reader know the writer is reasonable, but overusing such modifiers weakens an argument. Excessive qualification makes a writer sound hesitant. Like wordy phrases, qualifiers can add bulk without adding substance.

Wordy: *This rather serious breach of etiquette may possibly shake the very foundations of the corporate world.*

Concise: *This serious breach of etiquette may shake the foundations of the corporate world.*

Just as bad is the overuse of the word *very*. Some writers use this intensifying adverb before almost every adjective in an attempt to be more forceful. If a writer needs to add emphasis, she or he should look for a stronger adjective (or verb).

Weak: *Novak is a very good pianist.*

Strong: *Novak is a virtuoso pianist.* Or *Novak plays beautifully.*

Also, don't try to qualify words that are already absolute.

Wrong	Correct
more unique	unique
the very worst	the worst
completely full	full

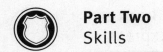

WRITE CLEAR, CONCISE REPORTS

At some point in the application and/or the exam process, you are going to have to write something. You may not see an essay portion on the test you take, but you will have to give extended answers to some questions in the application itself. You will also find yourself having to write various kinds of reports during your career as a police officer. Some exams will even have you write sample reports.

No one is expecting Pulitzer Prize material here. You just need to get your point across clearly and honestly—though using correct grammar also helps.

Here are some suggestions for writing effective responses:

Write an outline

Whether you're writing a sample report or a response to a question, developing a strong structure before you begin writing will save you time in the long run. It doesn't really matter what style you use to write your outline. You are the only one who is going to see it. But you should always start with an outline to keep your thoughts focused and organized.

First, write down the most important thing you want to say. Don't worry about how you write it now. It doesn't even have to be a complete sentence at this point. Just summarize your main point. Think of it as the direct answer to the question.

Next, you have to come up with some support for your main point. If your main point is the direct answer to the question, the supporting examples are the answers to the follow-up questions. The supporting material can be examples from your own experience or reasoning that you've worked out. The examples can be more or less separate, or one can build on top of another.

Finally, you need to wrap it up with a conclusion. You don't need to get fancy. You can just restate your original main point.

Be clear

Once you've got your outline finished, you are more than halfway there. All you have to do is flesh out the sentences or sentence fragments and you are done.

The big mistake people make here is that they get a little too fancy. Remember, you are writing to express, not impress. No one reading a police report cares about the writer's literary craft, so skip the 10-dollar words and the mile-long sentences. Just say what you want to say and stop.

Be active

Verbs can be categorized as active or passive. Some people think that the passive voice is more formal; it's really just blander and more boring. You will automatically sound like a better candidate if you just eliminate any passive verbs in favor of active verbs.

Here are some examples:

Passive: *I was introduced to the importance of hard work by my grandfather.*

Active: *My grandfather taught me the importance of hard work.*

Passive: *Offensive line is what I played for the All-Region football team during my senior year of high school.*

Active: *During my senior year in high school, I played offensive line for the All-Region football team.*

Passive: *My most difficult situation occurred shortly after my older brother was diagnosed with leukemia.*

Active: *I faced the most difficult period of my life after my older brother was diagnosed with leukemia.*

Give it a rest and reread

Once you have written your first draft, let it sit for a day or two and then come back to it. You will be able to see mistakes or awkward sentences that you didn't notice when you first wrote them down.

Obviously, on a timed test you won't have a couple of days to mull over what you've written. But you should always reread your written material before turning in the test. Look for misspellings and grammatical errors, along with holes in your logic and other structural mistakes.

USE STRONG LANGUAGE

The next group of principles aims at the goal of producing forceful writing with carefully shaped word usage and style. If a writer follows these principles, his or her writing will be much more convincing to the reader.

Avoid needlessly vague words

A writer should never ramble when crafting an essay. He or she should always choose specific, descriptive words. Vague language weakens writing because it forces the reader to guess what the writer means instead of concentrating fully on the essay's ideas and style.

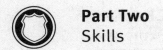
Weak: *Brown is highly educated.*

Forceful: *Brown has a master's degree in business administration.*

Weak: *She is a great communicator.*

Forceful: *She speaks persuasively.*

Notice that sometimes, to be more specific and concrete, a writer will have to use more words than one might with vague language. This principle is not in conflict with the general objective of concision. Being concise may mean eliminating unnecessary words. Avoiding vagueness may mean adding necessary words.

Avoid clichés

Clichés are overused expressions that may have once seemed colorful and powerful but are now dull and worn out. A reliance on clichés will suggest a writer is a lazy thinker.

Weak: *Performance in a crisis is the acid test for a leader.*

Forceful: *Performance in a crisis is the best indicator of a leader's abilities.*

Clichés can always be replaced with more imaginative and less-overused language.

Avoid jargon

Jargon includes two categories of words that you should avoid. First is the specialized vocabulary of a group, such as that used by doctors, lawyers, or baseball coaches. Second is the overly inflated and complex language that burdens many essays. A writer will not impress anyone with big words that do not fit the tone or context of the essay, especially if the writer misuses them.

If you are not certain of a word's meaning or appropriateness, leave it out. An appropriate word, even a simple one, will add impact to an argument.

Unnecessary: *The international banks are cognizant of the new law's significance.*

Forceful: *The international banks are aware of the new law's significance.*

Unnecessary: *The new law would negatively impact each of the nations involved.*

Forceful: *The new law would hurt each of the nations involved.*

The following are commonly used jargon words:

- prioritize
- optimize
- utilize
- finalize
- designate
- bottom line
- parameter
- time frame
- input/output
- maximize
- facilitate

Avoid slang and colloquialisms

Slang terms and colloquialisms can be confusing to readers because these expressions are not universally understood. Even worse, such informal writing may give readers the impression that you are poorly educated or arrogant.

Inappropriate: *He is really into gardening.*

Correct: *He enjoys gardening.*

Inappropriate: *She plays a wicked game of tennis.*

Correct: *She excels at tennis.*

Inappropriate: *Myra has got to go to Memphis for a week.*

Correct: *Myra must go to Memphis for a week.*

Inappropriate: *Joan has been doing science for eight years now.*

Correct: *Joan has been a scientist for eight years now.*

With a little thought, you will find the right word. Using informal language is risky. Play it safe by sticking to standard usage.

CREATE CLEAR SENTENCES

When completing a sentence or choosing from several sentences to select the most effective one, you must beware of two common writing errors: run-ons and sentence fragments. If you are familiar with what an *incorrect* sentence sounds like, it will set off alarms for you, and you will be able to quickly move on to find the right one.

Run-on sentences

When a sentence consists of more than one clause (a group of words that contains a subject and a verb), those clauses must be joined properly. It is never acceptable to hook two clauses together with a comma, as the "sentence" below does. That's called a run-on sentence.

Wrong: *Nietzsche moved to Basel in 1869, he planned to teach classical philology.*

There are a number of acceptable ways to fix a run-on.

Correct: *Nietzsche moved to Basel in 1869. He planned to teach classical philology.*

Also correct: *Nietzsche planned to teach classical philology; therefore, he moved to Basel in 1869.*

Also correct: *Nietzsche moved to Basel in 1869, and he planned to teach classical philology.* (The words *and, or, for, but, nor, so,* and *yet* are called coordinating conjunctions.)

Also correct: *Because Nietzsche planned to teach classical philology, he moved to Basel in 1869.* (The words *because, although, if, though,* etc. are called subordinating conjunctions.)

Also correct: *Nietzsche, who planned to teach classical philology, moved to Basel in 1869.* (The words *who, which, where, whom, that,* and *whose* are called relative pronouns.)

Sentence fragments

Sentence fragments are usually pretty easy to spot. When you read one, your reaction is usually, "Huh?" There is something crucial missing. In more technical terms, a sentence fragment is a group of words that looks like a sentence, but it is either grammatically or logically incomplete. Here is the grammatical test: to be a sentence, the group of words has to contain both a subject and a verb related to one another.

Take a look at this example:

The man in the lineup wearing the plaid shirt.

Well, you have a subject—"the man." And you seem to have a verb—"wearing." But "wearing the plaid shirt" really just modifies the subject, giving us more details about the man. There is no verb.

What about the man in the lineup? Did he do something? Or did someone do something to him? What was going on? Who knows?

You can complete the sentence by adding a verb:

The man in the lineup wearing the plaid shirt mumbled so much the witness couldn't understand him.

The man in the lineup wearing the plaid shirt was the witness's first choice.

But some sentence fragments do have a subject and verb; these are sentences that are logically incomplete. Look at this:

When the sergeant has to fill out a lot of paperwork.

There is the subject, "the sergeant." And there is a verb attached—"has to fill out a lot of paperwork." But what about that word "when" at the beginning of the sentence? That leads us to expect information that just isn't there. Here's how that fragment can be turned into a full sentence:

When the sergeant has to fill out a lot of paperwork, he gets very cranky.

The sentence may also be corrected by deleting "when":

The sergeant has to fill out a lot of paperwork.

USE CONTEXT TO DETERMINE THE MEANING OF A WORD

Vocabulary is an important part of being able to express yourself effectively. It's a good idea to read unfamiliar material with a dictionary close by. That way, you can easily look up any words you don't understand. But what if you aren't allowed to use a dictionary? In those situations, which include just about all standardized tests, you need to be able to make a good guess about the meaning of a word based on its context. Here is what we mean:

Even though they give her nightmares, Joyce likes gruesome movies.

Let's say you don't know exactly what *gruesome* means. But the sentence tells you that gruesome movies give Joyce nightmares, so it's a good bet that *gruesome* doesn't mean "romantic" or "funny." What kind of movies would give someone nightmares? Just using context and your own common sense, you can figure out that *gruesome* means something close to "scary" or "violent."

Once you are out of a testing situation, you can refine your definition by looking up those unfamiliar words in the dictionary. But your context definitions will keep you from getting stuck during a test.

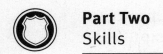

IDENTIFY THE CLEAREST AND MOST ACCURATE REPORT OF AN INCIDENT

When taking a police exam, there's a good chance you will be asked to identify the "best" version of an incident report after being provided the basic facts of the case. This is a way to test your writing ability without actually having you write. It aims to test your ability to identify good writing, as well as your ability to spot problems commonly made by those inexperienced with this unique form of writing.

Police incident reports should always focus on presenting facts clearly and completely. The writing style is plain, and for good reason: these reports are often critical elements in criminal investigations and subsequent court cases and may be scrutinized months or even years after they were written. An informally written report could call into question the legitimacy of the police work performed.

With this type of question, you may be presented with several pieces of information related to an incident. Here's an example:

Officer Church records the following information at a residence at which a woman reports a robbery:

- Location: 4949 Cherry Hill Lane
- Time: 8:15 a.m.
- Victim: Mrs. Alice Berry
- Crime: robbery
- Suspect: male, approx. 6 feet, covered in black clothing, except his hands, which are white
- Weapon: a switchblade knife
- Status of Suspect: fled on foot
- Items Missing: a watch, a ring, and six pairs of earrings

Now let's look at some options for how Officer Church might take these notes and shape them into in a report. Here's one option:

A watch, ring, and six pairs of earrings were stolen from Mrs. Alice Berry who warns that the armed and dangerous suspect, who is carrying a switchblade knife, fled on foot from her house at 4949 Cherry Hill Lane shortly after he robbed her, which happened at 8:15 a.m. Suspect is described as 6 feet tall, male, and covered in black clothing.

This option contains nearly all of the information in the notes. However, it omits the fact that the suspect's hands are visible and white—a potentially critical piece of information. The report also has a strange flow to it; the information is not presented as clearly as it could be, due mainly to the fact that it is mostly a single run-on sentence. Let's look at another option:

Shortly after 8:15 a.m., a six-foot-tall man robbed Mrs. Alice Berry at 4949 Cherry Hill Lane with a switchblade knife. He allegedly stole a watch and six pairs of earrings. The suspect fled on foot. He is described as wearing black all over his body except for his hands, which are exposed and white.

This option is written more clearly than the first option. The sentences are short and easy to follow. However, this option omits the fact that the perpetrator stole a ring. This may not seem all that important, but it could prove to be *very* important if the case later hinges upon identifying the stolen ring. Let's try one more:

A robbery suspect, approximately 6 feet tall and covered in black clothing with his white hands exposed, is fleeing on foot from 4949 Cherry Hill Lane, where Mrs. Alice Berry describes him as male and armed with a switchblade knife. The incident occurred at 8:15 a.m., and the suspect fled shortly thereafter.

Again, most of the report consists of a single, confusing sentence. More importantly, the report does not list the items that were stolen. Okay, let's take one last shot at this:

Mrs. Alice Berry was reportedly robbed at her residence, located at 4949 Cherry Hill Lane, at 8:15 a.m. The suspect, who is armed with a switchblade knife, reportedly stole a watch, a ring, and six pairs of earrings before fleeing on foot. The suspect is male, approximately 6 feet tall and covered in black clothing except for his exposed hands, which are white.

Finally! This version of the report contains all of the important information from the notes and presents it in a clear way.

When tackling a question like this, you should first check the answer choices to see which ones leave out important information. After you have ruled those out, read through the remaining choices to see which one presents the information most clearly and accurately, without throwing in unnecessary words.

TEST WHAT YOU LEARNED

Directions: Choose the ONE best answer for each question.

In each of the following sentences, choose the word or phrase that most nearly has the same meaning as the underlined word. Mark on your answer sheet the letter that identifies the correct choice.

1. The new policy aimed to <u>curtail</u> the prevalence of public drunkenness.

   (A) forbid

   (B) reduce

   (C) condemn

   (D) ignore

2. The suspect was attempting to <u>entice</u> minors with free cigarettes.

   (A) force

   (B) impress

   (C) tempt

   (D) provoke

Officer Escalante follows up on a report of a fire. She gathers the following information:

Location:	850 Hiram Boulevard
Time:	9:15 p.m.
Crime:	arson
Victim:	Jamal Ferrell
Suspect:	Kennedy Cochran
Damage:	carport destroyed by fire
Action Taken:	suspect arrested and taken into custody

3. Officer Escalante is writing her report. Which of the following expresses the information most clearly and accurately?

(A) Jamal Ferrell reported that at 9:15 p.m. at his home at 850 Hiram Boulevard, Kennedy Cochran started a fire that destroyed Ferrell's carport. Kennedy Cochran was arrested and was taken into custody.

(B) At 9:15 p.m., a fire lit by someone at 850 Hiram Boulevard destroyed a carport. The owner of the carport was Jamal Ferrell. The arsonist was Kennedy Cochran. Kennedy Cochran was taken into custody after having been arrested for arson.

(C) A carport at 850 Hiram Boulevard was destroyed by a fire lit by alleged arsonist Kennedy Cochran, who did not own the property. The owner is Jamal Ferrell, whose carport was destroyed at 9:15 p.m. Kennedy Cochran was arrested and taken into custody.

(D) Jamal Ferrell's carport was destroyed by arson at 850 Hiram Boulevard by a man he says is Kennedy Cochran, who was arrested and taken into custody. The fire destroyed the carport at 9:15 p.m., which was before Kennedy Cochran was arrested.

At the scene of an accident, Officer Broadbent gathers the following information:

Location:	intersection of Elderberry and Vincent Streets
Time:	7:30 p.m.
Occurrence:	automobile collision
Driver Struck:	Helen Sinclair
Driver at Fault:	Wade Wairubi
Damage:	Both cars were badly damaged and had to be towed away.
Action Taken:	Wade Wairubi was given a traffic ticket for failing to yield the right-of-way.

4. Back at the precinct, Officer Broadbent is attempting to write his report. Which of the following expresses the information most clearly and accurately?

   (A) Wade Wairubi should have yielded the right-of-way to Helen Sinclair. Since he did not, his automobile hit hers at the intersection of Elderberry and Vincent Streets, and he was given a traffic ticket. The collision occurred at 7:30 p.m.

   (B) At 7:30 a.m., at the intersection of Elderberry and Vincent Streets, Wade Wairubi's vehicle struck Helen Sinclair's after Mr. Wairubi failed to yield the right-of-way. Both cars were badly damaged. Mr. Wairubi was given a traffic ticket. The cars were towed away.

   (C) At the intersection of Elderberry and Vincent Streets, Wade Wairubi's and Helen Sinclair's vehicles were badly damaged and had to be towed away after Mr. Wairubi hit Ms. Sinclair after he failed to yield the right-of-way at 7:30, for which he was given a traffic ticket.

   (D) At 7:30 p.m., a vehicle driven by Wade Wairubi struck a vehicle driven by Helen Sinclair at the intersection of Elderberry and Vincent Streets. Both vehicles were badly damaged and had to be towed away. It was determined that Mr. Wairubi was at fault, and he was given a traffic ticket for failing to yield the right-of-way.

ANSWERS AND EXPLANATIONS

1. B

Learning Objective: Use context to determine the meaning of a word

Choice (B) is correct because both "curtail" and "reduce" mean "to make less." To forbid, Choice (A), is to prevent. To condemn, Choice (C), is to declare someone or something wrong or evil. To ignore, Choice (D), is to refuse to give attention.

2. C

Learning Objective: Use context to determine the meaning of a word

Choice (C) is correct because both "entice" and "tempt" mean "to lure." To use force, Choice (A), is to move someone or something with violence. To impress, Choice (B), is to deeply affect a person. To provoke, Choice (D), is to incite a person to anger.

3. A

Learning Objective: Identify the clearest and most accurate report of an incident

Choice (A) best presents the information completely, clearly, and accurately, without redundant, unclear, or missing information. Choice (B) is misleading. It states the fire was lit "by someone," and then later notes the arsonist is Kennedy Cochran. Choice (C) includes unnecessary information by stating Cochran is not the property owner. Finally, Choice (D) presents a confusing time line.

4. D

Learning Objective: Identify the clearest and most accurate report of an incident

Choice (D) best presents the information completely, clearly, and accurately, without redundant, unclear, or missing information. Choice (A) fails to mention the condition or whereabouts of the vehicles. Choice (B) incorrectly states the accident occurred in the morning (a.m.) rather than the evening (p.m.). Choice (C) fails to state morning or evening entirely and reports the order of events in reverse.

SELF-REFLECTION

As you have seen, there are a lot of rules to keep in mind when preparing a strong piece of writing, such as a forceful, concise, and correct police report. Problems such as wordiness, redundancies, needless qualifications, and vague language should be avoided. Inappropriate use of clichés, jargon, slang, and colloquialisms could also pose problems. All of these rules may seem a bit overwhelming at first, but practicing the kinds of questions that could appear on the police exam is a good way to get familiar with them.

Test What You Know score: _____ /4 correct

Test What You Learned score: _____ /4 correct

After working through the practice problems in this chapter, which of the Learning Objectives have you mastered? Place a check mark next to those objectives to keep track of your progress.

- ☐ Master writing techniques
- ☐ Write clear, concise reports
- ☐ Use strong language
- ☐ Create clear sentences
- ☐ Use context to determine the meaning of a word
- ☐ Identify the clearest and most accurate report of an incident

CHAPTER 8

Logic and Reasoning

You have probably taken an aptitude exam at some point in your school career, be it in grade school, the SAT or ACT, etc. Portions of these exams focus on abstract reasoning by including logic puzzles (e.g., making an inference from a set of conditions) and logical arguments (e.g., drawing a valid conclusion from a list of premises). These logical reasoning problems are distinctly different from more traditional mathematics problems in that they measure your ability to work with unfamiliar information. Indeed, these questions evaluate your ability to critically analyze and formulate/complete arguments as they arise in ordinary language.

LEARNING OBJECTIVES

In this chapter, you will review how to:

- ☐ Draw logical conclusions related to police scenarios

- ☐ Select the correct legal definition of a crime

- ☐ Make sound judgments regarding police scenarios

- ☐ Determine the best course of action in a police scenario

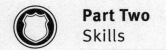

TEST WHAT YOU KNOW

Directions: Choose the ONE best answer for each question.

1. In the city, there is a marked increase in the number of bank robberies near the 1st and 15th of every month. Based on this information, which of the following is the most logical explanation?

    (A) The banks have fewer security guards on duty near the 1st and 15th of the month.

    (B) Many bank robbers have jobs that prevent them from robbing banks at other times of the month.

    (C) Banks see increased activity near the 1st and 15th of the month due to payroll traffic.

    (D) The phases of the moon affect the behavior of bank robbers in the city.

2. In State X, a person is guilty of unlawful use of credit card when, in the course of obtaining property or a service, he uses or displays a credit card which he knows to be revoked or canceled.

    Carla Jones attempts to pay for her purchases at a local pharmacy by presenting her Visa card, not realizing that her husband recently canceled that Visa account. Based only on the above definition, is Mrs. Jones guilty of unlawful use of credit card?

    (A) No, because she was unaware that the credit card was canceled.

    (B) Yes, because it is her responsibility to keep up with her credit card accounts.

    (C) No, but only because the card was rejected.

    (D) It is impossible to determine if she is guilty without knowing whether she paid for her purchases by some other means.

MISSING PERSON—The New York City Police Department classifies a missing person as any person missing from a New York City residence who is:

    i. Under 18 years of age, OR

    ii. Likely to commit suicide, OR

   iii. Mentally or physically handicapped, OR

   iv. Absent under suspicious circumstances, OR

    v. A possible victim of drowning.

3. According to this definition, which of the following should NOT be classified as a missing person?

(A) Calvin Colcheck, a 15-year-old male, is reported missing from his home in Queens by his parents. He was grounded three days earlier for receiving poor grades in mathematics and Spanish this semester.

(B) Mavis Moller, an 18-year-old female, is reported missing from her home in the Bronx. She just returned from an out-of-state conference.

(C) Daniel Donker, a 23-year-old mentally impaired male, is reported missing from the Manhattan facility where he lives. He was last seen following a parade passing down the street.

(D) Zelda Zimfield, a 24-year-old female, is reported missing from her Brooklyn home. Her friends report that she had been very depressed since the death of her sister last week.

During a simulation exercise, recruits learn that as officers, they may be required to aid in a situation involving radioactive contamination. Given that exposure to radioactive material is highly dangerous, ALL members of the service must follow these safety guidelines:

- All officers should use appropriate personal protective equipment when evaluating and treating patients/victims known or suspected to be contaminated with radioactive material.

- Pregnant officers should not work in:

  - Pre-decontamination areas

  - Decontamination areas

  - Areas where internally contaminated patients are cared for or domiciled

  - Areas where there are elevated levels of environmental radiation

- All officers responding to a radiation emergency should wear a personal radiation dosimeter to monitor dose. They should consult with a hospital radiation safety officer about type(s) and proper wearing of personal radiation dosimeters:

  - Dose rate meters (with or without alarms)

  - Accumulated dose meters (with or without alarms)

  - Finger ring dosimeters if the dose to hands or fingers is likely to be higher than the dose to the torso, where the main dosimeter is worn

4. Based on this information, it would be most accurate for recruits to conclude that the main reason behind these guidelines is

(A) keeping the situation confidential by restricting areas where officers can be.

(B) maintaining proper control of the situation to ensure no radioactive material is taken off-site.

(C) ensuring the safety of officers concerning radiation poisoning.

(D) controlling the situation to ensure that any data collected is as pure as possible.

The following pie chart shows the sources of funds to be collected by the National Highways Authority of India (NHAI) for its Phase II projects.

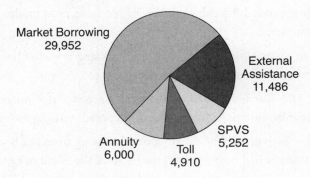

5. 10.4% of the funds will be arranged through which venue?

   (A) External assistance

   (B) Market borrowing

   (C) Tolls

   (D) Annuity

There are very few circumstances in which an officer may make an arrest. These are:

- If the officer personally observed a crime

- If the officer has probable cause to believe that the person arrested committed a crime

- If the officer has an arrest warrant issued by a judge

6. Based on these criteria, is it proper or improper for Officer Holston to arrest a scruffy man sitting on a curb, drinking from a bottle in a paper bag, who seems paranoid?

   (A) Improper, because the officer has no proof that the suspect committed a crime; this is merely suspicion based on appearance

   (B) Proper, because the suspect may be drinking alcohol, even if the paper bag is concealing it

   (C) Proper, because those who appear paranoid are a danger to the public

   (D) Improper, because the officer cannot prove the man is paranoid

Officer Pedro receives a radio call into headquarters for an aggravated assault. The dispatcher provides the following information: "Witness called in an altercation at 557 High Street. The aggressor has reportedly run from the scene and is described as a white male, tall, and wearing a yellow jersey and torn jeans, with a snake tattoo on his face."

7. Which of the following is the most important characteristic for which the officer should be on the lookout?

   (A) Yellow jersey

   (B) Face tattoo

   (C) Tall white male

   (D) Torn jeans

Officer Drake is assigned to patrol the streets of a certain section of her town. Her patrol area consists of two main streets, Route 10 and Route 22, parallel to each other and half a mile apart. Five residential streets run between these two main streets and are perpendicular to them: Bryan, Grange, Rockside, Indian Run, and Senn.

She reviews the area crime statistics for the past year prior to the start of duty. Reports indicate that yard vandalism was isolated to Grange Street and that petty theft (e.g., garden gnomes, bird feeders, etc.) was isolated to Rockside, on all days of the week. Both types of crime are believed to occur between 1 a.m. and 4 a.m. Illegal dragstrip racing has been reported along Route 10 in this area between 11 p.m. and 1 a.m. on the weekends. Teens have been reported to gather in groups and drink on the corners of Indian Run and Senn all days of the week, between 9 p.m. and midnight.

8. To cut down on dragstrip racing, she should patrol

   (A) Route 10 in this area between 10 p.m. and 2 a.m. on Saturdays.

   (B) Grange Street between 1 a.m. and 5 a.m. on Saturdays.

   (C) the corner of Indian Run and Senn between 11 p.m. and 1 a.m. on Thursdays.

   (D) Rockside Street between 1 a.m. and 4 a.m. on Thursdays.

ANSWERS AND EXPLANATIONS

1. C

Learning Objective: Make sound judgments regarding police scenarios

More people will visit a bank on payday, and based on a twice-monthly pay schedule, more people would naturally visit a bank near the 1st and 15th of every month. Choices (B) and (D) are unlikely and irrational and should be eliminated immediately. Choice (A) is wrong since there is no logical reason a bank would reduce the number of security guards on these two days each month.

2. A

Learning Objective: Select the correct legal definition of a crime

The answer is based <u>only on the definition</u>. Since she did not know the card was canceled, she is not guilty of unlawful use of credit card. The other choices introduce information beyond the scope of the definition, and such information cannot satisfy the criterion.

3. B

Learning Objective: Select the correct legal definition of a crime

To satisfy the given definition, only one of the five listed criteria must be satisfied, as indicated by the use of the word "or" separating all of the conditions. Mavis meets none of the criteria. In fact, the closest one to *possibly* satisfying it is condition (iv), but having been away at a conference is hardly suspicious. The person in Choice (A) satisfies condition (i), the person in Choice (C) satisfies condition (iii), and the person in Choice (D) satisfies condition (ii).

4. C

Learning Objective: Draw logical conclusions related to police scenarios

Surely, the safety of the officers on scene is a major priority of the force. So, Choice (C) is certainly reasonable. But is it the *most plausible* of all four interpretations provided? Well, Choice (A) concerns confidentiality, which the company undoubtedly values, but likely not secondarily to the safety of people exposed. Choice (B) is not sensible since these guidelines would not really prevent this from occurring. And Choice (D) is surely not a top priority, especially when the welfare of human lives is at stake.

5. D

Learning Objective: Draw logical conclusions related to police scenarios

The total amount is the sum of the funds from all sectors of the pie chart, namely 57,600. 6,000 represents 10.4% of the total amount.

6. A

Learning Objective: Determine the best course of action in a police scenario

An officer cannot arrest someone simply based on a hunch that he *might* be a criminal. Police officers must justify their arrest usually by providing tangible evidence that led them to probable cause. Choice (D) may appear to be a close runner-up, but "being paranoid" is not a crime, so whether the officer has proof of this would not be relevant to making an arrest.

7. B

Learning Objective: Determine the best course of action in a police scenario

The most unique characteristic is what the officer should be looking for. Tall white males and torn jeans are common. While yellow jerseys are arguably less common, snake tattoos on one's face are very rare. So this would be the characteristic to look for.

8. A

Learning Objective: Determine the best course of action in a police scenario

To use the statistics wisely, you need to identify the location where such illegal racing occurs. This information is provided in the sentence "Illegal dragstrip racing has been reported along Route 10 in this area between 11 p.m. and 1 a.m. on the weekends." So, the correct day will be a weekend day, and the correct time will encompass the times between 11 p.m. and 1 a.m.

DRAW LOGICAL CONCLUSIONS RELATED TO POLICE SCENARIOS

The skills involved in tackling logic and reasoning problems include drawing well-supported conclusions, identifying and applying principles and definitions, determining if a scenario satisfies a set of characteristics, and making common-sense inferences from a set of facts.

A portion of your police examination will assess your ability to process information logically, to formulate an easily understood synopsis of a situation, to correctly apply the *formal* definition of a crime to different scenarios, and to reason inductively and draw a plausible conclusion from a set of facts. The questions are based on short excerpts from various sources, including case studies, newspapers, and informal discourse.

Reasoning is the process of using existing knowledge to construct viable explanations or arguments, draw plausible conclusions, and make predictions. **Logic** can be viewed as the science of reasoning. We review some essential basics of logic, out of context, in this short section, and then dissect some of the common types of problems you will encounter on the exam in the short sections that follow.

The act of drawing conclusions from **premises**—information, facts, criteria, etc.—is called **inference**. For example, you see a large amount of water on the floor in the kitchen of a house and *infer* that either a pipe must have burst or the dishwasher malfunctioned.

The reasoning process starts with premises and produces an output, or conclusion. The main concern of logic is determining if the conclusion based on the input is correct. An **argument** is a sequence of statements, the last one of which is the conclusion: the beginning words of a conclusion are often *therefore, thus,* or *hence*. The input statements contributing to the formation of an argument should justify the conclusion.

Consider the following nonsensical, yet logical, argument:

All guinea pigs are birds.

All birds are Plutonians.

Therefore, all guinea pigs are Plutonians.

Though the statements themselves are not factually true, the argument is perfectly logical. The structure of the argument is: "All *p* are *q*. And all *q* are *s*. Therefore, all *p* are *s*."

The following is another valid argument, this time based on factual information:

All geckos are reptiles.

No reptiles are warm-blooded.

Thus, no geckos are warm-blooded.

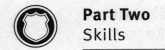

A twist that many people find unintuitive is that an argument formed using factual information can still be invalid. For example, consider the following argument:

Some birds are pets.

Some pets are cats.

Thus, some birds are cats.

The two premises are true. However, the final statement is not a logical conclusion that follows from these two statements, right?

Let us consider a more realistic scenario that involves making a logical conclusion:

Condominiums on the upper west side portion of the island cost less than condominiums on the east side of the island. Condominiums on the beach cost more than condominiums on the east side of the island. Of the three condominium locations, the beach condominiums cost the most.

This argument is valid and follows from the same logic used in our first example, but in a slightly different form. Precisely, "If $p < q$ and $q < s$, then $p < s$."

You are unlikely to encounter arguments like this on the exam. However, you will need to be able to ferret out logical reasoning from illogical reasoning, especially when on the job, taking reports from victims, assailants, burglars, witnesses, etc. We consider the main different types of questions you can expect on the exam in the next few sections. The underlying approach to solving these problems is rooted in these logic basics.

Sample reasoning questions

Inductive reasoning requires you to use pieces of information to draw a *likely* conclusion. These problems can take on different forms. We'll consider various sample questions below.

> During a seminar on traffic stop procedures, officers are urged to follow these guidelines when confronting a driver about a traffic violation:
>
> - Use a passenger-side approach so you are not blindsided by passing traffic.
> - Use all your patrol car's lighting to create a wall of light.
> - Call in the traffic stop before you even initiate the stop.
> - Remove occupants from the vehicle if the need arises for your safety.
> - Practice safe-searching techniques.

Based on this information, it would be most accurate for recruits to conclude that the main reason behind these guidelines is

(A) optimizing the number of traffic violations issued.

(B) ensuring the safety of officers issuing traffic violations.

(C) enabling officers to scan cars they pull over for wanted criminals.

(D) ensuring officers are not videotaped for wrongdoing while issuing a traffic violation.

Common sense suggests that Choice (B) is the most sensible choice here. Choice (A) would be self-serving for the department hosting the seminar. Choice (C) is not a likely consequence of following these guidelines. Choice (D) suggests a defensive action not characteristic of official department policy, and therefore would not be suitable for a seminar.

You might be asked to consider a situation presented graphically using bar graphs, pie graphs, or line graphs. Typically, you will be asked to provide a likely characterization of a scenario based on this information. For example, consider the following question:

Researchers have tracked the nature of violent crime in City X for 40 years. The categories of interest are murder, rape, robbery, and assault. The data they have gathered is summarized in the graph below:

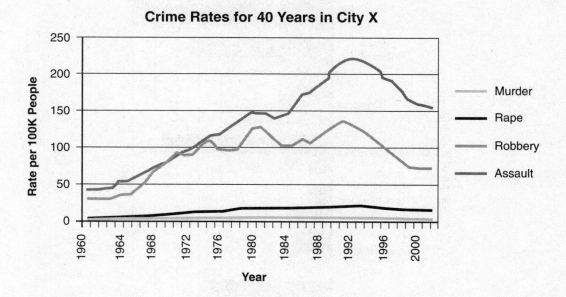

During which four-year time period does it appear that the rates of all forms of crime slowed down?

(A) 1980 to 1984

(B) 1964 to 1968

(C) 1992 to 1996

(D) 1974 to 1978

The correct time period will have all four graphs decreasing, or falling, from left to right. Choice (A) has the two main categories—robbery and assault—decreasing, but has rape on the rise. Choice (B) shows at least three of the four categories having an *increasing* rate. Choice (D) shows the rate at which assault and rape were both occurring as increasing. Finally, Choice (C) shows all four graphs decreasing from left to right and is therefore the correct answer.

A social scientist is interested in the types of bullying that occur for males and females, and if there is a marked difference. The results of the surveys she sent out are compiled in the following bar graph:

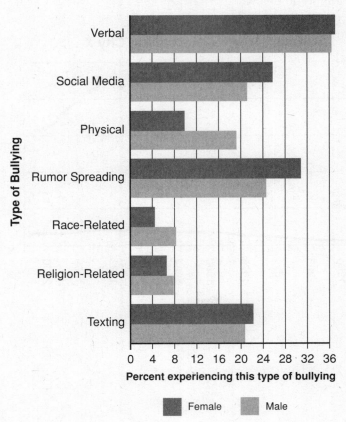

Bullying Occurrence in District X

For which of the following categories is the percent difference between the number of males and number of females experiencing that form of bullying the most distinct?

(A) Social media

(B) Physical

(C) Rumor spreading

(D) Race-related

Be careful here! You are asked for the largest *percent* difference. So, you must determine the difference in the lengths of the bars, and divide that by the length of the smaller bar, as follows:

Social media: $\dfrac{(26 - 22)}{22} = 0.18$ or 18%

Physical: $\dfrac{(19 - 10)}{10} = 0.9$ or about 90%

Rumor spreading: $\dfrac{(31 - 24)}{24} = 0.29$ or about 29%

Race-related: $\dfrac{(8 - 4)}{4} = 1$ or about 100%

So, the correct answer is Choice (D). About twice as many males are bullied because of their race.

SELECT THE CORRECT LEGAL DEFINITION OF A CRIME

There are numerous different crimes with which a person can be charged, and they all have specific criteria that must be met. As a police officer, you must know the statutes of your jurisdiction and be able to apply them accurately. Your ability to decipher if a scenario satisfies the criteria of a specific crime is important and will be assessed on the exam. The questions of this type will provide a definition and then ask you to make a judgment as to which scenario meets or does not meet the criteria. To do so, you must understand how to interpret a definition logically. This type of problem involves **deductive reasoning** since the conclusion is definitive and is based on facts presented. Let us consider several examples.

Consider the following definition:

*A person is guilty of **burglary in the third degree** when he knowingly enters or remains unlawfully in a building with intent to commit a crime therein.*

This definition comprises two distinct pieces, both of which are important.

i. The person unlawfully enters OR unlawfully remains in a building.

ii. The person *intends* to commit a crime.

Notice how *each and every word* of the definition is important and contributes meaningfully to the definition. Of note is the use of the word "or" in the first criterion. Logically, this criterion is satisfied if *either* condition holds; both do not need to hold for it to be satisfied! Also, there is an implied "and" between the criteria, meaning that both must be satisfied for a person to be guilty of this crime. If only one of the two is satisfied, then the person *cannot* be considered guilty of that specific crime.

A typical question would be as follows:

Question: Based <u>solely on this definition</u>, which of the following is the best example of burglary in the third degree?

Notice the underlined phrase. It is vital when working through this type of problem that you do not use other criteria beyond what is listed, even if other conditions of a scenario are illegal. Some choices will be included that provide information that breaks a *different* law but does NOT officially qualify as satisfying the given definition. The following are some standard choices:

(A) George, a bagger at Eagle Foods, climbs through an open window of the store after operating hours to retrieve his backpack, which he inadvertently left there after his shift.

(B) Peter enters the public library through a door that does not securely lock to steal several valuable DVDs and reference books.

(C) Monica, an employee of Hot Sam Pretzels, hides in the back room to sneak out the back exit to avoid encountering her boss, who she knows wants her to work an additional shift.

(D) Enrique climbs the exterior stairs of an office building so he can stargaze with his friends.

So, which is it? Choice (A) involves a person unlawfully entering the building, but there is no intent to commit a crime, so condition (ii) does not hold. Choice (C) does not satisfy the criteria since the person is *leaving* the building to simply avoid somebody—that's not a crime! Choice (D) does not involve the person *entering* the building. Even though it may be unlawful to be *on the grounds* after hours, this is not part of the criterion. Moreover, stargazing is not a crime. Finally, Choice (B) must be it! And common sense supports this choice. The person is entering a public building with the intention of stealing material from within the building. This is the correct choice.

Here is another example. Consider the following definition:

In State X, a person is guilty of **robbery in the third degree** *when he forcibly steals property.*

There are two distinct criteria in this definition:

  i. The person uses force of some kind, AND

  ii. The person steals property.

A typical question would be as follows:

> Based <u>solely on this definition</u>, which of the following is **least** likely to be an example of robbery in the third degree?
>
> (A) Randy pushes a teen off his motorbike and steals it.
>
> (B) Teri takes a package left by the mail carrier off her neighbor's doorstep and keeps it.
>
> (C) Scott pins a woman against the trunk of her SUV and takes her purse.
>
> (D) Dan grabs his roommate by the throat, shoves him onto the floor, and steals his wallet.

So, which is it this time? Choices (A), (C), and (D) all involve the assailant using force of some type and then taking something that is not theirs. Choice (B), however, does not involve the use of force. So, even though it *does* involve taking property that is not hers, this does not satisfy the definition of Robbery in the Third Degree.

The definitions can be more complicated. For instance, consider the following definition:

The crime of **statutory rape** *is committed when:*

  i. *A male or female, being 21 years of age or more, engages in sexual intercourse with a male or female 17 years of age or under, OR*

  ii. *A male or female, being 18 years of age or more, engages in sexual intercourse with a male or female 14 years of age or under, OR*

  iii. *A male or female, being 16 years of age or more, engages in sexual intercourse with a male or female 11 years of age or under.*

This definition involves three distinct sets of criteria, only one of which needs to be satisfied. And each of the three criteria is composed of three pieces of information (age of one person, age of the other person, and the act of sexual intercourse), ALL of which must be satisfied.

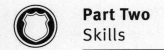

A typical question would be as follows:

> According to this definition, which of the following is the best example of statutory rape?
>
> (A) Theo, a 16-year-old male, engages in sexual intercourse with a 13-year-old female.
>
> (B) Henry, a 17-year-old male, engages in sexual intercourse with an 11-year-old female.
>
> (C) Nate, a 22-year-old male, engages in sexual intercourse with an 18-year-old female.
>
> (D) Ian, a 15-year-old male, engages in sexual intercourse with an 11-year-old female.

The only choice among these that satisfies the age combinations of one of the three distinct criteria comprising the definition of statutory rape is Choice (B). It satisfies criterion (iii).

Sometimes, there are different levels of a particular crime, and going from one level to another involves adding more criteria or strengthening existing ones. You must be able to distinguish between such levels by pinpointing their differences.

For example, consider the following two definitions:

i. *A person commits the offense of **stalking** when he or she follows, places under surveillance, or contacts another person at or about a place or places without the consent of the other person for the purpose of harassing and intimidating the other person.*

ii. *A person commits the offense of **aggravated stalking** when such person, in violation of a temporary restraining order, temporary protective order, permanent restraining order, permanent protective order, condition of probation, or condition of parole prohibiting this behavior, places under surveillance, or contacts another person at or about a place or places without the consent of the other person for the purpose of harassing and intimidating the other person.*

Here, the main difference is that a stalker guilty of *aggravated stalking* must violate a temporary or permanent restraining order or order of protection. Be certain not to introduce other criteria that are not already present in the definition, such as presuming that aggravated stalking involves a threat or injury that is more severe than is involved in non-aggravated stalking.

MAKE SOUND JUDGMENTS REGARDING POLICE SCENARIOS

Another type of problem you will encounter on the exam is one where you will need to make a judgment based on a situation. While certainly rooted in the law, these problems tend to resemble what you might think of as common-sense scenarios. Read the question carefully to make sure you completely understand the presented situation and use your judgment—trust yourself!

Let us consider several examples.

A school principal has been receiving emails and phone calls from parents about bullying in the school yard before the school bell rings in the morning. She asks the yard monitors to keep a close eye on student interaction prior to the first bell of the day. Which of the following situations should be reported by the yard monitors?

(A)   Four boys are playing two-on-two basketball and are discussing a potential foul.

(B)   Three kids are sitting in a group, engaged in a multiplayer online video game, jokingly heckling each other, sometimes using colorful language.

(C)   A young bespectacled girl sits in a corner playing with her iPhone and does not interact with any peers.

(D)   A taller girl seems to be in possession of a less popular, smaller girl's notebook, and the smaller girl seems distraught.

Choices (A) and (B) constitute normal child behavior. Choice (C) is arguably concerning, but it is not obvious that it is the result of bullying in the school yard. Choice (D) is the most apparent act of bullying of those listed.

The police department selects a particular sidearm as its department-issued weapon. Which of the following is the most logical reason for this?

(A)   The department does not want to waste time training officers on the use of more than one weapon.

(B)   The department selects the least expensive weapon available and orders it in bulk.

(C)   The manufacturer pays for the privilege of making the selected weapon.

(D)   The department selects the most efficient and accurate weapon available.

Choices (A) and (B) imply that saving money is more important than safety, efficiency, and accuracy, which is simply not true. Choice (C) is not a logical choice because police departments do not use weapons as a means of endorsing them, and manufacturers do not pay for the privilege. Choice (D) is the most sensible choice of those listed because it exemplifies a top priority of the police department.

Officer Bradford is told to focus her attention on drug dealing in her patrol area. Of the following, about which location should she be least concerned?

(A)   A bridge underpass where local teens often gather

(B)   An abandoned factory warehouse where drug arrests have been made in the past five years

(C)   A 24-hour community center staffed by social workers and medical staff

(D)   A back alley where prostitutes occasionally gather

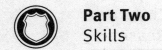
Choice (C) is the best choice here because it is unlikely someone would deal drugs in an active location full of people—both visitors and staff. Choices (A), (B), and (D) are all out-of-the-way places where few people would hang out.

> Officers Leeman and Rucko were dispatched to investigate a report of aggravated assault. They obtained the following information on scene:
>
> Date: May 20, 2018
> Victim: Bill Pincket
> Suspect: Samantha Downing, the victim's landlord
> Disposition: Suspect arrested
>
> Which of the following is an **incorrect** assumption based on the information obtained?
>
> (A) Samantha Downing and Bill Pincket are dating.
>
> (B) Samantha Downing assaulted Bill Pincket on May 20, 2018.
>
> (C) Samantha Downing is the landlord of Bill Pincket.
>
> (D) Samantha Downing was arrested.

To answer this type of question, study the given information carefully. Nowhere does it explicitly mention that Samantha Downing and Bill Pincket were dating. While this *might* very well be the case, it cannot be inferred from the given information, while all three of the other choices *can be*. So, Choice (A) is an incorrect assumption.

> On February 15, 2017, several jewelry store robberies were committed at different locations. Based on the descriptions provided by various eyewitnesses, it seems likely that the same person is responsible for all these robberies. Officers were given the following description of the suspect:
>
> *The suspect is a Latino male, partially bald with short black hair, weighing approximately 140 pounds and about 5 feet 6 inches tall, a dragon tattoo on his neck, and wearing a red hooded sweatshirt.*
>
> Officer Adamson has stopped five Latino males for questioning. Which of the following pieces of information should the officer consider the *most* useful in identifying the correct suspect?
>
> (A) The suspect is wearing a red hooded sweatshirt.
>
> (B) The suspect is partially bald with black hair.
>
> (C) The suspect has a dragon tattoo on his neck.
>
> (D) The suspect weighs 140 pounds and is about 5 feet 6 inches tall.

To answer this question, think to yourself, "Which of these pieces of information is the *most* unique and so, the *least* likely to appear on multiple suspects?" Choice (A) can be immediately discarded since such sweatshirts are very common. Choice (B) is not particularly unique, and the weight-height combination presented in Choice (D) is common. That leaves Choice (C), which is the most unique of those listed and would be impossible to hide or change in a short period of time.

Some problems, like the one below, require that you arrange a collection of actions in the most appropriate order.

> While on patrol at 2:00 a.m., Officer Kammen sees smoke coming off the bushes along the side of a house. As he pulls up to the house, he sees two teenagers bolt out of the yard and down the street. Which of the following is the best order of actions the officer should take?
>
> (A)   Alert the people in the house, assist with evacuating the house, radio for the fire department, radio the suspects' descriptions
>
> (B)   Radio the suspects' descriptions, assist with evacuating the house, alert the people in the house, radio for the fire department
>
> (C)   Radio for the fire department, alert the people in the house, assist with evacuating the house, radio the suspects' descriptions
>
> (D)   Alert the people in the house, radio the suspects' descriptions, assist with evacuating the house, radio for the fire department

The primary concern is the safety of the people in the house and the surrounding neighbors. So, Choice (B) can be eliminated. Likewise, once the officer has alerted people in the house as to the situation, it wouldn't be sensible for him to then change gears, radio headquarters, and then return to assist with the evacuation. So, Choice (D) can be eliminated. So, it's between Choices (A) and (C). This choice is tricky, but with the primary concern being the safety of people in the house, every second counts. So, Choice (A) is preferable over Choice (C).

DETERMINE THE BEST COURSE OF ACTION IN A POLICE SCENARIO

Proper/improper questions

As a police officer, you will have to abide by many rules that often will require you to make ethical decisions regarding proper and improper responses to scenarios. For instance, when is it appropriate for an officer to accept a gift? Is it more appropriate to arrest a suspect, let him or her go with a warning, or issue a fine? Is it ever appropriate to enter someone's house without explicit permission? The list goes on and on. Questions that assess proper and improper responses to different scenarios might be included on your police exam.

Let's look at a question. You might be given a sample scenario that looks like this:

Officer Wallace recently reviewed his department's policy on the scenarios for which it is appropriate to initiate a vehicle pursuit. The policy reads, "Officers may only initiate a vehicle pursuit when the driver of the vehicle-to-be-pursued has committed a serious crime and/or failure to pursue the vehicle is likely to be of greater danger to the public than the actual pursuit itself."

Given the above, you might be asked a question like this:

Based on this policy, is it proper or improper for Officer Wallace to initiate a vehicle pursuit of a driver who exceeds the speed limit in a school zone by 10 miles per hour?

(A) Proper, because driving over the speed limit is a serious crime that endangers all around you

(B) Proper, because performing a vehicle pursuit in a school zone does not put anyone at risk

(C) Improper, because driving only 10 miles over the speed limit is not a crime

(D) Improper, because a vehicle pursuit in this location could put children in harm's way

Questions of this type require an equal amount of common sense and adherence to the stated policy. The question is about whether driving *10 miles per hour over the speed limit* is a crime of sufficient seriousness worth tracking down that driver at all costs, including the potential lives of children in the school zone and other nearby drivers. The most common sense answer to this question is *no*. Yes, it is a crime, but not of sufficient seriousness as to warrant a vehicle pursuit. So, Choice (D) is the correct answer.

Logical judgment questions

A litany of procedures have been designed to ensure the safety of the officers, witnesses, and victims involved in various types of altercations, as well as to ensure the efficiency and accuracy with which incidents are addressed. As such, officers must be familiar with all these procedures and be able to correctly interpret them, which often involves knowing the correct order in which to perform a task.

As with all questions on your exam, you will be given all the information you need in order to answer a question. The test wants to determine your instincts, not your knowledge of police procedure.

For example, you might be given the following information to review:

Police officers are to handle radio calls and observational activities adhering to the following rules:

1. Be certain the scene is safe.

2. If medical attention is required, request fire rescue.

3. Get a brief synopsis of the incident, including a description of the suspect(s), weapon(s), vehicles, etc.

4. Relay this information to dispatch so that other police units can be notified.

5. Obtain a detailed report from the victim(s).

6. Question all witnesses.

7. Gather physical evidence.

8. Provide the victim with a report number of the incident.

9. Attempt to conclude the investigation with appropriate action.

After you review these facts, you will have to answer a question like the following:

> Officer MacKenzie is the first officer to arrive on the scene of an attempted carjacking in a concert parking lot. She spots the victim amidst broken glass from a shattered car window. The victim is hysterical, and his head is badly bruised. He is being comforted by two people. What is the first thing Officer MacKenzie should do?
>
> (A) Ask the victim to explain what happened.
>
> (B) Ask the two people comforting the victim to provide their accounts of what occurred.
>
> (C) Call for an ambulance.
>
> (D) Write notes about the scene.

To correctly determine the course of action, the officer must refer to the prescribed procedure. Use the information you are given—it is there for a reason. The exam is also testing your skills of comprehension in addition to your common sense.

The way to approach this problem is to determine which of the four choices occurs earliest in the list; this is the first course of action, of those listed, that the officer should take. In this case, Choice (C) is the earliest in the list. So, the correct answer is (C).

Time and place questions

As an officer, you will likely be assigned to patrol different neighborhoods and city sectors throughout your career. Each neighborhood is prone to different types of crime at different times of the day, so you will need to familiarize yourself with the statistics of your particular zone to efficiently serve the public. Specifically, you want to use your time wisely and patrol certain areas at certain times to minimize the number of incidents of a particular crime.

Let's take another look at the situation you saw in the Test What You Know section.

Officer Drake is assigned to patrol the streets of a certain section of her town. Her patrol area consists of two main streets, Route 10 and Route 22, parallel to each other and half a mile apart. Five residential streets run between these two main streets, perpendicular to them: Bryan, Grange, Rockside, Indian Run, and Senn.

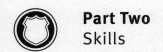

She reviews the area crime statistics for the past year prior to the start of duty. Reports indicate that yard vandalism was isolated to Grange Street and that petty theft (e.g., garden gnomes, bird feeders, etc.) was isolated to Rockside, on all days of the week. Both types of crime are believed to occur between 1 a.m. and 4 a.m. Illegal dragstrip racing has been reported along Route 10 in this area between 11 p.m. and 1 a.m. on the weekends. Teens have been reported to gather in groups and drink on the corners of Indian Run and Senn all days of the week, between 9 p.m. and midnight.

To reduce the number of occurrences of yard vandalism, she should patrol

(A) Route 10 in this area between 11 p.m. and 1 a.m.

(B) Grange Street between midnight and 5 a.m.

(C) the corners of Indian Run and Senn between 9 p.m. and midnight.

(D) Rockside Street between 1 a.m. and 4 a.m.

To use the statistics wisely, you need to identify the location where the yards are being vandalized and the time of day during which this occurs. This information is provided in the two adjacent sentences (key information in bold):

*Reports indicate that **yard vandalism was isolated to Grange Street** and that petty theft (e.g., garden gnomes, bird feeders, etc.) was isolated to Rockside. **Both types of crime** are believed to **occur between 1 a.m. and 4 a.m.***

Therefore, the correct answer is Choice (B)—its time range encompasses the times in the report. Note that Choice (D) also covers this time range, but at the wrong location for yard vandalism.

TEST WHAT YOU LEARNED

Directions: Choose the ONE best answer for each question.

A person is guilty of **petit larceny** when he steals property. A person is guilty of **robbery in the third degree** when he forcibly steals property.

1. Kyle steals his neighbor's mountain bike. Later that week, when the neighbor accuses him of stealing the mountain bike, he beats the neighbor unconscious. Based solely upon the above definitions, which of the following is true?

   (A) Kyle should be charged with robbery in the third degree.

   (B) Kyle should be charged with petit larceny.

   (C) Kyle should be charged with both petit larceny and robbery in the third degree.

   (D) Kyle should not be charged with either crime.

2. An industrial section of Officer Plack's patrol area has been hit by a recent rash of burglaries of large equipment. About which of the following scenarios should Officer Plack be most concerned while patrolling this industrial section?

   (A) A man dressed in black parked in a windowless van

   (B) A woman carrying a can of gasoline toward her small two-door Nissan car

   (C) Two men walking a dog and carrying toolboxes

   (D) A pair of teenagers skateboarding in the parking lot

3. Officer Watkins is sent to the elementary school following a call from the school principal, who reported seeing several teenagers spray-paint obscene phrases and pictures on the jungle gym in the school's playground. Officer Watkins asks the principal several questions. Which of the following is least likely to be among the questions asked?

   (A) "What time did the vandalism occur?"

   (B) "What did the suspects look like?"

   (C) "Did anyone else witness the vandalism?"

   (D) "For how many years have you been the principal at this school?"

Consider the following graph:

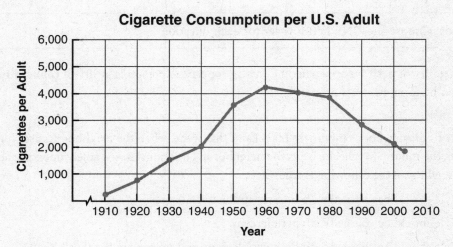

Cigarette Consumption per U.S. Adult

Source: U.S. Department of Health and Human Services

4. In which 10-year period did cigarette consumption increase at the greatest rate?

    (A) 1910 to 1920

    (B) 1940 to 1950

    (C) 1950 to 1960

    (D) 1980 to 1990

Breaking and entering is a specific type of property crime. It requires the following elements of proof:

  i. Unauthorized entry, AND

  ii. Entry is into a residence or building, AND

  iii. Entry involves using force, deceit, or property damage.

5. According to this definition, which of the following CANNOT be classified as breaking and entering?

    (A) Breaking a window on an office building while playing baseball in the parking lot

    (B) Prying open a back-alley entry door into a dance club after hours

    (C) Deceiving a security guard to gain unauthorized access to an area

    (D) Slightly pushing open a door to enter the building that has a sign saying "Authorized Personnel Only"

The Texas Code of Criminal Procedure states, "In making an arrest, all reasonable means are permitted to be used to effect it. No greater force, however, shall be resorted to than is necessary to secure the arrest and detention of the accused."

6. Based on this criterion, is it proper or improper for Officer Blake to push a suspect to the ground and handcuff her if she is flailing around due to being high on methadone after leaving her vehicle?

   (A) Proper. It is acceptable for an officer to tackle any suspect to the ground when making an arrest.

   (B) Improper. This is unnecessary use of force because the suspect was not aware of what she was doing while under the influence of drugs.

   (C) Proper. The suspect is acting unruly and so, to make the arrest, it is reasonable to restrain her in this manner.

   (D) Improper. An officer should never use physical force when making an arrest.

Police officers are to handle radio calls and observational activities while adhering to the following rules:

1. Be certain the scene is safe.
2. If medical attention is required, request fire rescue.
3. Get a brief synopsis of the incident, including a description of the suspect(s), weapon(s), vehicles, etc.
4. Relay this information to dispatch so that other police units can be notified.
5. Obtain a detailed report from the victim(s).
6. Question all witnesses.
7. Gather physical evidence.
8. Provide the victim with a report number of the incident.
9. Attempt to conclude the investigation with appropriate action.

7. Officer MacKenzie is the first officer to arrive on the scene of an attempted carjacking in a concert parking lot. She spots the victim amidst broken glass from a shattered car window. The victim is hysterical, and his head is badly bruised. He is being comforted by two people. What is most likely the LAST course of action that Officer MacKenzie should take?

   (A) Use the radio to contact headquarters to alert other officers in the vicinity to be on the lookout for the suspect.

   (B) Interview the two witnesses who were initially comforting the victim.

   (C) Collect the piece of ripped clothing the victim tore off the assailant.

   (D) Ask the victim for a detailed account of what happened.

Officer Guthrie is assigned to patrol a portion of the area between the boardwalk and Hill Street that lies between 30th Street and 75th Street. He reviews the crime statistics for the past year for the area prior to the start of duty. He finds that the majority of drug deals occurred during the weekend on the corner of 45th Street and Hill Street between 1 a.m. and 3 a.m. Vandals sprayed graffiti and broke windows on buildings along the boardwalk near 32nd and 33rd Streets between 12 a.m. and 3 a.m. after ladies' night on Thursday nights. All assaults, on every day of the week, occurred between 70th Street and 75th Street along Hill Street between 9 p.m. and 2 a.m. Parking violations occurred along the boardwalk during the morning hours when people were competing for parking spaces for their beach outings.

8. To reduce the number of buildings being vandalized, Officer Guthrie should patrol

   (A) the boardwalk in the morning on all weekdays.

   (B) between 70th Street and 75th Street along Hill Street between 9 p.m. and midnight on weekdays.

   (C) between 30th Street and 34th Street along the boardwalk from 11 p.m. to 3 a.m. on Thursdays.

   (D) the corner of 45th Street and Hill Street between 12 a.m. and 3 a.m. on Thursdays.

ANSWERS AND EXPLANATIONS

1. B

Learning Objective: Select the correct legal definition of a crime

While Kyle might be committing another crime when he "beats the neighbor unconscious," he is not committing robbery in the third degree because he is not forcibly stealing property. Now, had he beaten the neighbor *in the process of stealing* the mountain bike, then he would have been forcibly stealing property. In that case, he would have been committing robbery in the third degree.

2. A

Learning Objective: Make sound judgments regarding police scenarios

Since the thievery in this section has focused on large equipment, the only one of these scenarios involving a large enough vehicle in which to load such equipment is the van in Choice (A). So, the officer should be most concerned about such a scenario.

3. D

Learning Objective: Draw logical conclusions related to police scenarios

Choice (D) is correct because the number of years the principal has worked at the school won't help identify the vandals. The time of the vandalism (A), the suspects' appearance (B), and the presence of other witnesses (C) may help solve the crime.

4. B

Learning Objective: Draw logical conclusions related to police scenarios

Since you want the *maximum rate of increasing*, you want to find the 10-year span where the graph rises vertically by the largest amount. The graph goes *down* during the time period in Choice (D), so that can be eliminated immediately. So, you must choose from Choices (A), (B), and (C); here, the biggest increase occurs with Choice (B).

5. A

Learning Objective: Select the correct legal definition of a crime

While property damage was indeed done by the errant baseball into an office building, there is nothing mentioned about unauthorized entry into the building as a result. Since *all three* criteria must be satisfied, this scenario cannot be classified as breaking and entering. All other choices satisfy all three criteria.

6. C

Learning Objective: Determine the best course of action in a police scenario

The key here is to determine if the use of any force is warranted here, and if so, whether the level of force used is appropriate. Since the suspect was high on drugs, she needed to be restrained, so the use of force is appropriate, and pushing the suspect to the ground and cuffing her is a sufficient approach. Had the suspect been beaten prior to this, that would have constituted excessive force.

7. C

Learning Objective: Determine the best course of action in a police scenario

To correctly determine the course of action, the officer must refer to the prescribed procedure. The way to approach this problem is to determine which of the four choices occurs latest in the list; this is the last course of action, of those listed, that the officer should take. In this case, Choice (C) is the latest in the list.

8. C

Learning objective: Determine the best course of action in a police scenario

This is a lot of area to cover on patrol. To use the statistics wisely, you need to identify the location where the buildings are being vandalized, the time of day during which this occurs, and the day of the week. Buildings were vandalized on 32nd and 33rd Streets, along the boardwalk, on Thursdays between 12 a.m. and 3 a.m. Therefore, Choice (C) is the best answer.

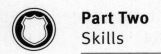

 **SELF-REFLECTION**

Now that you have concluded your work in this chapter, reflect on your ability to ferret out logical reasoning from illogical reasoning. Do you feel comfortable with deciphering whether a scenario satisfies the criteria of a specific crime? Can you distinguish between two seemingly similar crimes? Are you more aware of how to critically process given information and make a logical conclusion based solely on that information? Have you honed your ability to process data, information, and graphs sensibly and draw reasonable conclusions based on them? If you have answered yes to these questions, you are prepared for the logic questions you will encounter on the police exam! If not, look back at the chapter and hone in on what *exactly* continues to cause confusion, and practice those types of problems some more. This will ensure success on this part of the exam!

Test What You Know score: _____ /8 correct

Test What You Learned score: _____ /8 correct

After working through the practice problems in this chapter, which of the Learning Objectives have you mastered? Place a check mark next to those objectives to keep track of your progress.

- [ ] Draw logical conclusions related to police scenarios
- [ ] Select the correct legal definition of a crime
- [ ] Make sound judgments regarding police scenarios
- [ ] Determine the best course of action in a police scenario

CHAPTER 9

Mathematics

Some police exams may test basic mathematics to ensure you are comfortable working with numbers. This chapter reviews some of the building blocks of math. If you are comfortable with the concepts presented in this chapter, facing everyday problems that require a basic knowledge of addition, subtraction, multiplication, and division will present no challenge.

Most of you have encountered these rules and practices in school, though it may have been a while since you've reviewed the exact terms and concepts. For some of you, this chapter will just be a basic brushup of skills you are comfortable with. Others may have to study this chapter carefully to relearn the basics. As with grammar and spelling, no matter what your actual exam tests, reviewing this chapter and completing the practice questions can only enhance your confidence going into Test Day.

LEARNING OBJECTIVES

In this chapter, you will review how to:

- ❏ Approach math test questions strategically
- ❏ Apply mathematics concepts to law-enforcement scenarios
- ❏ Calculate area and perimeter

TEST WHAT YOU KNOW

Directions: Choose the ONE best answer for each question.

---

1. Mark can patrol the entirety of a park in 3 hours, and Kevin can patrol the entirety of the same park in 4 hours. How many hours would it take Mark and Kevin to patrol the park if they work together at their respective rates?

   (A) $\dfrac{3}{2}$

   (B) $\dfrac{12}{7}$

   (C) $\dfrac{10}{3}$

   (D) 4

2. Officer Grey regularly works patrol with Officer Krevoy. Yesterday, Officer Grey purchased coffees for both officers at a price of $4 each. Today, Officer Krevoy purchased coffees for the two at a different diner at the price of $3.50 each. How much more did Officer Grey spend?

   (A) $1

   (B) $3

   (C) $7

   (D) $8

3. A business owner claims that someone demanded a total of $100,000 in three payments or they would vandalize the store and hack into its website. The owner made a payment to the suspect of $30,000 before contacting police. If the next two payments were to be divided evenly, then what would be the amount of each payment?

   (A) $30,000

   (B) $35,000

   (C) $60,000

   (D) $70,000

4. A suspect has escaped a crime scene and your superior officer asks your team to search an area covering 15 city blocks by 20 city blocks. What is the total area of the space you are searching?

    (A) 35 square blocks

    (B) 70 square blocks

    (C) 140 square blocks

    (D) 300 square blocks

ANSWERS AND EXPLANATIONS

1.   B

Learning Objective: Approach math test questions strategically

If you use your mathematics strategies, you don't even need to technically solve this problem to find the answer. You are told the rates at which two officers can patrol a park separately. The correct answer represents how long it would take the two people to patrol the park together, each working at the same rate at which he works alone. If Mark, the faster officer, works completely on his own, he will complete the task in 3 hours. With help, he will take even less time to complete the job, so you can eliminate answer Choices (C) and (D), which are greater than 3. Since Kevin is slower than Mark, working together will take longer than half of 3 hours. Since (A) is half of 3, you can eliminate it. That leaves only answer Choice (B), which must be correct.

2.   A

Learning Objective: Apply mathematics concepts to law-enforcement scenarios

First, find the amount of money each officer spent separately. Officer Grey spent (2)($4) = $8. Officer Krevoy spent (2)($3.50) = $7. So, Officer Grey spent $8 − $7 = $1 more.

3.   B

Learning Objective: Apply mathematics concepts to law-enforcement scenarios

Subtracting the initial $30,000 payment yields $100,000 − $30,000 = $70,000. If this is divided over two payments, then that would make each payment $70,000 ÷ 2 = $35,000.

4.   D

Learning Objective: Calculate area and perimeter

Area = Length × Width. In this case, length = 15 blocks, and width = 20 blocks. So the area = 15 × 20, or 300 square blocks.

APPROACH MATH TEST QUESTIONS STRATEGICALLY

Working quickly and efficiently is essential to maximizing your score on the math questions you will face on your police exam. To accomplish this, use the following method:

1. Analyze the information given.

2. Identify what you are being asked for.

3. Solve strategically.

4. Confirm your answer.

Step 1. Analyze the information given

Read the entire question carefully before you start solving the problem. If you don't read the question carefully, you may make a careless mistake or overlook the simplest approach to answering the question.

Step 2. Identify what you are being asked for

Before you choose your approach, make sure you know what you're solving for. In other words, what does the correct answer choice represent? This is an important step to keep you from falling for tempting wrong answer choices. For example, if you are given an equation with two variables, x and y, identify whether you are solving for x, for y, or for something else. This step is important because your exam may give you wrong answer choices that represent the "right answer to the wrong question." That is, if you are asked to solve for x, one wrong answer choice might represent the value of y.

Step 3. Solve strategically

Once you understand what the question is asking you to solve, it's time to look for the most strategic approach. Use your analysis from Steps 1 and 2 to find the most efficient route to the correct answer. This step might involve performing calculations (that is, "doing the math"), or it might be the case that applying a strategy would get you to the correct answer more quickly. This chapter will discuss these strategic approaches.

Step 4. Confirm your answer

Reread the question as you select your answer. Make sure you are answering the question asked. If you notice that you missed something earlier, rework the problem and change your answer if necessary.

Here's an example of the steps in action:

> One bag contains 6 pieces of candy, another bag contains 8 pieces, and a third bag contains 16 pieces. What is the average number of pieces of candy in a single bag?
>
> (A) 6
>
> (B) 8
>
> (C) 10
>
> (D) 30

Step 1. Analyze the information given:

The question tells you the number of pieces of candy in three bags.

Step 2. Identify what you are being asked for:

You are being asked to calculate the average number of candies in one bag.

Step 3. Solve strategically:

Use the average formula:

$$\text{Average} = \frac{\text{Sum of terms}}{\text{\# of terms}}$$

$$\text{Average} = \frac{6 + 8 + 16}{3}$$

$$\text{Average} = \frac{30}{3} = 10$$

The average is 10, or Choice (C).

Step 4. Confirm your answer:

Don't rework the math from scratch; rather, ask yourself whether the answer makes sense given what you were asked for. Does 10 seem like a likely average given the numbers 6, 8, and 16?

Yes. Since the average of a set of numbers has a value that's between the smallest and largest numbers in the set, 10 makes sense as an answer.

Test strategies for approaching math problems

Several methods are extremely useful when you don't know—or don't have time to use—the textbook approach to solving the question. In addition, performing all the calculations called for in the question can often be more time-consuming than using a strategic approach and can increase the potential for mistakes.

Let's now explore four of those strategic methods:

1. Backsolving

2. Picking Numbers

3. Strategic Guessing

4. Estimation

Backsolving

Sometimes it's easiest to work backward from the answer choices. Since many math questions are word problems with numbers in the answer choices, you can often use this to your advantage by backsolving, or working backward from the available answer choices. After all, the test gives you the correct answer—it's just mixed in with the wrong answer choices. If you try an answer choice in the question and it fits with the information given, then you've got the right answer.

Here's how it works. When the answer choices are numbers, you can expect them to be arranged from small to large (or occasionally from large to small). Start by trying either Choice (B) or (C). If that number works when you plug it into the problem, you've found the correct answer. If it doesn't work, you can usually figure out whether to try a larger or smaller answer choice next. Even better, if you deduce that you need a smaller (or larger) number, and only one such smaller (or larger) number appears among the answer choices, that choice must be correct. You do not have to try that answer choice: simply select it and move on to the next question.

By backsolving strategically this way, you won't have to try out more than two answer choices before you zero in on the correct answer. To see an example of backsolving, check out the following problem and explanation.

> An appliance store reduced the price of a refrigerator by 20% and then raised the price by 10% from the lower price. What was the original price of the refrigerator, if the final price was $70.40?
>
> (A) $50
>
> (B) $70
>
> (C) $80
>
> (D) $100

Step 1. Analyze the information given:

The price of a refrigerator is reduced 20% and then that reduced price is raised 10%. The final price is $70.40.

Step 2. Identify what you are being asked for:

The correct answer represents the original price before the changes.

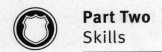
Step 3. Solve strategically:

To answer this question using algebra would be complex and time-consuming and would introduce many opportunities for errors. Instead, since all the answer choices are numbers, backsolve.

Start by trying out Choice (B), $70:

$70 reduced by 20%: $70 − $14 = $56

$56 raised by 10%: $56 + $5.60 = $61.60

That's lower than the final price of $70.40, so Choice (B) is too low. Now, you can eliminate both answer Choices (B) and (A).

Now try either (C) or (D). (D) is easier for a percent problem.

Reduce $100 by 20%: $100 − $20 = $80

Raise that $80 by 10%: $80 + $8 = $88

That final price is far too high, so (C) must be the correct answer.

Step 4. Confirm your answer:

The answer of $80 is the only one that is neither too large nor too small to yield the final price of $70.40 specified in the question. So, you're done!

In backsolving, when you start with Choice (B) or (C) and that answer doesn't work, you'll usually know which direction to go. For example, if the answer choices are listed smallest to largest and Choice (B) is too large when you plug it in, you will know that Choice (A) is the correct answer. If, on the other hand, Choice (B) is too small, you will know that the answer is Choice (C) or (D).

Picking numbers

Another strategy that comes in handy on many math questions is picking numbers. Just because the question contains numbers in the answer choices, that doesn't mean that you can always backsolve. There may be numbers in the answer choices, but sometimes you won't have enough information in the question to easily match up an answer choice to a specific value in the question stem.

For example, a problem might present an equation with many variables, or it might give you information about percentages of some unknown quantity and ask you for another percent. If the test maker hasn't provided you with a quantity that would be really helpful to have in order to solve the problem, you may be able to simply pick a value to assign to that unknown. The other case in which you can pick numbers is when there are variables in the answer choices.

When you are picking numbers, be sure that the numbers you select are permissible (following the rules of the problem) and manageable (easy to work with). In general, it's a good idea to avoid picking -1, 0, or 1 because they have unique number properties that can skew your results.

Here's a great example showing how picking numbers can make an abstract problem concrete.

When n is divided by 14, the remainder is 9. What is the remainder when n is divided by 7?

(A) 1

(B) 2

(C) 3

(D) 4

Step 1. Analyze the information given:

An unknown number, n, is 9 larger than a multiple of 14.

Step 2. Identify what you are being asked for:

The correct answer represents the remainder when n is divided by 7.

Step 3. Solve strategically:

To make this abstract question concrete, pick a number for n that leaves a remainder of 9 when divided by 14. The most manageable number to pick that is also permissible in the problem is $n = 23$ (because $14 + 9 = 23$).

Now try out your number: $23 \div 7 = 3$ with a remainder of 2.

Therefore, Choice (B) is the correct answer.

Step 4. Confirm your answer:

Briefly look back over the math to check that you are solving for the correct value. Confirm, and you're all set!

When there are variables in the problem and in the answer choices, you can pick numbers for those variables. Evaluate the expression in the question stem using your chosen numbers, and then evaluate each answer choice using the same numbers. Your goal is to find the answer that yields the same numerical result as the one you calculated using your chosen numbers. When you use this method, you must evaluate all of the answer choices. If more than one yields the same numerical result, choose a different set of numbers to evaluate only the remaining choices that gave matching solutions with the first set of numbers that you chose.

To solve problems containing variables in the question stem and answer choices using picking numbers, start by picking permissible and manageable numbers for the variables. Answer the question using the numbers you've picked. This answer is your target number. Then substitute the numbers you picked for the variables into the answer choices. You are looking for the answer choice that gives you the target number.

Take a look at this example:

For all r, s, t, and u, what does $r(t + u) - s(t + u)$ equal?

(A) $(r + s)(t + u)$

(B) $(r - s)(t - u)$

(C) $(r + s)(t - u)$

(D) $(r - s)(t + u)$

Step 1. Analyze the information given:

You are given an algebraic expression and asked to find an equivalent expression.

Step 2. Identify what you are being asked for:

The correct answer simplifies the expression $r(t + u) - s(t + u)$.

Step 3. Solve strategically:

Since you are given no values for any of the four variables, you can pick numbers for each of them.

Some good numbers to pick here are $r = 5$, $s = 4$, $t = 3$, and $u = 2$. You can, however, use any permissible and manageable numbers you wish.

Replacing the variables in the expressions with the numbers picked yields the following:

$$5(3 + 2) - 4(3 + 2) = 25 - 20 = 5$$

Then replace the variables in each answer choice to see which choice gives the target number of 5:

(A) $(r + s)(t + u)(5 + 4)(3 + 2) = (9)(5) = 45$ Incorrect

(B) $(r - s)(t - u)(5 - 4)(3 - 2) = (1)(1) = 1$ Incorrect

(C) $(r + s)(t - u)(5 + 4)(3 - 2) = (9)(1) = 9$ Incorrect

(D) $(r - s)(t + u)(5 - 4)(3 + 2) = (1)(5) = 5$ Correct

Step 4. Confirm your answer:

In this example, only Choice (D) works. If more than one choice gives a correct answer, you need to pick another set of numbers and try only those answer choices again.

Strategic guessing

Sometimes you can determine the characteristics of a correct answer without doing a lot of calculations. Study the example below.

> After eating 25% of the pretzels, Sonya had 42 left. How many pretzels did Sonya have originally?
>
> (A) 50
>
> (B) 54
>
> (C) 56
>
> (D) 58

Step 1. Analyze the information given:

Original # of pretzels − 25% of pretzels = 42

Step 2. Identify what you are being asked for:

The correct answer represents the original number of pretzels before Sonya ate any.

Step 3. Solve strategically:

Because 25% is the same as one-quarter, the correct answer must be divisible by 4 with no remainder. If the number of pretzels Sonia started with was not divisible by 4, and she then ate $\frac{1}{4}$ of the pretzels, she'd be left with fractions of pretzels left over. Of the answer choices, only Choice (C), 56, is evenly divisible by 4, so it has to be the correct answer.

Step 4. Confirm your answer:

One-quarter of 56 is 14, and 56 − 14 = 42, the number of pretzels Sonya had left.

If at all possible, try to avoid doing extensive calculations; rather, see if you can eliminate some answer choices based on logic.

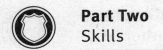
Estimation

There is no rule that says you have to use just one approach to get the correct answer. Study the example below.

> Shoshanna bought a new cell phone, cell phone case, and wall charger. The cell phone cost $149.99, the case cost $19.99, and the wall charger cost $29.99. If tax on each of these items was 9.5%, which of the following is closest to the total amount Shoshanna spent?
>
> (A) $180
>
> (B) $200
>
> (C) $205
>
> (D) $220

Step 1. Analyze the information given:

You are told the prices of three items that Shoshanna purchased, plus a sales tax rate.

Step 2. Identify what you are being asked for:

You are asked to find the answer that is closest to the total amount Shoshanna paid for her purchases.

Step 3. Solve strategically:

Because you are asked for the closest amount, you do not have to use an exact calculation to find the correct answer. Estimation will work well. Round the prices for each item before tax to the nearest dollar.

Shoshanna spent $150 + $20 + $30 = $200 before tax. You can eliminate Choices (A) and (B) because they are too small. Now round the tax rate to 10%. Because 10% of $200 is $20, Shoshanna spent about $200 + $20 = $220 in total. Choice (D) is correct.

Step 4. Confirm your answer:

Check that you did the arithmetic correctly and that the answer makes sense. All the other answer choices are too low to be close to what she spent.

Sometimes, you'll find that you have to make a guess, but don't guess at random. Narrow down the answer choices to increase your odds of guessing the correct one. First, eliminate answer choices you know are wrong. Next, avoid answer choices that don't make logical sense. Finally, choose one of the remaining answer choices.

APPLY MATHEMATICS CONCEPTS TO LAW-ENFORCEMENT SCENARIOS

Some police exams may test basic mathematics to ensure you are comfortable working with numbers. This chapter reviews some of the building blocks of math. If you are comfortable with the concepts presented in this chapter, facing everyday problems that require a basic knowledge of addition, subtraction, multiplication, and division will be a smooth process.

Most of you have encountered these rules and practices in school, though it may have been a while since you've reviewed the exact terms and concepts. For some of you, this chapter will just be a basic brushup of skills you are comfortable with. Others may have to study this chapter carefully to relearn the basics. Like grammar and spelling, no matter what your actual exam tests, reviewing this chapter and completing the practice questions can only enhance your confidence going into Test Day.

Arithmetic definitions

Familiarize yourself with these key terms and concepts so you don't come across any surprises when you take your exam.

Integers: all whole numbers, including zero, and their negative counterparts

Examples: −900, −3, 0, 1, 54

Addends: any number added to another in an equation

Example:

$$1 + 2 = 3$$

In this equation, 1 and 2 are the addends.

Fractions: a number that is written in the form $\frac{A}{B}$, where A is the numerator and B is the denominator

Example:

$$-\frac{5}{6}, \ -\frac{3}{17}, \ \frac{1}{2}, \ \frac{899}{901}$$

An improper fraction has a numerator with a greater absolute value than that of the denominator.

Example:

$$-\frac{65}{64}, \ \frac{9}{8}, \ \frac{57}{10}$$

A mixed number consists of a whole number and a fraction.

Example:

$$-1\frac{1}{64},\ 1\frac{1}{8},\ 5\frac{7}{10}$$

An improper fraction can be converted to a mixed number and vice versa.

Example:

$$2\frac{3}{5} = \frac{13}{5}$$

Positive/negative: Numbers greater than 0 are positive numbers; numbers less than 0 are negative numbers. 0 is neither positive nor negative.

Examples:

Positive:

$$\frac{7}{8},\ 1,\ 5.6,\ 900$$

Negative:

$$-64,\ -40,\ -1.11,\ -\frac{3}{16}$$

Even/odd: An even number is an integer that is a multiple of 2; an odd number is an integer that is not a multiple of 2. Fractions and mixed numbers are neither even nor odd.

Examples:

Even numbers: $-8, -2, 0, 12, 188$

Odd numbers: $-17, -1, 3, 9, 457$

Factor: a positive integer that divides evenly into a given number

Example:

The complete list of factors of 12: 1, 2, 3, 4, 6, 12

Prime number: an integer greater than 1 that has no factors other than 1 and itself; 2 is the only even prime number

Examples: 2, 3, 5, 7, 11, 59, 83

Consecutive numbers: numbers that follow one after another, in order, without skipping any

In a series of consecutive numbers, the differences between any consecutive numbers are equal.

Examples:

Consecutive integers: 3, 4, 5, 6

Consecutive even integers: 2, 4, 6, 8, 10

Consecutive multiples of −9: −9, −18, −27, −36

Multiple: A multiple of a number is the product of that number and an integer.

Example:

Some multiples of 12: 0, 12, 24, 60

Order of operations

No matter what line of work you are in, you will always encounter formulas in everyday life. When traveling abroad, you may need to convert a temperature from degrees Celsius to degrees Fahrenheit to better understand it. You may need to calculate the perimeter or area of a room in order to accurately describe it. Formulas exist for all kinds of situations.

When simplifying a mathematical expression after you have plugged values into your formula, you do not simply work from left to right as you do when you read a book. Just as there are rules for driving an automobile, there are rules for order when performing arithmetic operations. There is a predetermined order of operations used to evaluate expressions. Perhaps you remember the mnemonic for remembering the order of operations: **PEMDAS**. Some of you may have used the memory tool "Please Excuse My Dear Aunt Sally" to recall the correct order.

The order of operations is:

P: Parentheses (grouping symbols)

E: Exponents

MD: Multiply and Divide from left to right

AS: Add and Subtract from left to right

The P in PEMDAS stands for parentheses, or grouping symbols. Grouping symbols include parentheses, brackets, the absolute value symbol, and a fraction bar. So, to simplify $\dfrac{18 + 10^2 - 4 \times 2}{20 - 27 \div 3}$, treat the fraction bar as a grouping symbol and first evaluate the top (the numerator) and then the bottom (the denominator). Then you will divide the numerator by the denominator for the final step.

To simplify the numerator, first simplify your exponent: $10^2 = 100$. Second, multiply 4 times 2 to get 8. The top is now $18 + 100 - 8$. Evaluate from left to right: $118 - 8 = 110$. To simplify the denominator, first divide 27 by 3 to get 9. Then subtract: $20 - 9 = 11$. Finally, divide 110 by 11 to get 10.

When plugging numbers into formulas, a working knowledge of the order of operations is essential. For example, to convert a temperature from degrees Fahrenheit to degrees Celsius, you use the formula $C = \frac{5}{9}(F - 32)$, where F is the degrees in Fahrenheit and C is the degrees in Celsius. If you have a temperature of 77 degrees Fahrenheit, and you want to know the equivalent degrees in Celsius, substitute in 77 for F in the formula: $C = \frac{5}{9}(77 - 32)$. First, subtract 32 from 77, because parentheses are evaluated first: $C = \frac{5}{9}(45)$. Now multiply $\frac{5}{9}$ by 45 (or $5 \times 45 \div 9$) to get 25 degrees Celsius.

Number properties

There are common properties of numbers that are frequently used to make adding and multiplying easier. You most likely use these properties without even realizing it when you do mental arithmetic or when you add a column of numbers. These properties give you the license to change the order of operations in certain situations. In addition to making addition and multiplication of number terms easier to calculate, these three properties are frequently used in solving algebraic equations.

The commutative property of addition

The commutative property of addition states that changing the order of the addends in a sum does not change the sum: $a + b = b + a$, where a and b are any real numbers.

For example:

$$12.3 + 6.9 + 7.7 = 12.3 + 7.7 + 6.9$$

The order of operations would dictate that 12.3 would first be added to 6.9. But the addition is easier if you first add 12.3 to 7.7 because the sum will equal a whole number. The commutative property gives you this freedom.

The commutative property of multiplication

Similar to the commutative property of addition, the commutative property of multiplication states that changing the order of the factors in a product does not change the product: $a \times b = b \times a$, where a and b are any real numbers.

For example:

$$2 \times 8 \times 5 \times 7 = 2 \times 7 \times 8 \times 5$$

If you scan a group of factors to find subproducts to equal 10, 100, or 1,000, it is easiest to multiply these factors first. The commutative property allows you to make these changes to the order of operations.

The associative property

The associative property also pertains to either the addends in a sum or the factors in a product. The associative property of addition or multiplication states that changing the grouping (parentheses or brackets) of addends in a sum or the grouping of factors in a product does not change the resulting sum or product:

$a + (b + c) = (a + b) + c$, where a, b, and c are any real numbers.

$a \times (b \times c) = (a \times b) \times c$, where a, b, and c are any real numbers.

For example, to add $9.8 + (10.2 + 6.1) + 4.9$, the order of operations would call for you to evaluate inside the parentheses first and then to add from left to right. But the sum of 9.8 and 10.2 is 20, and the sum of 6.1 and 4.9 is 11. The associative property allows you to change the grouping by adding: $(9.8 + 10.2) + (6.1 + 4.9)$, to get $20 + 11 = 31$. Notice in the example that the order of the addends did not change, just the grouping.

You can also use a combination of the properties. For example, to simplify the expression $2.1 + 8.07 + 7.9 + 24.93$, scan the addends and recognize that $(2.1 + 7.9)$ and $(8.07 + 24.93)$ will produce whole numbers. Use the commutative property to get $2.1 + 7.9 + 8.07 + 24.93$. Then use the associative property to get $(2.1 + 7.9) + (8.07 + 24.93)$. Now the addition is easy to finish: $10 + 33 = 43$.

The distributive property

The distributive property involves two operations: addition and multiplication or subtraction and multiplication.

The distributive property of multiplication over addition or subtraction states that multiplication distributes over addition and subtraction:

$a \times (b + c) = (a \times b) + (a \times c)$, where a, b, and c are real numbers.

$a \times (b - c) = (a \times b) - (a \times c)$, where a, b, and c are real numbers.

For example, if you want to multiply 16 by 8, you may not know the multiples of 16. However, you do know the multiples of 10 and 6. The distributive property allows you to rewrite 8×16 as $8 \times (10 + 6)$, or simply $8(10 + 6)$. Because multiplication distributes over addition, this problem becomes $(8 \times 10) + (8 \times 6)$, which can be evaluated as $80 + 48 = 128$. Likewise, 8×16 could be written as $8 \times (20 - 4)$ or:

$$(8 \times 20) - (8 \times 4) = 160 - 32 = 128$$

You can also use the distributive property in reverse. For example, if you were instructed to simplify $(12 \times 6.4) + (12 \times 3.6)$, order of operations would have you evaluate parentheses first, which involves decimal multiplication. If you notice that both terms are multiplied by 12, use the distributive property to factor out the 12:

$$(12 \times 6.4) + (12 \times 3.6) = 12 \times (6.4 + 3.6) = 12 \times 10 = 120$$

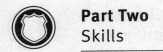

CALCULATE AREA AND PERIMETER

When writing a report, investigating a crime scene, or just making observations, it will be important for you to be able to calculate (even if you're just estimating) areas and perimeters of rooms, open areas such as parks, and other types of spaces. Here's a quick review of how to calculate the area and perimeter of spaces.

Area

Mathematically speaking, the area of a space is the two-dimensional surface occupied by that space. You will likely encounter areas when reporting square footages of a room or building. Area is a fairly easy formula to remember, particularly since most rooms, buildings, parking lots, etc., are approximate squares or rectangles. Triangles and circles get a bit trickier. But how often do you encounter a triangular room or a circular parking lot? For these reasons, let's focus solely on squares and rectangles.

In the example below, the room's dimensions are 15 feet by 22 feet. Assuming that the parallel walls are the same size, the area of this room is calculated by multiplying the length (l) times the width (w) or 15 feet $\times$ 22 feet = 330 feet^2.

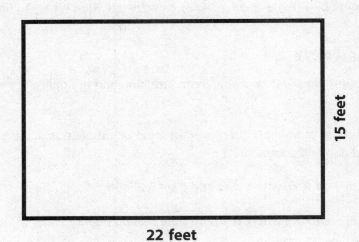

22 feet

Calculating the area of a square space is even simpler. Since a square has four equal sides, you simply square the length of one side, often written as s^2. So, for the square playground below, the calculation for its area would be $(40 \text{ feet})^2 = 1{,}600 \text{ feet}^2$.

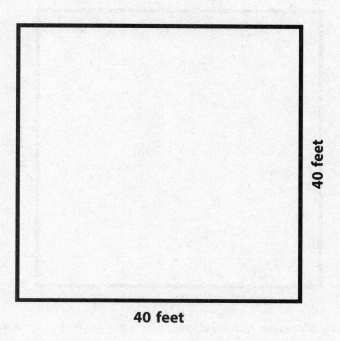

40 feet

Perimeter

Perimeter is a term you've likely heard on TV cop shows. "Secure the perimeter of the park with 20 officers." You know what a perimeter is—the outer edge of a space—but do you remember how to calculate it? Let's use the room and the playground examples from above.

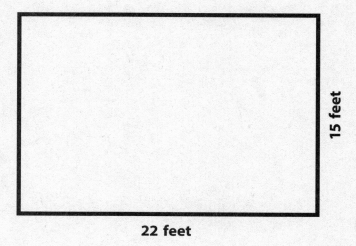

22 feet

A perimeter of a shape is the sum of all its sides. So, in this case, the perimeter of this room = 22 feet + 15 feet + 22 feet + 15 feet, simplified as 2 × (22 feet + 15 feet) = 74 feet.

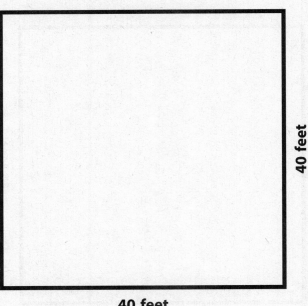

40 feet

40 feet

Likewise, the perimeter of the playground above is 40 feet + 40 feet + 40 feet + 40 feet, simplified as 4 × 40 feet = 160 feet.

TEST WHAT YOU LEARNED

Directions: Choose the ONE best answer for each question.

1. A business owner reports that his cash register value was reduced to 25% of its previous value after a robbery. If the value before the robbery was $2,200, what is the value now?

   (A) $500

   (B) $550

   (C) $1,000

   (D) $2,750

2. A large number of suspects are arrested at a midnight dance party. Each police van can transport 10 suspects, and a total of 3 vans were required. If one of the vans only transported 4 suspects, then how many total suspects were arrested at the dance party?

   (A) 12

   (B) 24

   (C) 26

   (D) 30

3. Starting from the second floor, a suspect on foot takes an elevator down 1 floor, up 14 floors, down 6 floors, and then down another 2 floors. On what floor does this suspect end up?

   (A) 2nd

   (B) 5th

   (C) 7th

   (D) 21st

4. Your team has been asked to secure the perimeter of the outside of a building. The base of the building is 100 feet by 78 feet. What is the total perimeter of the building?

   (A) 178 feet²

   (B) 356 feet

   (C) 3,900 feet

   (D) 7,800 feet²

ANSWERS AND EXPLANATIONS

1. B

Learning Objective: Approach math test questions strategically

Before you begin to calculate, see which clearly wrong answer choices you can eliminate. If the amount of money in the cash register was reduced, the total money in there now cannot exceed the original amount—you can eliminate (D). You are given that the reduced amount is 25% of the original. Choice (C) looks closer to 50% than 25%, so you can eliminate it as well. Now that only two choices remain, you can calculate. Half of $2,200 is $1,100 (50%), and then half of $1,100 is $550 (25%).

2. B

Learning Objective: Apply mathematics concepts to law-enforcement scenarios

Two of the vans were full, so that is $2 \times 10 = 20$ people transported. Then the third van had 4 people, for a total of $20 + 4 = 24$ people transported.

3. C

Learning Objective: Apply mathematics concepts to law-enforcement scenarios

Write an expression for the elevator trip that starts at the second floor: $2 - 1 + 14 - 6 - 2$. Then work the equation out:

$$2 - 1 = 1$$
$$1 + 14 = 15$$
$$15 - 6 = 9$$
$$9 - 2 = 7$$

The person ended up on the seventh floor.

4. B

Learning Objective: Calculate area and perimeter

The perimeter of the building is the sum of all its sides, so 100 feet + 100 feet + 78 feet + 78 feet = 356 feet. Choices (C) and (D) are in the wrong units for a perimeter, while (A) is obviously too small.

SELF-REFLECTION

Once you have the building blocks of mathematics that we present in this chapter down, you should be able to tackle any question that comes your way on your police exam.

Test What You Know score: _____ /4 correct

Test What You Learned score: _____ /4 correct

After working through the practice problems in this chapter, which of the Learning Objectives have you mastered? Place a check mark next to those objectives to keep track of your progress.

- ☐ Approach math test questions strategically
- ☐ Apply mathematics concepts to law-enforcement scenarios
- ☐ Calculate area and perimeter

CHAPTER 10

Spatial Orientation, Memorization, and Visualization

One of the requirements for being a police officer is vision correctable to 20/20. Well, that perfect vision won't do you any good if you can't use it intelligently. That's where questions about spatial orientation, visualization, and observation come in.

As a police officer, you need to be able to observe a scene and sort through all the thousands of details to come up with the relevant information. You also must do it quickly—almost unconsciously. Of course, you will develop this skill with experience, but the program you are applying to wants to know whether you've got the basics in place already. These question types will test your attention to detail, your memory, and your ability to see beyond what is right in front of you to predict what might happen.

LEARNING OBJECTIVES

In this chapter, you will review how to:

- ☐ Read maps to find the quickest route
- ☐ Memorize elements of street scenes
- ☐ Recognize and identify facial features
- ☐ Visualize patterns
- ☐ Identify identical patterns and objects

TEST WHAT YOU KNOW

Directions: Choose the ONE best answer for each question.

Please use the following map to answer questions 1–3.

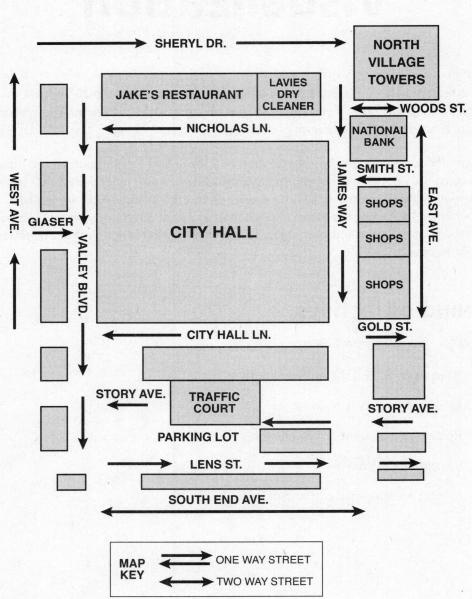

1. Officer Jones is parked on the southeast corner of Lens Street between James Way and East Avenue filling out his memo book. He receives a radio transmission of a disorderly person at the corner of Valley Boulevard and City Hall Lane. Which of the following is the shortest route to the location, following all traffic regulations?

    (A) East on Lens Street, north on East Avenue, then west on Gold Street, west on City Hall Lane to Valley Boulevard

    (B) East on Lens Street, then north on East Avenue, west on Smith Street, north on James Way, west on Nicholas Lane, and south on Valley Boulevard to City Hall Lane

    (C) East on Lens Street, north on East Avenue, west on Woods Street, south on James Way, west on Nicholas Lane, south on Valley Boulevard to City Hall Lane

    (D) East on Lens Street, south on East Avenue, west on South End Avenue, north on West Avenue, east on Giaser Street, and south on Valley Boulevard to City Hall Lane

2. While on routine patrol, Officer Girardi is at the intersection of Giaser Street and Valley Boulevard when he gets dispatched to a vehicle accident at the intersection of Woods Street and James Way. Which of the following is the shortest route to the location, following all traffic regulations?

    (A) South on Valley Boulevard, west on City Hall Lane, north on West Avenue, east on Sheryl Drive, then south onto James Way to Woods Street

    (B) South on Valley Boulevard, east on City Hall Lane onto Gold Street, north on East Avenue, then east on Woods Street to James Way

    (C) South on Valley Boulevard, east on South End Avenue, north on East Avenue, then west onto Woods Street and James Way

    (D) North on Valley Boulevard, east on Sheryl Drive, and south on James Way to Woods Street

3. Officer Quint is on Gold Street when he is dispatched for a medical call at the corner of Sheryl Drive and James Way. Which of the following is the shortest route to the location, following all traffic regulations?

    (A) East on Gold Street, south on East Avenue, west on South End Avenue, north on West Avenue, and east on Sheryl Drive to James Way

    (B) East on Gold Street, north to East Avenue, west on Woods Street, south on James Way, west on Nicholas Lane, north on West Avenue, east on Sheryl Drive to James Way

    (C) West on Gold Street, east on City Hall Lane, north on West Avenue, and east on Sheryl drive to Woods Avenue

    (D) East on Gold Street, north on East Avenue, west on Smith Street, south on James Way, west on City Hall Lane, on West Avenue, and east on Sheryl Drive to James Way

Questions 4–6

Study the photograph below very carefully for five minutes. You will be asked three detailed questions about this image. Once you have finished looking at this photograph, cover it over. You will not be able to look back at it again.

4. What are the last four numbers of the telephone number of the billboard on the wall?

   (A) 0306

   (B) 0303

   (C) 0203

   (D) 0207

5. What is the name of the gas station?

   (A) Shell

   (B) Mobil

   (C) Exxon

   (D) Gulf

6. What is the name of the street crossing New Main Street?

    (A) Park Hill Street

    (B) Park Hill Avenue

    (C) Main Avenue

    (D) Center Street

Use the below image for question 7.

7. Which face below is an exact representation of the face above?

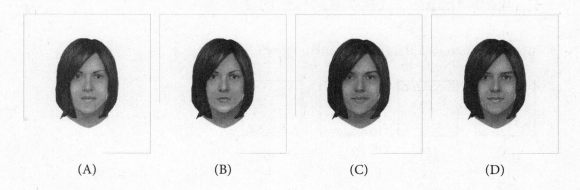

(A) (B) (C) (D)

Use the below figure for question 8.

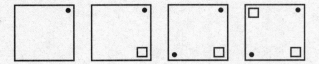

8. Choose the next logical step to the pattern above.

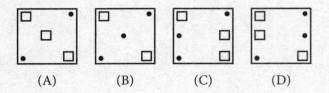

(A)   (B)   (C)   (D)

Use the below figure for question 9.

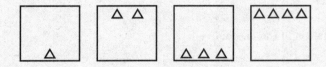

9. Choose the next logical step to the pattern above.

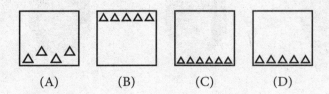

(A)   (B)   (C)   (D)

Use the following information to answer the question below.

The suspect first ran southbound on 104th Terrace but heard sirens on the road coming toward him. He turned around, ran in the opposite direction for two blocks, then quickly turned right and ran straight, across an open field.

10. According to this information, the suspect was last seen heading:

(A) north

(B) south

(C) east

(D) west

Use the below text for question 11.

wwvw_=-pqpq;S5$nmvnm

11. Select the choice below that is an exact match for the string of characters above.

(A) wwvw_=-pqpq;S5$mnvnm

(B) wwvw_=-pqpq;S5$nmvnm

(C) wwvw_=_pqpq;S5$nmvnm

(D) wwvw_=-pqpq;S$5nmvnm

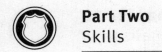

ANSWERS AND EXPLANATIONS

1. D

Learning Objective: Read maps to find the quickest route

Choice (D) is the quickest route. Choice (A) is the wrong way on Gold Street. Choice (B) is the wrong way on James Street. Choice (C) is too long.

2. A

Learning Objective: Read maps to find the quickest route

Choice (A) is the quickest route. Choice (B) is the wrong way on City Hall Lane. Choice (C) is too long. Choice (D) is the wrong way on Valley Boulevard.

3. B

Learning Objective: Read maps to find the quickest route

Choice (B) is the quickest route. Choice (A) is too long. Choice (C) is the wrong way on Gold Street. Choice (D) is too long.

4. B

Learning Objective: Memorize elements of street scenes

Choice (B) is correct. The last four digits of the advertised phone number are 0303. When looking at a street scene, keep in mind that your test can ask about any element in the scene, down to the smallest detail.

5. D

Learning Objective: Memorize elements of street scenes

Choice (D) is correct. A Gulf gas station sign is visible on the right side of the photo. It's not enough to know that the scene contains a gas station; you should always notice and remember specific details like names.

6. B

Learning Objective: Memorize elements of street scenes

Choice (B) is correct. Park Hill Avenue intersects New Main Street. If you see text in a street scene, assume there will be a question asking about it. Be careful to distinguish streets from avenues, highways from parkways, etc.

7. B

Learning Objective: Recognize and identify facial features

Choice (B) is correct because it is the only face that exactly matches the original face. In this case, the woman's mouth is irregular and/or fuller in Choices (A), (C), and (D).

8. B

Learning Objective: Visualize patterns

The first box starts off with a dot. The pattern then adds a square, then a dot, then another square. So the correct answer, Choice (B), will add another dot.

9. D

Learning Objective: Visualize patterns

Here, the pattern of triangles increases by one every box, and the placement of the triangles switches from down, to up, to down, to up. The correct answer, Choice (D), has five triangles at the bottom of the box.

10. C

Learning Objective: Visualize patterns

The correct answer is Choice (C). The suspect starts out running south, but then turns around and runs north. Then the suspect makes a right turn, which means he is running eastbound.

11. B

Learning Objective: Identify identical patterns and objects

Choice (B) is correct because it is the only answer choice that exactly matches the original string of characters. Choice (A) transposes the first "n" and "m." Choice (C) has an underscore where the hyphen should be. Choice (D) transposes the "$" and "5."

READ MAPS TO FIND THE QUICKEST ROUTE

Reading maps and knowing how to get from one place to another is crucial in law enforcement. Spatial orientation, particularly through map reading, most likely will show up in some form on your police exam. The good news is that doing well on these questions does not involve memorization. Your key goal is simply knowing how to get from one location to another in the shortest route possible. These exam questions will test you on how well you understand map locations and directions.

Here are some key tips for you to follow to find success on spatial orientation questions.

Review all map elements before you answer any questions

First and foremost, always read the directions and map elements carefully—make sure you have a good sense of what you're looking at and the rules you need to know and follow. All maps represent direction, streets, and location elements differently, so you want to make sure you understand what is being represented symbolically.

The compass

When looking at any map there will always be a compass or part of one. Check the compass and get familiar with the directions it lays out for the map you are observing. If there is only a partial compass, as it may just point north, then fill in the rest of the compass with south, east, and west. (If you are able to write in a test booklet, sketch directly within; if not, sketch out a full compass on your scratch paper.) Do *not* try to use your memory on this, even if you think you have a fantastic sense of direction. During the test, it is better to have something to look at and use as a point of reference.

Another important feature you need to be aware of is corners. Remember, there are four corners to every location. If the question is asking you to go to the northeast corner of a particular intersection, first look at your compass above the map and figure out which corner you need to focus on.

Locations and Streets

After making sure you understand the compass, you want to carefully review the map. Take a moment to study it. Take note of key locations: banks, hospitals, a police station, or a firehouse. Know where they are in relation to each other. Sometimes, a map may note that the building entrance is on a specific side. Take note of where these entrances are, if they are shown.

After that, you need to look at the streets and take very close notice of any one-way or two-way streets. There may be a ledger at the top or bottom of the given map that will show all map symbols and what they represent. For street direction, representation may be as simple as a line with an arrow pointing in a single direction for a one-way street and a line with arrows on both sides for a two-way street. Take note of dead-end streets and streets that are interrupted by a building or structure but resume on the other side.

Approach each question thoughtfully

There are really no secret tricks to this exercise—you just have to read carefully and avoid careless mistakes. Once you have the map elements down, you can make your way to the questions, which will ask you to find the most efficient route from Point A to Point B.

Don't rush, and don't make assumptions—when asked for the quickest route, take the time to sketch out the routes you are considering on your exam if you are permitted to write on it. Use a pencil, and erase if you need to. Too many marks and cross-outs will clutter your map and your brain, so aim to keep your sketching as clean and neat as possible. If you cannot write on the test booklet, use scrap paper, and sketch it out that way.

Take each answer choice one by one, and either keep for later review or eliminate. For example, if one of the choices suggests going down a one-way street the wrong way, cross that off and move on. Several choices will most likely be correct with regard to getting to the destination given to you. But remember, you are looking for the *shortest route possible* to the location. If a choice seems correct, don't rush to select it and move on—it may get you there, but not by the shortest route.

Do not make snap assumptions without really studying the given map. One common mistake is assuming that the highway is always the fastest way to get to a location. For example, if one of the choices has a highway or a major boulevard and does not violate any traffic regulations, don't automatically choose it. These questions do not typically factor different speed limits into the premise. Even if you might be able to travel faster on a main road in the real world, these questions ask specifically about the *shortest* route. Think: Even if this is a highway or major road, is it a little out of the way as compared to another choice? It does not matter how fast you may be able to drive on a larger road—you are looking for the shortest route.

Abide by all traffic laws

For the most part, you must follow all traffic regulations. You are not at the point in your police career yet where you might have to go down the wrong way on a one-way street, or drive through small alleyways, or even cut across sidewalks for high priority and emergency calls. During the test, obey all laws unless you are strictly directed to do otherwise.

Practice

Let's look at another map so you can practice and become more comfortable when learning how to read and interpret one on the fly. Take a few minutes to assess the following map. Then, we'll walk through some practice questions together.

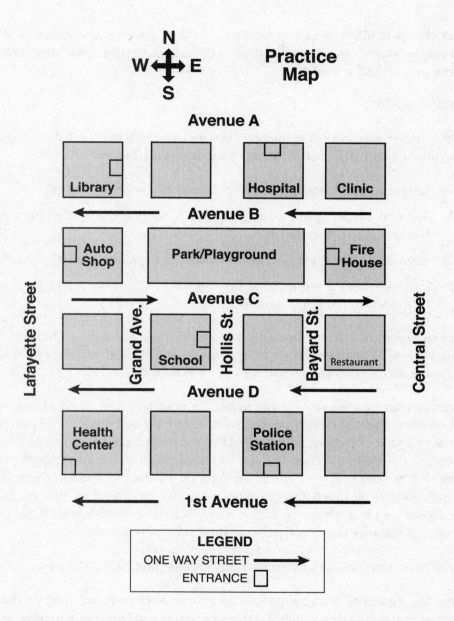

You are standing in front of the police station when a man on foot stops and asks you to help him find the library. You should tell him to

(A) walk across the street to the library.

(B) walk south to Avenue C, make a right and walk west on Avenue C, and then make a right on Grand Avenue and walk up to the library.

(C) walk north to Avenue B, then west on Avenue B to the end of the park, and then walk north for half a block.

(D) walk north to Avenue B, then west on Avenue B to Lafayette Street, and then walk north for half a block.

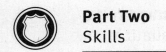
The correct choice is (C). It takes you right to Avenue B, where you would walk westbound. Remember you are walking, not driving. At the end of the park, turn right, and then walk one block up to the entrance on Grand Avenue.

Let's try another one.

> After responding to a call at the firehouse, you are ready to drive back to the police station for the end of your shift. What is the quickest legal route?
>
> (A)   South on Bayard Street, west on 1st Avenue to the police station
>
> (B)   North on Bayard Street, west on Avenue A, south on Lafayette Street, east on 1st Avenue to the police station
>
> (C)   North on Bayard Street, east on 1st Avenue to the police station
>
> (D)   South on Bayard Street, west on Avenue C, south on Grand Avenue, east on 1st Avenue to the police station

The correct answer is (A). It is the shortest legal route to the police station. Choice (B) is not only long but goes the wrong the way on 1st Avenue. Choice (C) will lead you away from 1st Avenue, not toward it. Choice (D) takes you the wrong way on Avenue C.

With this specific map, here are some things to keep in mind. If the question involves walking, like our first one, it does not matter which way you walk. You are allowed to walk both ways on a street. However, make sure the map shows no indication that the street is closed off owing to construction. Also, be careful if the street is a dead end and you need to get to the other side. If the question calls for you to walk, also read the choices carefully. Do not let the wording throw you off. For instance, "walk north *to* Avenue B, then west on Avenue B." You may think that you cannot walk on Avenue B twice, but it is not saying that. It is saying walk north *to* Avenue B. Also, be careful and take notice of entrance points and on what streets they are located.

Now that you have these tips, let's try another practice question for the same map.

> You are dispatched from the police station to an altercation occurring on the northeast corner of the public park. Which is the most direct and legal route to drive there?
>
> (A)   East to Central Street, north on Central Street to Avenue B, west on Avenue B to Grand Avenue
>
> (B)   West to Grand Avenue, north on Grand Avenue to Avenue B
>
> (C)   East to Bayard Street, north on Bayard Street to Avenue B, west to Grand Avenue
>
> (D)   West to Hollis Street, north on Hollis Street to Avenue C, east on Avenue C to Bayard Street

The correct answer is (B). Both Choices (A) and (C) take you the wrong way on 1st Avenue. Choice (D) gets you to the southeast corner of the park instead of the northeast corner.

This question has you leaving the entrance point of the police station. The correct choice assumes you are going west on 1st Avenue, which is why it is not stated in any of the answers. Be careful, because Choices (A) and (C) do not say to go east *on* 1st Avenue, they say to go east *to* another street.

When you are driving around your own neighborhood, think and visualize routes, directions, and how would you get from one location to another the quickest way. Instead of just using GPS, start sharpening your mind and think about directions.

MEMORIZE ELEMENTS OF STREET SCENES

Many police exams will start with an image you will have time to study. Then a series of questions will test your memory and observation skills. The majority of these questions will require you to study an illustration or photo of a street scene, like the one you just practiced in the Test What You Know section.

You will be given a certain length of time to look at the scene and then be asked to answer several questions about details shown. If you are lucky, you already have a good memory, but you can always sharpen it. Even if your memory isn't so great, you can learn better memory skills.

Do not just stare at the picture. Remember, they will have a page full of details to look at, and you need to know them. Methodically start looking at the picture. Make sure you cover it from top to bottom. Do not think that because something is on top of the page they will not ask about it. Everything is in play.

Think of the image you are given as a movie scene, and focus on the three basics you would find in any movie: setting, characters, and action.

Setting:

- Take note of any numbers, such as street addresses and license plate numbers.

- Look for other useful identifiers—business signs, names on buildings, statues, or other land-marks. Carefully read all that you see, and remember all details you can.

- Does the area seem prosperous or struggling? Crowded or deserted? Can you tell whether it's a weekday or weekend, daytime or evening or night?

- Pay attention to the streets and the direction the cars or buses are pointed in.

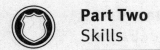

Characters:

- How many people are there?

- Ages? Genders?

- What is each person wearing?

- Use two words to describe the physical appearance of each person. For instance, "tall, hairy man" or "plump, elderly woman."

- If one of the characters has an especially distinctive physical characteristic, note it: "tall, hairy man with eye patch."

- What about their facial expressions?

- What, if anything, is each character carrying?

Action:

- What is each person doing?

- Group them, using your two-word descriptions: "Tall, hairy man escorting plump, elderly woman across the intersection."

- What can you infer about the relationships among the members of the group? Are they boss/coworkers, friends, spouses, strangers?

- Are any of the groups interacting? For instance, "Tall, hairy man escorting plump, elderly woman across intersection. Young, slender man with blond ponytail is running behind them, reaching toward her shopping bag."

You should also look for numbers of all kinds: clocks (and, of course, note the time), any visible license plates, and addresses. Make sure you also take notice of specific numbers of objects: How many cars are parked on the street? How many people are on the corner?

The best way to prepare for this kind of test is to practice noticing *everything* around you in the time leading up to your exam. For the next few days, make a point of going through this exercise with as many things as you can—news photographs, advertisements, even the crowd in a movie theater or sports arena. Do this often enough, and it will become second nature.

Let's walk through some examples together.

For this picture, you might be asked any of the following questions:

- What time was it when this photograph was taken?

- What is a description of the car waiting at the traffic light?

- How many floors is the parking garage?

- What type of establishment is advertised on the corner of the parking garage?

- What traffic law is in place for the rightmost lane of the road?

Yes, there is a lot to remember, but five minutes is a long time. Scan the picture, try to take everything in that you can, and then start zooming in on particular items. Do not get caught up in staring at just one item. A good tip to remember is to try to memorize information in some sort of order—top to bottom or left to right.

Here is another picture with some great signage.

For this picture you might see questions like:

- What is the price of regular gas?

- According to the sign, what type of fuel is being sold at the gas station?

- What is the speed limit?

- What does the sign on the lawn say?

If it is an indoor scene, there will be a good probability that it will be a sketch of a crime scene. All the same rules apply as in street scenes: Look at calendars, clocks, and anything out of place. Look for weapons, and start associating items with each other and their locations.

Note: This type of question tends to come at the beginning of most police exams because everyone is starting off at the same time and the proctor has to time the exercise for everyone. At this point, your anxiety and nerves are all built up. Go in expecting this question type to come first—don't let it catch you off guard. Take a deep breath. Relax and concentrate all your energy into focusing on the picture.

No matter what type of memorization exercise you are given, once the proctor collects the memorization image or booklet, start writing down notes on what you can remember (if that is permitted).

RECOGNIZE AND IDENTIFY FACIAL FEATURES

Another type of exam question you might see will test your ability to recognize faces, no matter how they are altered. These questions may come in the form of "wanted" posters or simply pictures of faces with different options for comparison. You will then have to match the original face from the choices provided. This can be challenging because the options might alter the appearance of the original face, hairstyle, and facial hair.

If you do come across this category, you should do the following:

- Focus on facial characteristics that can't easily be changed: nose breadth and length, the shape of the chin, the size of the eyes, how far apart the eyes are set, and the way the ears are set on the head.

- Don't be distracted by differences (or similarities) in qualities that are easier to manipulate: hair length, color, and texture; facial hair; size and shape of eyebrows; and general shape of the face, which can be affected by weight gain or loss. Even eye color can be disguised with contacts. Just realize that anything that *can* be changed might be changed. Elements like these are diversions to throw you off.

- Don't rush your decision. Take your time and evaluate all your choices. Stick to the underlying facial structure, and the right choice will pop out at you.

Keep this main point in mind: your one goal is to match the facial structure with the original. Start with the eyes, nose, and mouth. Here, process of elimination is extremely important. Some of the changes may be subtle, so pay attention to detail. Once any of those features do not match exactly, cross it off—you can even cover it up if you think having many pictures in front of you will cause you to get distracted.

Let's take a look at John's face:

Now let's try to find the face that exactly matches the image of John's face on the previous page. Is this it?

It's very similar, as we would expect. However, if you look at the lips, you can see that they are different. The upper lip in the second image is less pronounced and does not have as much of a downturn at the edges.

What about this face—is this our John?

The lips now match, but something else seems different. The nose is thinner and the nostrils are more flared. This isn't John.

What about this guy?

The nose and face are a match for John. But those eyes are definitely not the same as in the original picture.

Let's try one more:

There's John! Finally, we have a perfect match of the original image.

Let's take a look at Troy:

Certain questions might tell you that the original suspect has since grown facial hair (or maybe changed hairstyles). You will then be given an array of choices that look like the original picture, but with different hair. Your job will be to pick the face that is the same as the original.

Is this Troy?

No, look at the lips in each picture. They do not match.

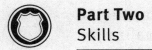

Is *this* Troy?

No, this choice is wrong because the eyebrows, lips, and nose are slightly different.

This must be Troy:

Yes, this image is correct.

As you can see, once you know what to look for, you can eliminate obviously wrong answers and find your way to the right one.

Study tips for memorization and visualization questions

So, how do you prepare for these parts of the test? As is the key with most police officer skills questions, you simply must practice. Every day, develop your ability to describe people, places, and things in detail.

Throughout your day, if you have a few minutes, play a game with yourself. Look at someone nearby, turn away, and describe him or her. Sneak a peek and see if you are correct. Keep doing this to develop your talent for noticing all the features of a person's face.

Play games with your family and friends. At the dinner table, sit down and look at everyone quickly. Then, close your eyes and describe what they are wearing. This sounds simple, but it is not. If you are a passenger in a car, turn away and describe the car next to you or the one that just passed you. Look at the license plate number and repeat it five minutes later without writing it down. Anything you can think of to train your mind in memorization will prepare you for this part of the test.

VISUALIZE PATTERNS

Visualization questions on your police exam will test your ability to recognize and predict patterns. You will be asked to mentally rearrange images so they match up with a given pattern structure.

Once again, the key to approaching this section is to slow down and take each part of the question step by step, especially if pattern recognition is not your strong point. Do not panic, and be methodical. Paying close attention to details is extremely important—if something is given to you, you can be sure it's an important detail to notice.

As you saw in the Test What You Know section, one possible question type will test you on how patterns and objects look when they are moved and rearranged. These questions require you to form mental images of how a picture will look as it changes.

Let's look at a sample question. Which of the following boxes is the next element in the given pattern?

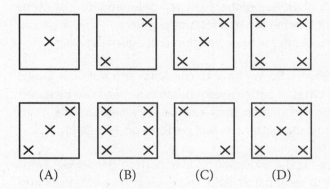

This example is a more basic question, but it gives you a good idea of how you will have to think to answer this question type successfully. In each box, you see an X. As the pattern progresses, an X is added to every box. So, the next element to this pattern is Choice (D), the box with five Xs.

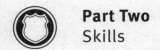

Let's look at another visualization question.

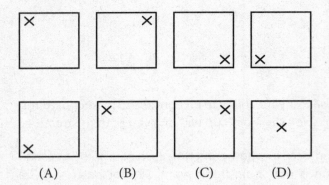

(A)   (B)   (C)   (D)

Right away, we see that there is only one X in each of the boxes, so we are not really looking for any type of number building or sequential ordering. But we do see the X moving its position in each box. How it is moving? It looks like it's traveling around the corners. In what direction is it traveling? Here, we see that the X is moving in clockwise fashion. So, the best answer is Choice (B).

Since there are no hard and fast rules to these question types, it's hard to know how to prepare—unlike math questions, you can't really memorize rules. You just need to train your brain on how to visualize objects and how they look when they change. Now, like anything else, this section may come more easily to some than others. That's okay! Remember, you will only see a few of these questions on the test. The exam writers are not looking for architects or engineers—they are looking for future police officers. They are simply looking for basic imaging and reasoning skills.

Visualization questions are, in essence, brainteasers. So, we have to condition and train our brains to these types of questions. Oftentimes these types of pattern-recognition questions can be found in IQ tests. Searching the Internet for pattern-recognition tests can be very helpful. The more practice you have with these kinds of questions, the better you will perform on Test Day.

Use everything to your advantage to practice for these questions. Play pattern games like word search or Sudoku, which may be found in your local paper. Also, there are plenty of games and apps that focus on pattern building and sequential ordering. Dedicate a few hours a week to training your mind for this section of the test. That way, when someone asks you why you are playing games on your phone, you can honestly say that you are studying!

IDENTIFY IDENTICAL PATTERNS AND OBJECTS

Flexibility of closure

Flexibility of closure is the ability to discern identifiable objects or patterns when they are mixed in with noise or other distracting material. Look at the design below:

Can you identify the three shapes that are repeated throughout the design? With test items such as this, you will have to choose the one correct shape out of a set of four possible shapes. This means that three of the shapes will not appear in the design at all; if you are unsure about which shape appears in the design, you can look for answer choices that are unusual or distinctive, and might be easy to rule out. This can help you narrow down your choices.

In flexibility of closure items, the correct answer choice might not appear *exactly* as it appears in the design, i.e., it might be smaller or even rotated. However, it will always remain proportional to the design. For example, which of the following two shapes appears in the design above?

Although the moon on the left is very similar to a shape found in the design, it has been squashed and has a much thicker line compared to the proportions in the original. The moon on the right is correct because it matches the shape found in the design, proportions and all.

Which of these two shapes is found in the design?

Again, both choices closely resemble shapes in the design. However, the arrow on the right has a much longer head, a slightly different shape, and is generally thicker than the arrow found in the design. The arrow on the left is correct because it matches the arrow in the design, even though none of the arrows in the design point straight up.

One more: which of these two shapes is found in the design?

As usual, the shapes are quite similar. In this case, it helps to count the number of points on the star in the design. The original shape is an eight-pointed star, which matches on the right. The star on the left has 10 points.

Flexibility of closure items might look intimidating at first, but with a little practice, you can learn to "see through the noise" and recognize the most important elements. If you are unsure of the correct answer, try mentally placing each of the shape choices into the design and see if you can find a match. Just remember to always check the proportions of the shapes to make sure they are consistent.

Selective attention

Another question type that relies upon your ability to spot patterns is called *selective attention*. Selective attention questions may ask you to match a string of letters, numbers, and symbols with an exact match from a set of four possible answers. Sounds easy, right? Not so fast. Here's an example of what you might encounter in a typical selective attention question:

yv^wwv^<O_dhlbbdpq"!ilo0'

Which of these choices is an exact match for the string above?

(A) yv^wvw^<O_dhlbbdpq"!ilo0'

(B) yv^wwv^<O_dhlbbdpq'!ilo0'

(C) yv^wwv^<O_dhlbbdpq"!ilo0'

(D) yv^wwv^<O_dhlbbdpq"i!lo0'

All of the answers are so similar that they require serious scrutiny to find the differences. Be careful with letters and symbols that are similar but not the same, such as the capital letter O and the number zero. Also, watch for letters whose order can be easily confused when placed near each other, such as *n* and *m*, *v* and *w*, or *p* and *q*. Since spotting differences near the beginning and end of the string is easier, expect to have to focus harder on the middle of each string, where incorrect characters are more likely to hide.

Were you able to spot which answer choice matches the original string? In Choice (A), a *v* and a *w* have switched places near the beginning of the string. In Choice (B), a double-quote mark has been replaced with a single-quote mark. In Choice (D), an exclamation point and a letter *i* have been transposed. Choice (C) is the correct answer.

TEST WHAT YOU LEARNED

Directions: Choose the ONE best answer for each question.

Please use the following map to answer questions 1–3. NOTE: Arrows indicate the direction of traffic.

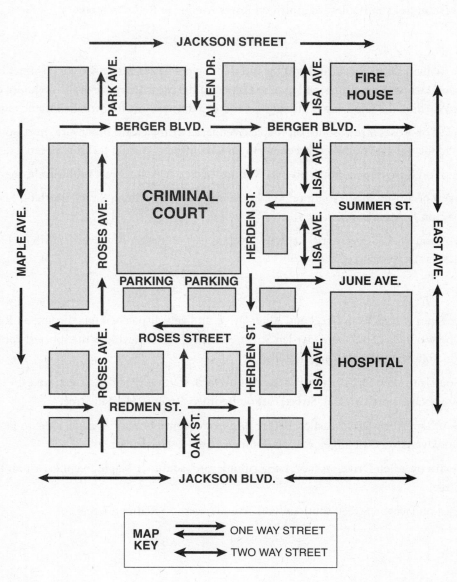

1. Officer Sanchez is finishing up a report at Berger Boulevard and Allen Drive when he receives a call for a lost child at Redmen Street and Roses Avenue. Which of the following is the shortest route for Officer Sanchez to reach the location, following all traffic regulations?

   (A) East on Berger Boulevard, south on East Avenue, west on Jackson Boulevard, north on Roses Avenue to Redmen Street

   (B) East on Berger Boulevard, south on Lisa Avenue, west on Jackson Boulevard, north on Roses Avenue to Redmen Street

   (C) East on Berger Boulevard, south on Herden Street, west on Jackson Boulevard, north on Roses Avenue to Redmen Street

   (D) East on Berger Boulevard, south on Lisa Avenue, east on June Avenue, south on East Avenue, west on Jackson Boulevard, north on Roses Avenue to Redmen Street

2. Officer Williams is on patrol and is at the intersection of Herden Street and Roses Street facing westbound when she is dispatched to take a report at the north entrance of the firehouse on Jackson Street. Which of the following is the shortest route to the location, following all traffic regulations?

   (A) West on Roses Street, south on Maple Avenue, east on Jackson Boulevard, north on East Avenue, west on Summer Street, north on Lisa Avenue, east on Jackson Street

   (B) East on Roses Street, north on Lisa Avenue, east on Jackson Street to the firehouse

   (C) West on Roses Street, south on Maple Avenue, east on Redmen Street, north on Lisa Avenue, east on Jackson Street

   (D) West on Roses Street, north on Roses Avenue, east on Berger Boulevard, north on Lisa Avenue, east on Jackson Street

3. Officer Jones is at Jackson Street and Allen Drive, and gets dispatched to a dispute on Redmen Street between Oak Street and Herden Street. Which of the following is the shortest route to the location, following all traffic regulations?

   (A) South on Allen Drive, east on Berger Boulevard, south on Herden Street, west on Jackson Boulevard, north on Oak Street, east on Redmen Street to Herden Street

   (B) South on Allen Drive, east on Berger Boulevard, south on Lisa Avenue, west on Jackson Boulevard, on Oak Street, east on Redmen Street to Herden Street

   (C) South on Allen Drive, west on Berger Boulevard, south on Maple Avenue, east on Redmen Street

   (D) East on Jackson Street, south on East Avenue, west on Redmen Street

Questions 4–6

Study the photograph very carefully for five minutes. You will be asked three detailed questions about this image. Once you have finished looking at this photograph, you will not be able to look back at it again.

4. Which way is the one-way sign pointing on Main Street?

    (A) Straight

    (B) Left

    (C) Right

    (D) The sign is not on Main Street.

5. What is the word in the middle of "Daisy's _____ Shop"?

    (A) Designer

    (B) Optical

    (C) Gift

    (D) Hallmark

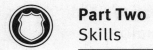
6. Which store has the most people in front of it?

   (A) A1 Gift Shop

   (B) Daisy's

   (C) The beauty supply shop

   (D) Designer Optical

The woman shown here has since changed her hairstyle.

7. Which face below represents the same woman with a different hairstyle?

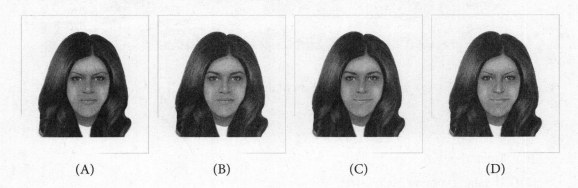

| (A) | (B) | (C) | (D) |

Use the figure below to answer question 8.

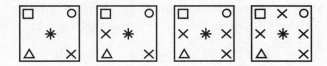

8. Choose the next logical step in the pattern above.

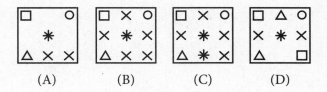

      (A)   (B)   (C)   (D)

Use the figure below to answer question 9.

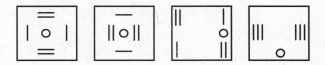

9. Choose the next logical step in the pattern above.

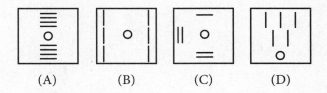

      (A)   (B)   (C)   (D)

Use the text below to answer question 10.

ppdqpd[0ocO@]\bddpqdb

10. Select the choice below that is an exact match for the string of characters above.

    (A) ppdqpd[Ooc0@]\bddpqdb

    (B) ppdpqd[0ocO@]\bddpqdb

    (C) ppdqpd[0ocO@]\bdbpqdb

    (D) ppdqpd[0ocO@]\bddpqdb

Use the following information to answer question 11.

Police Officer Cho is in pursuit of a suspect driving eastbound on Riverside Drive. The suspect makes a quick right and then an immediate left, driving the wrong way down a one-way street. He turns left again, finding himself stuck, facing a dead end.

11. According to this information, the suspect is facing which direction?

(A) North

(B) South

(C) East

(D) West

ANSWERS AND EXPLANATIONS

1. C

Learning Objective: Read maps to find the quickest route

Choice (C) is correct. This is the most efficient route. Choices (A), (B), and (D) are too long.

2. D

Learning Objective: Read maps to find the quickest route

Choice (D) is correct. Choices (A) and (C) are too long; Choice (B) is the wrong way on Roses Street.

3. A

Learning Objective: Read maps to find the quickest route

Choice A is correct. Choice (B) is too long. Choice (C) is the wrong way on Berger Boulevard. Choice (D) is impossible because Officer Jones cannot travel west on Redmen Street from East Avenue. The hospital is in the way.

4. B

Learning Objective: Memorize elements of street scenes

Choice (B) is correct. The one-way sign is pointing to the left. Always look at street signs; don't just note their presence, but also what they say and the directions they give.

5. D

Learning Objective: Memorize elements of street scenes

Choice (D) is correct. Daisy runs a Hallmark shop. Read all text elements carefully: storefronts, traffic signs, license plates, etc.

6. B

Learning Objective: Memorize elements of street scenes

Choice (B) is correct. There are four people in front of Daisy's, and one man near the beauty supply shop. There are no other people in the photograph.

7. A

Learning Objective: Recognize and identify facial features

Choice A is correct. Choice (A) is the only option that is the same face as the original, but with a new hairstyle. The women in Choices (B) and (C) both have thicker eyebrows, and the woman in Choice (D) has a thinner, wider mouth.

8. B

Learning Objective: Visualize patterns

Choice (B) is correct. The number of Xs in every box increases by one in each image. Choice (B) is the only option with five Xs. The rest of the elements in the box are just a distraction.

9. B

Learning Objective: Visualize patterns

Choice (B) is correct. Every box has six lines and a circle. They are moved around, but the numbers stay the same. While Choice (B) maintains the six lines, the other choices have either five or eight lines.

10. D

Learning Objective: Visualize patterns

Choice (D) is correct. It is the only answer choice that is an exact match for the original string of characters. In Choice (A), a letter "O" is in place of the number "0." Choice (B) transposes the "q" and "p." Choice (C) replaces the fourth "d" with a "b."

11. A

Learning Objective: Visualize patterns

The correct answer is (A). The suspect starts out driving east and then makes a quick right, which means he's then driving south. He then makes two lefts: after the first left he is driving east again, and after the second he is driving north.

 **SELF-REFLECTION**

The main way to get better with questions that test your skills of spatial orientation (map reading), memorization, facial recognition, and visualization is to practice. The more familiar you are with the types of questions you will face on Test Day, the more prepared you will be to approach them with confidence.

Test What You Know score: _____ /11 correct

Test What You Learned score: _____ /11 correct

After working through the practice problems in this chapter, which of the Learning Objectives have you mastered? Place a check mark next to those objectives to keep track of your progress.

- ☐ Read maps to find the quickest route
- ☐ Memorize elements of street scenes
- ☐ Recognize and identify facial features
- ☐ Visualize patterns
- ☐ Identify identical patterns and objects

CHAPTER 11

Information Management and Problem Sensitivity

On questions that test your information management skills (sometimes referred to as information ordering), the goal is to logically put sequences in order. Most of the time, these questions will come in the form of actions that took place during an event or procedures or rules that need to be followed in a certain order.

Other items, sometimes labeled as problem sensitivity questions, give you police scenarios to interpret. You will be asked to come up with a plan to respond to the situation at hand. These questions test your common sense and logical reasoning.

LEARNING OBJECTIVES

In this chapter, you will review how to:

- ☐ Order and manage facts logically

- ☐ Find the most appropriate response to police scenarios

- ☐ Identify the most/least meaningful details in a police scenario

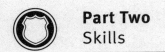

TEST WHAT YOU KNOW

Directions: Choose the ONE best answer for each question.

Police Officer Rodriguez responds to a robbery. The following six statements appear in the victim's account of the incident:

1. The man ran back to the north, up Dupree Street.

2. I just left the check cashing store and was walking south on Dupree Street.

3. The man in the black jacket said, "Hey, wanna see something?" Then he pulled out a knife at least 6 inches long.

4. A man in a black jacket approached from the convenience store at the corner and started walking alongside me.

5. The man demanded my wallet, so I gave it to him.

6. I stopped at the closest place I could, a fast-food restaurant, and called the police.

1. What is the most logical order of these statements?

   (A) 1, 3, 4, 5, 6, 2

   (B) 3, 4, 1, 5, 2, 6

   (C) 2, 4, 3, 5, 1, 6

   (D) 2, 1, 6, 4, 3, 5

Police Officer Martin responds to an assault call. The victim's account includes the following six statements:

1. I got up, went inside the convenience store, and asked the cashier to call the police.

2. The man walked up to me and punched me in the face, knocking me to the ground. He said, "It's my business now," and then walked away down Maine, southbound.

3. I was putting air in my tires with a manual pump, and I had my driver-side door open with the radio playing.

4. I had my car parked in the parking lot at the convenience store on the corner of Maine and Sparta.

5. He said, "Turn that junk down, man." I told him to mind his own business.

6. A large man, about 6 feet 4 inches and 300 lb, came out of the convenience store and walked past my car.

2. What is the most logical order of these statements?

    (A) 4, 3, 6, 5, 2, 1

    (B) 4, 5, 6, 3, 1, 2

    (C) 6, 2, 4, 3, 5, 1

    (D) 5, 3, 4, 1, 2, 6

Answer this question on the basis of the following.

A police officer is required to report dangerous situations immediately to the station house in closest proximity.

3. Which of the following situations would most likely require an officer to report as dangerous?

    (A) An abnormally large amount of garbage piled up at a sidewalk curb

    (B) A group of teenagers conversing loudly on a street corner

    (C) A significant amount of fresh graffiti on the perimeter wall of a park

    (D) A chemical spill on a street next to a school

4. A tractor trailer is disabled on the side of the highway. Which of the following is the most appropriate first action for the officer?

    (A) Call for backup.

    (B) Set up flares 300 feet behind the truck.

    (C) Ask the operator for his license.

    (D) Conduct an inspection of the truck for violations.

ANSWERS AND EXPLANATIONS

1. C

Learning Objective: Order and manage facts logically

The correct answer is (C). Choices (A) and (B) seem to start in the middle or end of the story and can therefore be ruled out. The second statement in Choice (D) refers to "the man" running away, but no man appears in the first statement, and no incident has yet occurred, so this choice can be eliminated. Reading through the statements in the order shown in Choice (C) provides a logical, coherent account of the robbery.

2. A

Learning Objective: Order and manage facts logically

The correct answer is (A). Sentence 4 clearly makes sense as the first statement. Choice (D) can be eliminated because sentence 5 does not make sense as the first statement. The second statement in Choice (C) covers the assault, but it skips over details in the other statements that must happen first. The second statement in Choice (B) refers to "he," but no other person has been introduced yet, so you can rule this one out. Looking at Choice (A), ordering the statements in this way provides a logical and coherent account of the victim's experience.

3. D

Learning Objective: Find the most appropriate response to police scenarios

The correct answer is (D). Choices (A), (B), and (C) are all situations that could potentially require attention, but only Choice (D) represents a situation that should be reported immediately as dangerous.

4. B

Learning objective: Find the most appropriate response for police scenarios

The correct answer is (B). Aside from Choice (A), which seems unnecessary, all of the answer choices are good responses, and all might be conducted by the officer at some point. However, the question asks for the most appropriate first action, and for safety reasons, it would make the most sense to set up the flares first before performing other actions.

ORDER AND MANAGE FACTS LOGICALLY

Information management questions ask you to determine the appropriate order of steps in a police scenario. You will be presented with all the facts you need to know to answer the question, and then you have to select the most logical way to present those facts.

Because the information can be wordy and detailed, these questions might take up more time than other more direct test questions. However, this is not to say that you should rush through them: you don't want to miss a key detail because you skimmed a paragraph too quickly. Trust us: you will have ample time to complete your exam, especially if you are familiar with the question types you will see on Test Day. Read on for some strategies to help you not only save time, but also conserve your energy and concentration as you go through the examination.

For ordering questions, use logic and process of elimination

Let's walk through a sample question together so you can get an idea of the best way to approach one. Say you are given the following scenario:

Officer Marks is interviewing the victim of a robbery. The following six statements appear in the victim's account of the incident.

1. I told him that I wasn't ignoring him, and I held up my phone to show him I was listening to music.

2. I was walking along Fifth Street, wearing earbuds and listening to music on my phone.

3. The shouting was coming from a guy right behind me. He said, "Hey! Why are you ignoring me?"

4. I heard someone shouting, so I paused my music and took out one of my earbuds.

5. I went into the nearest store, a restaurant, and called the police.

6. The man grabbed my phone and shouted, "That's what you get!" Then he ran off to the north and turned west on State Avenue.

What is the most logical order of these statements?

(A) 1, 5, 6, 3, 2, 4

(B) 4, 2, 6, 3, 1, 5

(C) 2, 4, 3, 1, 6, 5

(D) 2, 3, 4, 5, 1, 6

Here, you are to pick the correct choice for the sequence of events. What is the proper order? Process of elimination, as in all parts of the test, will be extremely useful here. But don't underestimate your own keen sense of how a story is told.

Instead of reading all the sentences from 1–6, *first* look at your choices, (A) through (D). Take a look at the first number in each of these answers. There is a good chance that at least some of the numbers will be different. Read each sentence that corresponds to the first numbers. Are any obviously incorrect? Is it clear that one comes before the others?

Choice (A) does not seem like a correct answer, because the first statement appears to start in the middle of the story. For Choice (B), it's hard to tell if the answer is good yet or not. For Choices (C) and (D), however, the first statement definitely feels like the start of a story. It sets the scene of the incident and explains what the victim was doing before the incident occurred.

So, we've already ruled out Choice (A). Let's look at the second statement in the remaining answer choices and see if we can narrow it down further. For Choice (B), the second statement is the same as the first statement in the other two answer choices. We liked that statement in the other answer choices, and the fact that it appears near the beginning in this answer choice means that this could still be a good possibility. For Choice (C), the second statement is the same as the first statement in Choice (B). Again, it's difficult to tell which of these two is better, but so far, they are both pretty good choices. For Choice (D), the second statement refers to "the shouting," as if shouting has already been mentioned; however, shouting is not mentioned in the first statement. Let's rule this one out.

Now we've cut our answer choices in half, giving us much better odds. Let's look at the third statement in the remaining choices. In Choice (B), the third statement describes the actual theft. Hmm … your keen sense of how a story develops might be tingling by now. If the theft occurs in the third statement, what happens in the remaining three statements? Let's stay on Choice (B) and look at what happens next. Sure enough, the fourth and fifth statements appear to contain details that wouldn't make sense if they happened *after* the theft, especially since the thief has already run off! It looks like we can eliminate Choice (B).

Just to make sure, take a look at your preferred answer choice and read through the story in the order shown. Does it all make sense? Do any details seem to be out of place? Looking at Choice (C) above, all the details fit together perfectly, and the story makes sense. Choice (C) is correct.

If more than one choice has the same first number, don't assume it's the right one! For example, if Choices (A), (B), and (C) all have number 3 as the first statement, make *sure* that Statement 3 makes sense as the first step. You still need to evaluate the first statement of Choice (D), because it might make sense, too.

Another way to use the process of elimination when faced with several answer choices that have the same first number is to move right to examining the last number. Chances are, these will be different. Read the sentences that correspond to the final number and determine which one makes the most logical sense for the last sentence. If any sentence does not fit as the final step, eliminate that choice.

Always remember: take it step-by-step, number-by-number, and eliminate along the way. Eventually, this process of elimination will guide you to the correct answer, as there will only be one left to choose from.

FIND THE MOST APPROPRIATE RESPONSE TO POLICE SCENARIOS

On just about any police exam, you will be presented with real-life police scenarios to test how you would respond to situations that might come up on the job. To answer scenario-based questions correctly, you must identify a problem (or parts of the problem) and then select the best solution from the choices given; this is sometimes described as *problem sensitivity*. These questions test your common sense and logical reasoning skills. This can sometimes cross over to what is known as deductive reasoning.

Questions of this type differ from exam to exam. They may take the form of "Which of the following actions would you take in the given situation?" or "What problem can you foresee happening in this scenario, and how would you correct it?" You may also be given a specific law enforcement guideline and asked which scenario would require you to respond in a certain way.

These questions often intimidate test takers, who, for the most part, have not yet had *any* real-life policing experience. Here's a little secret: the test makers know that. If you find yourself getting nervous, keep repeating to yourself this fact: you do *not* need to have police experience or be familiar with police procedures to answer these questions correctly. However, you will need to read carefully, think logically, and pay attention to details in order to select the best answer among the choices presented to you.

Let's look at a question. Say you are given the following scenario:

Police officers often respond to calls about lost or missing children and have to follow proper procedures and make decisions on how to handle and investigate these calls. An officer receives a call about a missing 5-year-old.

A question accompanying this information might be worded as follows:

With which of the following actions should the officer start his investigation?

(A) Search all hospitals in the vicinity

(B) Question neighbors if and when they have seen the child

(C) Obtain a description of the child and the clothes he was wearing and a picture, if possible

(D) Transmit an all-points bulletin over the radio about the missing child

The first thing you need to do is make sure you understand what the question is asking. For this question, you want to provide the most logical choice for how the officer will begin an investigation of a missing child. Chances are, all answer choices presented to you will be good, common-sense actions. But even good choices may not be the right answer. Never just choose the answer that seems the most lawful and move on—take it step-by-step, and use process of elimination.

Would Choice (A) be the most logical step to do first? Probably not: you may do that later on, but definitely not first. You need to gather important details first, before you begin a search. Choices (B) and (D) are also great actions to take. However, how can you question neighbors or transmit a bulletin if you do not even know whom you are looking for? Choice (C) is the most logical answer: you want to find out whom you are looking for before you can put effort into looking for him.

For this type of question, the answer is really in the stem of the question: someone is missing. When in doubt, assume you have to find out the following pieces of information in this order:

1. Who

2. What

3. When

4. Where

5. How

Keeping this in mind should help guide you through these question types.

The test will offer concise and basic scenarios for you to read, with a clear, correct answer among the choices. It is not trying to trick you—it just is testing your ability to read a situation, understand it, and pick out the most important information you must seek out to do your job.

IDENTIFY THE MOST/LEAST MEANINGFUL DETAILS IN A POLICE SCENARIO

Another common question type accompanies a scenario filled with details. These test your reading comprehension skills (see chapter 6 to brush up!), because you must identify key details from the information presented that will lead you to the most logical outcome. The difficult part of these questions is recognizing which details are important. Always refer back to the details of the story after you read and understand what the question is asking. Then, use process of elimination.

Let's look at a passage.

In the middle of the afternoon, two men wearing masks and gloves walked into a check-cashing store. When they entered the store, there were three customers waiting in line. One of the men threw all three against the wall and kept them at gunpoint. The other masked man walked up to the counter that had bulletproof glass and pointed a firearm at the teller. He then told the teller not to step on the alarm button, which is located on the floor behind the counter. The perpetrator then stated, "I know you got a money delivery an hour ago. Fill up this bag or we will shoot the customers." The teller unlocked the secured door and filled the bag with the money.

The other masked man ordered the customers to empty their wallets and purses. The robber then walked up to a female customer, made lewd remarks, and ripped her blouse. The female slapped the robber across the face, catching her nail by his eye under the mask, which caused a slight scratch and some bleeding. The robber then threw her to the ground and kicked her. At this time, the other masked man yelled, "Tommy, stop. Leave her alone!" At this point, the bag was filled with the money, and they both fled the store with the bag.

Answer the following question based on the above information.

Based on the information provided, which of the following is MOST likely to be true?

(A) The perpetrators had been watching the delivery times for the store.

(B) The perpetrator was bluffing when he said he knew the store recently received a money delivery.

(C) At least one of the perpetrators is or was an employee at the check-cashing store.

(D) The perpetrator personally knew the female customer who slapped him.

Based on the scenario given, what can the police assume from the statements and actions of the robbers? Let's review. As the robbers entered the store, one of them threw the customers against the wall. This behavior does not really tell us anything in particular.

As we read on, we learn about the robber who approached the counter. The robber tells the teller not to step on the alarm button. We have to assume he somehow knows that a) such a button exists and b) it is on the floor, because he cannot see past the counter. The next thing he states is, "I know you got a money delivery an hour ago." Therefore, we need to put these two pieces of information together to guide us to the correct answer.

Choice (A) states that the robber has been watching the times of the delivery. That may well be true, as he knew about the timing of the last delivery. However, it does not explain how he knew about the alarm button. Choice (B), which states the perpetrator was bluffing when he said he knew the store recently received a money delivery, is not the best answer. The robber was very specific in his language about the timing of the money delivery. This small but significant detail eliminates this choice. Finally, Choice (D) is just an assumption that does not really fit into the details of the crime. Therefore, logically speaking, considering only the information given, the correct choice is (C).

This leads us to the following question.

What is the most reliable physical evidence the police can use to investigate this crime?

(A)   None, because the perpetrators wore masks and gloves

(B)   Video recording from the check-cashing store's surveillance camera

(C)   A cell phone picture from one of the victims

(D)   DNA from the victim's fingernail

This question asks about physical evidence that may have been left behind. As with all scenario-based questions, look to what you are given, and *only* to what you are given. The answer can always be found in the passage, and you cannot assume anything that is not there on the test.

We know in the scenario there was a physical altercation, and that would be where we would look for and find the physical evidence.

Choice (A) is not the best answer. Yes, you were given the fact that the robbers wore masks and gloves to throw you off, but that does not mean no physical evidence was left behind. *Never* just mark (A) if it looks "okay" and move on. Read on to make sure there is not a better choice.

Choice (B) can be eliminated because the scenario never states that there are cameras at the store—remember, no assumptions! Eliminate and move on. Same for Choice (C)—you are never told that one of the victims took a cell phone picture. One very well might have, but you can *only* answer questions based on what is given to you.

Choice (D) is the best and most logical answer. What happened, and how did physical evidence get left behind? The details of the story tell us that the victim scratched one of the robbers and cut him with her fingernail. The correct answer matches the details of the story.

When you are dealing with scenario-based questions, it is not a bad idea to skim over the questions first, before you go on to read the passage. Doing so will help you to focus on the information in the story you will need to answer the specific questions, and not get distracted by unnecessary information. Unless you are a speedy reader, it can be a waste of your time to exert energy into reading the scenario without even knowing what the test is looking for.

Elimination is your friend for all of these question types. Rule out the choices that have nothing to do with the question or are based on information not included in the passage. Keep in mind that no matter what format your test uses, there has to be a clear-cut right answer.

TEST WHAT YOU LEARNED

Directions: Choose the ONE best answer for each question.

Police Officer Jeter responds to the local pharmacy for a larceny report. The witness account contains the following six statements:

1. The cashier chased the suspects out of the store.

2. Two young males with hoodies entered the store and began to walk around.

3. One of the males began stuffing items from the shelf into his pockets.

4. One of the males approached the counter and began to ask questions while the other walked around.

5. One of the workers observed both of them in the corner talking before splitting up.

6. The cashier noticed what was happening and shouted at the male to put the items back.

1. Which of the following is the most logical order for the details in Officer Jeter's report?

    (A) 3, 4, 2, 5, 1, 6

    (B) 2, 5, 4, 3, 6, 1

    (C) 2, 4, 5, 6, 1, 3

    (D) 5, 3, 6, 4, 2, 1

Answer this question on the basis of the following.

A police officer may have to place traffic cones on the roadway to mark potential safety hazards.

2. Which of the following situations would most likely require an officer to place a traffic cone on the roadway?

    (A) A car has stalled in a store parking lot.

    (B) A truck has parked illegally in front of a residence.

    (C) A deep pothole has opened up in the middle of a paved street.

    (D) A panhandler has been seen standing on the median of a busy street, begging for change.

3. For which of the following should an officer tape off and block pedestrian traffic from the sidewalk?

   (A) The facade of a building falling off into the street

   (B) A traffic accident on the street

   (C) An ambulance responding to a medical call

   (D) A dispute between two individuals in front of a store

Use the following passage to answer questions 4–6.

You receive and respond to a radio transmission about a home invasion. You approach the house and determine it is safe to enter. As you enter the house, you are approached by a married couple who state that a male posing as a gas and electric utility repairman rang the doorbell. When the wife opened the door, the male, wearing the exact uniform of the local utility company, entered the house stating that he had to check the gas lines for a possible leak. The wife noticed he had an identification badge on him, but it was upside down. Once the door closed, he brandished a firearm. The husband then walked into the kitchen, where he was confronted by the perpetrator.

The perpetrator placed the husband and wife in chairs, tied them up, and duct-taped their mouths. The husband noticed that the perpetrator walked with a slight limp and did not wear any gloves when applying the tape, but then put on gloves to search the house. The intruder ransacked the house, taking cash, jewelry, and two laptop computers. He then fled the scene. The husband managed to free himself, untie his wife, and call 911.

4. On which of the following would you MOST likely find the fingerprints of the perpetrator?

   (A) The duct tape

   (B) The rope

   (C) The jewelry box

   (D) The bedroom dresser drawer

5. Which of the following details would be MOST helpful in identifying the perpetrator?

   (A) He had a firearm.

   (B) His badge was upside down.

   (C) He tied the couple up in the kitchen.

   (D) He walked with a limp.

6. What evidence or information would be the most essential clue to this investigation?

    (A) The victims were bound and gagged.

    (B) The perpetrator possessed a firearm.

    (C) The perpetrator was wearing a gas and electric utility uniform.

    (D) The perpetrator stated there was a gas leak to gain entry.

ANSWERS AND EXPLANATIONS

1. B

Learning Objective: Order and manage facts logically

Sentence 2 makes the most sense for the first action. So, right away, you can eliminate Choices (A) and (D). You can then look at the last action for both to see which one makes the most sense. Sentence 1 makes the most sense as the last action to happen, making Choice (B) the correct answer.

2. C

Learning Objective: Find the most appropriate response to police scenarios

Choices (A) and (B) do not appear to represent safety hazards. Choice (D) may represent a safety hazard, but placing a traffic cone does not seem like an appropriate solution.

3. A

Learning Objective: Find the most appropriate response for police scenarios

Only one choice affects the safety of pedestrians walking on the sidewalk—the possibility of falling debris from a facade that has already fallen. Choices (B) and (C) affect the street, but not pedestrian traffic. Choice (D) does not pose a threat to pedestrians.

4. A

Learning Objective: Identify the most/least meaningful details in a police scenario

The scenario tells you that the intruder put on gloves after taping up the victims. Your best chance of retrieving fingerprints is from the glue side of the duct tape.

5. D

Learning Objective: Identify the most/least meaningful details in a police scenario

Some of the other choices may be important during the investigation, but knowing that the intruder has a limp would be a big part of putting a description together. A limp is a physical element that can be easily seen and recognized.

6. C

Learning Objective: Identify the most/least meaningful details in a police scenario

The other details given are important in the investigation, but the detail that the intruder was wearing a utility uniform would be the most logical starting point for the police.

 **SELF-REFLECTION**

When you get to questions testing your knowledge of police information, what you are given can sometimes seem long and complex. But always remember that ALL the information you need to answer the questions is right there on the test in front of you.

Use process of elimination wherever you can: not only will you increase your chances of doing well, but you will also save a tremendous amount of time on the test. Even though you will have plenty of time given to you, saving time and energy will only benefit you in the long run.

Also remember that there is only one best and most correct answer. Do not get overwhelmed by all the details presented to you.

Test What You Know score: _____ /4 correct

Test What You Learned score: _____ /6 correct

After working through the practice problems in this chapter, which of the Learning Objectives have you mastered? Place a check mark next to those objectives to keep track of your progress.

- [ ] Order and manage facts logically
- [ ] Find the most appropriate response to police scenarios
- [ ] Identify the most/least meaningful details in a police scenario

Practice Exams

Practice Exam 1

POLICE EXAM
Time—2 hours
Number of questions—100

A CALCULATOR MAY NOT BE USED ON THIS EXAM.

> **Directions:** Choose the ONE best answer for each question.

Questions 1–10

Study the photograph below very carefully for five minutes. You will be asked 10 detailed questions about this image. Once you have finished looking at this photograph, you will not be able to look back at it again.

Practice Exam 1

1. What is the name of the fabric store in the photo?

   (A) Viking Fabric

   (B) Billie's Designer Fabrics

   (C) Fabrics and Notions

   (D) Rose Fabrics

2. In how many places does the phone number for the nail salon appear?

   (A) 0

   (B) 1

   (C) 2

   (D) 3

3. According to the signage, what is located on the second floor above the nail salon?

   (A) Wildtrout Gallery

   (B) Spa & Waxing

   (C) Orphic Property Management

   (D) The Real Estate Guide

4. What is the phone number for the nail salon?

   (A) (748) 360-6188

   (B) (778) 748-6188

   (C) (360) 778-6188

   (D) (360) 748-6188

5. How many trash cans appear in the photo?

   (A) 0

   (B) 1

   (C) 2

   (D) 3

6. Which of the following is located closest to the entrance of the fabric store?

   (A) A trash can

   (B) A bicycle rack

   (C) A U.S. mail drop box

   (D) A sandwich board sign

7. What is the address listed for Orphic Property Management?

    (A) 778 N. Market Blvd.

    (B) 748 N. Market Blvd.

    (C) 618 S. Market Blvd.

    (D) 360 N. Market Blvd.

8. Which of the following words does NOT appear on the "Space for Lease" sign?

    (A) Retail

    (B) Residential

    (C) Professional

    (D) Office

9. Which of the following brands does NOT appear on the sign for the fabric store?

    (A) Husqvarna

    (B) Viking

    (C) White

    (D) Singer

10. According to the "Space for Lease" sign, how many square feet are available?

    (A) Up to 2,000 square feet

    (B) Up to 3,000 square feet

    (C) Up to 4,000 square feet

    (D) Up to 5,000 square feet

Questions 11–19

Read the short scenarios, and then select the best answer to the following questions.

The vehicle maintenance division is replacing the data terminals in all department squad cars. They can replace three data terminals per day. The department has 42 squad cars that need new data terminals.

11. How many days would it take to replace the data terminals in all of the department's squad cars?

    (A) 7 days

    (B) 12 days

    (C) 14 days

    (D) 18 days

A shoe store owner reported a burglary, and Officer Brandt responded to take a report. The owner stated that the following items were missing:

- 3 pairs of sneakers worth $75 each
- 2 pairs of loafers worth $80 each
- 4 pairs of designer pumps worth $200 each
- 2 pairs of boots worth $150 each

12. What is the total value of the stolen items?
    (A) $1,010
    (B) $1,485
    (C) $1,600
    (D) $1,725

In his first week on the job, Officer Sanchez wrote 26 incident reports. The following week, he only wrote half as many. For weeks three and four, he wrote 15 reports each week.

13. How many incident reports did Officer Sanchez write in his first month?
    (A) 56
    (B) 69
    (C) 75
    (D) 81

A group of 50 volunteers has shown up to help with a search for a missing boy. Officer Lopez has been put in charge of performing a straight-line sweep search of a field that measures 350 feet in width.

14. Approximately how many feet apart should each volunteer stand to provide even coverage across the width of the field during the sweep search?
    (A) 5 feet apart
    (B) 6 feet apart
    (C) 7 feet apart
    (D) 8 feet apart

Officer Engelhard responds to a reported theft from a pawn shop. The pawn shop owner lists the following items as stolen:

- 1 computer worth $400
- 2 guitars worth $120 each
- 1 television worth $350
- 1 trombone worth $75
- 3 watches worth $60 each

15. What is the total value of the stolen items?

    (A) $1,005

    (B) $1,125

    (C) $1,245

    (D) $1,475

Officer Deschutes responded to a reported theft from a coin change machine at an arcade. The machine had been pried open and all of the coin change was removed. Paper bills were stored in a separate secure hopper and were not taken. According to an employee, the machine had been fully stocked with 50 dollars in quarters, 10 dollars in dimes, and 5 dollars in nickels at the beginning of the night. According to the machine's recorded transaction logs, the machine dispensed 20 quarters, 10 dimes, and 40 nickels in legitimate transactions prior to the theft.

16. Assuming the witness statement and the machine's transaction logs were correct, what was the value of the coins taken by the thief?

    (A) $39

    (B) $45

    (C) $51

    (D) $57

Officer Wayne is putting together handouts for a presentation at the local school. He is giving the presentation to five different classes. The first class has 50 students, the second and third classes each have 35 students, the fourth class has 40 students, and the fifth class has 45 students.

17. How many handouts does Officer Wayne need to cover all the students in his presentations?

    (A) 170

    (B) 205

    (C) 220

    (D) 245

Officer Carmona responded to a reported theft at a computer store. The manager of the store stated that 16 identical computers were stolen, with a total value of $24,000.

18. What is the value of each stolen computer?

    (A) $750

    (B) $1,000

    (C) $1,200

    (D) $1,500

Officer Dobbs responded to a reported theft at a phone store. According to an employee, four identical phones were stolen along with several chargers and phone cases. The chargers and phone cases were valued at $200 total. The total value of the stolen items was $1,800.

19. What is the value of each stolen phone?

    (A) $250

    (B) $400

    (C) $500

    (D) $600

Questions 20–27

In each of the following sentences, choose the word or phrase that most nearly has the same meaning as the underlined word.

20. The <u>assailant</u> fled north along Canal Street.

    (A) attacker

    (B) victim

    (C) witness

    (D) critic

21. The witness later claimed that he was <u>coerced</u> into testifying.

    (A) bribed

    (B) forced

    (C) convinced

    (D) assisted

22. The officer felt that the presentation would <u>deter</u> any future incidents at the school.

    (A) facilitate

    (B) solve

    (C) postpone

    (D) prevent

23. The protesters <u>congregated</u> near the entrance to City Hall.

    (A) shouted

    (B) dispersed

    (C) gathered

    (D) attacked

24. The woman claimed that she and her husband had been <u>estranged</u> for six months.

    (A) married

    (B) separated

    (C) in hiding

    (D) abnormal

25. The man in the street was <u>hindering</u> the flow of traffic.

    (A) blocking

    (B) facilitating

    (C) directing

    (D) observing

26. The officer's order to disperse had an <u>adverse</u> effect on the crowd.

    (A) unforeseen

    (B) expected

    (C) encouraging

    (D) negative

27. The suspect <u>ingested</u> approximately three pills in front of the officer.

    (A) sold

    (B) threw out

    (C) swallowed

    (D) pocketed

Questions 28–35

In the following sentences, choose the correct option to fill in the blank for each sentence.

28. After the championship, two cars were destroyed in the _____ chaos.

    (A) insuing

    (B) ensuing

    (C) ensueing

    (D) insueing

29. The difference between the real and counterfeit bill was _____.

    (A) inperceptible

    (B) inperceptable

    (C) imperceptible

    (D) imperceptable

30. The witness made a _____ attempt to run after the suspect's car.

    (A) futile

    (B) fudile

    (C) feudal

    (D) futal

31. The statement the suspect made to his lawyer was _____.

    (A) confedential

    (B) confidential

    (C) confidencial

    (D) confadenshal

32. Three different firearms _____ found in the suspect's vehicle.

    (A) was

    (B) is

    (C) were

    (D) where

33. The three men lost _____ wallets at some point during the concert.

    (A) they're

    (B) there

    (C) his

    (D) their

34. The suspect was _____ victim was taken to the hospital.

    (A) arrested, and the

    (B) arrested, the

    (C) arrested however the

    (D) arrested: and the

35. The suspect was questioned _____ he matched the description given by a witness.

    (A) therefore

    (B) however

    (C) then

    (D) because

Part Three
Practice Exams

Practice Exam 1

Questions 36–43

Read the short scenarios, and then select the best answer to the following questions.

Officer Jones is dispatched to an apartment building where a section of the parking deck has collapsed, and she gathers the following information:

Location:	Waterfront Apartments
Time:	5:15 a.m.
Problem:	section of parking deck collapsed
Damage:	10 cars destroyed
Injuries:	none

36. Officer Jones must write her report. Which of the following expresses the information most clearly and accurately?

(A) At 5:15, 10 cars were destroyed by a collapsing section of the parking deck at Waterfront Apartments.

(B) At 5:15, 10 cars were destroyed but no one was injured when a section of the parking deck collapsed. The cars were parked in the parking deck at Waterfront Apartments.

(C) At 5:15 a.m., a section of the parking deck at Waterfront Apartments collapsed, destroying 10 cars. No one was injured.

(D) At 5:15 a.m., Waterfront Apartments' parking deck collapsed in one section but did not cause anyone to be injured except for the cars.

Officer Greene is dispatched to a residence at which a "peeping Tom" has been reported. There, Officer Greene gathers the following information:

Location:	14 Liberty Avenue
Time:	8:15 p.m.
Incident:	A man was seen peering in the bathroom window.
Victim:	Rachel Winters, resident
Suspect:	short, heavyset male, wearing a stocking cap
Location of Suspect:	fled on foot in unknown direction

37. Officer Greene must prepare a report on the incident. Which of the following expresses the information most clearly and accurately?

    (A) A short, heavyset man in a stocking cap peered in the window of Rachel Winters's bathroom at 14 Liberty Avenue. The man fled on foot shortly after 8:15 p.m.

    (B) At 8:15 p.m., Rachel Winters reported that in her bathroom window at 14 Liberty Avenue a man was peering in. He was heavyset, Ms. Winters said, and short. He also wore a stocking cap. He fled on foot in an unknown direction.

    (C) Rachel Winters reported that at 8:15 p.m., she saw a short, heavyset man, who was wearing a stocking cap, peering in her bathroom window at 14 Liberty Avenue. The suspect fled in an unknown direction.

    (D) A short, heavyset man in a stocking cap was reported by Rachel Winters to have been peering into her bathroom window at 14 Liberty Avenue at 8:15 p.m. The man fled on foot in an unknown direction.

Officer Flanagan responds to a call from a worker at a fast-food restaurant who explains that an elderly man has collapsed at his table. Officer Flanagan gathers the following information:

Location:	Burger Binge
Time:	1:00 p.m.
Victim:	Timothy Sanderson, age 81
Suffering From:	heart attack, according to paramedics
Action Taken:	Mr. Sanderson taken by ambulance to the hospital

38. Officer Flanagan is writing his report. Which of the following expresses the information most clearly and accurately?

   (A) At 1:00 p.m. at Burger Binge, Timothy Sanderson, age 81, collapsed from what paramedics later determined was a heart attack. Mr. Sanderson was taken by ambulance to the hospital.

   (B) At 1:00 p.m., a man eating at Burger Binge had a heart attack and collapsed on his table. The man, 81-year-old Timothy Sanderson, was taken to the hospital by an ambulance, whose paramedics were the ones that determined that it was a heart attack.

   (C) Timothy Sanderson, 81, had a heart attack at Burger Binge at 1:00 p.m. He was taken to the hospital.

   (D) At Burger Binge, 81-year-old Timothy Sanderson was taken by ambulance to the hospital after paramedics determined that what caused his collapse was a heart attack that occurred when he collapsed on his table.

Officer Major responds to a report of the smell of natural gas at an apartment building, where he gathers the following information:

Location: Bear Village Apartments

Time: 8:00 p.m.

Caller: Paula Oak

Problem: The smell of natural gas was permeating her apartment.

Action Taken: The gas company was contacted; an emergency repair person arrived in minutes and fixed the leak.

39. Officer Major is writing his report. Which of the following expresses the information most clearly and accurately?

(A) At 8:00 p.m., Paula Oak reported that the smell of natural gas was permeating her apartment. The gas company was contacted, and an emergency repair person arrived in minutes and fixed the leak.

(B) At 8:00 p.m., Paula Oak reported that the smell of natural gas was permeating her apartment at Bear Village Apartments. The gas company was contacted.

(C) At 8:00 p.m., Paula Oak reported that the smell of natural gas was permeating her apartment at Bear Village Apartments. The gas company was contacted, and an emergency repair person arrived in minutes and fixed the leak.

(D) At 8:00 p.m., Paula Oak reported smelling natural gas. The gas company was contacted, and an emergency repair person arrived in minutes to fix the leak, which was causing the smell at Bear Village Apartments.

Officer Robinson responds to a call from a man who reports that a woman tried to sell drugs to him. Officer Robinson gathers the following information:

Location:	Silver Screen Multiplex
Time:	midnight
Person Reporting Incident:	Danny Singh
Crime:	attempting to sell drugs
Suspect:	40-year-old woman
Location of Suspect:	left the theater lot in a white Lincoln

40. Officer Robinson must write a report on the incident. Which of the following expresses the information most clearly and accurately?

(A) At midnight, at Silver Screen Multiplex, a woman of about 40 years old tried to sell drugs to Danny Singh. The woman left the theater lot in a white Lincoln, according to Danny Singh, to whom the woman tried to sell the drugs.

(B) Danny Singh reported that at midnight at the Silver Screen Multiplex, a woman around 40 years of age attempted to sell him drugs, then left the theater lot in a white Lincoln.

(C) Danny Singh reported that, at midnight, a woman tried to sell him drugs. The woman then left the theater lot in a white Lincoln, after which time Mr. Singh called the police to report the attempted sale.

(D) At the Silver Screen Multiplex at midnight, a 40-year-old woman attempted to sell Danny Singh some drugs. The woman was described as 40 years old, and left the theater in a white car.

Officer Petty responds to the scene of a reported domestic dispute, where she gathers the following information:

Location:	88 DeVaro
Time:	3:30 p.m.
Incident:	loud fighting and crashing sounds coming from the house
Person Reporting Incident:	Chung Lee, a neighbor
Residents at 88 DeVaro:	Jay and Ida Lindsay
Action Taken:	The couple explained that they were practicing judo together; no action taken.

41. Officer Petty has to write her report. Which of the following expresses the information most clearly and accurately?

(A) At 3:30 p.m., Chung Lee reported that loud fighting and crashing sounds were coming from his neighbors' house at 88 DeVaro. The residents, Jay and Ida Lindsay, explained that they were practicing judo together, so no action was taken.

(B) At 88 DeVaro, a judo practice session between Jay and Ida Lindsay, the residents, alarmed their neighbor, Chung Lee, who called the police. No action was taken.

(C) Chung Lee reported that his neighbors at 88 DeVaro were fighting and that crashing sounds were loudly coming from their house at 3:30 p.m. Jay and Ida Lindsay said they were just practicing judo.

(D) Jay and Ida Lindsay were practicing judo in their home at 88 DeVaro, causing loud fighting and crashing sounds to be heard by their neighbor, Chung Lee, who became concerned and called the police. No action was taken.

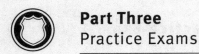
Practice Exam 1

Officer London is stopped by a girl who asks that he take her friend, who has been stung multiple times by hornets, to the hospital. At the hospital, Officer London gathers the following information:

Victim: Reggie Planks, age 8

Condition: stable after a severe allergic reaction to hornet stings

Friend: Hanna Reynolds, age 7

Action Taken: Hanna Reynolds provided Reggie Planks's phone number, and his parents were contacted.

42. Officer London must fill out his report. Which of the following expresses the information most clearly and accurately?

(A) After suffering a severe allergic reaction to multiple hornet stings, Reggie Planks, age 8, is in stable condition. His parents were contacted.

(B) Reggie Planks, age 8, was stung multiple times by hornets and suffered a severe allergic reaction. Reggie was taken to the hospital, where he is in stable condition. His friend, Hanna Reynolds, provided Reggie's phone number, and his parents were contacted.

(C) Hanna Reynolds, age 8 and a friend of hornet sting victim Reggie Planks, age 7, provided Reggie's phone number so that his parents could be contacted after Reggie suffered a severe allergic reaction. Reggie is now in stable condition.

(D) In stable condition after suffering a severe allergic reaction to multiple hornet stings, the parents of Reggie Planks, age 8, have been contacted, thanks to his friend Hanna Reynolds, age 7, who provided their phone number.

Officer Westover arrives at a residence that has been spray-painted with obscenities. At the residence, Officer Westover gathers the following information:

Location:	#15 Tanner Circle
Crime:	vandalism; house was spray-painted with obscenities
Victim:	Mrs. Hersch
Suspect:	Grant Patrick
Witness:	Geri Budd, a neighbor
Status of Suspect:	arrested

43. Officer Westover must write her report. Which of the following expresses the information most clearly and accurately?

   (A) Mrs. Hersch's home at #15 Tanner Circle was reportedly vandalized by Grant Patrick, who spray-painted obscenities on the house while a neighbor was watching. Mr. Patrick was arrested.

   (B) Geri Budd, who lives near Hersch's home at #15 Tanner Circle, witnessed Grant Patrick spray-painting the Hersch residence with obscenities. Mr. Patrick was arrested.

   (C) Grant Patrick was arrested after a witness, Mrs. Hersch's neighbor Geri Budd, saw him spray-paint obscenities onto the house at #15 Tanner Circle, where Mrs. Hersch lives.

   (D) At #15 Tanner Circle, Mrs. Hersch reported that her neighbor, Geri Budd, had seen Grant Patrick spray-paint Mrs. Hersch's house with obscenities. Mr. Patrick was arrested.

Questions 44–46

To answer questions 44–46, use the information in the following passage.

Police Officers Jennings and Lincoln were working a 4:00 p.m. to midnight tour of duty on Friday, December 5, when they were assigned to investigate a burglary. At 7:00 p.m., they were told to respond to 35-45 Grand Street, Apartment 1402, and to speak to the complainant, Ms. Phoebe Frost. Upon arrival, Officer Jennings interviewed Ms. Frost, who stated that when she returned home from work at approximately 6:10 p.m., she was unable to unlock her door because the keyhole had been stuffed with chewing gum. The building superintendent wasn't home, so she had a cup of coffee at the diner on the corner. When she returned to the building, the superintendent had arrived home and was able to open the door for her. Once she entered her apartment, she saw that her TV and DVD player were gone, and her jewelry box had been emptied and was lying on the floor. She immediately left the apartment and called the police from the super's apartment.

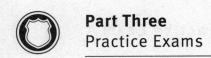

Officer Lincoln, who is qualified in fingerprint recovery, dusted the jewelry box and the front door in an attempt to recover any fingerprints that the burglar may have left. The officers also interviewed several other residents of the floor: Mrs. Lenore Caputo, who lives in Apartment 1404 next door to Ms. Frost; Ms. Frida Kalish, who lives in Apartment 1400 on the other side of Ms. Frost; and Mr. William Babbit, who lives in Apartment 1407 across the hall. None of the individuals had been at home during the day, and none had seen or heard anything unusual. Mrs. Caputo had come home earliest, at about 4:30 p.m. Ms. Kalish had returned at 5:45, and Mr. Babbit between 5:45 and 6:00.

At 4:30 in the afternoon on Saturday, December 6, Officers Jennings and Lincoln responded to Apartment 1514 in the same building on a call of burglary. The complainant, Ms. Lee Chung, stated that she left her apartment at about 2:00 to go shopping and run errands. When she returned home, she discovered that the lock on her apartment door had been stuffed with chewing gum. She found the super, who let her in. She discovered that her apartment had been burglarized. Her TV and DVD player were missing, along with her laptop computer, her answering machine, and her microwave oven. Officer Lincoln dusted for prints, focusing on the front door and a dresser, which had been left with its drawers ajar. The officers interviewed several neighbors: Mr. Stuart Lyon in Apartment 1512 next door, Mrs. Eunice Colón in Apartment 1516, and Ms. Petra Gruber in Apartment 1520 across the hall. Ms. Gruber had been home studying all afternoon but had heard nothing; Mr. Lyon had just returned from a trip to Washington, D.C., and hadn't been home; Mrs. Colón had heard "suspicious footsteps" at approximately 3:00 p.m. but hadn't seen anyone when she looked through the apartment door's peephole.

At the precinct, Detective Melendez was assigned to investigate the burglaries. Three days after the second burglary, Mr. Allen Hunt of the fingerprint identification unit informed Detective Melendez that the prints matched those of Peter Reilly, whose last known address was 355 Gavel Street, Apartment 1705. Later that evening, after obtaining an arrest warrant, Detective Melendez arrested Peter Reilly for the burglaries.

44. Who lived on the same floor as Ms. Frost?

    (A) Mrs. Eunice Colón

    (B) Mr. Allen Hunt

    (C) Mr. William Babbit

    (D) Mr. Stuart Lyon

45. When was the suspect arrested?

    (A) December 9

    (B) December 5

    (C) December 6

    (D) December 12

46. Why was Ms. Chung unable to unlock her door?

  (A) The lock was stuffed with chewing gum.

  (B) A pickpocket had stolen her key.

  (C) The lock had been loosened so it no longer worked.

  (D) The lock was stuffed with toothpicks.

Questions 47–49

To answer questions 47–49, use the information in the following passage.

Officers Scanlon and McCoy were in a patrol car when they were called to the scene of a vehicle/pedestrian accident at the intersection of 14th Avenue and Cavalcade Street. When the officers arrived at the scene, they saw that the injured pedestrian was being tended to by paramedics. Several people were gathered at the corners of the intersection. The driver of the car had parked to the side on Cavalcade Street. Officers in another patrol car began directing traffic, and Officers Scanlon and McCoy interviewed the driver and the witnesses.

The driver, Mr. Pierre Toulouse, said he'd been driving his Ford Taurus northbound on Cavalcade. As he neared the intersection, the light turned yellow; he'd just noticed this when the pedestrian ran in front of the car. Mr. Toulouse said he slammed on the brakes but was unable to stop. He said he wasn't sure exactly how fast he was traveling, but was certain that it was no more than 30 mph. His insurance and registration were current, but his driver's license had expired on his last birthday. Mr. Toulouse said he'd simply forgotten to renew it; a license check showed no outstanding violations.

Several of the bystanders said they'd witnessed the incident. Ms. Amy Presser said she'd been waiting at the southeast corner to cross Cavalcade. She happened to be looking south and saw the Taurus approaching the intersection. She stated that the car's speed was "about normal" and that she'd seen the light turn yellow just as the car entered the intersection. She had not seen the pedestrian until the car began braking and struck him.

Mr. Augustin Lantos also had been waiting to cross Cavalcade but on the corner opposite Ms. Presser. He said he'd seen the Ford "out of the corner of his eye," but he couldn't tell how fast it had been traveling. He had seen the pedestrian approaching the corner; Mr. Lantos said the young man was running along the sidewalk, carrying a basketball.

The young man glanced both ways at the intersection but ran into the street without pausing. Mr. Lantos turned his head as the pedestrian left the curb and did not see the collision. Mr. Lantos said he'd seen young people jaywalking at this intersection many times, often headed for the basketball courts in the nearby park, and he had been "expecting something like this to happen one of these days."

Mr. Ben Klein had been standing at the bus stop on the west side of Cavalcade, about midway down the block. He had noticed the Taurus as it went through the intersection of Cavalcade and 13th Avenue; he said the car seemed to be traveling at a moderate speed. His view of the collision was blocked by parked cars.

Ms. Nanette Guidry had left the deli at the southeast corner of Cavalcade and 14th Avenue shortly before the Taurus struck the pedestrian. She said the young man had brushed against her as he was running toward the intersection, and she was irritated that he didn't apologize. She was about to cross 14th Avenue and had turned to the left to check traffic when she saw the young man being struck by the Taurus; she said that just prior to the collision, she'd seen the Taurus out of the corner of her eye, and it had been "flying along very fast."

Before the paramedics took the pedestrian to the hospital, one of them reported to Officer McCoy. The pedestrian's name was Lenny McGraw; he had a broken femur and possible internal injuries. He was conscious but unable to answer any questions.

47. Who was driving the Ford Taurus involved in the incident?

   (A) Mr. Ben Klein

   (B) Mr. Augustin Lantos

   (C) Mr. Lenny McGraw

   (D) Mr. Pierre Toulouse

48. In which direction was the driver traveling?

   (A) Northbound on 14th Avenue

   (B) Eastbound on Cavalcade

   (C) Northbound on Cavalcade

   (D) Southbound on 14th Avenue

49. How many people witnessed the accident?

   (A) Four people, all of whom witnessed the car strike the pedestrian

   (B) Four people, two of whom witnessed the car strike the pedestrian

   (C) Four people, three of whom witnessed the car strike the pedestrian

   (D) Four people, none of whom witnessed the car strike the pedestrian

Questions 50–52

For questions 50–52, select the object that is included in the figure below. Only ONE of the answer choices for each question is included in the figure. Objects may be larger, smaller, mirrored, or rotated in the picture, but the proportions will be identical.

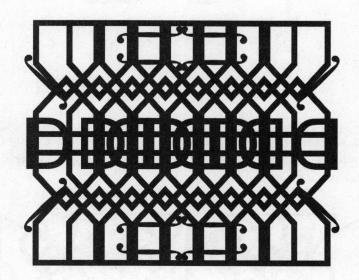

50.

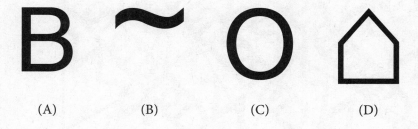

(A)   (B)   (C)   (D)

51.

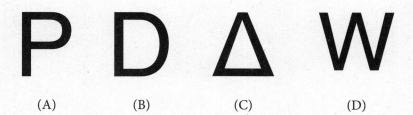

(A)   (B)   (C)   (D)

52.

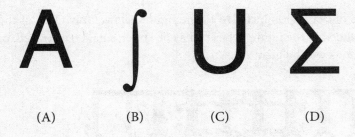

(A)   (B)   (C)   (D)

Questions 53–55

For questions 53–55, select the object that is included in the figure below. Only ONE of the answer choices for each question is included in the figure. Objects may be larger, smaller, mirrored, or rotated in the picture, but the proportions will be identical.

53.

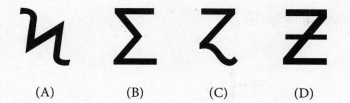

(A)   (B)   (C)   (D)

54.

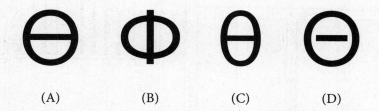

(A)   (B)   (C)   (D)

55.

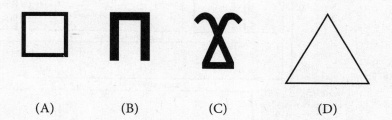

(A)   (B)   (C)   (D)

Questions 56–57

Please use the following map for questions 56–57.

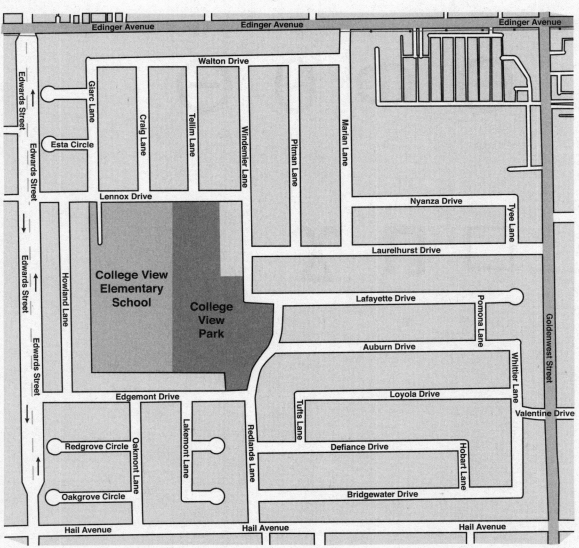

Officer Kazan has been dispatched to a home at the corner of Auburn Drive and Whittier Lane. She is currently located at the intersection of Windemeir Lane and Lennox Drive.

56. Which of the following would be the shortest (least distance) route for Officer Kazan to take to the incident scene?

(A) South on Windemeir Lane, east on Laurelhurst Drive, south on Goldenwest Street, west on Valentine Drive, north on Whittier Lane

(B) South on Windemeir Lane, east on Lafayette Drive, south on Redlands Lane, east on Auburn Drive

(C) South on Windemeir Lane, east on Lafayette Drive, south on Pomona Lane, east on Auburn Drive

(D) South on Windemeir Lane, east on Lafayette Drive, south on Redlands Lane, east on Bridgewater Drive, north on Whittier Lane

Officer Davis has been dispatched to a home at the intersection of Oakmont Lane and Oakgrove Circle. He is currently located at the intersection of Craig Lane and Walton Drive.

57. Which of the following would be the shortest (least distance) route for Officer Davis to take to the incident scene?

(A) South on Craig Lane, west on Lennox Drive, south on Edwards Street, east on Heil Avenue, north on Oakmont Lane

(B) West on Walton Drive, south on Giarc Lane, west on Lennox Drive, south on Howland Lane, east on Edgemont Drive, south on Oakmont Lane

(C) South on Craig Lane, east on Lennox Drive, south on Windemeir Lane, east on Lafayette Drive, south on Redlands Lane, west on Edgemont Drive, south on Oakmont Lane

(D) East on Walton Drive, north on Marian Lane, west on Edinger Avenue, south on Edwards Street, east on Edgemont Drive, south on Oakmont Lane

Questions 58–59

Please use the following map for questions 58–59.

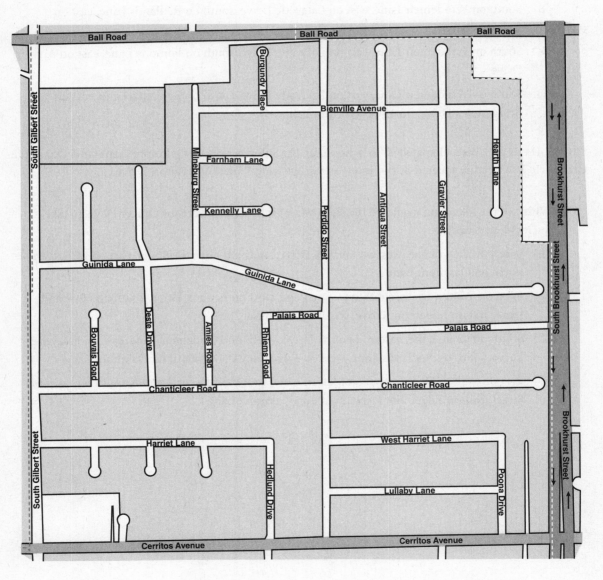

Officer Kovacs has been dispatched to a home at the intersection of Guinida Lane and Deste Drive. He is currently located at the intersection of Ball Road and Perdido Street.

58. Which of the following would be the shortest (least distance) route for Officer Kovacs to take to the incident scene?

(A) South on Perdido Street, west on Bienville Avenue, south on Milneburg Street, west on Guinida Lane

(B) South on Perdido Street, west on Guinida Lane

(C) West on Ball Road, south on South Gilbert Street, east on Guinida Lane

(D) South on Perdido Street, east on Bienville Avenue, South on Antigua Street, west on Guinida Lane

Officer Bentley has been dispatched to a home at the intersection of Harriet Lane and South Gilbert Street. She is currently located at the intersection of Bienville Avenue and Gravier Street.

59. Which of the following would be the shortest (least distance) route for Officer Bentley to take to the incident scene?

(A) West on Bienville Avenue, north on Perdido Street, west on Ball Road, south on South Gilbert Street

(B) West on Bienville Avenue, south on Perdido Street, west on Chanticleer Road, south on South Gilbert Street

(C) South on Gravier Street, west on Guinida Lane, south on South Gilbert Street

(D) West on Bienville Avenue, south on Perdido Street, west on Cerritos Avenue, north on South Gilbert Street

Questions 60–61

Please use the following map for questions 60–61. NOTE: Direction arrows indicate flow of traffic.

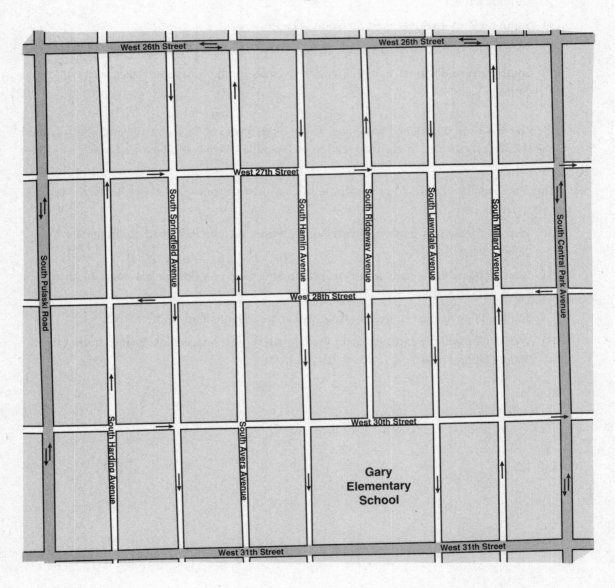

Officer Keyes has been dispatched to a home at the intersection of West 27th Street and South Hamlin Avenue. He is currently located at the intersection of West 30th Street and South Lawndale Avenue.

60. Which of the following would be the shortest (least distance) route for Officer Keyes to take, while following the flow of traffic?

(A) South on South Lawndale Avenue, west on West 31st Street, north on South Pulaski Road, east on West 27th Street

(B) East on West 30th Street, north on South Central Park Avenue, west on West 26th Street, south on South Hamlin Avenue

(C) West on West 30th Street, north on South Avers Avenue, east on West 27th Street

(D) East on West 30th Street, north on South Millard Avenue, west on West 28th Street, north on South Avers Avenue, east on West 27th Street

According to witness statements, a robbery suspect was seen running northbound on South Ridgeway Avenue. The suspect turned left on West 28th Street, traveled three blocks, turned left again, and ran two more blocks before the trail was lost.

61. At which intersection was the suspect last seen?

(A) West 31st Street and South Springfield Avenue

(B) West 30th Street and South Pulaski Road

(C) West 26th Street and South Springfield Avenue

(D) West 26th Street and South Central Park Avenue

Questions 62–66

Read the definitions, and then select the best answer to the following questions.

In State X, the crime of auto stripping is defined in the following ways:

- Auto stripping in the third degree occurs when a person removes or destroys any part of a vehicle without the owner's permission.

- Auto stripping in the second degree occurs when a person removes or destroys any part of two or more vehicles without the owners' permission, and the total value of the parts removed or destroyed is greater than $1,000.

- Auto stripping in the first degree occurs when a person removes or destroys any part of three or more vehicles without the owners' permission, and the total value of the parts removed or destroyed is greater than $3,000.

62. According to the definition given, which of the following is the best example of auto stripping in the second degree?

(A) A man removes all four tires from his ex-girlfriend's car, including rims valued at $1,500 total.

(B) A woman breaks the windows out of her neighbor's two vehicles during an argument, causing $800 in damage.

(C) A man removes stereo systems from four vehicles, valued at $2,000 total.

(D) A man removes hood ornaments from at least 20 cars in his neighborhood, causing $4,000 in damage.

In State X, the crime of computer tampering in the third degree is defined as any one of the following:

- Accessing a computer or computer network without authorization with the intent to commit a felony

- Accessing a computer or computer network without authorization and altering computer material

- Accessing a computer or computer network without authorization and destroying computer data or programs, causing at least $1,000 in damages

63. According to the definition given, which of the following is the best example of computer tampering in the third degree?

(A) A woman uses her personal computer to run an illegal online gambling operation, which is a felony.

(B) A man accesses his wife's email account to read messages she sent to a former boyfriend.

(C) A man attempts to fix his friend's computer at her request, but accidentally erases computer programs valued at $1,000.

(D) A woman facing termination secretly deletes software from her employer's computer network, causing $1,500 in damages.

In State X, the crime of grand larceny in the fourth degree is defined as theft involving at least one of the following conditions:

- The property is valued at more than $1,000.
- The property consists of records kept by elected officials.
- The property consists of a credit or debit card.
- The property is forcibly taken from another person.
- The property consists of one or more firearms.

64. According to the definition given, which of the following is NOT an example of grand larceny in the fourth degree?

   (A) A man borrows a camera worth $800 from a friend, but loses it and refuses to pay the owner back for it.

   (B) A woman removes printouts of the mayor's expense reports from his desk in City Hall.

   (C) A woman secretly takes her sister's credit card and uses it to buy $400 worth of clothing at the mall.

   (D) A man grabs a woman's purse at a busy intersection and runs off but later discovers the purse only contains $50 and some personal effects.

In State X, the crime of disorderly conduct occurs when a person, through recklessness or intent to cause public inconvenience, does at least one of the following:

   • Engages in a fight or threatening behavior

   • Creates a noise nuisance

   • Disturbs the lawful assembly of other people without authority

   • Blocks the traffic flow of vehicles or pedestrians

65. According to the definition given, which of the following is NOT an example of disorderly conduct?

   (A) A woman punches a stranger at the mall after he insults her child.

   (B) A man refuses to turn down his loud music despite complaints from neighbors.

   (C) A woman stages an impromptu pantomime performance in the park plaza without first notifying park personnel.

   (D) A man blocks an intersection and demands that drivers pay him a toll to use the road.

Practice Exam 1

In State X, the crime of loitering is defined as any one of the following actions:

- Remaining in a public place for the purpose of gambling with dice, cards, or similar items
- Remaining on school grounds without a legitimate purpose or written permission from school officials
- Remaining in a bus, train, or subway station for the purpose of selling goods or services
- Remaining in a bus, train, or subway station for the purpose of providing entertainment in exchange for tips or donations

66. According to the definition given, which of the following is the best example of loitering?

   (A) A man carries playing cards on his way to a poker match at a friend's house.

   (B) A man approaches travelers in the bus station and attempts to sell them coupon books for local businesses.

   (C) A woman waits in the train station to meet a business acquaintance for lunch.

   (D) A man sits parked in the school parking lot waiting for his daughter to finish class so he can drive her home.

Questions 67–70

Look at the provided image, and then select the best corresponding image to answer each question.

67. Which face below is an exact representation of the face above?

   (A)   (B)   (C)   (D)

The woman shown here has since changed her hairstyle.

68. Which face below represents the same woman with a different hairstyle?

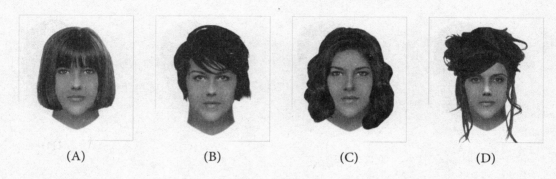

(A)   (B)   (C)   (D)

The man shown here has since grown facial hair.

69. Which face below represents the same man with facial hair?

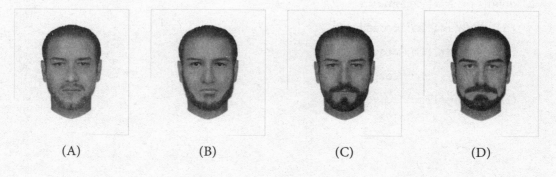

(A)   (B)   (C)   (D)

70. Which face below is an exact representation of the face above?

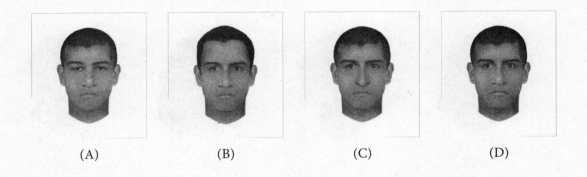

(A)   (B)   (C)   (D)

Questions 71–74

Questions 71–74 each contain a set of letters, symbols, and numbers. Please choose only ONE option for each that contains the exact same pattern of letters, symbols, and numbers.

71. YIiO0hggGBmnn;sWvvVw6bp9

    (A) YIi0OhggGBmnn;sWvvVw6bp9

    (B) YIiO0hggGBmnn;sWvvVw6bp9

    (C) YIiO0hggGBmmn;sWvvVw6bp9

    (D) YIiO0hggGBmnn;sWwvVw6bp9

72. dbbd[+rTHy/x]ccogqp\./un

    (A) dbdb[+rTHy/x]ccogqp\./un

    (B) dbbd{+rTHy/x}ccogqp\./un

    (C) dbbd[+rTHy/x]coogqp\./un

    (D) dbbd[+rTHy/x]ccogqp\./un

73. Hi4&;xx><-jgpq\$tRd"!li"

   (A) Hi4&;xx><-jgpq\$tRd"!li"

   (B) Hi4&;xx><-jgpq\$tRd"!il"

   (C) Hi4&;xx<>-jgpq\$tRd"!li"

   (D) Hi4&;xx><-jgpq\StRd"!li"

74. YvWVum%,uw#dpbqB3EH=s_wO

   (A) YvWVum%,uw#dpbqB3EH=s_wO

   (B) YvWVum%;uw#dpbqB3EH=s_wO

   (C) YvWVum%,uw#dpbqB3EH=s_w0

   (D) YvVWum%,uw#dpbqB3EH=s_wO

Questions 75–77

Read the short scenarios, and then place the statements in the most logical order.

Officer Aquino is interviewing the victim of a robbery. The following six statements appeared in the victim's account of the incident.

1. As I reached in my pocket for my phone, a man came behind me and pressed the point of a knife into my lower back.

2. I ran back into the gym and told an employee what had just happened.

3. The woman dropped my phone to the ground and smashed it under her foot, then fled with the man south down First Street.

4. I walked out of the gym where I had spinning class and headed to my car at the far end of the parking lot.

5. The man demanded my wallet, and the woman demanded my phone, so I complied.

6. A woman approached me and asked if she could use my phone to report a car accident.

75. What is the most logical order of these statements?

   (A) 4, 1, 5, 6, 3, 2

   (B) 6, 2, 4, 1, 5, 3

   (C) 4, 6, 1, 5, 3, 2

   (D) 1, 6, 3, 5, 4, 2

Officer Tran is interviewing a witness who saw a murder victim shortly before she was killed. The following six statements appeared in the witness's account of the incident.

1. I asked Melissa what she'd been up to, and she looked kind of scared. She said, "Not much. But we gotta take off. I'll text you later."

2. On Tuesday night, I saw Melissa at the convenience store with a guy I didn't recognize. He was about 6 feet tall, with very short black hair and a large mole on his right temple.

3. I texted Melissa an hour later just to check in, but she never responded.

4. Melissa and the guy walked out to the parking lot, and I could see they were arguing about something next to their car, which was a black SUV. I assume it was his car, because I haven't seen it before.

5. I haven't seen Melissa around much lately, and I assumed it was because she had a new boyfriend.

6. The guy opened the passenger door and pushed Melissa into the car. I heard her yell something at him, but I couldn't make out the words.

76. What is the most logical order of these statements?

    (A) 2, 4, 6, 1, 5, 3

    (B) 1, 5, 4, 6, 2, 3

    (C) 2, 3, 5, 1, 4, 6

    (D) 5, 2, 1, 4, 6, 3

In the aftermath of a bombing at a popular holiday parade, Officer Nilsson is interviewing a witness who may have seen the bomber prior to the blast. The following six statements appeared in the witness's account of the incident.

1. As the Santa's Workshop float approached, I saw a bright flash and heard a deafening boom. It knocked me to the floor.

2. I was watching the parade from the window of my fourth-story apartment, like I do every year. The parade route goes right down my street.

3. The man in the blue sweatshirt moved quickly through the crowd of spectators and turned north at the Foster Street intersection, leaving my view.

4. After the float with the dancing snowflakes passed by, I saw a man in a blue hooded sweatshirt drop a black duffle bag near the curb on the opposite side of the street.

5. The crowds along the sidewalk were somewhat smaller than usual, probably because of the very cold weather.

6. When I looked out the window again, there was a cloud of smoke in the street, and I could hear people screaming.

77. What is the most logical order of these statements?

(A) 5, 2, 3, 4, 1, 6

(B) 2, 5, 4, 3, 1, 6

(C) 4, 5, 3, 1, 2, 6

(D) 1, 2, 4, 6, 5, 3

Questions 78–80

Use the following charts to answer questions 78–80.

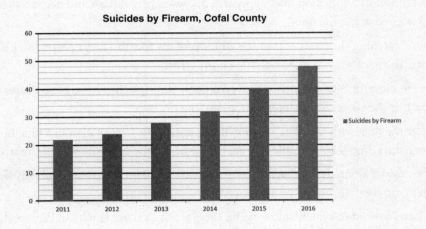

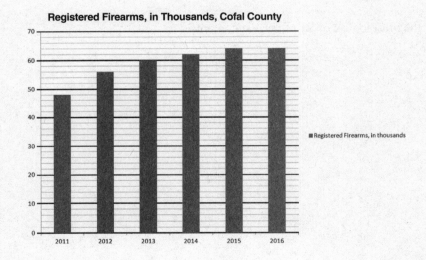

78. If the number of suicides by firearm increases by the same number as the previous two years, what will be the number of suicides by firearm in 2017?

    (A) 52

    (B) 56

    (C) 60

    (D) 64

79. How many suicides by firearm occurred in the same year that the number of firearms registrations first reached 60,000?

   (A) 22

   (B) 24

   (C) 28

   (D) 32

80. Which time span shows no increase in registered firearms in Cofal County?

   (A) 2010 to 2011

   (B) 2014 to 2015

   (C) 2015 to 2016

   (D) 2016 to present day

Questions 81–83

Read the descriptions of a duty an officer may be called upon to perform, and then select the best answer to the following questions.

A police officer may have to order a crowd to disperse in cases of unlawful assembly or instances where the crowd poses a safety hazard to themselves or others.

81. For which of the following should an officer issue an order for a crowd to disperse?

   (A) A group of sports fans is standing in the middle of a street, blocking traffic, celebrating their team's victory.

   (B) A group of protesters gathers on the sidewalk in front of City Hall to demand the mayor's resignation.

   (C) A group of picketers marches outside the entrance of a company headquarters building to call for higher wages.

   (D) A group of tourists follows a tour guide through the streets of downtown.

A police officer may be called upon to evacuate people from a dangerous area.

82. From which of the following should an officer evacuate people?

   (A) An office building with a broken heating system

   (B) A school conducting a fire drill

   (C) A sold-out rock concert delayed by rain

   (D) An office that has received a bomb threat

A police officer may be called upon to help mediate disputes between individuals.

83. Which of the following disputes would an officer be most likely to help mediate?

   (A) A disagreement between an employer and employee over job performance

   (B) A discussion between friends over where to eat dinner

   (C) A dispute between criminals over how to divide their drug profits

   (D) An argument between a cashier and a customer over whether an item was correctly paid for

Questions 84–86

Use the following passage to answer questions 84–86.

On September 21, 2017, at 6:38 p.m., Mr. Hari Reddy contacted the Bridgetown Police Department after he returned to his home at 538 Oakwood Lane to find that it had been burglarized. The front door was still locked, but the rear sliding glass door in the dining room was open and undamaged, despite being left closed and locked. The only missing items were taken from a wall safe in the victim's bedroom, which was concealed behind a large framed landscape print. The wall safe was opened without evidence of force. The stolen items included a large number of various gold coins valued at approximately $22,000 as well as an antique watch valued at $1,000. In the garage, a small window at the back of the building was broken. Mr. Reddy reported that the window had been intact when he left for work. No blood evidence was found among the broken glass.

84. Based only on the information provided, which of the following is most likely to be true?

   (A) There were several burglars working together.

   (B) The burglar was familiar with the Reddy home.

   (C) The burglar parked his getaway car on the next block over.

   (D) The burglar was in the house for at least 20 minutes.

85. Which of the following is the most likely route taken by the burglar through the house?

   (A) Dining room to master bedroom to garage

   (B) Master bedroom to garage to dining room

   (C) Back door to master bedroom to front door

   (D) Garage to master bedroom to dining room

86. Which of the following pieces of evidence would most likely incriminate the burglar?

(A) A match of a suspect's fingerprints to fingerprints found on the picture glass in the master bedroom

(B) A comparison of the garage door damage to similar damage in a previous burglary with a known suspect

(C) Transaction receipts indicating a suspect has recently sold a large quantity of gold coins to a local dealer

(D) A match between a suspect's car and a witness description of a strange car in the area just before the burglary

Questions 87–88

Read the short scenarios, and then select the best answer to the following questions.

The suspect first ran northbound on Spring Street, but was startled by a large group of people approaching. He turned around and doubled back toward the victim, running past the victim in the opposite direction for about a block, before turning to his left and disappearing around a corner.

87. According to this information, the suspect was last seen heading:

(A) north

(B) south

(C) east

(D) west

The suspect was observed by witnesses traveling eastbound on Travis Lane. The suspect then turned right at the corner of Fox Avenue, ran for two more blocks, and turned right again.

88. According to this information, the suspect was last seen heading:

(A) west

(B) north

(C) south

(D) east

Questions 89–91

For each question below, please choose the line that contains the misspelled word, grammatical error, or punctuation error by choosing the correct Roman numeral line number. Only one of the lines will contain an error.

89. I.   Officer Danko approached a group of youths standing near the entrance to the Dubois

    II. Corner Store. One of the youths, Andrew Hunter, fled to the south as Danko approached,

    III. leading the officer to engage in persuit. Hunter attempted to climb a chain-link fence on

    IV. Downey Street between Elm and Willow Lanes, but Danko was able to apprehend him.

    (A) Line I
    (B) Line II
    (C) Line III
    (D) Line IV

90. I.   Community outreach is an important part of police work. Officer Trevins visits local

    II. elementary schools and gives presentations about the dangers of drugs. Trevins is often

    III. later approached by teachers and students alike. Who tell her that her visits have made

    IV. a profound impact on the students. Many even say they want to become police officers!

    (A) Line I
    (B) Line II
    (C) Line III
    (D) Line IV

91. I.   According to several witnesses, a dark blue Mercedes turned right onto Hoover at a high

    II. rate of speed, and a passenger fired three shots at a crowd in front of the club before

    III. speeding away. Though no identification of the suspects could be made, several witnesses

    IV. indicated that the suspects was likely members of the Eighth Street Slayers, a local gang.

    (A) Line I
    (B) Line II
    (C) Line III
    (D) Line IV

Questions 92–93

Read the short traffic accident scenarios, and then choose the diagram that best answers the question.

Officer Mead responded to a traffic accident. According to a witness, the driver of a sedan (Vehicle #1) was traveling northbound on First Street and made a left turn onto Elm Road in front of a southbound bus (Vehicle #2), even though he was required to yield to oncoming traffic. Vehicle #2 struck Vehicle #1 on the passenger side of Vehicle #1's front end.

92. Which of the following diagrams accurately depicts the witness statement?

(A)

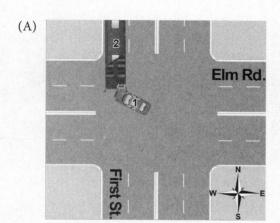

(C)

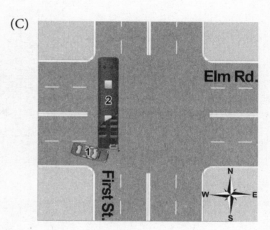

(B)

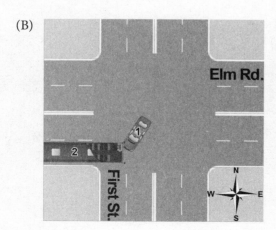

(D)

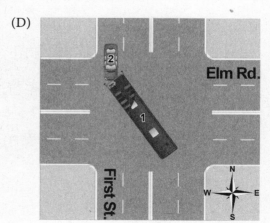

Officer Park responded to a traffic accident. According to a witness, the driver of a sedan (Vehicle 1) was facing eastbound on Dire Avenue, waiting to turn left onto Lemon Street. The driver of a hatchback (Vehicle #2), also eastbound on Dire Avenue, did not see that Vehicle #1 was stopped and rear-ended Vehicle #1. The collision pushed Vehicle #1 into oncoming traffic, where a station wagon (Vehicle #3) struck Vehicle #1 in the front end.

93. Which of the following diagrams accurately depicts the witness statement?

(A)

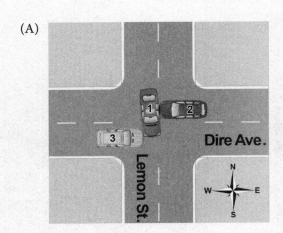

(C)

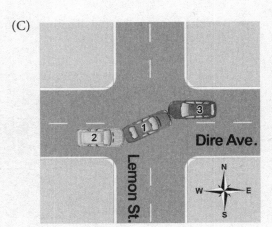

(B)

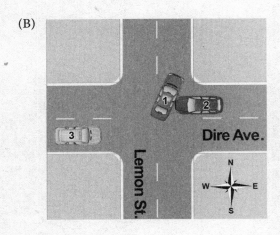

(D)

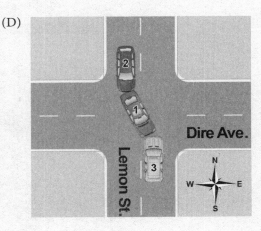

Questions 94–100

Read the short scenarios, and then select the best answer to the following questions.

Officer Curry observes that a great number of larcenies have been occurring in different sections of the area he patrols. He has determined that bicycles are stolen from the high-school quad, newspapers are stolen from the business district, and hats are stolen from the shopping district. Bicycles are stolen between 1:00 p.m. and 3:30 p.m., newspapers are stolen between 6:00 a.m. and 10:30 a.m., and hats are stolen between 10:00 a.m. and 4:00 p.m. Bicycles are stolen on Wednesdays and Fridays; newspapers on Mondays, Tuesdays, and Thursdays; and hats on Thursdays.

94. Based on the information provided, which of the following patrol schedules would enable Officer Curry to most effectively reduce the number of hats stolen?

   (A) The shopping district, Wednesdays and Fridays, 9:00 a.m. to 5:00 p.m.

   (B) The shopping district, Thursdays, 9:30 a.m. to 5:15 p.m.

   (C) The business district, Thursdays, 10:00 p.m. to 4:00 a.m.

   (D) The business district, weekdays, 10:00 a.m. to 4:00 p.m.

95. Based on the information provided, which of the following patrol schedules would be least effective in reducing the number of bicycles stolen?

   (A) The high-school quad, weekdays, 10:00 a.m. to noon

   (B) The high-school quad, weekdays, 10:00 a.m. to 4:00 p.m.

   (C) The high-school quad, Wednesdays and Fridays, noon to 4:00 p.m.

   (D) The high-school quad, Wednesdays and Fridays, 9:00 a.m. to 3:30 p.m.

Several burglaries were committed in the same four-block area over the course of a month. Based on descriptions of eyewitnesses, it is believed that the same person committed all of the burglaries. Officers are provided with the following description: Caucasian male with short-cropped brown hair, approximately 6 feet tall and 180 lb, with a deep scar on his left cheek.

96. Officer Shanks stops four males for questioning. Which one of the items of information provided by witnesses should Officer Shanks consider the most helpful in identifying the suspect?

   (A) The suspect is Caucasian.

   (B) The suspect is 6 feet tall.

   (C) The suspect has short-cropped brown hair.

   (D) The suspect has a deep scar on his left cheek.

Several assaults were committed around town over the course of a month. Based on descriptions of eyewitnesses, it is believed that the same person committed all of the assaults. Officers are provided with the following description: Asian male with long black hair in a ponytail, braces on his teeth, approximately five and a half feet tall and 130 lb, wearing tan cargo shorts.

97. Officer DeLeon stops four Asian males for questioning. Which one of the items of information provided by witnesses should Officer DeLeon consider the most helpful in identifying the suspect?

    (A) The suspect wears his hair in a ponytail.

    (B) The suspect has braces on his teeth.

    (C) The suspect weighs about 130 lb.

    (D) The suspect is wearing tan cargo shorts.

Several car thefts were committed around town over the course of a week. Based on descriptions of eyewitnesses, it is believed that the same person committed all of the thefts. Officers are provided with the following description: female with hair covered by a blue bandanna, approximately 5 feet tall and 120 lb, three piercings on her left eyebrow, wearing bright pink fingernail polish.

98. Officer Sparks stops four females for questioning. Which one of the items of information provided by witnesses should Officer Sparks consider the most helpful in identifying the suspect?

    (A) The suspect has three piercings on her left eyebrow.

    (B) The suspect's hair is covered by a blue bandana.

    (C) The suspect is approximately 5 feet tall.

    (D) The suspect is wearing bright pink fingernail polish.

Mrs. Hancock, who lives at 3075 Teak Street, returns home from taking her kids to school and finds her expensive brick mailbox broken and laying on her front lawn. She calls the police. When Officer Lee arrives, Mrs. Hancock shows him the damage and says she is certain that her neighbor's 20-year-old son, Ronnie Fielding, is guilty because he speeds around the neighborhood recklessly and has never held down a job.

Mrs. Hancock gives Officer Lee a description of Ronnie and tells him that Ronnie and his parents live around the corner, at 2828 Oak Drive, and that Ronnie drives a red Jeep with an obscene cartoon sticker on his rear bumper. Officer Lee writes down the information and calls in an alert for Ronnie Fielding and his vehicle. He then returns to the station house.

99. Officer Lee's actions were:

 (A) improper, because Officer Lee should have stayed around and asked Mrs. Hancock to list other neighbors with bad reputations

 (B) improper, because Officer Lee should have visited the Fielding residence in an attempt to question Ronnie as to whether or not he might have been involved

 (C) proper, because Mrs. Hancock's instincts were probably correct, since she knows her neighborhood, and Ronnie Fielding could cause more damage to personal property if a concentrated effort to apprehend him is not made

 (D) proper, because even if Ronnie Fielding is not guilty, Mrs. Hancock's suspicion is the only lead Officer Lee has, and he needs to get back to the precinct right away to type up his report

A speeding motorist, driving down a busy road in a shopping district, refuses to pull over, even after Officer Sandoval indicates by flashing lights and several amplified verbal announcements that the motorist should do so. Officer Sandoval leans out of his window and fires a shot at the motorist's left front tire.

100. Officer Sandoval's actions were:

 (A) proper, because the motorist is dangerous and should be stopped immediately

 (B) proper, because this will deter others from attempting to evade a pursuing officer in the future

 (C) improper, because his actions might have endangered the lives of innocent people on this busy stretch of road

 (D) improper, because Officer Sandoval should have taken a shot at the rear tire, which would stop the vehicle more safely

STOP

END OF EXAM

ANSWER KEY

1. B	26. D	51. B	76. D
2. C	27. C	52. B	77. B
3. A	28. B	53. A	78. B
4. D	29. C	54. C	79. C
5. B	30. A	55. D	80. C
6. C	31. B	56. C	81. A
7. A	32. C	57. B	82. D
8. C	33. D	58. A	83. D
9. D	34. A	59. B	84. B
10. D	35. D	60. D	85. D
11. C	36. C	61. A	86. A
12. B	37. D	62. C	87. C
13. B	38. A	63. D	88. A
14. C	39. C	64. A	89. C
15. C	40. B	65. C	90. C
16. D	41. A	66. B	91. D
17. B	42. B	67. B	92. A
18. D	43. D	68. A	93. C
19. B	44. C	69. C	94. B
20. A	45. A	70. D	95. A
21. B	46. A	71. B	96. D
22. D	47. D	72. D	97. B
23. C	48. C	73. A	98. A
24. B	49. B	74. A	99. B
25. A	50. D	75. C	100. C

ANSWERS AND EXPLANATIONS

1. B

Choice (B) is correct because the name of the store, Billie's Designer Fabrics, appears on two signs out front.

2. C

Choice (C) is correct because the phone number for the nail salon appears on the store's main sign and on a sandwich-board sign on the sidewalk.

3. A

Choice (A) is correct because a sign for "Wildtrout Gallery" appears on the marquee in front of the nail salon, with an arrow pointing up.

4. D

Choice (D) is correct because the phone number for the nail salon is (360) 748-6188.

5. B

Choice (B) is correct because there is one trash can in the photo.

6. C

Choice (C) is correct because, although all the items appear in the photo, the U.S. mail drop box is closest to the entrance to the fabric store.

7. A

Choice (A) is correct because the address listed for Orphic Property Management is 778 N. Market Blvd.

8. C

Choice (C) is correct because the word "Professional" does not appear on the "Space for Lease" sign.

9. D

Choice (D) is correct because Singer does not appear on the sign for the fabric store.

10. D

Choice (D) is correct because the sign reads "Up to 5,000 sq ft available."

11. C

Choice (C) is correct because, at a rate of three terminals per day, it would take (42 ÷ 3) days, or 14 days, to replace all the terminals.

12. B

Choice (B) is correct because $(3 \times 75) + (2 \times 80) + (4 \times 200) + (2 \times 150) = \$1,485$.

13. B

Choice (B) is correct because Officer Sanchez wrote 26 reports in week one, 13 reports in week two, 15 reports in week three, and 15 reports in week four. Therefore, $26 + 13 + 15 + 15 = 69$ reports.

14. C

Choice (C) is correct because the 350 feet is divided by 50 volunteers, leaving 7 feet between each volunteer ($350 \div 50 = 7$).

15. C

Choice (C) is correct because $400 + (2 \times 120) + 350 + 75 + (3 \times 60) = \$1,245$.

16. D

Choice (D) is correct because the coins in the machine at the beginning of the night had a total value of $65, and $8 in transactions occurred before the theft. So, $65 – $8 = $57 in coins taken.

17. B

Choice (B) is correct because there are 50 students in the first class, 35 students in the second class, 35 students in the third class, 40 students in the fourth class, and 45 students in the fifth class. So, $50 + 35 + 35 + 40 + 45 = 205$ students.

18. D

Choice (D) is correct because the total value of the 16 computers was $24,000, and $24,000 ÷ 16 = $1,500 per computer.

19. B

Choice (B) is correct because the total value of the items was $1,800, and the chargers and phone cases were valued at $200, so the total value of the phones was $1,600. This means each phone was valued at $1,600 ÷ 4 = $400.

20. A

Choice (A) is correct because an assailant is a person who attacks another person violently. A victim is the person who was attacked. A witness is a person who saw the attack. Finally, a critic is a person who expressed an opinion or judgment about the attack.

21. B

Choice (B) is correct because to "coerce" or "force" someone is to compel them, perhaps using violence, to testify. To "bribe" the witness is to offer him money or favors in return for his testimony. To "convince" him is to argue or reason with him, and to "assist" is to help or support him.

22. D

Choice (D) is correct because "deter" and "prevent" both mean "to discourage" or "stop" something from happening. "Facilitate" means "to make easier" or "help." To "solve" means "to find a solution." Finally, to "postpone" means "to delay."

23. C

Choice (C) is correct because "congregate" and "gather" both mean "to collect." To "disperse" means "to break up," and to "attack" means "to assail."

24. B

Choice (B) is correct because "estranged" and "separated" both mean "to be apart." To be "married" is to be legally joined in matrimony. To be "in hiding" means "to be out of sight." To be "abnormal" means "to be unusual."

25. A

Choice (A) is correct because both "hinder" and "block" mean "to slow or inhibit progress." "Facilitate" means "to help." "Direct" means "to instruct." "Observe" means "to watch."

26. D

Choice (D) is correct because both "adverse" and "negative" mean "harmful" or "disagreeable." An "unforeseen" effect is one that was not expected or anticipated. "Encouraging" means "inspiring or urging."

27. C

Choice (C) is correct because "ingest" and "swallow" both mean "to take in." To "sell" means "to trade for money." To "throw out" means "to discard." To "pocket" means "to keep or put away."

28. B

Choice (B) is correct because "ensuing" is the correctly spelled option.

29. C

Choice (C) is correct because "imperceptible" is the correctly spelled option.

30. A

Choice (A) is correct because "futile" is the correctly spelled option.

31. B

Choice (B) is correct because "confidential" is the correctly spelled option.

32. C

Choice (C) is correct because the subject of the sentence, "firearms," is plural, and therefore the verb must agree with the plural form.

33. D

Choice (D) is correct because the sentence requires a plural possessive, since the wallets belong to three different men.

34. A

Choice (A) is correct because a conjunction, "and," is required to join the two ideas in this sentence. Further, a comma is the correct punctuation before a conjunction, not a colon as in Choice (D).

35. D

Choice (D) is correct because the second half of the sentence explains why the suspect was questioned, making "because" the correct choice.

36. C

Choice (C) is correct because it best presents the information completely, clearly, and accurately, without redundant, unclear, or missing information. Choices (A) and (B) fail to mention the collapse happened in the morning (a.m.), and Choice (D) awkwardly states that the cars were "injured" rather than "damaged" or "destroyed," and doesn't state how many cars were affected.

37. D

Choice (D) is correct because it best presents the information completely, clearly, and accurately, without redundant, unclear, or missing information. Choice (A) doesn't state who reported the incident. Choices (B) and (C) present all of the information, but in a jumbled and confusing manner.

38. A

Choice (A) is correct because it best presents the information completely, clearly, and accurately, without redundant, unclear, or missing information. Choice (B) is repetitive and rambling. Choice (C) leaves out too much information, such as Mr. Sanderson's collapse and the arrival of the ambulance. Choice (D) confuses the timeline of events.

39. C

Choice (C) is correct because it best presents the information completely, clearly, and accurately, without redundant, unclear, or missing information. Choice (A) fails to mention the location of the incident. Choice (B) doesn't explain that the leak was fixed, and Choice (D) doesn't link Ms. Oak's apartment to Bear Village Apartments.

40. B

Choice (B) is correct because it best presents the information completely, clearly, and accurately, without redundant, unclear, or missing information. Choice (A) is repetitive, mentioning Mr. Singh, the woman, and the attempted sale multiple times. Choice (C) doesn't mention the location or the description of the woman ("40-year-old"). Choice (D) describes the woman twice and never mentions Mr. Singh is the person reporting the incident.

41. A

Choice (A) is correct because it best presents the information completely, clearly, and accurately, without redundant, unclear, or missing information. Choice (B) doesn't explain why the judo practice alarmed Mr. Lee or mention the time of the incident. Choice (C) is rambling and doesn't mention the outcome: that no action was taken. Choice (D) is also rambling but, more importantly, never mentions the time of the incident.

42. B

Choice (B) is correct because it best presents the information completely, clearly, and accurately, without redundant, unclear, or missing information. Choice (A) doesn't mention that Reggie was taken to the hospital or even the existence of Hanna Reynolds. Choice (C) confuses Reggie and Hanna's ages, contains poor punctuation, and also never mentions the hospital. It also makes Hanna providing the phone number the subject of the sentence, and not poor Reggie. Choice (D) makes it sound like Reggie's parents were stung by bees, also confusing the subject.

43. D

Choice (D) is correct because it best presents the information completely, clearly, and accurately, without redundant, unclear, or missing information. Choice (A) doesn't name Geri Budd as the witness. Choice (B) makes Ms. Budd the subject and doesn't properly name Mrs. Hersch. Choice (C) is concise and includes all of the information, but it's written awkwardly and presents the events out of order. Further, none of these choices state who reported the incident to the police.

44. C

Choice (C) is correct because the passage describes him as one of the "other residents of the floor."

45. A

Choice (A) is correct because the suspect was arrested three days after the second burglary, which occurred on December 6.

46. A

Choice (A) is correct because the passage states that "the lock on her apartment door had been stuffed with chewing gum."

47. D

Choice (D) is correct because the passage states that Pierre Toulouse had been "driving his Ford Taurus northbound on Cavalcade."

48. C

Choice (C) is correct because the passage states that the driver had been traveling "northbound on Cavalcade."

49. B

Choice (B) is correct because, although they are witnesses, Augustin Lantos "did not see the collision," and Ben Klein's "view of the collision was blocked by parked cars."

50. D

Choice (D) is correct because it is the only shape found in the design.

51. B

Choice (B) is correct because it is the only shape found in the design.

52. B

Choice (B) is correct because it is the only shape found in the design.

53. A

Choice (A) is correct because it is the only shape found in the design.

54. C

Choice (C) is correct because it is the only shape found in the design.

55. D

Choice (D) is correct because it is the only shape found in the design.

56. C

Choice (C) is correct because it provides the shortest distance route to the destination.

57. B

Choice (B) is correct because it provides the shortest distance route to the destination.

58. A

Choice (A) is correct because it provides the shortest distance route to the destination.

59. B

Choice (B) is correct because it provides the shortest distance route to the destination.

60. D

Choice (D) is correct because it provides the shortest distance route to the destination. Note that because the area has a number of one-way streets, a direct route to the incident is not possible.

61. A

Choice (A) is correct because the suspect traveled three blocks along West 28th Street, which put him at the intersection of West 28th and South Springfield Avenue. He then turned left and proceeded southbound on South Springfield Avenue for two more blocks, which put him at South Springfield and West 31st Street when the trail was lost.

62. C

Choice (C) is correct because it meets all the parameters of the crime, while the others do not. The man in Choice (A) only damages one car, and two or more are required for auto stripping in the second degree. The woman in Choice (B) damages two vehicles, but the damage only amounts to $800, not the required $1,000. The man in Choice (D) causes far too much damage to be auto stripping in the second degree. His crime is in the first degree.

63. D

Choice (D) is correct because it meets all the parameters of the crime, while the others do not. Although the woman in Choice (A) commits a felony (illegal gambling), she is using her personal computer. The man's actions in Choice (B) are immoral, but he has no intent to commit a felony, he has not altered any material, and he has not destroyed any data or programs resulting in $1,000 in damages. Finally, the man in Choice (C) made a mistake and caused more than $1,500 in damage, but he accessed the computer with permission. Only the woman in Choice (D) accessed the computer without permission, altered or destroyed data, and caused over $1,000 in damages.

64. A

Choice (A) is correct because it does not meet the parameters of the crime, while the others do. The man is responsible for the borrowed camera, and he is being unfair in refusing to repay his friend, but he has not committed grand larceny.

65. C

Choice (C) is correct because it does not meet the parameters of the crime, while the others do. While the woman's performance may be annoying to passersby, it is not threatening, does not create a noise nuisance, does not disturb anyone else from assembling, and does not impede traffic.

66. B

Choice (B) is correct because it meets all the parameters of the crime, while the others do not. The man in Choice (A) is not gambling in a public place. The woman in Choice (C) is not selling anything or trying to earn money at the train station. The man in Choice (D) has a "legitimate purpose" for being on school grounds.

67. B

Choice (B) is correct because it is the only face that exactly matches the original face. Choice (A) has the wrong hairline. Choice (C) has a more defined and sharp brow. Choice (D) has a slightly narrower and less bulbous nose.

68. A

Choice (A) is correct because it is the only face that exactly matches the original face, aside from the hairstyle. Choice (B) has different eyes and a narrower mouth. Choice (C) has a rounder nose and fuller lips. Choice (D) has smaller eyes and a more upturned nose.

69. C

Choice (C) is correct because it is the only face that exactly matches the original face, aside from the facial hair. Choice (A) has a narrower nose. Choice (B) has a downturned mouth and bigger eyes. Choice (D) has thicker brows, bigger eyes, and a more elongated nose.

70. D

Choice (D) is correct because it is the only face that exactly matches the original face. Choice (A) has smaller eyes. Choice (B) has a different hairline. Choice (C) has a longer, downturned nose.

71. B

Choice (B) is correct because it is the only option that exactly matches the original. Choice (A) transposes the "O" and "0." Choice (C) has two "m's" instead of two "n's." Choice (D) reads "Wwv" instead of "Wvv."

72. D

Choice (D) is correct because it is the only option that exactly matches the original. Choice (A) has a "d" in place of the second "b." Choice (B) has a "{" in place of the "[." Choice (C) reads "coo" instead of "cco."

73. A

Choice (A) is correct because it is the only option that exactly matches the original. Choice (B) transposes the "l" and the "i." Choice (C) transposes the ">" and the "<." Choice (D) replaces the "$" with an "S."

74. A

Choice (A) is correct because it is the only option that exactly matches the original. Choice (B) replaces the comma with a semicolon. Choice (C) replaces the "O" with a "0." Choice (D) transposes the "W" and "V."

75. C

Choice (C) is correct because it presents events in the most logical order. Choice (A) describes the woman appearing and demanding the victim's phone (5) before she approaches the victim (6). Choice (B) describes the victim running to tell a gym employee (2) that a woman asked to use his phone (6). Choice (D) describes the woman approaching to ask for the phone (6) while the victim is already being mugged at knifepoint (1).

76. D

Choice (D) is correct because it presents events in the most logical order. Choice (A) describes the witness talking to Melissa (1) after she's already been pushed into the car (6). Choice (B) describes the witness talking to Melissa (1) before we know when or where we are (2). Choice (C) describes the witness texting Melissa out of concern (3) before even speaking to her or witnessing the argument (1).

77. B

Choice (B) is correct because it presents events in the most logical order. Choice (A) describes the crowds (5) before we know where the witness is (2). Choice (C) doesn't tell us where the witness is until after the bombing occurs. Choice (D) has the bomb go off (1) before the man in the blue hooded sweatshirt drops it off (4).

78. B

Choice (B) is correct because the number of suicides by firearm increased by 8 in 2015 (to 40) and by 8 again in 2016 (to 48). An increase by the same number would result in 56 suicides by firearm in 2017.

79. C

Choice (C) is correct because firearms registrations first reached 60,000 in 2013, and that same year, there were 28 suicides by firearm.

80. C

Choice (C) is correct because the only time span that shows no increase in registered firearms is 2015 to 2016; data before 2011 and after 2016 is not shown. In 2014 to 2015, there is an increase of firearms by 2,000.

81. A

Choice (A) is correct because the group of sports fans poses a safety hazard by standing in the street and blocking traffic. The protesters, picketers, and tour group are all examples of lawful assembly.

82. D

Choice (D) is correct because only the bomb threat poses an immediate threat requiring evacuation.

83. D

Choice (D) is correct because it is the dispute that a police officer would most likely help mediate. This situation could potentially escalate and would benefit from an impartial third party.

84. B

Choice (B) is correct because the burglar only stole items from a wall safe that was locked and hidden from view. It is most likely that the burglar was already familiar with the Reddy home.

85. D

Choice (D) is correct because the garage was the only location that showed any sign of forced entry; therefore, it is the most likely entry point for the burglar. The burglar would then have stolen the items from the master bedroom before leaving out the sliding door in the dining room without causing any further damage.

86. A

Choice (A) is correct because fingerprints on the picture glass in the bedroom would place the suspect at the scene of the crime. Choices (B) and (C) could simply be coincidental, and Choice (D) is not firm evidence. Just because the suspect has a car seen in the area does not mean she or he is the burglar.

87. C

Choice (C) is correct because the suspect originally headed north but turned and ran back toward the victim. At this point, he was heading south, and then turned to his left, or east.

88. A

Choice (A) is correct because the suspect was originally heading east. He then turned right, or south, and turned right again, or west.

89. C

Choice (C) is correct because in Line III, the word "pursuit" is misspelled.

90. C

Choice (C) is correct because in Line III, a sentence is fragmented by the incorrect use of a period.

91. D

Choice (D) is correct because in Line IV, the verb "was" does not match the plural noun "suspects," and is therefore incorrect.

92. A

Choice (A) is correct because it most accurately illustrates the witness's account of the accident. Choice (B) depicts Vehicle #1 traveling southbound on First Street rather than northbound and making a right turn instead of a left. Choice (C) depicts Vehicle #1 making a right turn onto First Street from Elm Road. Choice (D) mislabels Vehicle #1 and Vehicle #2.

93. C

Choice (C) is correct because it most accurately illustrates the witness's account of the accident. Choice (A) depicts Vehicle #1 traveling southbound on Lemon Street instead of waiting on Dire Avenue. Choice (B) depicts Vehicle #1 traveling northbound on Lemon Street. Choice (D) depicts Vehicle #1 traveling southbound on Lemon Street.

94. B

Choice (B) is correct because hats are only stolen in the shopping district, and only on Thursdays.

95. A

Choice (A) is correct because bicycles are stolen between 1:00 p.m. and 3:30 p.m., making a patrol from 10:00 a.m. until noon the least effective.

96. D

Choice (D) is correct because a deep scar on the cheek is unusual and difficult to hide or change.

97. B

Choice (B) is correct because braces are uncommon and would be difficult to hide or change.

98. A

Choice (A) is correct because eyebrow piercings are unusual and would be difficult to hide or change.

99. B

Choice (B) is correct because the officer did not investigate the crime sufficiently to identify Ronnie Fielding as the perpetrator.

100. C

Choice (C) is correct because Officer Sandoval unnecessarily endangered the lives of innocent people by discharging his firearm.

Practice Exam 2

POLICE EXAM
Time—2 hours
Number of questions—100

A CALCULATOR MAY NOT BE USED ON THIS EXAM.

Directions: Choose the ONE best answer for each question.

Questions 1–10

Study the photograph very carefully for five minutes. You will be asked 10 detailed questions about this image. Once you have finished looking at this photograph, you will not be able to look back at it again.

1. What services does the laundromat advertise on its awning?

   (A) Coin-Op - Dry Cleaners - Wash & Fold

   (B) Dry Cleaners - Linen Service - Free Delivery

   (C) Dry Cleaners - Drop Off - Self Service

   (D) Coin-Op - Self Service - Drop Off

2. Of the three cars parked next to each other on the street, which one has an open window?

   (A) The car in front.

   (B) The car in the middle.

   (C) The car in back.

   (D) None of the three cars has an open window.

3. How many parking regulation signs are visible on the block?

   (A) Zero

   (B) One

   (C) Two

   (D) Three

4. Why is there bunting above one of the storefronts on the street?

   (A) It is there to advertise a block party.

   (B) One of the stores is having a Grand Opening.

   (C) One of the stores is having a Fourth of July sale.

   (D) One of the stores is hosting a birthday party.

5. What is the name of the second store in from the street corner?

   (A) Farmacia

   (B) Comercial Mexicana

   (C) La Paz

   (D) La Plaza

6. A person descending the only visible fire escape in the photograph would end up in front of which store?

   (A) La Plaza

   (B) Laundromat

   (C) Pagos Express

   (D) The corner pharmacy

7. Which of the following most accurately describes the people standing on the corner by a vehicle?

   (A) One adult woman and a child

   (B) One adult woman and two children

   (C) Two adult women and a child

   (D) Two adult women and two children

8. What is the largest number of satellite dishes in any one apartment window?

   (A) One

   (B) Two

   (C) Three

   (D) Four

9. How many second-story windows are open?

   (A) Zero

   (B) One

   (C) Two

   (D) Three

10. Which store is advertising an ATM?

    (A) Pagos Express

    (B) Laundromat

    (C) Deli Grocery Comercial Mexicana

    (D) La Plaza

Questions 11–19

Read the short scenarios, and then select the best answer to the following questions.

11. A busy urban toll bridge receives an average of about 36,000 paid crossings each weekday morning during the rush hour period between 7:00 a.m. and 9:00 a.m. Approximately how many vehicles enter the bridge per minute during the morning rush?

    (A) 60

    (B) 180

    (C) 300

    (D) 600

12. Authorities are tracking a vehicle headed west along the interstate highway. The automobile travels 216 miles in the course of four hours. If the vehicle maintains its same rate, how far will it have gone after six hours?

    (A) 288

    (B) 324

    (C) 348

    (D) 384

13. A local bank branch reported the disappearance of 5% of its total daily income on February 18. An investigation revealed that Kim Fein, a teller at the branch, made a deposit of $725 into her own account that afternoon. The deposit would appear to implicate Fein in possible embezzlement, especially because the bank branch's receipts for the day totaled:

    (A) $1,450

    (B) $7,250

    (C) $14,500

    (D) $21,750

14. How much alcohol is there in a 40-ounce bottle of malt liquor, if its ratio of alcohol by volume (ABV) is 6%?

    (A) 0.64 oz

    (B) 1.6 oz

    (C) 2.0 oz

    (D) 2.4 oz

15. William's gross pay for the month of April was $2,916.66. After deductions of $447.25 for federal tax withholding, $223.12 for FICA, and $81.66 for state and local taxes, what was William's take-home pay?

    (A) $2,164.63

    (B) $2,246.29

    (C) $2,327.95

    (D) $2,469.41

16. Pacific standard time (PST) in Los Angeles is three hours earlier than Eastern Standard Time (EST) in New York. A plane leaves Los Angeles at 5:30 p.m. PST and arrives in New York City at 12:45 a.m. EST. How long did the flight take?

    (A) 4 hours, 15 minutes

    (B) 4 hours, 45 minutes

    (C) 6 hours, 45 minutes

    (D) 7 hours, 15 minutes

17. A fruit vendor purchased six 40-pound boxes of peaches for $45 per box. The fruit inside one of the boxes was moldy and had to be discarded. In order to meet his target profit of 10% above cost, at what price per pound would he need to sell the remaining peaches?

    (A) $0.75

    (B) $1.25

    (C) $1.50

    (D) $1.75

18. In one jurisdiction in Massachusetts, speeding ticket fines are assessed at a rate determined, in part by the recorded speed. A base rate of $75 is assessed for the initial 10 miles per hour (mph) above the posted speed limit. Each additional mile per hour is assessed at $12.50. For a motorist caught driving at 72 mph in a 55 mph zone, what would be the amount of the assessed fine?

    (A) $112.50

    (B) $150.00

    (C) $162.50

    (D) $212.50

19. In 2010, the population of town A was 9,400 and the population of town B was 7,600. In every year since 2010, the population of town A decreased by 100 and the population of town B increased by 100. Assuming that in each case the rate continues, in what year will the two populations be equal?

    (A) 2019

    (B) 2020

    (C) 2027

    (D) 2028

Questions 20–27

In each of the following sentences, choose the word or phrase that most nearly has the same meaning as the underlined word.

20. A man was charged with <u>fabricating</u> title documents in order to gain possession of a residence.

    (A) constructing

    (B) falsifying

    (C) issuing

    (D) forging

21. The presence of police in uniform appeared to <u>augment</u> the tensions in the auditorium.

    (A) mollify

    (B) replicate

    (C) exacerbate

    (D) polarize

22. An expert witness was brought in to <u>authenticate</u> the claims made by the defendant.

    (A) reconcile

    (B) verify

    (C) elucidate

    (D) implicate

23. A Yemeni <u>national</u> was briefly detained by airport officials.

    (A) official

    (B) partisan

    (C) citizen

    (D) ethnic

24. The suspect proved <u>intractable</u> under intensive questioning.

    (A) undisciplined

    (B) uncooperative

    (C) irrational

    (D) pliable

25. Warren said the dispute was a result of his neighbor's <u>belligerent</u> nature.

    (A) stubborn

    (B) boisterous

    (C) impassioned

    (D) argumentative

26. The district attorney argued that the coworker's testimony was <u>immaterial</u> to the case for the prosecution.

    (A) irrelevant

    (B) intangible

    (C) indispensable

    (D) circumstantial

27. Investigators were looking into the <u>source</u> of the stolen artifacts.

    (A) progeny

    (B) propinquity

    (C) provenance

    (D) predecessor

Questions 28–35

In the following sentences, choose the correct option to fill in the blank for each sentence.

28. The two officers _____ the suspect on foot.

    (A) persued

    (B) purcued

    (C) pursued

    (D) persood

29. Yolanda Sanchez reported that several valuable items _____ from her residence.

    (A) stolen

    (B) been stolen

    (C) had been stolen

    (D) are stolen

30. Dwight Jackson and his girlfriend _____ they saw their neighbor return to the building around 10:30 in the evening.

    (A) claims

    (B) claim

    (C) claiming

    (D) is claiming

31. If a motorist is driving erratically, there is a high _____ the individual is under the influence of drugs or alcohol.

    (A) probbability

    (B) probabillity

    (C) probabbility

    (D) probability

32. The _____ mother worked at Fairchild Elementary School.

   (A) child

   (B) childs

   (C) child's

   (D) childs'

33. Before reporting the item as missing, Mrs. Rogers searched the apartment, _____ the contents of her handbag, and telephoned her daughter to question her.

   (A) empty

   (B) emptied

   (C) empties

   (D) emptying

34. It appears the handgun was not in the hand of _____ owner at the time the crime was committed.

   (A) its

   (B) it's

   (C) their

   (D) an

35. The tall man _____ a black fedora hat.

   (A) with

   (B) in

   (C) wearing

   (D) was wearing

Questions 36–43

Read the short scenarios, and then select the best answer to the following questions.

Officer Holmes reports to the scene of a fire. He gathers the following information:

Location: 1515 Armory Boulevard

Time: 11:00 p.m.

Incident: Fire destroyed one floor of an office building.

Injuries: none, building was empty

Cause of Fire: under investigation; faulty wiring is suspected

36. Officer Holmes is writing a report on the incident. Which of the following expresses the information most clearly and accurately?

(A) At 11:00 p.m., a fire caused by faulty wiring destroyed one floor of an office building at 1515 Armory Boulevard. The building was empty, so no one was injured.

(B) Faulty wiring is suspected in a fire that destroyed one floor of an office building at 1515 Armory Boulevard. The cause of the fire, that injured no one, is under investigation.

(C) At 11:00 p.m. at 1515 Armory Boulevard, one floor of an office building was destroyed by a fire whose cause, which is under investigation, is suspected to have been faulty wiring. The building was empty, and no one was injured.

(D) Faulty wiring may have caused the fire at 11:00 p.m. at 1515 Armory Boulevard that injured no one because the office building was empty. Officially, the cause is under investigation.

Officer Barghouti was dispatched to the scene of an explosion, where she gathered the following information:

Location:	Fountain Park
Time:	3:00 p.m.
Incident:	A fountain exploded.
Injuries:	Three people were hospitalized.
Witness:	Mr. Barber saw a tall man wearing blue jeans place a small box in the water a few minutes before the explosion.
Status of Suspect:	left the park on foot; current location unknown

37. Officer Barghouti must write her report. Which of the following expresses the information most clearly and accurately?

(A) At 3:00 p.m., a fountain exploded. Three people were injured and hospitalized. Mr. Barber stated that he saw a tall man place a small box in the water a few minutes before the explosion. The suspect then left the park on foot; his current location is unknown.

(B) An explosion in a fountain at Fountain Park was reported at 3:00 p.m. Three people were injured and hospitalized. A witness, Mr. Barber, stated that he saw a tall man wearing blue jeans place a small box in the water a few minutes before the explosion. The suspect left the park on foot; his current location is unknown.

(C) Three people were injured and hospitalized as a result of an explosion at Fountain Park, just before which a tall man wearing blue jeans placed a small box in the water, according to Mr. Barber. The suspect's current location is unknown.

(D) At 3:00 p.m., three people were injured and hospitalized after a fountain at Fountain Park exploded, which happened just a few minutes after a tall man wearing blue jeans placed a small box in the water, according to a witness. The suspect then left the park on foot.

Practice Exam 2

Officer Seymour responded to a report of an underage driver and gathered the following information:

Location:	Castle Island subdivision
Time:	4:15 p.m.
Police Contacted By:	Dr. Ronald, a resident
Incident:	A child was seen driving a yellow convertible through the neighborhood.
Action Taken:	The child and vehicle were not found.

38. Officer Seymour is writing his report. Which of the following expresses the information most clearly and accurately?

    (A) At 4:15 p.m., Dr. Ronald, a resident of Castle Island subdivision, reported seeing a child driving a yellow convertible through the neighborhood. The child and vehicle in question were not found.

    (B) Dr. Ronald, a Castle Island resident, reported seeing a child driving a yellow convertible through the neighborhood. The time that Dr. Ronald reported this was at 4:15 p.m. The child and vehicle in question, as described by Dr. Ronald, were not found.

    (C) In Castle Island subdivision, Dr. Ronald, a resident, reported seeing a child driving a yellow convertible through the neighborhood. The car and child were not found.

    (D) A child driving a convertible through Castle Island subdivision was reported by Dr. Ronald, a resident there, at 4:15 p.m. The child was not found who was reported to have been doing the driving.

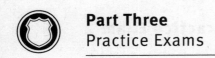

Officer Schofield responds to a report of a robbery and gathers the following information:

Location: Anderson Arms Apartments, manager's office

Time: 5:00 p.m.

Incident: Victim was robbed at knifepoint.

Victim: Henry Anderson, assistant manager

Amount Stolen: $3,000 from the office's petty cash drawer

Suspect: short female wearing black coveralls

39. Officer Schofield must write her report. Which of the following expresses the information most clearly and accurately?

(A) Henry Anderson stated that at 5:00 at the manager's office at Anderson Arms Apartments, where he is assistant manager, he was robbed at knifepoint by a short female wearing black coveralls, who stole $3,000 from the office's petty cash drawer.

(B) Henry Anderson stated that at 5:00 p.m. at the manager's office at Anderson Arms Apartments, where he is the assistant manager, he was robbed at knifepoint by a short female wearing black coveralls, who stole $3,000 from the office's petty cash drawer.

(C) Henry Anderson stated that at 5:00 p.m. at the manager's office at Anderson Arms Apartments, he was robbed at knifepoint by a short female wearing black coveralls, who stole $3,000 from the office petty cash drawer.

(D) Henry Anderson stated that at 5:00 p.m. at the manager's office at Anderson Arms Apartments, where he is the assistant manager, he was robbed by a short female wearing black coveralls, who stole $3,000 from the office's petty cash drawer.

Officer Chimimanda was sent to investigate a report of an aggressive stray dog and gathered the following information:

Location:	Big Movies' parking lot
Time:	1:30 p.m.
Incident:	An aggressive stray dog was seen there.
Police Contacted By:	Ralph Miller, an employee
Action Taken:	Animal was found and animal control was notified.

40. Officer Chimimanda is writing his report. Which of the following expresses the information most clearly and accurately?

(A) Ralph Miller reported seeing an aggressive stray dog in the parking lot of Big Movies, where he works. The animal was found and animal control was notified.

(B) At 1:30 p.m., Ralph Miller reported seeing a stray dog in the parking lot of Big Movies, where he works. The animal was found and animal control was notified.

(C) Ralph Miller reported at 1:30 p.m. that he had seen an aggressive stray dog in the parking lot of Big Movies. The animal was found.

(D) At 1:30 p.m., Ralph Miller reported seeing an aggressive stray dog in the parking lot of Big Movies, where he works. The animal was found and animal control was notified.

Officer Gupta arrived at the scene of an auto accident, where she gathered the following information:

Location:	corner of Hickory Street and First Avenue
Time:	5:00 p.m.
Driver and Vehicle:	Mr. Rasmussen, driving a white Ford minivan
Incident:	A falling rock crashed through Mr. Rasmussen's windshield, causing him to drive off the road into a ditch.
Injuries:	Mr. Rasmussen suffered cuts and bruises.

41. Officer Gupta is writing her report. Which of the following expresses the information most clearly and accurately?

   (A) Mr. Rasmussen stated that at 5:00 p.m., at the corner of Hickory Street and First Avenue, a falling rock crashed through the windshield of his white Ford minivan, causing him to drive off the road into a ditch. He suffered cuts and bruises.

   (B) At 5:00 p.m., a falling rock crashed through the window of Mr. Rasmussen's white Ford minivan, causing him to drive off the road into a ditch and causing him to suffer cuts and bruises.

   (C) At the corner of Hickory Street and First Avenue, a falling rock crashed through the windshield of the white minivan being driven by Mr. Rasmussen, who suffered cuts and bruises. As a result, Mr. Rasmussen drove off the road into a ditch.

   (D) A falling rock crashed through his windshield, according to Mr. Rasmussen, at 5:00 p.m., causing him to drive off the road into a ditch in his white Ford minivan and giving him, as a result, cuts and bruises. This was at the corner of Hickory Street with First Avenue.

Officer Cassel responded to a report of a dispute. He gathered the following information:

Location:	Dizzy's Vintage Records
Time:	3:15 p.m.
Police Contacted By:	Dizzy Smith, owner
Incident:	Two customers were fighting over a record.
Action Taken:	Customers were removed from the store.

42. Officer Cassel is writing his report. Which of the following expresses the information most clearly and accurately?

(A) Dizzy Smith's Dizzy's Vintage Records was the scene of two customers fighting over a record who were, after it was reported at 3:15 p.m., ejected from the store, Dizzy's Vintage Records.

(B) At 3:15 p.m., two customers' fighting, over a record, was reported by Dizzy Smith, the owner of Dizzy's Vintage Records, where the fight was. The customers who were doing the said fighting were kicked out of the store.

(C) Dizzy Smith reported at 3:15 that his store, Dizzy's Vintage Records, was where two customers were fighting over a record who were later removed from the store after he reported the fight.

(D) At 3:15 p.m., Dizzy Smith reported that two customers were fighting over a record at Dizzy's Vintage Records, which he owns. The customers were removed from the store.

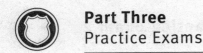

Officer Welch was dispatched to the scene of a reported assault, where she gathered the following information:

Location:	Puente Real Estate Agency
Time:	6:00 p.m.
Police Contacted By:	Ellie Puente, owner
Incident:	A prospective renter struck real estate agent John Sears in the face.
Injury:	black eye
Suspect:	Cary Kearns
Location of Suspect:	unknown

43. Officer Welch is writing her report. Which of the following expresses the information most clearly and accurately?

(A) At Puente Real Estate Agency, which Ellie Puente owns, and where she reported the incident, a prospective renter named Cary Kearns struck real estate agent John Sears. He, Mr. Sears, was struck in the face, causing him to end up with a black eye. The suspect's location is unknown.

(B) At 6:00 p.m. at Puente Real Estate Agency, a prospective renter named Cary Kearns, whose location is unknown now, struck real estate agent John Sears in the face. This was reported by Ellie Puente, who happens to own Puente Real Estate, where it happened and which employs Mr. Sears as the real estate agent who suffered a black eye. The suspect's location is unknown.

(C) Ellie Puente reported that at 6:00 p.m. at Puente Real Estate Agency, which she owns, a prospective renter named Cary Kearns struck real estate agent John Sears in the face. Mr. Sears suffered a black eye. The suspect's location is unknown.

(D) Ellie Puente reported that at 6:00 p.m. at Puente Real Estate Agency, which she owns, a perspective renter named Cary Kearns, whose location is unknown, struck tenant John Sears in the face. Mr. Sears suffered a black eye.

Questions 44–46

To answer questions 44–46, use the information in the following passage.

Police Officers Nunez and Vasquez were dispatched to the Downtown Cellular mobile phone store at 1453 Eastern Boulevard, where an assault and robbery had taken place several minutes earlier. Arriving at 4:20 p.m., the officers found the store in disarray with broken glass on the floor and display cases damaged. They proceeded to interview the store's owner, Ahmed Mahmoud. He said he was managing the store with his brother, Rafik, when two young men entered the shop seeking to sell a mobile device. The young men became enraged, Mahmoud said, after being told the business did not purchase cell phones. A female customer was in the store at the time, Mahmoud said, and the two suspects began directing hostile comments at her. One of them eventually grabbed the woman by the arm, prompting Rafik Mahmoud to order both young men out of the shop immediately.

According to Ahmed Mahmoud's account, as the two suspects neared the door, one of them produced a switchblade and attempted to stab Rafik in the gut. He blocked the thrust of the knife, according to his brother, but in doing so received a stab wound to the left hand. Rafik Mahmoud and the two suspects continued grappling outside on the street. Moments later, the proprietor saw the young men re-enter the shop holding a brick that may have been lying in the street. They proceeded to smash several glass cases and shelves and exit with a number of mobile phones worth a total of more than $1,000.

Lashawn Richards approached Officer Nunez while the two officers were questioning the store owner. She said she had been in the salon next door to Downtown Cellular when the incident took place and came outside to investigate the commotion. She heard the two young men yelling to a third person sitting in a parked car on the other side of the boulevard. Richards managed to take a picture of the suspects on her mobile phone. She then ducked back into the salon for her safety, she said. She watched the suspects run past the salon's window as they fled the scene on foot. The vehicle whose driver they had spoken to, a blue sport utility vehicle, drove away at the same time, she said. The officers arrived approximately 10 minutes later by Richards's estimate.

At 5:25 p.m., the two officers heard over the radio that two adolescent suspects had been detained in connection with a robbery at a cell phone outlet.

44. At about what time did the two suspects enter Downtown Cellular?

    (A) 3:15 p.m.

    (B) 4:00 p.m.

    (C) 4:20 p.m.

    (D) 5:25 p.m.

45. According to his brother's account, why did Rafik Mahmoud attempt to evict the two suspects from the store?

    (A) The young men were angry that the proprietors didn't want to buy their mobile phone.

    (B) One of them stabbed Mahmoud in the hand.

    (C) One of them grabbed a female customer inside the store.

    (D) Both of them threatened Lashawn Richards.

46. Based on the information provided, which of the following people is most likely an accomplice to the crime?

    (A) Rafik Mahmoud

    (B) Lashawn Richards

    (C) The woman in the phone store

    (D) The driver of the blue sport utility vehicle

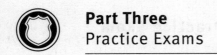
Practice Exam 2

Questions 47–49

To answer questions 47–49, use the information in the following passage.

The majority of domestic abuse victims are women, but women can also be perpetrators of violence against intimate partners. A more common scenario is for men to accuse their female partners of verbal or psychological abuse. However, in some cases these domestic disputes cross the line from words to physical confrontation. Women in quarrels with a spouse or lover may use a weapon either to defend themselves or to threaten harm against their partner. Men are often too embarrassed to report instances in which they have been battered by a female partner.

Officers Bryant Porter and Marlene Martinez responded on a recent Thursday to a call related to a domestic dispute at 504 Monroe Road. A neighbor, Mrs. Renee Erickson of 506 Monroe Road, had placed the call at 5:13 p.m., saying she heard a loud argument and the sound of breaking glass from the adjacent row house. No such sounds were audible as the officers approached the house. Carolina Fuentes answered the door. Her pink blouse had several small but visible blood stains. Stepping inside, the officers found a great deal of broken glass.

After a moment, the Mrs. Fuentes' husband, Bernardo Fuentes, emerged from the bathroom, wearing a white undershirt, khaki slacks with a brown leather belt, and brown loafers. He was pressing a towel against his temple to stanch the flow of blood, and several small puncture wounds were visible on his neck.

At first, Mr. Fuentes denied that his wife had caused these injuries, but Mrs. Fuentes admitted coming at him while holding the neck of a broken bottle. The woman explained that the couple had been in a heated argument about money and overdue bills. Mr. Fuentes, she said, had smashed a coffee mug and two empty liquor bottles onto the floor of the couple's living room. At that point, Mrs. Fuentes said, she picked up a broken bottle by the neck and threatened him with it.

"I told her to put it down," her husband interjected, "and went over to take it from her." Both parties affirmed that Mrs. Fuentes struck her husband with the glass while the pair struggled. Officer Martinez asked the woman whether her husband had tried to injure her during the altercation. "No, ma'am," she said. "He tried to stop me, but I was too strong and too mad." Officer Martinez then handcuffed Mrs. Fuentes and placed her under arrest for misdemeanor domestic battery.

47. Who called the police to report this domestic dispute?

(A) Marlene Martinez

(B) Renee Erickson

(C) Carolina Fuentes

(D) Bernardo Fuentes

48. What was the evidence that the wife was guilty of domestic battery?

    (A) The husband accused the wife of stabbing him.

    (B) The wife confessed to stabbing her husband.

    (C) The husband accused the wife of stabbing him, and his head and neck were bleeding.

    (D) The wife confessed to stabbing her husband, and his head and neck were bleeding.

49. Why did the officers arrest the wife rather than both spouses?

    (A) Both the husband and wife denied the husband hit her, but the wife admitted stabbing the husband with a broken bottle.

    (B) The wife threatened to gouge out her husband's eyes.

    (C) The husband and wife attacked each other, but only the wife landed a damaging blow.

    (D) The wife started the argument in the first place.

Questions 50–52

For questions 50–52, select the object that is included in the figure below. Only ONE of the answer choices for each question is included in the figure. Objects may be larger, smaller, mirrored, or rotated in the picture, but the proportions will be identical.

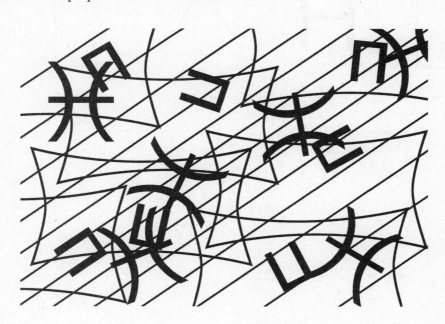

50.

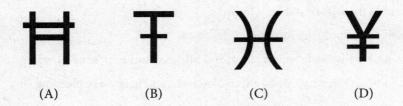

(A)   (B)   (C)   (D)

51.

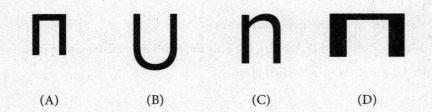

(A)   (B)   (C)   (D)

52.

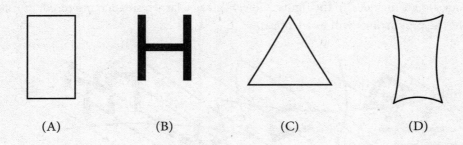

(A)   (B)   (C)   (D)

Questions 53–55

For questions 53–55, select the object that is included in the figure below. Only ONE of the answer choices for each question is included in the figure. Objects may be larger, smaller, mirrored, or rotated in the picture, but the proportions will be identical.

53.

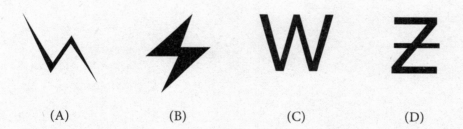

(A)   (B)   (C)   (D)

54.

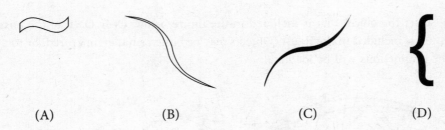

(A)   (B)   (C)   (D)

55.

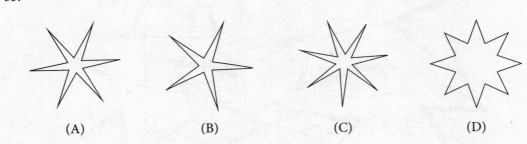

(A)   (B)   (C)   (D)

Practice Exam 2

Questions 56–57

Please use the following map for questions 56–57. NOTE: Direction arrows indicate flow of traffic.

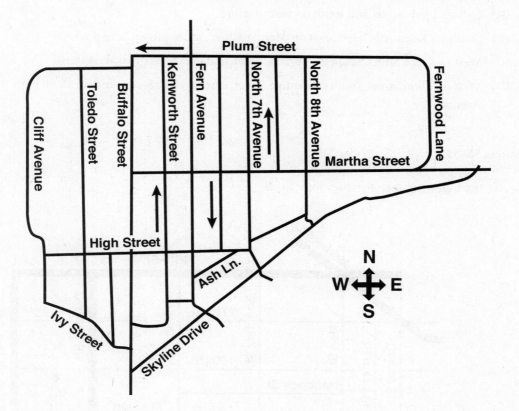

56. You are currently at the intersection of Ivy Street and Toledo Street, and you are dispatched to the scene of an assault at Martha Street and North 7th Avenue. Which of the following is the shortest route to the scene?

(A) East on Ivy Street, north on Buffalo Street, and east on Martha Street

(B) East on Ivy Street, south on Buffalo Street, northeast on Skyline Drive, and north on North 7th Avenue

(C) West on Ivy Street, north on Cliff Avenue, east on High Street, and north on North 7th Avenue

(D) North on Toledo Street and east on Martha Street

57. You are currently at the intersection of Plum Street and Kenworth Street when you hear about a robbery in progress at Skyline Drive and Fern Avenue. Which of the following is the shortest route to take in your squad car, obeying all traffic regulations?

(A) East on Plum Street and south on Fern Avenue

(B) South on Kenworth Street, east on Martha Street, and south on Fern Avenue

(C) West on Plum Street, south on Buffalo Street, and northeast on Skyline Drive

(D) West on Plum Street, south on Buffalo Street, east on High Street, and south on Fern Avenue

Questions 58–59

Please use the following map for questions 58–59.

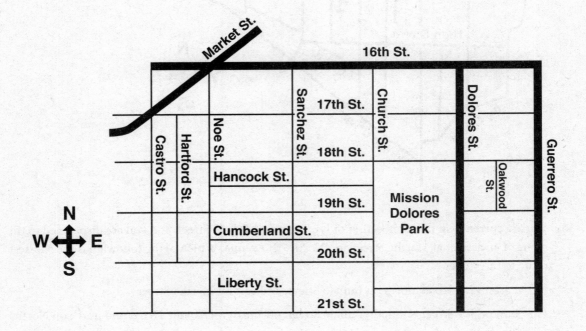

Practice Exam 2

58. You are at the intersection of 17th Street and Dolores Street when you are dispatched to Cumberland Street between Sanchez and Noe Streets. Which of the following is the shortest route to the scene?

    (A) South on Dolores Street, west on Cumberland Street

    (B) South on Dolores Street, west on 20th Street, north on Sanchez Street, west on Cumberland Street

    (C) West on 17th Street, south on Noe Street, east on Cumberland Street

    (D) West on 17th Street, south on Sanchez Street, west on Cumberland Street

59. Your squad car is currently parked near the intersection of Hancock and Noe Streets, facing west. Dolores Street is closed to all traffic between 18th and 20th Streets, including all intersections, for a special event in Mission Dolores Park. You are dispatched to a crime in progress on Oakwood Street. Which of the following is the shortest driving route to the scene?

    (A) North on Noe Street, east on 18th Street, south on Oakwood Street

    (B) North on Noe Street, east on 17th Street, south on Guerrero Street, west on 18th Street, south on Oakwood Street

    (C) South on Noe Street, east on 21st Street, north on Guerrero Street, west on 19th Street, north on Oakwood Street

    (D) East on Hancock Street, north on Church Street, east on 18th Street, south on Oakwood Street

Practice Exam 2

Questions 60–61

Please use the following map for questions 60–61. NOTE: Direction arrows indicate flow of traffic.

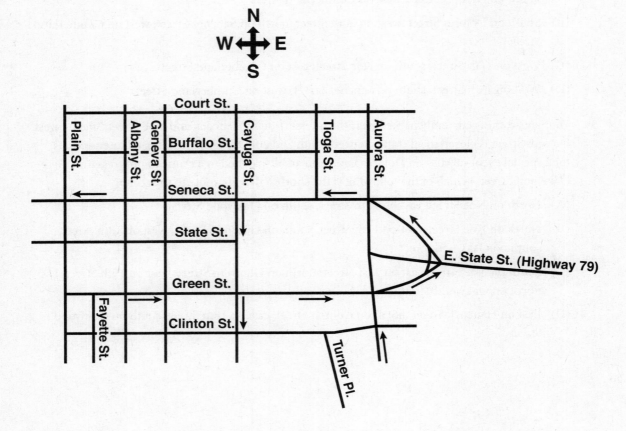

60. You are currently at the intersection of Green and Albany Streets when you are summoned to an incident on Seneca Street between Tioga and Aurora Streets. Which of the following is the shortest driving route to the scene, obeying all traffic regulations?

(A) East on Green Street, north on Aurora Street, west on Seneca Street

(B) North on Albany Street, east on Buffalo Street, south on Tioga Street

(C) East on Green Street, north on Cayuga Street, east on Seneca Street

(D) East on Green Street, north on Aurora Street, west on Buffalo Street, south on Tioga Street

61. You are currently entering town from the east on Highway 79. Which of the following is the shortest route to your destination on Fayette and Clinton Streets?

   (A) West on E. State Street (Highway 79), north on Aurora Street, west on Buffalo Street, south on Cayuga Street, west on Clinton Street

   (B) West/northwest on E. State Street (Highway 79), west on Seneca Street, south on Cayuga Street, west on Clinton Street

   (C) West on E. State Street (Highway 79), south on Aurora Street, west on Clinton Street

   (D) West/northwest on E. State Street (Highway 79), west on Seneca Street, south on Plain Street, east on Green Street, south on Fayette Street

Questions 62–66

Read the definitions, and then select the best answer to the following questions.

In State X, a person is guilty of sports bribe receiving when, being a sports participant, he solicits, accepts, or agrees to accept any benefit from another person upon an agreement that he will be influenced not to give his best efforts in a sports contest; or, being a sports official, he solicits, accepts, or agrees to accept any benefit from another person upon an agreement that he will perform his duties improperly.

62. Given the above definition alone, which of the following is the best example of sports bribe receiving?

   (A) Johnny, a soccer referee, is offered $100 to overlook fouls committed by the Stanford Stingers' star forward, but he refuses.

   (B) Sven accepts $50 from a parent to umpire a baseball game in a new kids' league.

   (C) Joey, a guard for State College's basketball team, accepts a new car from a gambler in return for intentionally getting himself thrown out of a game by committing too many fouls.

   (D) During a softball game, the ball hits Sylvia in the eye. Following doctor's orders, Sylvia sits out the next game, and her parents console her with a new glove.

In State X, a person is guilty of aggravated disorderly conduct when he makes unreasonable noise while at a lawfully assembled religious service or within 100 feet thereof, with intent to cause annoyance.

63. Based solely upon this definition, which of the following is the best example of aggravated disorderly conduct?

   (A) In the midst of a heated sermon, Reverend Hightower yells at his congregation.

   (B) During his ex-girlfriend's wedding, Greg drives in circles around the parking lot of the church with his stereo blaring and his windows down.

   (C) A. J., an 18-month-old baby, begins to cry loudly during mass.

   (D) Emotionally driven to commit her life to the church, Ada runs screaming down the aisle during a service and throws herself on the altar.

In State X, a person is guilty of harassment in the first degree when he intentionally and repeatedly harasses another person by following such person or by repeatedly committing acts that place such person in reasonable fear of physical injury.

64. Given this definition alone, which of the following is the best example of harassment in the first degree?

(A) Josh accompanies his girlfriend to school after a series of early-morning rapes are reported along her route.

(B) Moira follows her ex-boyfriend to his chess club meetings several nights in a row then waits outside during his meetings, swinging a crowbar and yelling about his lack of loyalty.

(C) Trevor surprises his mother by picking her up from school five days in a row.

(D) One evening, Dale follows his father, whom he suspects is having an affair, to determine where he is going.

In State X, a person is guilty of hindering prosecution in the third degree when she intentionally harbors or conceals a person who has committed a felony.

65. Xavier is guilty of a felony and is running from the police. Based solely upon the above definition, which of the following is the best example of hindering prosecution in the third degree?

(A) Xavier's mother goes to her condo at the beach for the weekend, and Xavier hides in her basement, without her knowledge, while she is gone.

(B) Xavier's former business partner pays for Xavier's wife to have her teeth fixed out of consideration to her and her family.

(C) Xavier's brother picks Xavier up at their mother's house and takes him to his house, where he hides Xavier in a secret underground apartment.

(D) Xavier's former parole officer provides the police with records, phone numbers, and addresses of all of Xavier's known associates.

In State X, a person is guilty of fraudulently obtaining a signature when, with intent to defraud or to acquire a substantial benefit, he obtains a signature of a person to a written document by means of any misrepresentation of fact that he knows to be false.

66. Cassandra tells her boss that the paper she has placed in front of him is another copy of his consent form for his son's class trip, when she knows that the paper is actually a revised copy of her employment contract. This revised contract, which she has not discussed with her boss, grants her a substantial cash bonus immediately upon being signed, in addition to an immediate one-month vacation. Based solely upon the above definition, which of the following is true?

    (A) Cassandra should be charged with fraudulently obtaining a signature.

    (B) Cassandra should not be charged with any crime.

    (C) Cassandra should be charged with fraudulently obtaining a signature only if she attempts to claim any of the benefits granted to her in the revised contract.

    (D) Cassandra should be charged with fraudulently obtaining a signature only if, upon looking over the contract, her boss determines that she does not deserve the perks outlined in the new contract.

Questions 67–70

Look at the provided image, and then select the best corresponding image to answer each question.

67. Which face below is an exact representation of the face above?

(A)   (B)   (C)   (D)

The woman shown here has since changed her hairstyle.

68. Which face below represents the same woman with a different hairstyle?

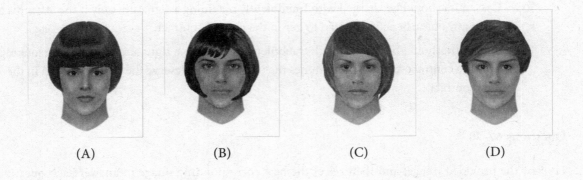

(A)   (B)   (C)   (D)

The man shown here has since grown facial hair.

69. Which face below represents the same man with facial hair?

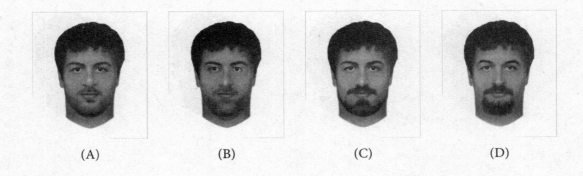

(A)   (B)   (C)   (D)

Use the below image for question 70.

70. Which face below is an exact representation of the face above?

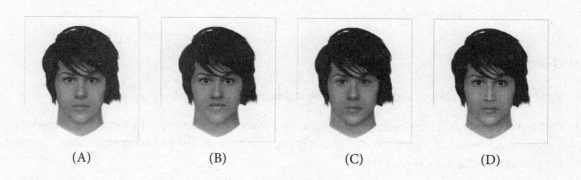

(A)   (B)   (C)   (D)

Questions 71–74

Questions 71–74 each contain a set of letters, symbols, and numbers. Please choose only ONE option for each that contains the exact same pattern of letters, symbols, and numbers.

71. HEn%AA74#qú!8O{7g)-+Nøfk

 (A) HEN%AA74#qú!8O{7g)-+Nøfk

 (B) HEn%AA74#qú!80(7g)-+Nøfk

 (C) HEn%AA74#qú!8O{7g)-+Nøfk

 (D) HEn%AA74#qú!8O{7g)-+Nofk

72. Iu9^5@¿qqeY9ġh8?)"Thê62x

 (A) Iu9^5@¿qqeY9ġh8?)"Thê62x

 (B) Iu9^5@?qqeY9ġh8?)'Thê62x

 (C) Iu9^5@¿qqeY9ġh8?)The62xx

 (D) Iu9^5@¿queY9gh8?)"Thê62x

73. $Ö6b([in5;:il1iti[ZIiů3+

   (A) $Ö6b[(in5;:il1iti[ZIiů3+

   (B) $Ö6b([in5::il1iti[ZIíů3+

   (C) $Ö6b([in5;:ili1ti[ZIiu3+

   (D) $Ö6b([in5;:il1iti[ZIiů3+

74. &""<=696nnmbdĄAΛ:;\VW/}{

   (A) &""<=696nmmbdĄAΛ:;\VV/}{

   (B) &'"<=696nnmdbĄAΛ:;\VW/}{

   (C) &""<=696nnmbdĄAΛ:;\VW/}{

   (D) &""<=696nnmbdĄĄΛ;:\VW/}(

Questions 75–77

Read the short scenarios, and then place the statements in the most logical order.

Officer Fontana is interviewing Enrique Padilla, who witnessed an attempted robbery on Thursday night inside the convenience store at South 7th Street and Lee Avenue. The following statements appeared in his account of what took place.

1. The guy gets free and tries to throw a punch across the counter.

2. The other guy chased him out on the street but he got away.

3. I came to the store to buy a six-pack of beer. There was another guy in the place, not very tall, but muscular.

4. He doesn't pull a weapon or anything. Then I heard the two guys yelling at each other, and the clerk is trying to force the drawer shut and trap his hands.

5. Another worker comes out from the back of the place and he's running toward him, and the guy just bounces out the door.

6. The man brought one or two little items to the counter and when the guy behind the counter opens the register, this guy reaches across with both hands to grab the money out of it.

75. What is the MOST logical order of these statements?

   (A) 3, 1, 5, 6, 2, 4

   (B) 3, 6, 4, 1, 5, 2

   (C) 6, 5, 3, 1, 4, 2

   (D) 3, 4, 1, 6, 5, 2

Officer Kim is taking a statement from Wesley Washington after issuing a citation to his neighbors for disturbing the peace last Friday night. The following statements appeared in Washington's account of the evening's events:

1. When I got to my door, I could see out on my porch—the shared porch for the two apartments—that three people, who sounded very drunk, were having a loud conversation.

2. I went back in and banged on the ceiling, but that had no effect. After a while, I heard the sound of glass breaking out on the street, over and over.

3. It was getting late, and the music was so loud I couldn't hear my TV even with the sound up high. I said enough is enough and went to say something.

4. I realized they were chucking beer bottles out the window onto the sidewalk. That's when I called you guys.

5. So, I had second thoughts about going and confronting my neighbors whom I don't really know.

6. I was home watching TV and heard the neighbors having a party. I could hear their hip-hop through my walls. I work Saturdays, so I wanted to get a decent night's sleep.

76. What is the MOST logical order of these statements?

(A) 3, 6, 4, 1, 5, 2

(B) 6, 1, 5, 2, 3, 4

(C) 6, 1, 2, 4, 3, 5

(D) 6, 3, 1, 5, 2, 4

Officer Smith is taking a statement from Robert Rose after a domestic dispute in which Mr. Rose's ex-wife called the police. The following statements are excerpted from his remarks:

1. We have joint custody of our daughter and it's my day with her, but for some reason I said she could stop off at her mother's house for an hour after school, and I'd pick her up.

2. She says there's a violent man in her house. I didn't do anything violent or threatening.

3. But as soon as I talked back and raised my voice a little, she walks over to the phone and calls 911.

4. I should have known better than to go into my ex-wife's house. When she gets on the warpath, there's no telling what she'll do.

5. I tried to suggest she should shut up and not talk about this in front of the kid.

6. As soon as I step inside the door, my ex starts insulting me and accusing me of neglect and child abuse and all this garbage.

77. What is the MOST logical order of these statements?

    (A) 1, 2, 3, 5, 6, 4

    (B) 1, 6, 2, 3, 4, 5

    (C) 4, 1, 6, 5, 3, 2

    (D) 4, 3, 6, 1, 5, 2

Questions 78–80

Use the following charts to answer questions 78–80.

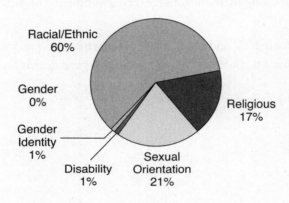

U.S. Bias Crimes, 2013

Source: FBI

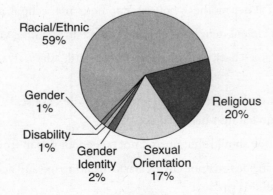

U.S. Bias Crimes, 2015

Source: FBI

78. Which category of bias crime increased the most, measured by proportion, between 2013 and 2015?

    (A) Racial/ethnic

    (B) Religious

    (C) Sexual orientation

    (D) Gender identity

79. Which category of bias crime decreased the most between 2013 and 2015?

    (A) Racial/ethnic

    (B) Religious

    (C) Sexual orientation

    (D) Gender identity

80. If religious hate crimes continued to increase at the same rate over the next two years, what would be the percentage of religious bias crimes in 2017?

    (A) 21%

    (B) 23%

    (C) 25%

    (D) 26%

Questions 81–83

Read the descriptions of a duty an officer may be called upon to perform, and then select the best answer to the following questions.

Police officers may have to take special efforts to ensure or promote the flow of traffic on streets and roadways.

81. Which of the following would NOT be appropriate activity for a police officer?

    (A) Pushing a stalled car to the side of a busy road

    (B) Clearing the way for an ambulance to move through heavy traffic

    (C) Dispersing a group of demonstrators who are deliberately blocking a busy intersection

    (D) Directing automotive traffic to drive on a city sidewalk when the street is blocked by an accident or other hazard

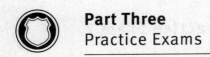
Practice Exam 2

A police officer is required to report dangerous situations immediately to the station house in closest proximity.

82. Which of the following situations should an officer report immediately?

(A) Five young men are running down a commercial street.

(B) A loose dog is behaving aggressively and foaming at the mouth.

(C) An unattended child falls off a bicycle.

(D) Teenagers have opened a fire hydrant on a summer afternoon.

Police officers may need to provide first aid in an emergency if they are the first to arrive on a scene.

83. In which situation should an officer provide immediate first aid while awaiting emergency medical personnel?

(A) A person bleeding heavily from a wound to the leg

(B) A child complaining of stomach pains

(C) A man passed out in an alley

(D) An elderly woman stating that she is short of breath

Questions 84–86

Use the following passage to answer questions 84–86.

On December 29, the exclusive French restaurant Grenoble reported the theft of several bottles of expensive wine. Although only a handful of bottles had disappeared from the restaurant's wine cellar, they were all from elite French vineyards and had a combined retail value of more than $10,000. Henri LaCroix, owner of Grenoble, told the police the premium wines were not kept under lock and key but stored in the cellar among the rest of the collection. They had been found missing during the restaurant's weekly inventory check. LaCroix speculated that the theft may have taken place on Christmas Day, the one day of the year when the restaurant is closed. However, he admitted that a relatively large number of restaurant employees and other people could have gained sufficient familiarity with the restaurant's layout to plan the heist. No evidence of forced entry was found.

84. Which of the following pieces of evidence would MOST likely convince a jury that a defendant had committed this crime?

(A) The defendant possessed one bottle each of two of the wines reported stolen in his or her personal collection.

(B) Fingerprints matching the defendant's were found on the restaurant's cellar door.

(C) The defendant is seen alone in surveillance video footage taken inside the restaurant on December 25.

(D) The defendant made a wine delivery to the restaurant on December 23.

85. Which of the following would be LEAST likely to suggest that a defendant was familiar with the restaurant's most expensive wines and their location in the cellar?

    (A) The defendant worked at the restaurant as a prep cook.

    (B) The defendant visited the restaurant during the daytime, on the pretext of planning a private party, and was given a tour of the wine cellar.

    (C) The defendant was a wine expert who carefully studied the restaurant's wine list.

    (D) The defendant had a prior conviction for burglary.

86. Based only on the information given in the passage, which of the following statements is MOST likely to be true about the incident?

    (A) The thief gained access to the cellar during the restaurant's normal hours of operation.

    (B) The thief either works in the restaurant or has an accomplice employed there.

    (C) The owner is implicated in the theft and is trying to shift the blame to someone else.

    (D) The thief was aware that the restaurant only checked its wine inventory once a week.

Questions 87–88

Read the short scenarios, and then select the best answer to the following questions.

87. Late one afternoon, you are on a coffee break inside a convenience store in an unfamiliar section of town. You receive a radio report that a wanted criminal suspect has just been spotted two blocks north of your location. You are momentarily blinded by a strong sun as you exit the store. What do you do?

    (A) Run two blocks to the left.

    (B) Run two blocks to the right.

    (C) Run straight out the door, across the street, and two blocks farther.

    (D) Turn right, go to the nearest corner, turn right again, and run two blocks.

A suspect took off running eastward through a crowd on South Street while Officer West gave chase. She turned right at the intersection and left at the next one, eluding capture when Officer West became entangled in a dog's leash. The suspect turned left again on Broad Street and disappeared into the crowd.

88. According to this description, the suspect was last seen heading:

    (A) east

    (B) west

    (C) north

    (D) south

Questions 89–91

For each question below, please choose the line that contains the misspelled word, grammatical error, or punctuation error by choosing the correct Roman numeral line number. Only one of the lines will contain an error.

89. I.   After a resident at the Creekside Manor apartment complex reported

II. a burglary, Officer Greene searched the two residential buildings as well

III. upon surrounding property. In the woods behind the complex, he found

IV. eight marijuana plants, each about 5 feet in height, in plastic containers.

(A) Line I

(B) Line II

(C) Line III

(D) Line IV

90. I.   Research conducted at Columbia Law School suggests that increasing

II. racial diversity among police forces, to match the diversity found in the

III. urban populations those forces serve, may be among the most effective

IV. ways to reduce the number of racially charged incidence of police violence.

(A) Line I

(B) Line II

(C) Line III

(D) Line IV

91. I.   The nation's largest law enforcement union, the National Fraternal

II. Order of Police, endorsed Donald Trump in the 2016 presidential election.

III. Shortly after the ballotting, the union released a list of policy proposals

IV. it hoped the administration would implement in its first 100 days.

(A) Line I

(B) Line II

(C) Line III

(D) Line IV

Questions 92–93

Read the short traffic accident scenarios, and then choose the diagram that best answers the question.

Officer Contreras responded to the scene of a traffic accident. According to a witness, the driver of a sedan (Vehicle 1) was traveling east on Ball Blvd. in the right-hand lane and attempted to turn right onto Hobie St. while the light was red. The driver began to turn before ensuring there was no oncoming traffic. He did not see the southbound vehicle approaching (Vehicle 2), which struck Vehicle 1 on the front driver side.

92. Which of the following diagrams accurately depicts the witness statement?

(A)

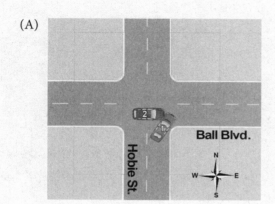

(C)

(B)

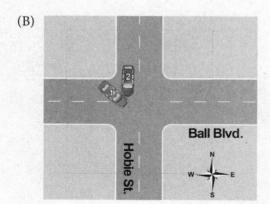

(D)

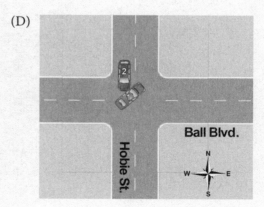

Officer Ellis responded to the scene of a traffic accident. According to a witness, the driver of a sedan (Vehicle 1) was traveling northbound on Chance Lane, approaching a T-intersection with Trager Street. The driver of Vehicle 1 did not appear aware that Chance Lane was ending and drove straight through the T-intersection. The front end of Vehicle 1 passed into a culvert on the north side of Trager Street before the driver was able to stop; the back half of Vehicle 1 remained in the roadway. Another sedan (Vehicle 2) was approaching the T-intersection westbound on Trager and had to swerve into the eastbound traffic lane to avoid colliding with Vehicle 1. Vehicle 2 collided with a hatchback (Vehicle 3), which was traveling east on Trager.

93. Which of the following diagrams accurately depicts the witness statement?

(A)

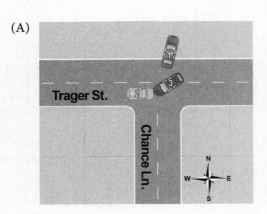

(C)

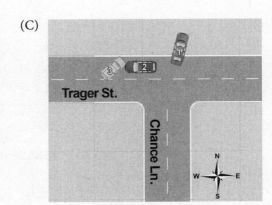

(B)

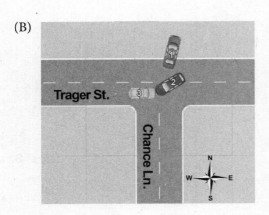

(D)

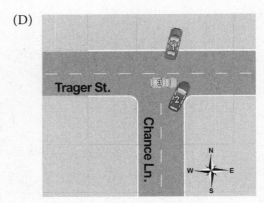

Questions 94–95

Answer these questions on the basis of the following list of recently recorded crimes.

Date	Day	Time	Type of Crime	Location
4/19	Wednesday	4:30 p.m.	Assault	689 Powell Ave.
4/19	Wednesday	10:15 p.m.	Burglary	2121 Suburban Ave.
4/21	Friday	11:45 p.m.	Att. Rape	114 St. Joseph St.
4/22	Saturday	2:15 a.m.	Rape	841 Powell Ave.
4/23	Sunday	10:45 p.m.	Burglary	1776 Suburban Ave.
4/24	Monday	5:15 p.m.	Assault	2533 Suburban Ave.
4/26	Wednesday	11:30 p.m.	Burglary	2614 Suburban Ave.
4/26	Wednesday	1:40 a.m.	Burglary	234 St. Joseph St.
4/27	Thursday	6:45 p.m.	Assault	821 Powell Ave.
4/28	Friday	12:30 a.m.	Att. Rape	102 St. Joseph St.
4/29	Saturday	1:25 a.m.	Att. Rape	205 St. Joseph St.
4/29	Saturday	4:00 a.m.	Burglary	45 Brown Lane

94. A police patrol would be most likely to reduce the number of burglaries by patrolling:

    (A) Suburban Avenue between 2:00 p.m. and 8:00 p.m. on Wednesdays and Thursdays

    (B) Brown Lane between midnight and 6 a.m. on Saturdays and Sundays

    (C) Suburban Avenue between 8:00 p.m. and 2:00 a.m. on Tuesdays and Wednesdays

    (D) St. Joseph Street between 8:00 p.m. and 2:00 a.m. on Fridays and Saturdays

95. A police patrol would be most likely to reduce the number of attempted rapes by patrolling:

    (A) St. Joseph Street between 8:00 p.m. and 2:00 a.m. on Fridays and Saturdays

    (B) St. Joseph Street between midnight and 6:00 a.m. on Saturdays and Sundays

    (C) Powell Avenue between midnight and 6:00 a.m. on Saturdays and Sundays

    (D) Suburban Avenue between 8:00 p.m. and 2:00 a.m. on Wednesdays and Thursdays

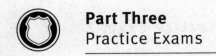
Practice Exam 2

Questions 96–100

Read the short scenarios, and then select the best answer to the following questions.

Police are searching for a suspect believed to have carried out two armed robberies in the past week. Witnesses have provided the following description: a Caucasian male, about 5 feet 9 inches tall, with long blond hair, a missing top tooth, and wearing several rings on both hands. He was last seen wearing a black down vest, blue jeans, and brown leather boots.

96. Which of these details would be most helpful in identifying the suspect among individuals detained for questioning?

 (A) About 5 feet 9 inches tall

 (B) Wearing a black down vest

 (C) A missing top tooth

 (D) Rings on both hands

Witnesses have offered the following description of a man wanted in connection with a rape reported earlier this week: Middle Eastern or Indian in descent, about 5 feet 5 inches tall, 160 pounds, slightly cross-eyed, wearing a grey and green Baja-style woolen hooded jacket.

97. Which of these details would be most helpful in identifying the suspect among individuals detained for questioning?

 (A) Middle Eastern or Indian descent

 (B) Slightly cross-eyed

 (C) Wearing a grey and green Baja-style woolen hooded jacket

 (D) About 5 feet 5 inches tall

Witnesses have offered the following description of a suspect wanted for blackmail and attempted murder: a white male approximately 30 years of age, about 6 feet 4 inches tall, 200 pounds, wearing dark glasses, a goatee beard, light brown hair, brown eyes, last seen wearing a navy blue tailored suit and dress shoes.

98. Which of these details would be most helpful in identifying the suspect among individuals detained for questioning?

 (A) Approximately 30 years of age

 (B) About 6 feet 4 inches tall

 (C) Goatee beard

 (D) Wearing a navy blue tailored suit and dress shoes

Officer Rush was off duty, unarmed, and eating lunch on the third-floor terrace of a restaurant when she witnessed a robbery on the first floor of a business across the street. Officer Rush immediately reported the robbery by using her cellular phone to call the precinct and was instructed to follow the suspect and stay in touch with the precinct. Officer Rush did as she was instructed, maintaining a safe distance since she was unarmed, but the suspect eluded her when he ran into a crowd of people.

99. Officer Rush's actions were

   (A) improper, because the suspect got away.

   (B) proper, because she reported the crime and followed the instructions of her supervisor.

   (C) improper, because she should have had a gun with her.

   (D) proper, but only because she was not hurt.

Just as Officer Sharma pulled a motorist over for exceeding the speed limit by seven miles per hour, a car sped by him from which a passenger was firing bullets in random directions. Officer Sharma got back into his patrol car and called in to report the situation as he turned on his lights and sirens and began pursuing the speeding vehicle.

100. Officer Sharma's actions were

   (A) improper, because his first order of business was to complete his exchange with the motorist he had pulled over.

   (B) proper, because he reported the dangerous situation and took immediate action to protect the public from it.

   (C) improper, because he should have immediately begun firing shots at the passenger who was firing the bullets from the second car.

   (D) proper, because the driver he had pulled over was going fewer than 10 miles above the speed limit anyway.

STOP

END OF EXAM

ANSWER KEY

1.	C	26.	A	51.	A	76.	D
2.	A	27.	C	52.	D	77.	C
3.	C	28.	C	53.	A	78.	D
4.	B	29.	C	54.	B	79.	C
5.	D	30.	B	55.	C	80.	B
6.	C	31.	D	56.	A	81.	D
7.	C	32.	C	57.	D	82.	B
8.	C	33.	B	58.	D	83.	A
9.	B	34.	A	59.	B	84.	C
10.	B	35.	D	60.	A	85.	D
11.	C	36.	C	61.	B	86.	B
12.	B	37.	B	62.	C	87.	B
13.	C	38.	A	63.	B	88.	C
14.	D	39.	B	64.	B	89.	C
15.	A	40.	D	65.	C	90.	D
16.	A	41.	A	66.	A	91.	C
17.	C	42.	D	67.	B	92.	C
18.	C	43.	C	68.	D	93.	B
19.	A	44.	B	69.	C	94.	C
20.	D	45.	C	70.	A	95.	A
21.	C	46.	D	71.	C	96.	C
22.	B	47.	B	72.	A	97.	B
23.	C	48.	D	73.	D	98.	B
24.	B	49.	A	74.	C	99.	B
25.	D	50.	C	75.	B	100.	B

ANSWERS AND EXPLANATIONS

1. C

Choice (C) is correct because it includes the correct language found on the sign.

2. A

Choice (A) is correct because the driver's window of the car in front is open.

3. C

Choice (C) is correct because a 1-hour parking sign is located in front of Pagus Express, and a No Parking sign is in front of the laundromat.

4. B

Choice (B) is correct because the storefront sign says "Grand Opening."

5. D

Choice (D) is correct because the store name is La Plaza.

6. C

Choice (C) is correct; the ladder of the fire escape partially obscures the awning of Pagos Express.

7. C

Choice (C) is correct because one child, along with two women holding handbags, are clearly visible in front of the automobile. The head of an adult can be seen behind the car, but it is not clear whether that person is with the others.

8. C

Choice (C) is correct because three satellite dishes in a row can be seen on the second story above the pharmacy.

9. B

Choice (B) is correct because there is an open window above Pagos Express, visible through the ladder of the fire escape.

10. B

Choice (B) is correct because part of a sign reading "ATM" can be seen in the laundromat window.

11. C

Choice (C) is correct because it represents the average per-minute total over a period of two hours (or 120 minutes). Divide the number of crossings (36,000) by 120. 36,000 divided by 120 equals 300.

12. B

Choice (B) is correct because the car's rate is 54 miles per hour ($54 \times 4 = 216$), and after six hours it will have traveled 324 miles ($54 \times 6 = 324$).

13. C

Choice (C) is correct because $725 is 5% (1/20) of $14,500.

14. D

Choice (D) is correct because 40 oz $\times$ 0.06 = 2.4 oz.

15. A

Choice (A) is correct because the total deductions ($447.25 + $223.12 + $81.66) for the month equal $752.03, and subtracting that amount from the gross pay figure ($2,916.66) leaves a net (take-home) income of $2,164.63.

16. A

Choice (A) is correct because it was 8:30 p.m. EST when the plane took off, so the plane was in the air 4 hours, 15 minutes when it landed at 12:45 a.m. EST.

17. C

Choice (C) is correct because the vendor spent a total of $270 ($45 $\times$ 6) to buy the peaches, but could only sell five boxes, or 200 pounds (5 $\times$ 40). To reach a 10% profit above cost, he must earn above $297 (10% of $270 is $27, and $270 plus $27 equals $297). At a cost of $1.50 per pound, he will earn $300 for selling all the peaches (200 $\times$ $1.50 = $300).

18. C

Choice (C) is correct. For speeding tickets assessed in a 55 mph zone, the calculation is done by multiplying $12.50 by each mph above 65 mph and adding the base fine of $75. In this case, the driver was caught going 7 mph above 65 mph, so $87.50 ($12.50 × 7) is assessed above the $75 base rate, for a total of $162.50.

19. A

Choice (A) is correct because the difference between the two towns' populations, as of 2010, is 1,800, and since that difference shrinks by 200 each year, the populations will equalize in nine years, or in 2019.

20. D

Choice (D) is correct because in this sentence, "fabricating" is closest in meaning to "forging." "Constructing" and "issuing" fail to make clear that the title documents are phony, while "falsifying" suggests adulterating or corrupting what may once have been legitimate documents.

21. C

Choice (C) is correct because in this sentence, "augment" is closest in meaning to "exacerbate." "Mollify" has the opposite meaning; "polarize" means to divide into starkly opposed groups; "replicate" means to reproduce.

22. B

Choice (B) is correct because in this sentence, "authenticate" is closest in meaning to "verify." Both mean "to prove" or "to establish the truth." "Reconcile" means "to resolve or settle," "elucidate" is to "clarify," and "implicate" means "to imply."

23. C

Choice (C) is correct because in this sentence, "national" is closest in meaning to "citizen." A "national," in this usage, means a citizen of a particular nation. The word does not suggest any particular "ethnic" or "partisan" affiliation and does not, like "official," connote that the individual is in government service.

24. B

Choice (B) is correct because in this sentence, "intractable" is closest in meaning to "uncooperative." "Pliable" has the opposite meaning. "Undisciplined" means out of control while "irrational" means lacking in logical coherence.

25. D

Choice (D) is correct because "belligerent" means "quick to fight," so "argumentative" is a close synonym. "Stubborn" means "unyielding," "boisterous" means "rowdy," and "impassioned" means "filled with passion or zeal."

26. A

Choice (A) is correct because "immaterial" and "irrelevant" are close synonyms. They both mean "of little or no consequence." "Intangible" means "not able to be felt by touch." "Indispensable" means "necessary" or "essential." "Circumstantial" means "dependent on circumstances."

27. C

Choice (C) is correct because "provenance" refers to the origin and prior ownership of something, such as an artwork or historical artifact, and is thus the closest synonym of "source" in this context. "Predecessor" refers to something that has been followed or replaced by something else. "Progeny" means "descendants." "Propinquity" means "proximity" or "closeness."

28. C

Choice (C) is correct because "pursued" is the correct spelling.

29. C

Choice (C) is correct because the sentence is in the past tense and requires the passive voice, so among the answer choices only "had been stolen" is grammatically correct.

30. B

Choice (B) is correct because the subject "Dwight Jackson and his girlfriend" is plural. Therefore, both "claims" and "is claiming," which are singular verb forms, do not agree. "Claiming" is missing a modifying verb.

31. D

Choice (D) is correct because "probability" is the correct spelling.

32. C

Choice (C) is correct because an apostrophe is needed between the word "child" and the final "s" to show correct usage of the possessive form.

33. B

Choice (B) is the correct choice since the past-tense form of "emptied" matches that of "searched" and "telephoned." The sentence is an example of parallelism.

34. A

Choice (A) is correct because the sentence requires the singular possessive "its," rather than the plural "their" or the more vague "an." The contraction "it's" (for "it is") is incorrect.

35. D

Choice (D) is correct because among the answer choices, only "was wearing" makes the sentence grammatically correct. The other choices would result in a sentence fragment—that is, a sentence missing a verb.

36. C

Choice (C) is correct because it best presents the information completely, clearly, and accurately, without redundant, unclear, or missing information. Choice (A) inaccurately depicts the fire's cause as certain. Choice (B) omits the time of the incident. Choice (D) omits the damage to the building.

37. B

Choice (B) is correct because it best presents the information completely, clearly, and accurately, without redundant, unclear, or missing information. Choice (A) omits the location of the incident; choice (C) omits the time; choice (D) omits the name of the witness.

38. A

Choice (A) is correct because it best presents the information completely, clearly, and accurately, without redundant, unclear, or missing information. Choice (C) omits the incident time; choice (D) omits the color of the vehicle. Choice (B) is written less clearly and economically than Choice (A).

39. B

Choice (B) is correct because it best presents the information completely, clearly, and accurately, without redundant, unclear, or missing information. Choice (A) omits "p.m." from the time; Choice (C) omits Henry Anderson's job of assistant manager; Choice (D) omits the weapon used in the robbery.

40. D

Choice (D) is correct because it best presents the information completely, clearly, and accurately, without redundant, unclear, or missing information. Choice (A) omits the incident time; Choice (B) neglects to describe the dog as aggressive; Choice (C) omits part of the action taken.

41. A

Choice (A) is correct because it best presents the information completely, clearly, and accurately, without redundant, unclear, or missing information. Choice (B) omits the incident location; Choice (C) omits the time and vehicle make; Choice (D) is fully accurate but is written less clearly than Choice (A).

42. D

Choice (D) is correct because it best presents the information completely, clearly, and accurately, without redundant, unclear, or missing information. Choice (A) is repetitive and difficult to read; Choice (B) is also repetitive and contains grammatical errors; Choice (C) omits "p.m." from the time.

43. C

Choice (C) is correct because it best presents the information completely, clearly, and accurately, without redundant, unclear, or missing information. Choice (A) omits the incident time; Choice (D) misstates the occupation of the victim and contains a misspelled word; Choice (B) is accurate but is written less economically than Choice (C).

44. B

Choice (B) is correct because the officers reached the crime scene at 4:20 p.m. and were told the suspects had fled 10 minutes earlier, so 4:00 p.m. is the best estimate for the time of the incident.

45. C

Choice (C) is correct because it accurately describes the sequence of events. The suspects' interaction with the woman happened after the exchange about selling their mobile phone. The stabbing took place afterward, and there is no evidence that Lashawn Richards was threatened.

46. D

Choice (D) is correct because, according to the passage, the suspects were seen talking to the driver of the blue sport utility vehicle after the incident, and the driver left the scene at the same time as the suspects.

47. B

Choice (B) is correct because the second paragraph states that the next-door neighbor, Mrs. Renee Erickson, placed the call.

48. D

Choice (D) is the best answer because the wife's admission confirms the physical evidence of the husband's injury.

49. A

Choice (A) is correct because the passage states both parties denied the husband tried to injure the wife.

50. C

Choice (C) is correct because it is the only shape found in the design.

51. A

Choice (A) is correct because it is the only shape found in the design.

52. D

Choice (D) is correct because it is the only shape found in the design.

53. A

Choice (A) is correct because it is the only shape found in the design.

54. B

Choice (B) is correct because it is the only shape found in the design.

55. C

Choice (C) is correct because it is the only shape found in the design.

56. A

Choice (A) is correct because it describes the shortest route. Choices (B) and (C) involve brief turns in the wrong direction; Choice (D) is not possible.

57. D

Choice (D) is correct because it describes the shortest permissible route. Choices (A) and (B) are against one-way traffic regulations; Choice (C) is less direct.

58. D

Choice (D) is correct because it describes the shortest route. Choice (A) is impossible, and Choices (B) and (C) require traveling one block out of the way.

59. B

Choice (B) is correct because it describes the shortest permissible route. Choices (A) and (D) are not possible due to the obstruction at Dolores Street. Compared to Choice (B), Choice (C) requires driving one additional block out of the way.

60. A

Choice (A) is correct because it describes the shortest permissible route. Choice (C) violates one-way regulations, while Choices (B) and (D) bring the driver only to the nearest intersection rather than directly to the scene.

61. B

Choice (B) is correct because it describes the shortest permissible route. Choice (C) violates one-way regulations. Choices (A) and (D) involve driving several blocks out of the way.

62. C

Choice (C) is correct because it is the only choice that fits the description for sports bribe receiving. In Choice (A), a referee refuses to accept a bribe. In Choice (B), there is no suggestion that the umpire is paid to behave improperly. The situation in Choice (D) is not relevant to the statute.

63. B

Choice (B) is correct because it is the only choice in which the person displays intent to cause annoyance. Choices (A) and (D) involve participants behaving within the expected norms of a religious service, while Choice (C) involves an infant.

64. B

Choice (B) is correct because the person involved repeatedly and intentionally engages in threatening behavior with a weapon. Choices (A) and (C) involve benevolent behavior, while Choice (D) involves a single instance of following but no explicitly threatening behavior.

65. C

Choice (C) is correct because it is the only choice that fits the terms of the statute. In Choice (A), the mother is not hiding the felon knowingly. Choices (B) and (D) do not relate to the statute.

66. A

Choice (A) is correct because Cassandra had a clear intent "to acquire a substantial benefit" and obtained her boss's signature by means of conscious "misrepresentation of fact."

67. B

Choice (B) is correct because it is the only face that exactly matches the original face. Choice (A) has a broader nose, Choice (C) has thinner lips, and Choice (D) has thicker eyebrows.

68. D

Choice (D) is correct because it is the only face that exactly matches the original face, except for the hairstyle. Choice (A) has a narrower mouth, Choice (B) has lighter eyes, and Choice (C) has thinner eyebrows and a more pronounced mouth.

69. C

Choice (C) is correct because it is the only face that exactly matches the original face, except for the facial hair. Choice (A) has a bigger nose, Choice (B) has smaller eyes, and Choice (D) has wider set, arched eyebrows.

70. A

Choice (A) is correct because it is the only face that exactly matches the original face. Choice (B) has fuller lips, Choice (C) has smaller eyes, and Choice (D) has a narrower nose.

71. C

Choice (C) is correct because it is the only option that exactly matches the original. Choice (A) capitalizes the lowercase "n," Choice (B) replaces the "O" with an "0," and Choice (D) replaces the "Ø" with an "o."

72. A

Choice (A) is correct because it is the only option that exactly matches the original. Choice (B) replaces the "¿" with a "?," Choice (C) omits the quotation marks, and Choice (D) replaces the "ǵ" with a "g."

73. D

Choice (D) is correct because it is the only option that exactly matches the original. Choice (A) transposes the "(" and "[," Choice (B) replaces the semicolon with a colon, and Choice (C) replaces the "1" with a "i."

74. C

Choice (C) is correct because it is the only option that exactly matches the original. Choice (A) replaces the second "n" with an "m," Choice (B) replaces the rounded quotation marks with an apostrophe and squared quotation marks, and Choice (D) transposes the colon and semicolon.

75. B

Choice (B) is correct because it places the events in their logical sequence: the robbery attempt (6), the scuffle between the robber and the clerk (4, 1), the second worker's intervention (5), and the thief's escape (2).

76. D

Choice (D) is correct because it places the events in their most logical sequence: setting the scene of the noisy party (6, 3), Washington's hesitation to confront his neighbors personally (1, 5), and his choice to call the police after hearing thrown glass bottles landing on the sidewalk (2, 4).

77. C

Choice (C) is correct because it orders these statements in the most logical manner, first describing what preceded the incident (1), then narrating the incident chronologically (6, 5, 3).

78. D

Choice (D) is correct because while religious hate crimes increased from 17% to 20%, an increase of 17.6%, crimes based on gender identity increased from 1% to 2%, an increase of 100%—in other words, they doubled.

79. C

Choice (C) is correct because in either numerical or proportional terms, sexual orientation crimes decreased the most between the two measurements.

80. B

Choice (B) is correct because religious hate crimes increased by 3%, so another 3% increase would take them to 23%.

81. D

Choice (D) is correct because it is unsafe to direct cars onto sidewalks and into pedestrian traffic. When a hazard blocks all traffic on a street, officers should close the street and establish a detour to redirect traffic.

82. B

Choice (B) is correct because a dog displaying these symptoms could have rabies and pose a deadly danger to humans and other animals. The other choices are not necessarily life-threatening situations.

83. A

Choice (A) is correct because a person bleeding heavily requires immediate assistance. The child complaining of stomach pains, Choice (B), does not represent a medical emergency. The officer should first evaluate the unconscious man in Choice (C) to determine if he is in any immediate danger. The woman described in Choice (D) is able to speak, so before applying first aid the officer should question her to determine whether her shortness of breath might be life-threatening.

84. C

Choice (C) is correct because it would place the defendant at the scene of the crime at a time when the restaurant was closed and, presumably, nobody else was present.

85. D

Choice (D) is correct because even though a prior burglary conviction could help convince a jury of an individual's guilt, it does not by itself provide evidence that the individual had the knowledge of or access to the expensive wines surrounded by less valuable bottles in the restaurant cellar.

86. B

Choice (B) is correct because there is no evidence of forced entry, so it is likely the thief had access to the restaurant key no matter when the crime took place.

87. B

Choice (B) is correct because the strong late afternoon sun in your eyes as you exit the store indicates you are facing west. Turn right to run north.

88. C

Choice (C) is correct because the suspect was originally heading east. She then turned right, or to the south, then left, or to the east, then left again, or to the north.

89. C

Choice (C) is correct because Line III should begin "as the surrounding property."

90. D

Choice (D) is correct because Line IV should conclude "incidents of police violence."

91. C

Choice (C) is correct because the word "balloting" is misspelled in Line III.

92. C

Choice (C) is correct because it most accurately illustrates the witness's account of the accident. Choice (A) depicts Vehicle #1 traveling north on Hobie St instead of east on Ball Blvd. Choice (B) depicts Vehicle #1 in the left-hand lane instead of the right. Choice (D) depicts Vehicle #1 making a left turn instead of a right.

93. B

Choice (B) is correct because it most accurately illustrates the witness's account of the accident. Choice (A) misrepresents Vehicle #3 as Vehicle #2. Choice (C) doesn't show Vehicle #2 swerving. Choice (D) shows Vehicle #2 northbound on Chance Ln. instead of westbound on Trager St.

94. C

Choice (C) is correct because three of the five reported burglaries took place on Suburban Avenue, two of them on Wednesday evenings after 10:00 p.m.

95. A

Choice (A) is the best of the available choices because three of the four rape incidents took place on St. Joseph Street, and all four occurred between 11:45 p.m. and 2:15 a.m. on Fridays or Saturdays.

96. C

Choice (C) is correct because among these details, a missing top tooth would be both the most unusual and the hardest to conceal or alter.

97. B

Choice (B) is correct because among these details, being cross-eyed would be both the most unusual and the hardest to conceal or alter.

98. B

Choice (B) is correct because among these details, a height of 6 feet 4 inches would be both the most unusual and the hardest to conceal or alter.

99. B

Choice (B) is correct because the officer cannot be blamed for not having her gun while off duty nor for losing the suspect in a crowd. Her actions would arguably have been appropriate even if she had been hurt.

100. B

Choice (B) is correct because the firing of bullets from a passing car was unmistakably a higher priority than a routine speeding ticket. Firing at the car himself would have been extremely dangerous and would have threatened the lives of other citizens.

Practice Exam 3

POLICE EXAM
Time—2 hours
Number of questions—100

A CALCULATOR MAY NOT BE USED ON THIS EXAM.

Directions: Choose the ONE best answer for each question.

Questions 1–10

Study the photograph very carefully for five minutes. You will be asked 10 detailed questions about this image. Once you have finished looking at this photograph, you will not be able to look back at it again.

1. How many windows are found on the second story of the building?

   (A) 4

   (B) 5

   (C) 6

   (D) 7

2. How many air conditioners are in the photograph?

   (A) 1

   (B) 2

   (C) 3

   (D) 4

3. What is the address of Gene Reed?

   (A) 49

   (B) 47

   (C) 74

   (D) 79

4. What is the name of the business to the left of Gene Reed?

   (A) Thieves Market

   (B) Antiques Market

   (C) Thieves Antiques

   (D) Market Antiques

5. How many garbage cans are in the photograph?

   (A) 0

   (B) 1

   (C) 2

   (D) 3

6. What word is written vertically in the middle of the photograph?

   (A) Gene

   (B) Thieves

   (C) Market

   (D) Antiques

7. What is the price of the beer on the sign in the window?

   (A) $4.99

   (B) $8.99

   (C) $10.99

   (D) $12.99

8. Which of the following beer brands is NOT depicted in the window?

   (A) Bud

   (B) Miller

   (C) Corona

   (D) Bud Light

9. How many people are in the photograph?

   (A) 0

   (B) 1

   (C) 2

   (D) 3

10. What word best describes the awning above Gene Reed?

    (A) Torn

    (B) Striped

    (C) Missing

    (D) Rolled up

Questions 11–19

Read the short scenarios, and then select the best answer to the following questions.

Officer Katz was given the assignment of distributing 40 body cameras equally among 8 different squads in the precinct.

11. Which choice correctly states the number of body cameras distributed to each squad?

    (A) 4

    (B) 5

    (C) 8

    (D) 10

Sergeant Rudd has arrested Jessica Wilson, a shoplifter at Lyon's Boutique. Ms. Wilson had the following stolen items in her possession:

- Two dresses each valued at $499
- Three pant suits each valued at $899
- Five scarves each valued at $75
- Six shirts each valued at $129

12. Which of the following is the total value of the stolen property?

    (A) $1,602

    (B) $2,659

    (C) $4,700

    (D) $4,844

A condo owner reports the following items stolen from her residence:

- Large screen television: $1,200
- Laptop computer: $3,000
- DVD player: $55
- Diamond earrings: $999
- Diamond bracelet: $1,100
- Cash: $4,256

Later, the condo owner reports that the diamond earrings were found in a dresser drawer.

13. What is the total value of the items stolen?

    (A) $8,511

    (B) $8,610

    (C) $9,611

    (D) $10,610

When Detective Hawthorne is leaving a crime scene, a woman approaches him while carrying a bag. The woman introduces herself as Marian Lewis and says she is a jeweler. Mrs. Lewis explains that she found the bag on the sidewalk in front of her shop when she arrived this morning. Mrs. Lewis has prepared a list of contents of the bag and their estimated value and shows it to Detective Hawthorne. The list reads:

- One platinum men's watch: $4,450
- Two gold ladies' dress watches: $2,200 (each watch)
- One heavy sterling silver bracelet with charms: $500
- One diamond tennis bracelet: $1,800
- Three pearl rings in white gold settings: $3,800
- Two diamond solitaire necklaces: $2,500 (each necklace)

14. What is the total value of the jewelry in the bag?
    (A) $15,250
    (B) $17,450
    (C) $19,950
    (D) $21,500

A truck driver making deliveries for a liquor distributor reports that his truck has been stolen while he was on his route. He is not exactly sure how much merchandise is missing because his delivery book was inside the truck. When he picked up his truck in the morning, his full load was worth about $18,000, and the driver estimates that he made about one-third of his deliveries.

15. About how much was the liquor in the stolen truck worth?
    (A) $3,000
    (B) $5,000
    (C) $6,000
    (D) $12,000

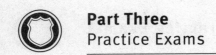
A storage warehouse manager finds that one of the storage spaces has been broken into and robbed. When she files a report, she gives a list of the items prepared by the storage unit tenant to the officer. The list includes the items stolen and their value.

- Four men's tuxedos: $2,000 (total)
- One wedding dress: $1,850
- Two women's leather jackets: $450 (each)
- Four first edition signed books: $800 (total)
- One leather recliner: $1,150
- Four Victorian lamps: $250 (each)
- One sterling silver tea set: $500

16. What is the total value of the missing merchandise?

(A) $7,250

(B) $7,950

(C) $8,200

(D) $9,050

A study shows that 2.5% of drivers stopped by police on the road on Super Bowl Sunday are driving while impaired by alcohol or drugs.

17. Using the data from this study, if a police department stops 3,800 drivers on Super Bowl Sunday, about how many of these drivers would be impaired?

(A) 8

(B) 38

(C) 76

(D) 95

The owner of an appliance store reported a break-in and gave the police the following list of items stolen and their value:

- Five 36-inch HD televisions: $350 (each)
- Three microwave ovens: $135 (each)
- Three laptop computers: $1,500 (each)
- Two red stand mixers: $325 (total)

The owner later amended his report after he learned that an employee put aside one laptop in a locked storage area for a customer.

18. What is the total value of the missing merchandise?

    (A) $4,780

    (B) $5,480

    (C) $5,560

    (D) $6,280

According to one study about City X, the annual rate of car thefts is 4.5 thefts per 1,000 cars.

19. If last year's car registration records show 150,000 cars, how many car thefts would be expected?

    (A) 67.5

    (B) 600

    (C) 675

    (D) 6,750

Questions 20–27

In each of the following sentences, choose the word or phrase that most nearly has the same meaning as the underlined word.

20. The witness <u>corroborated</u> another witness's description of the suspect.

    (A) validated

    (B) disproved

    (C) enhanced

    (D) challenged

21. The officer was <u>undeterred</u> in his investigation into the missing person case with few solid leads.

    (A) careless

    (B) practical

    (C) surprised

    (D) persistent

22. Because the suspect wanted to hide the truth from the officer, she told him a <u>blatant</u> lie.

    (A) obvious

    (B) slight

    (C) creative

    (D) dangerous

23. The officers thought it was best to be <u>cautious</u> when approaching the house where a robbery was allegedly in progress.

    (A) open

    (B) hostile

    (C) careful

    (D) excited

24. The suspect <u>proclaimed</u> that he was innocent during his interview with the detectives.

    (A) found

    (B) stated

    (C) showed

    (D) suggested

25. The victim was from out of town and fell for the <u>ruse</u>.

    (A) trick

    (B) display

    (C) description

    (D) opportunity

26. The case suffered in court because the lawyer argued that it was based on <u>hearsay</u>.

    (A) fact

    (B) trust

    (C) rumor

    (D) examples

27. Because the officer's search warrant was <u>flawed</u>, the suspect was released without being charged.

    (A) memorized

    (B) dismissed

    (C) mislaid

    (D) faulty

Questions 28–35

In the following sentences, choose the correct option to fill in the blank for each sentence.

28. The detective _____ the situation before questioning the suspect.
    (A) analized
    (B) analezed
    (C) analyzed
    (D) analizied

29. Before making an arrest, the officer should _____ the suspect's story.
    (A) verify
    (B) verified
    (C) be verified
    (D) had been verifying

30. The most _____ way to gather information from witnesses is to listen.
    (A) efectiv
    (B) afektiv
    (C) affactive
    (D) effective

31. It was _____ word against the word of other suspects.
    (A) their
    (B) there
    (C) theyre
    (D) they're

32. The detective _____ one suspect after the witness took part in a line-up.
    (A) eliminetd
    (B) eleminatd
    (C) eliminated
    (D) eleminated

33. Because the victim had been knocked unconscious, she waited a week before _____ a police report.

    (A) filleing

    (B) fileing

    (C) filling

    (D) filing

34. Before the police sergeant arrived at the _____, it had been established as the scene of the crime.

    (A) sit

    (B) site

    (C) sight

    (D) sighte

35. The officer took a moment to calm the _____ teenager.

    (A) frighten

    (B) frightens

    (C) frightened

    (D) be frightening

Questions 36–43

Read the short scenarios, and then select the best answer to the following questions.

Officer Thomas is dispatched to a residence where a larceny has been reported. She gathers the following information:

Location:	7845 Mesa Boulevard
Time:	8:30 a.m.
Crime:	larceny
Victim:	Ms. Torres
Item Missing:	gas grill
Suspect:	Terrence Edwards (victim reports seeing him take the grill)
Location of the Suspect:	unknown

36. Officer Thomas is writing her report. Which choice expresses the information most clearly and accurately?

   (A) Terrence Edwards stole a gas grill from Ms. Torres at 8:30 a.m. Terrence Edwards's location since stealing the grill from 7845 Mesa Boulevard is unknown.

   (B) At 8:30 a.m., a gas grill was stolen from Ms. Torres, who reported seeing Terrence Edwards, whose location is unknown, stealing the grill.

   (C) From 7845 Mesa Boulevard, the home of Ms. Torres, a gas grill was stolen at 8:30 a.m. The location of the suspect, whom Ms. Torres saw stealing the grill, is unknown.

   (D) Ms. Torres reported that at 8:30 a.m., she saw Terrence Edwards steal a gas grill from her residence at 7845 Mesa Boulevard. Terrence Edwards's location is unknown.

Officer Rosales is dispatched to the scene of a collision between two delivery trucks. He gathers the following information:

Location:	the intersection of Bernice Lane and 45th Street
Time:	7:15 a.m.
Incident:	Two delivery trucks collided.
Drivers:	Pablo Ford and Joseph Bandy
Action Taken:	Both drivers were issued traffic tickets.

37. Officer Rosales is writing his report on the incident. Which of the following expresses the information most clearly and accurately?

   (A) At 7:15 a.m. at the intersection of Bernice Lane and 45th Street, two delivery trucks collided. Both drivers, Pablo Ford and Joseph Bandy, were issued traffic citations.

   (B) Pablo Ford and Joseph Bandy were both issued traffic tickets shortly after their two delivery trucks collided. The accident occurred at the intersection of Bernice Lane and 45th Street.

   (C) Two delivery trucks, driven by Pablo Ford and Peter Josephs, at the intersection of Bernice Lane and 45th Street at 7:15 a.m. Both drivers, Mr. Ford and Mr. Josephs, were issued traffic tickets.

   (D) At the intersection of Bernice Lane and 45th Street, a collision occurred. The two vehicles were both delivery trucks, and the drivers, Pablo Ford and Joseph Bandy, were issued traffic tickets.

Officer Knowles is responding to a call from a man who is stuck on his roof. She gathers the following information:

Location:	3545 East Congress Avenue
Time:	2 p.m.
Resident:	Mr. Blair
Situation:	Mr. Blair, home alone, was stuck on his roof after his ladder fell.
Caller:	Mr. Blair used his cell phone.
Action Taken:	Ladder was replaced, and Mr. Blair safely climbed down.

38. Officer Knowles is writing her report. Which choice expresses the information most clearly and accurately?

(A) Mr. Blair was stuck on his roof when his ladder fell at 2 p.m. He was home alone and safely climbed down when his ladder was replaced after he used his cell phone to call the police.

(B) Mr. Blair was stuck on his roof at 3545 East Congress Avenue after his ladder fell at 2 p.m. He was home alone, so he used his cell phone to contact the police. His ladder was replaced, and he safely climbed down.

(C) Mr. Blair was helped safely down his ladder after it was replaced at his home at 3545 East Congress Avenue. Mr. Blair was on his roof when his ladder fell, and was home alone, but used his cell phone to call the police.

(D) At 3545 East Congress Avenue, Mr. Blair used his cell phone to call the police after his ladder fell, leaving him stuck on his roof. He was home alone. The ladder was replaced, and then Mr. Blair, who was no longer stuck, safely climbed down.

Officer Iba is dispatched to a candy factory where a man has reportedly been beaten. Officer Iba gathers the following information:

Location: Tim's Treats, 78 Pascale Road

Time: 5 p.m.

Crime: assault

Victim: Michael O'Dell, employee

Suspect: Eric Kennedy, supervisor

Status of Suspect: confessed, was arrested, and is in custody

39. Officer Iba must prepare an initial report on the incident. Which choice expresses the information most clearly and accurately?

(A) Michael O'Dell reported that at 5 p.m. at Tim's Treats, which is located at 78 Pascale Road and at which Mr. O'Dell is an employee, he was beaten by Eric Kennedy, his supervisor. Mr. Kennedy confessed, was arrested, and is in custody.

(B) Michael O'Dell, an employee of Tim's Treats, was beaten at 5 p.m. at the location of Tim's Treats at 78 Pascale Road by his supervisor. The supervisor confessed and was arrested.

(C) Eric Kennedy, a supervisor at Tim's Treats at 78 Pascale Road, beat an employee at Tim's Treats at 5 p.m. Mr. Kennedy confessed. Mr. Kennedy was arrested and is in custody.

(D) At 5 p.m., at the location of Tim's Treats, which is at 78 Pascale Road, a supervisor, Eric Kennedy, beat up an employee, Michael O'Dell. Mr. Kennedy is in custody.

Officer Branaugh was dispatched to the scene of a bicycle accident, where he gathered the following information:

Location:	the corner of Dover Road and Christopher Street
Time:	9:30 p.m.
Police Contacted By:	Jonas Pollack
Incident:	Two cyclists collided as each rounded the corner and slid on the road, which was wet because of a recent storm.
Injuries:	Both suffered several broken bones and are currently hospitalized.

40. Officer Branaugh is writing his report. Which choice expresses the information most clearly and accurately?

(A) Jonas Pollack reported seeing two cyclists collide as each rounded the corner of Dover Road and Christopher Street and slipped on the road, which was wet because of a recent storm.

(B) Jonas Pollack reported at 9:30 p.m. that he had seen two cyclists collide as each rounded the corner of Dover Road and Christopher Street. Both cyclists suffered several broken bones and are currently hospitalized.

(C) At 9:30 p.m., Jonas Pollack reported seeing two cyclists collide as each rounded a corner and slipped on the road, which was wet due to a recent storm. Both cyclists suffered several broken bones and are currently hospitalized.

(D) At 9:30 p.m., Jonas Pollack reported seeing two cyclists slip on the road and collide as each rounded the corner of Dover Road and Christopher Street, which was wet due to a recent storm. Both cyclists suffered several broken bones and are currently hospitalized.

Officer Ng was sent to investigate a report that two women had attempted to sneak into a movie, and she gathered the following information:

Location:	Queen City Cinemas
Time:	8:30 p.m.
Police Contacted By:	Matthew Grey, manager
Incident:	Two women attempted to sneak into a movie without paying.
Suspects:	Josie and Rachelle Joseph
Action Taken:	Both women confessed and were arrested.

41. Officer Ng is writing her report. Which choice expresses the information most clearly and accurately?

   (A) Josie and Rachelle Joseph were caught by Queen City Cinemas manager Matthew Gray trying to sneak into a movie without paying. The women confessed and were arrested.

   (B) Josie and Rachelle Joseph were caught by Queen City Cinemas manager Matthew Grey trying to sneak into a movie without paying. Mr. Grey reported the incident at 8:30 p.m.

   (C) At 8:30 a.m., Matthew Grey, the manager, reported that Josie and Rachelle Joseph attempted to sneak into a movie at the Queen City Cinemas without paying. Both women confessed and were arrested.

   (D) At 8:30 p.m., Matthew Grey reported that two women had attempted to sneak into a movie without paying at the Queen City Cinemas, which Mr. Grey manages. The two women, Josie and Rachelle Joseph, confessed and were arrested.

Officer Burton responded to a report of a man firing a pistol in the air at a public park and gathered the following information:

Location:	Lone Pines Park
Time:	7 a.m.
Police Contacted By:	Ms. Mowbery, a park attendant
Incident:	A man was repeatedly firing a pistol into the air.
Injuries:	none
Action Taken:	The man, Daniel Williamson, was arrested.

42. Officer Burton is writing his report. Which choice expresses the information most clearly and accurately?

(A) At 7 a.m., Ms. Mowbery reported that a man was repeatedly firing a pistol into the air at Lone Pines Park, where Ms. Mowbery is a park attendant. There were no injuries. The man, Daniel Williamson, was arrested.

(B) Ms. Mowbery reported at 7 a.m. that a man was repeatedly firing a pistol into the air at Lone Pines Park, where Ms. Mowbery is a park attendant. The man, Daniel Williamson, was arrested.

(C) Ms. Mowbery reported that a man was repeatedly firing a pistol into the air at Lone Pines Park, where Ms. Mowbery is a park attendant. The man, Daniel Williamson, was arrested.

(D) At 7 a.m., Ms. Mowbery reported that a man was repeatedly firing a pistol into the air. There were no injuries. The man, Daniel Williamson, was arrested.

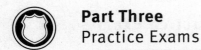

Officer Cherry was patrolling a downtown street when she saw someone cross the street at a point where there was no crosswalk. She noted the following information:

Location: the middle of the 1500 block of Meredith Street

Time: 11 a.m.

Violation: jaywalking

Action Taken: Stephanie Fulton, the jaywalker, was given a verbal warning.

43. Officer Cherry is writing her report. Which choice expresses the information most clearly and accurately?

   (A) Stephanie Fulton jaywalked. She crossed the street in the middle of the 1500 block of Meredith Street, so she was given a verbal warning.

   (B) Stephanie Fulton received a traffic ticket for jaywalking after crossing the street in the middle of the 1500 block of Meredith Street at 11 a.m.

   (C) At 11 a.m., Stephanie Fulton crossed the street in the middle of the 1500 block of Meredith Street. She was given a verbal warning for jaywalking.

   (D) At 11 a.m., Stephanie Fulton crossed the street in the middle of the 1500 block of Meredith Street and received a verbal warning for jaywalking. This was at 12 p.m.

Questions 44–46

To answer questions 44–46, use the information in the following passage.

Officers Donna McLaughlin and Nathan Taylor are called to the scene of a vehicle/bicycle accident on June 21 at 9:30 a.m. The accident took place near the intersection of Woodward Street, a one-way northbound street, and Third Avenue, a two-way, east-west street. When the officers arrive, they find a silver Lexus sedan double-parked in the far left lane of Woodward. The Lexus has damage to the inside of the passenger side door. When they move in front of the Lexus, they see a blue bicycle with a bent front tire and damage to the handlebars on the ground.

Officers McLaughlin and Taylor take the statements of all involved. The driver of the Lexus, Jonah Wylie, tells Officer McLaughlin that he was dropping off his girlfriend, Sabrina Bright, for work. When she opened the door, the rider of the bicycle, Ellie Dodson, struck the door and was thrown partially in the adjoining lane on the right. Ellie was knocked off her bike but landed in a sitting position. She has visible lacerations and a potentially broken arm. Two pedestrians, John Featherstone and Lloyd Thompson, told Officer Taylor that they were walking west on Third Avenue toward the corner of Third and Woodward. They saw the accident take place and helped Ellie to the sidewalk. Jonah and Lloyd both called 911 on their cell phones to report the accident and Ellie's injuries.

While waiting for the paramedics to arrive, Officer McLaughlin takes a statement from Ellie. Ellie explains that she saw the car door open in front of her and tried to brake but could not stop in time. She also states that the Lexus did not have its flashing lights on to indicate that it was temporarily parked. This fact was confirmed by another witness, Janice DiMauro, who was walking north on Woodward toward the corner of Third. She saw that the Lexus was double-parked for a few minutes without its flashers on and wondered if it would be ticketed. Janice also told officers that she saw a cab nearly hit Ellie on her bike moments before the accident; it was American Cab Company car 272. When Officer Taylor interviews Sabrina, she confirms Jonah's story and tells the officer that she had not seen Ellie nor her bike before she opened the passenger door. The officers later learn that Ellie was treated for a broken arm from the accident.

44. In which direction was Ellie traveling on her bike?

    (A) North

    (B) South

    (C) East

    (D) West

45. When Officers McLaughlin and Taylor arrive at the scene, they see which of the following?

    (A) A blue Lexus without damage and a damaged silver bicycle lying in the road

    (B) A blue Lexus without damage and a silver bicycle without damage lying in the road

    (C) A silver Lexus with minor damage to the passenger door and a damaged blue bicycle lying in the road

    (D) A silver Lexus with minor damage to the passenger door and blue bicycle without damage lying in the road

46. Which pair of people called the authorities to report the accident?

    (A) Jonah Wylie and Sabrina Bright

    (B) Jonah Wylie and Lloyd Thompson

    (C) Janice DiMauro and John Featherstone

    (D) John Featherstone and Lloyd Thompson

Questions 47–49

To answer questions 47–49, use the information in the following passage.

At 10:30 p.m., Officers Roque Lewis and Tania Lipton were parked in front of 727 Allandale Avenue when they received a radio call of a family dispute at 717 Metric Avenue, Apartment 345. The radio dispatcher informed the officers that the call came from Ms. Cassie Ballard, who lives in Apartment 343. When the officers arrived at Apartment 345 on the third floor, they heard yelling and screaming. When they knocked on the door, a woman answered. She was wearing a red T-shirt and denim jeans, and was sobbing. The officers could hear a man in the background shouting and slamming cabinet doors in the kitchen.

The woman, Janelle Fisher, informed the officers that her husband, Wayne Fisher, was in her apartment. The couple was in the process of getting divorced, and she had moved to the present apartment four months earlier. She explained that her husband had arrived at her door at 9:45 p.m. He was intoxicated and yelled his demands to see his children. After Janelle's efforts to get him to go home failed, she let him inside so that the neighbors would not be disturbed. Inside, Wayne continued to demand to see the children. When she told him they were staying with her parents, he accused her of lying and threatened her with bodily harm if she did not let him see them. The argument continued until police arrived.

Janelle told the officers that she had an order of protection issued by Family Court. This order stated that Wayne Fisher was not to be seen anywhere near his wife, including her residence and place of employment. Janelle told the officer that she wanted her husband arrested for violating the order of protection. Officer Lipton asked to see the order. While Janelle was retrieving the order, Wayne came out of the kitchen. He was walking unsteadily and smelled of alcohol. He was wearing a green baseball cap, a white polo shirt, and tan khakis; there was a large stain on his left pant leg. He told Officer Lewis that his wife had invited him in and that he had a right to be there and a right to see his children. When Janelle returned, Officer Lipton quickly read the order of protection and told Officer Lewis that the order was valid. Officer Lewis ordered Wayne Fisher to turn around with his hands behind his back, handcuffed him, and placed him under arrest.

47. Which of the following persons first made authorities aware of the domestic dispute?

(A) Roque Lewis

(B) Wayne Fisher

(C) Janelle Fisher

(D) Cassie Ballard

48. Where did the police officers respond to a disturbance?

(A) 345 Allandale Avenue

(B) 727 Allandale Avenue

(C) 717 Metric Avenue, Apartment 345

(D) 717 Metric Avenue, Apartment 343

49. Which of the following best describes why Wayne Fisher was arrested?

(A) He was drunk, which indicated he was likely to act foolishly.

(B) He was wearing stained clothing, which showed his lack of control.

(C) He was violating a valid court order by his presence at his wife's apartment.

(D) He was disturbing Janelle Fisher's neighbors, which was threatening the peace.

Questions 50–52

For questions 50–52, select the object that is included in the figure below. Only ONE of the answer choices for each question is included in the figure. Objects may be larger, smaller, mirrored, or rotated in the picture, but the proportions will be identical.

50.

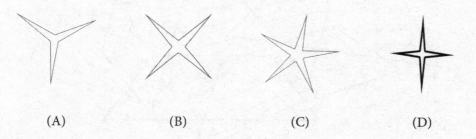

(A)   (B)   (C)   (D)

51.

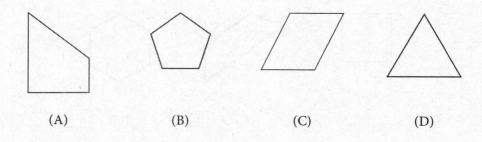

(A)   (B)   (C)   (D)

52.

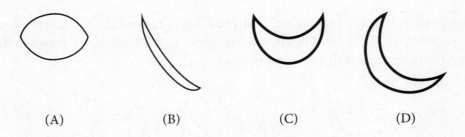

(A)   (B)   (C)   (D)

Questions 53–55

For questions 53–55, select the object that is included in the figure below. Only ONE of the answer choices for each question is included in the figure. Objects may be larger, smaller, mirrored, or rotated in the picture, but the proportions will be identical.

53.

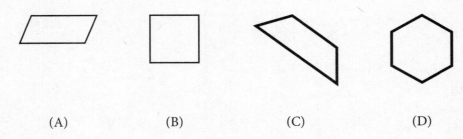

(A)   (B)   (C)   (D)

54.

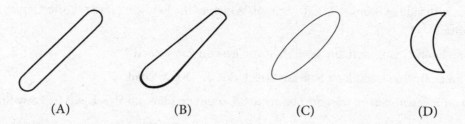

(A)   (B)   (C)   (D)

55.

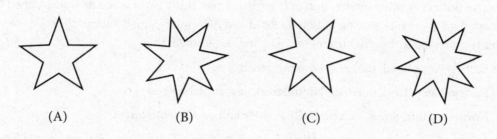

(A)   (B)   (C)   (D)

Questions 56 and 57

Please use the following map to answer questions 56 and 57.

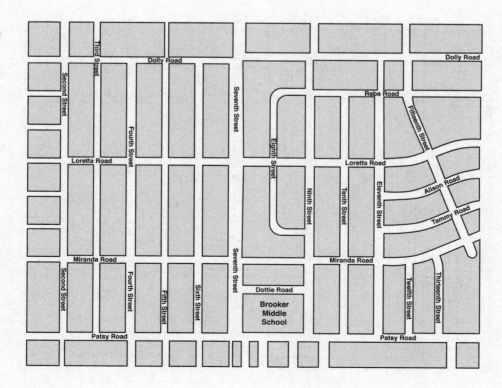

56. Officer Schultz is at the intersection of Dolly Road and Fifteenth Street when she is dispatched to a call at the north side of Brooker Middle School. Which of the following is the shortest route to the destination?

(A) West on Dolly Road, south on Seventh Street, east on Patsy Road

(B) West on Dolly Road, south on Seventh Street, east on Dottie Road

(C) South on Fifteenth Street, west on Tammy Road, south on Eleventh Street, east on Patsy Road

(D) South on Fifteenth Street, west on Miranda Road, south on Ninth Street, west on Patsy Road

57. Detective Bonner is at the intersection of Patsy Road and Third Street when he is dispatched to a car accident at the intersection of Loretta Road and Eleventh Street. Which of the following routes is shortest between his current location and the accident?

(A) East on Patsy Road, north on Eleventh Street

(B) East on Patsy Road, north on Ninth Street, east on Reba Road

(C) North on Third Street, east on Dolly Road, south on Eleventh Street

(D) North on Third Street, east on Miranda Road, north on Tenth Street, east on Loretta Road

Questions 58 and 59

Please use the following map to answer questions 58 and 59.

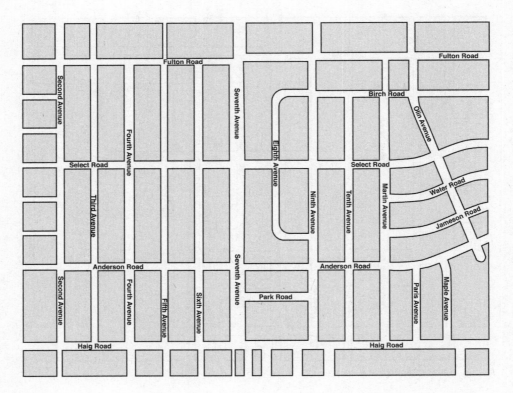

58. Officer Bennett is at the intersection of Birch Road and Olin Avenue. He is dispatched to the scene of a robbery at Anderson Road and Fourth Avenue. Martin Avenue is closed for construction between Birch Road and Anderson Road. Which of the following would be the shortest route for Officer Bennett to take to the scene of the larceny?

    (A) South on Olin Avenue, west on Anderson Road

    (B) West on Birch Road, south on Tenth Avenue, west on Anderson Road

    (C) West on Birch Road, south on Eighth Avenue, west on Anderson Road

    (D) North on Olin Avenue, west on Fulton Road, south on Seventh Avenue, west on Anderson Road

59. There is a report of an armed robbery near the corner of Olin Avenue and Jameson Road. Officer Michaels is being dispatched to the scene. She is currently at the intersection of Fulton Road and Third Avenue. Olin Avenue is closed for construction between Fulton Road and Water Road. Which of the following is the shortest route to the scene of the incident?

    (A) East on Fulton Road, south on Seventh Avenue, east on Anderson Road, north on Olin Avenue

    (B) South on Third Avenue, east on Anderson Road, north on Martin Avenue, east on Jameson Road

    (C) East on Fulton Road, south on Martin Avenue, east on Jameson Road

    (D) East on Fulton Road, south on Martin Avenue, east on Birch Road, south on Olin Avenue

Questions 60 and 61

Please use the following map to answer questions 60 and 61.

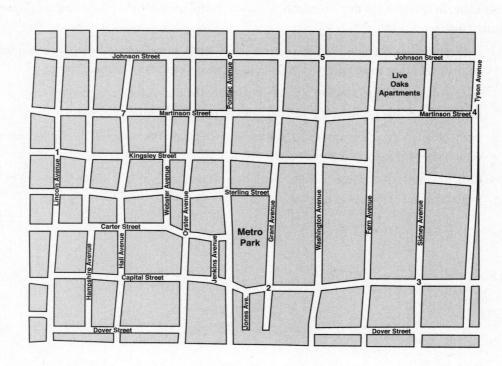

60. If you are located at the Live Oaks Apartments, then travel west on Martinson Street, south on Hampshire Avenue, east on Capital Street, and then turn south on Grant Avenue, you will be closest to which point?

   (A) 4

   (B) 3

   (C) 2

   (D) 1

61. If you are located at point 5, then travel west on Johnson Street, south on Oyster Avenue, west on Carter Street, and turn north on Hall Avenue and travel three blocks, you will be closest to which point?

   (A) 1

   (B) 2

   (C) 6

   (D) 7

Questions 62–66

Read the definitions, and then select the best answer to the following questions.

In State X, a person is guilty of hazing in the first degree when a person intentionally or recklessly engages in conduct that creates a substantial risk of physical injury to another person during the course of an initiation or affiliation with any organization.

62. Only using information in this definition, which of the following is the best example of hazing in the first degree?

   (A) Jessica Topham, the president of a sorority, tells the freshman girls who want to join the sorority that they must take part in a vodka-drinking contest to become sisters.

   (B) Nate Samuels, the president of a fraternity, invites the fraternity's new pledges to go on a guided white-water rafting trip to celebrate their brotherhood.

   (C) Jason Sloan, a church youth leader, organizes a Saturday afternoon hiking trip for the newest members of the youth group.

   (D) Nancy Gamble, the head of a women's club, arranges for an indoor smoking area to be used voluntarily by members as needed.

In State X, a person is guilty of promoting a suicide attempt by intentionally causing or aiding another person to attempt suicide.

63. Considering only this definition, which of the following is NOT an example of promoting a suicide attempt?

    (A) Scott lends a gun to his uncle so he can shoot nuisance birds on his property; the uncle shoots himself instead.

    (B) Donna jumps from a 15th floor ledge after being helped onto the ledge by her cousin Missy, who knew Donna was planning on jumping.

    (C) Marta dies of carbon monoxide poisoning after being shown how to kill herself in this manner by her friend Ruth, who knew Marta was having suicidal thoughts.

    (D) Billy has told Allison that he wants to die, and Allison helps him figure out the number of prescription pills needed to stop his heart. He swallows the pills but is resuscitated at the hospital.

In State X, a person is guilty of appearance in public under the influence of narcotics or a drug other than alcohol when a person appears in public under the influence of narcotics or a drug other than alcohol to the degree that the person may endanger himself or herself or other persons or property, or annoy persons in his or her vicinity.

64. Which of the following is the best example of appearance in public under the influence of narcotics or a drug other than alcohol?

    (A) After drinking eight beers at a wedding reception in a public park, Lottie gets into an argument with the maid of honor and punches her.

    (B) After drinking 10 cocktails, Martha drunkenly stumbles onto the sidewalk and into people walking the other way.

    (C) After taking a hallucinogenic drug, Jeffrey panics at a public bus stop and screams incessantly.

    (D) After consuming a marijuana edible, Gregory lies on a hammock in his backyard.

In State X, a person is guilty of loitering in the first degree when a person loiters or remains in any place with one or more persons for the purpose of unlawfully using or possessing a controlled substance.

Terry sits on a bench in a public park for an extended period of time, waiting for a quiet moment to use a drug that is legally defined as a controlled substance. Officer Beverly arrests Terry, and Terry is subsequently charged with loitering in the first degree.

65. Only considering the definition above, is Terry guilty as charged?

    (A) Yes, because he was in a public park.

    (B) Yes, because he remained in one place.

    (C) No, because he was alone.

    (D) No, because he did not use the substance.

In City X, a missing person is classified as any person who has been missing from a residence in City X and who is at least one of the following: under the age of 18, likely to commit suicide, absent under suspicious circumstances, a possible victim of drowning, or mentally or physically disabled.

66. Using only the information in this definition, which of the following would best be classified as a missing person?

(A) Juliet is a 17-year-old female who has been reported missing from her home in City X after getting into an argument with her parents and leaving home four days earlier.

(B) Johnny is a 25-year-old male who has been reported missing from his home in City X after taking a handgun to a shooting range.

(C) Mariclaire is a 19-year-old female who has been reported missing from her home near City X after taking a long morning run.

(D) Bob is an 18-year-old male who has been reported missing from his home in City X after returning home from a vacation.

Questions 67–70

Look at the provided image, and then select the best corresponding image to answer each question.

67. Which face below is an exact representation of the face above?

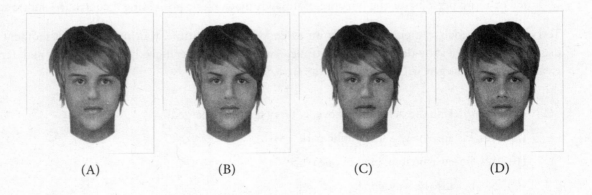

(A)   (B)   (C)   (D)

Practice Exam 3

68. Which face below is an exact representation of the face above?

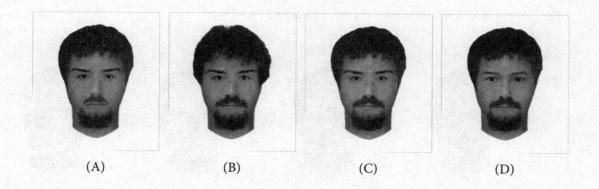

(A)   (B)   (C)   (D)

The man shown here has since grown facial hair.

69.   Which face below represents the same man with facial hair?

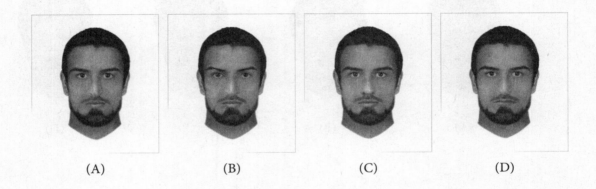

(A)   (B)   (C)   (D)

The woman shown here has since changed her hairstyle.

70. Which face below represents the same woman with a different hairstyle?

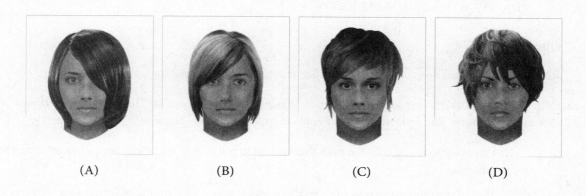

| (A) | (B) | (C) | (D) |

Questions 71–74

Questions 71–74 each contain a set of letters, symbols, and numbers. Please choose only ONE option for each that contains the exact same pattern of letters, symbols, and numbers.

71. &|0N,ñ0jkdajkalKI+#O0;;.<|x>

   (A) &|0N,ñ0jkdajkalKI+#O0;;.<|x>

   (B) &|0N.ñ0jkdajkalKI+#O0;;.<|x>

   (C) &|0N,ñ0jkdajkalKI+#OO;;.<|x>

   (D) &|0N,ñ0jkdajkalKI+#O0;:.<|x>

72. 7*Bb%%#@\?/"ll={*}6.8.wu_¥x

   (A) 7*Bb%%#@\?/'ll={*}6.8.wu_¥x

   (B) 7•Bb%%#@\?/"ll={*}6.8.wu_¥x

   (C) 7*Bb%%#@\?/"ll={*}6.8.wu_¥x

   (D) 7*Bb%%#@\¿/"ll={*}6.8.wu_¥x

73. !¡$[31}M,x (86)_=__+wu!ßðéʃ˜ol>

    (A) !¡$[31]M,x (86)_=__+wu!ßðéʃ˜ol>

    (B) !¡$[31]M,x (86)_=__+wu!ßðéʃ˜ol>

    (C) !¡$[31]M,x (86)_=__+wu!ßðeʃ˜ol>

    (D) !¡$[31]M,x (86)_=_-+wu!ßðéʃ˜ol>

74. √©ʃ¨Δ°R#:;:≠ᵃUUMm$§/|/XYW™ø∞

    (A) √©ʃ¨Δ°R#:;:≠ᵃUUMm$§/|/XYW™ø∞

    (B) √©ʃ¨Δ°R#:;:≠ᵃUUMm$§/l/XYW™ø∞

    (C) √©ʃ¨Δ°R#:,:≠ᵃUUMm$§/|/XYW™ø∞

    (D) √©ʃ¨Δ°R#:;:≠ᵃUUMm$S/|/XYW™ø∞

Questions 75–77

Read the short scenarios, and then place the statements in the most logical order.

Officer Walsh-Perkins is interviewing Janice Washington, the owner of Hair by Janice. She was the victim of a battery. The following six statements appeared in her account of the incident.

1. I went outside and told the man that he had to leave, or I would call the police to report his loitering.

2. Two of my employees told me that there was a man sitting on the ground in the parking lot next to the salon. They told me he was talking to himself and asked them for money.

3. I had just arrived at the salon early to prepare for the arrival of a bridal party who were getting their hair done for a wedding.

4. Another stylist came out with her cell phone and called 911 when she saw I was bleeding.

5. The man got up and laughed at me, then struck me in the nose.

6. A passerby saw the man hit me and came over to intervene. When the man saw the passerby, who was bigger than he was, he ran away.

75. What is the MOST logical order of these statements?

    (A) 3, 2, 1, 5, 6, 4

    (B) 2, 1, 3, 5, 4, 6

    (C) 1, 3, 5, 2, 6, 4

    (D) 4, 2, 3, 1, 5, 6

Practice Exam 3

Detective Rushing is interviewing the victim of an attempted kidnapping. The following six statements appeared in her account of the incident.

1. I tried to hit and kick my attacker as he dragged me from my car, but I could not shake him off.

2. Before he could put me in his car, headlights shined on us from a vehicle driving through the parking garage. My attacker released me as soon as he saw the headlights. Then he jumped in his car and quickly drove away.

3. I had just finished shopping and left the shopping center a few minutes after the last store closed. I was the last shopper I saw leaving the center and heading to the parking garage.

4. When I arrived at my car, I felt someone grab me from behind and put their hand over my mouth to keep me quiet.

5. I walked to my car, which was located on the fourth floor.

6. As I was being dragged, I could see he was trying to bring me to a brown car that had heavily tinted windows and an open back door.

76. What is the MOST logical order of these statements?

    (A) 1, 3, 5, 4, 2, 6

    (B) 2, 4, 3, 1, 5, 6

    (C) 3, 5, 4, 1, 6, 2

    (D) 4, 3, 6, 5, 4, 1

Officer Larson is interviewing Derrick, a witness to an attempted robbery. The following six statements appeared in Derrick's account of the incident.

1. When I neared the door of the store, I noticed through the glass that Myra was chatting with the store's owner, Mr. Sam.

2. After the robber left, Mr. Sam collapsed, and I called 911 because of the incident and because I was worried about Mr. Sam having a heart attack.

3. Mr. Sam reached to open the cash register when the robber noticed that I had walked inside and saw his face.

4. It was about noon when I walked to the corner store to get a snack on my lunch hour. I saw a woman I know from my office building, Myra, walk in ahead of me.

5. The robber ran out the door before Mr. Sam had a chance to open the register. He nearly ran into Myra as she walked back to the office.

6. As I walked inside, Myra walked out and a man started waving a gun at Mr. Sam and demanded the money in the cash register.

77. What is the MOST logical order of these statements?

   (A) 1, 4, 5, 6, 3, 2

   (B) 4, 1, 6, 3, 5, 2

   (C) 2, 3, 4, 5, 6, 1

   (D) 3, 1, 2, 4, 5, 6

Questions 78–80

Read the descriptions of a duty an officer may be called upon to perform, and then select the best answer to the following questions.

A police officer may have to place traffic cones on a roadway to warn motorists about hazardous areas on the road.

78. In which of the following situations should an officer place a traffic cone on the road?

   (A) Outside a park with a one-lane road

   (B) Over a filled-in pothole on a country road

   (C) Near a sharp turn on a road before a bridge

   (D) Before a road affected by a broken water main

A police officer sometimes is called upon to evacuate people from dangerous areas.

79. In which of the following situations should an officer evacuate people?

   (A) An office building with a gas leak

   (B) A crowded bar just before closing

   (C) An elementary school during a tornado drill

   (D) A parking garage with a stalled vehicle blocking traffic

A police officer on traffic patrol sometimes is called upon to determine which driver is creating danger on the road.

80. In which of the following situations should an officer be concerned because of a dangerous driver?

   (A) A driver who swerves a few inches into another lane after sneezing

   (B) A driver who changes lanes on a busy street several times without signaling

   (C) A driver who does not immediately turn on windshield wipers when rain starts to fall

   (D) A driver who does not dim car lights when the officer's patrol car approaches in an oncoming lane of traffic

Practice Exam 3

Questions 81–83

Please use the following information to answer questions 81–83.

You have been dispatched to the scene of a burglary in a hotel suite. Ms. Jansen returned to her suite to find the door ajar and her contents in disarray. An outside window has a crack in one corner, and the lock to one of the bedrooms has been broken. Ms. Jansen reports that her laptop, a pair of earrings, and one of her purses with a wallet inside are missing. A water glass next to the bed has been broken, and a few drops of blood are found on one of the shards. A witness, Mr. Smith, reports that he saw a young woman leaving the room an hour earlier carrying a backpack.

81. Which of the following pieces of evidence would MOST likely incriminate the burglar?

   (A) The clothing worn by a suspect when apprehended

   (B) Surveillance footage that comes from security cameras in the hallway

   (C) The information from the key card related to the last time the room was entered

   (D) The model of laptop carried by a suspect in a backpack matches the one that was stolen from the hotel room

82. Which of the following pieces of evidence would LEAST likely convince a jury that a defendant had committed this crime?

   (A) The fact that the defendant was seen carrying a purse that matched the description of the one reported stolen by the victim

   (B) The fact that the defendant had sold a pair of earrings that matched the stolen pair to a pawnbroker

   (C) The fact that the defendant matched the description given by the witness

   (D) The fact that the defendant had previously been convicted of burglary

83. Based only on the information given in the passage, which of the following statements is MOST likely to be true about the incident?

   (A) The intruder believed that items of value were located in the bedroom with the broken lock.

   (B) The intruder intended to break the water glass during the incident.

   (C) The intruder wanted to steal information to steal the victim's identity.

   (D) The intruder tried to break the window to enter the hotel room.

Questions 84–85

Read the short scenarios, and then select the best answer to the following questions.

Officer Emmanuel questioned Ms. Barber, the secretary at the business located on the third floor of a small office building, after she reported that a suspect stole her purse off her desk when she had her back briefly turned to the office door. Ms. Barber explained that she saw the suspect run out of the office. Looking out of a window, she saw the suspect run southbound, make a left turn, run three more blocks, and make another left turn.

84. Using this information, what would be the most correct to radio that the perpetrator was last seen traveling?

   (A) North

   (B) South

   (C) East

   (D) West

Officer Garrett questioned Mr. Williams, the owner of a corner grocery store. Mr. Williams explained to the officer that he saw the suspect shoplift items. Following the suspect on the street, he saw the suspect run west for a block, make a right turn, run two more blocks, and make another right turn before losing him.

85. Using this information, what would be the most correct to radio that the perpetrator was last seen traveling?

   (A) North

   (B) South

   (C) East

   (D) West

Questions 86–88

For each question below, please choose the line that contains the misspelled word, grammatical error, or punctuation error by choosing the correct Roman numeral line number. Only one of the lines will contain an error.

86.　I.　While on foot patrol one day, Officer Thomas observed a young child

　　II.　playing alone in the park. She was to young to be on her own, and the

　　III.　officer could not see anyone watching her. As Officer Thomas talked

　　IV.　to the girl, her frantic mother found her and saw that she was safe.

　　(A)　Line I

　　(B)　Line II

　　(C)　Line III

　　(D)　Line IV

87.　I.　During her presentation at a local elementary school, Officer Samuels

　　II.　was asked by a student why she had joined the police force. The officer

　　III.　explained to the student that she "liked to help others when they

　　IV.　need help.' The student said she wanted to do that when she grew up.

　　(A)　Line I

　　(B)　Line II

　　(C)　Line III

　　(D)　Line IV

88.　I.　As a young man gave a statement about his car being burglarized,

　　II.　he described the damage that was done to the interior. He also listed

　　III.　what is stolen, including his wallet, passport, and suitcase that was

　　IV.　packed for his trip. Only his empty backpack remained untouched.

　　(A)　Line I

　　(B)　Line II

　　(C)　Line III

　　(D)　Line IV

Questions 89–90

Read the short traffic accident scenarios, and then choose the diagram that best answers the question.

Officer Nolan is called to the scene of a vehicle accident on Palace Avenue and 47th Street. The male driver of Vehicle #2 tells Officer Nolan that he was traveling west on Palace Avenue when Vehicle #3, which was traveling north on 47th Street, ran a stop sign at Palace Avenue, hit Vehicle #2, then hit Vehicle #1, which was traveling south on 47th Street.

89. Which diagram is the MOST consistent with the driver's statement?

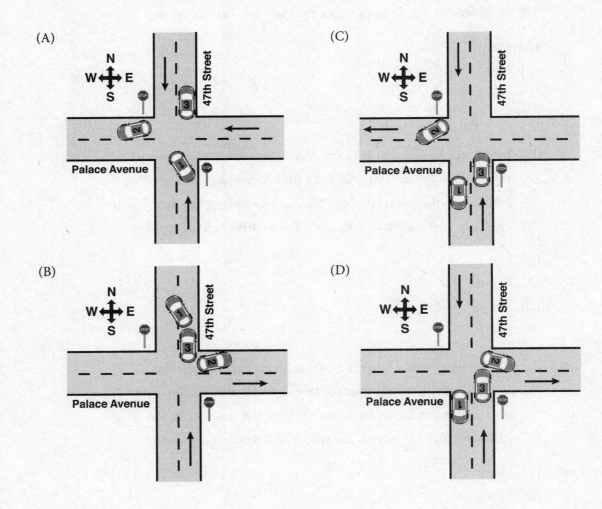

Officer Rumi is called to the scene of a vehicle accident on Sabine Street and First Avenue. The female driver of Vehicle #1 tells Officer Rumi that she was traveling south on Sabine Street when Vehicle #2, which was also traveling south on Sabine Street, hit her vehicle from behind when she was stopped at a stop light. Vehicle #1 was pushed into the intersection where she hit Vehicle #3, which was traveling east on First Avenue through the intersection.

90. Which diagram is MOST consistent with the driver's statement?

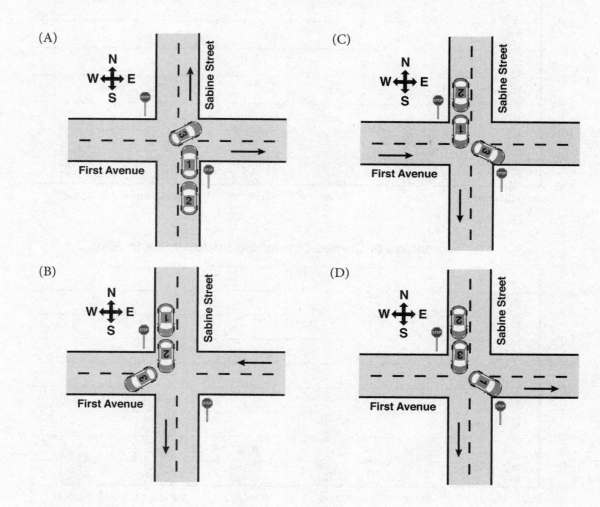

Questions 91–93

Use the bar graphs to answer questions 91–93.

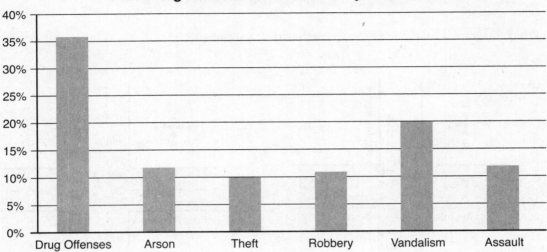

Percentage of Crimes Committed by Juveniles in 2014

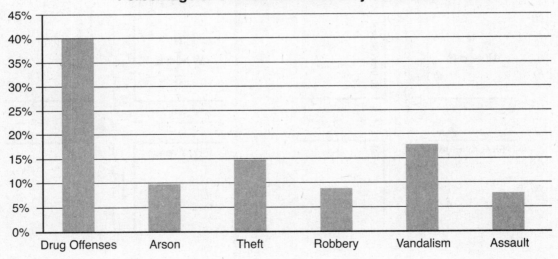

Percentage of Crimes Committed by Juveniles in 2016

91. The two bar charts describe the percentages of crimes committed by juveniles by category in 2014 and 2016 in one city. How many of the categories saw an increase between 2014 and 2016?

(A) One

(B) Two

(C) Three

(D) Four

92. If the vandalism category changed at the same rate from 2016 to 2018 as it did from 2014 to 2016, what would be the percentage of vandalism offenses in 2018?

    (A) 14%

    (B) 15%

    (C) 16%

    (D) 17%

93. Which category of juvenile crime had the largest increase between 2014 and 2016?

    (A) Vandalism

    (B) Robbery

    (C) Theft

    (D) Arson

Questions 94–100

Read the short scenarios, and then select the best answer to the following questions.

Officer Vandy is assigned to the Jenkins Housing Development located on 73rd Street and Enfield Avenue. Officer Vandy has studied the crime statistics of the six buildings in the development for the spring of 2019. All of the rapes took place at 75 Enfield Avenue. All of the robberies took place at 240 73rd Street. All of the larcenies took place outside of 242 73rd Avenue. All of the assaults took place at 73 Enfield Avenue. All of the rapes took place between 6 and 8 a.m. All of the robberies took place between 10 a.m. and 3 p.m. All of the larcenies took place between 4 and 6 p.m. All of the assaults took place between 9 a.m. and noon.

When Officer Vandy is working a 7 a.m. to 5 p.m. shift, he must divide his time between the four buildings to prevent these crimes.

94. Which location and time should he patrol to reduce the number of larcenies?

    (A) 240 73rd Street from 7 a.m. to 8 a.m.

    (B) 242 73rd Avenue from 4 p.m. to 5 p.m.

    (C) 73 Enfield Avenue from noon to 3 p.m.

    (D) 75 Enfield Avenue from 10 a.m. to 3 p.m.

95. Which location and time should he patrol to reduce the number of assaults?

    (A) 240 73rd Street from 9 a.m. to 10 a.m.

    (B) 242 73rd Avenue from 4 p.m. to 5 p.m.

    (C) 75 Enfield Avenue from 1 p.m. to 3 p.m.

    (D) 73 Enfield Avenue from 10 a.m. to noon

On June 26, 2017, three assaults were committed in a short period of time in close proximity. The descriptions of eyewitnesses have led officers to believe that the same person committed all three assaults. Police officers have been given the following description: The suspect is a Hispanic male, 5 feet 7 inches tall, approximately 160 lb, long straight hair that is tied back, a missing pinkie finger, wearing a black long-sleeved T-shirt.

96. Officer Jones has stopped four Hispanic males for questioning. Which of the following items of information provided by witnesses should Officer Jones consider the MOST helpful in identifying the suspect?

    (A) The suspect has long straight hair.

    (B) The suspect is missing a pinkie finger.

    (C) The suspect weighs approximately 160 lb.

    (D) The suspect is wearing a black long-sleeved T-shirt.

Over 10 days in August 2018, a series of robberies took place on the same city block. The descriptions of eyewitnesses have led officers to believe that the same person committed these robberies. Police officers have been given the following description: a black male, 5 feet 9 inches tall, approximately 200 lb, graying beard and mustache, a parrot tattoo on his forearm, wearing a dark-colored T-shirt.

97. Officer Beverly has stopped four black males for questioning. Which of the following items of information provided by witnesses should Officer Beverly consider the MOST helpful in identifying the suspect?

    (A) The suspect is 5 feet 9 inches tall.

    (B) The suspect weighs approximately 200 lb.

    (C) The suspect has a parrot tattoo on his forearm.

    (D) The suspect has a graying beard and mustache.

In January 2017, a series of rapes were committed in an area near a college campus. The descriptions of victims have led officers to believe that the same person committed these rapes. Police officers have been given the following description: a white male, 6 feet 1 inch tall, approximately 175 lb, curly brown hair, a deep scar on the right side of his neck, and wears plastic sunglasses and a gold-colored wristwatch.

98. Officer Patrelli has stopped four white males for questioning. Which of the following items of information provided by witnesses should Officer Patrelli consider the MOST helpful in identifying the suspect?

    (A) The suspect has a deep scar on the right side of his neck.

    (B) The suspect is wearing a gold-colored watch.

    (C) The suspect weighs approximately 175 lb.

    (D) The suspect is wearing plastic sunglasses.

Officer Martinez overhears a conversation between two of his supervisors in which they discuss the fact that forensic evidence points to a famous suspect in a sexual assault case, but that the individual has a solid alibi for the time of the assault. Officer Martinez believes that his supervisors are attempting to cover for the suspect, so he anonymously reports the information to a reporter. After a front-page article goes viral, the suspect dies from a self-inflicted gunshot wound to the head.

99. Officer Martinez's actions were

    (A) proper, because the suicide proves the suspect was guilty.

    (B) proper, because the case is now closed and focus can shift to other cases.

    (C) improper, because the officer should have investigated the outside pressure before leaking information.

    (D) improper, because leaking information about an ongoing investigation to the media without permission is unethical and dangerous.

Officer Sterling encounters a young woman, who appears to be under the legal drinking age, leaving a liquor store with a six-pack of beer. Officer Sterling asks the young woman to show her identification, and the young woman complies. Her identification proves that she is over the legal drinking age, so the officer thanks her and tells her she is free to go.

100. Officer Sterling's actions were

    (A) proper, because the young woman complied with the officer's request.

    (B) proper, because the officer had reason to believe that the young woman was breaking the law.

    (C) improper, because the officer should have interrogated both the young woman and the store clerk.

    (D) improper, because the officer should not have approached the young woman because she was not breaking the law.

STOP

END OF EXAM

ANSWER KEY

1. C	26. C	51. A	76. C
2. A	27. D	52. D	77. B
3. C	28. C	53. C	78. D
4. A	29. A	54. A	79. A
5. C	30. D	55. C	80. B
6. D	31. A	56. B	81. B
7. C	32. C	57. A	82. D
8. B	33. D	58. B	83. A
9. B	34. B	59. C	84. A
10. B	35. C	60. C	85. C
11. B	36. D	61. D	86. B
12. D	37. A	62. A	87. D
13. C	38. B	63. A	88. C
14. C	39. A	64. C	89. A
15. D	40. D	65. C	90. C
16. C	41. D	66. A	91. B
17. D	42. A	67. B	92. C
18. B	43. C	68. C	93. C
19. C	44. A	69. A	94. B
20. A	45. C	70. A	95. D
21. D	46. B	71. A	96. B
22. A	47. D	72. C	97. C
23. C	48. C	73. B	98. A
24. B	49. C	74. A	99. D
25. A	50. B	75. A	100. B

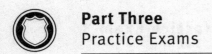

ANSWERS AND EXPLANATIONS

1. C

Choice (C) is correct because there are six windows on the second floor.

2. A

Choice (A) is correct because there is one air conditioner in the photograph.

3. C

Choice (C) is correct because that is the address number on the business.

4. A

Choice (A) is correct because Thieves Market is listed on the building.

5. C

Choice (C) is correct because there are two garbage cans in this photograph.

6. D

Choice (D) is correct because the word in this location is "Antiques."

7. C

Choice (C) is correct because the sign says "10.99."

8. B

Choice (B) is correct because the other three brands are mentioned in the window on the far right.

9. B

Choice (B) is correct because there is one person in the photograph, right in front of Gene Reed.

10. B

Choice (B) is correct because the awning is vertically striped just above the shop.

11. B

Choice (B) is correct because dividing 40 body cameras by 8 squads equals 5.

12. D

Choice (D) is correct because $2 \times \$499 = \$998$; $3 \times \$899 = \$2,697$, $5 \times \$75 = \$375$, and $6 \times \$129 = \$774$, which adds up to $4,844.

13. C

Choice (C) is correct because the sum of $1,200, $3,000, $55, $1,100, and $4,256 is $9,611 (ignoring the $999 earrings, which were found).

14. C

Choice (C) is correct because $19,950 is the sum of each item as listed. Remember to read the information provided carefully, and note whether the value given is for *each* item or the *total* of all items.

15. D

Choice (D) is correct because one-third of $18,000 is $6,000, so the remaining amount would be $12,000.

16. C

Choice (C) is correct because the value of the missing merchandise adds up to $8,200.

17. D

Choice (D) is correct because $2.5\% \times 3,800 = 95$.

18. B

Choice (B) is correct because the total value of the merchandise is $5,480, which excludes one laptop that was found to not have been stolen.

19. C

Choice (C) is correct. To arrive at this answer, first divide the 150,000 cars by the 1,000 cars used to find the 4.5 rate. $150,000 \div 1,000 = 150$. Then multiply the rate of car thefts (4.5) by 150. $4.5 \times 150 = 675$.

20. A

Choice (A) is correct because in this sentence, "corroborated" is closest in meaning to "validated." It does not mean "enhanced" or "added to," nor "challenged" or "disproved," which are negative and do not correctly define the word.

21. D

Choice (D) is correct because in this sentence, "undeterred" is closest in meaning to "persistent." "Careless" means sloppy or not doing a good job, while "surprised" is a reaction to something unexpected. "Practical" means realistic, which is not a definition of "undeterred."

22. A

Choice (A) is correct because in this sentence, "blatant" is closest in meaning to "obvious." "Slight" means minimal or small, while "creative" means something that has been formed in a positively imaginative way. "Dangerous" means with potential negative consequences, but a blatant lie does not have to be dangerous.

23. C

Choice (C) is correct because in this sentence, "cautious" is closest in meaning to "careful." "Open" implies that the officers were vulnerable, which does not fit the sentence. "Hostile" and "excited" also imply emotions that are not logical considering the circumstances.

24. B

Choice (B) is correct because in this sentence, "proclaimed" is closest in meaning to "stated." Though "showed" and "suggested" mean something similar, these words do not mean the same thing as "proclaimed." "Found" means "discovered," which is unrelated.

25. A

Choice (A) is correct because in this sentence, "ruse" is closest in meaning to "trick." A ruse is a trick, con, or scam. "Opportunity" may mean "a favorable time or chance," but it does not describe tricking someone. "Display" and "description" are words that describe actions that affect other people, but these words do not mean the same thing as "ruse."

26. C

Choice (C) is correct because in this sentence, "hearsay" is closest in meaning to "rumor." "Hearsay" refers to secondhand information, which is what a rumor is. "Facts" and "examples" are not hearsay because facts are known truths and examples are given to illustrate a point. "Trust" is not related to the meaning of "hearsay."

27. D

Choice (D) is correct because in this sentence, "flawed" is closest in meaning to "faulty." Although "dismissed" and "mislaid" could be correct in the proper context, they do not mean the same thing as "flawed." "Memorized" is not related to the meaning of "flawed."

28. C

Choice (C) is correct because the correct spelling of the word is "analyzed."

29. A

Choice (A) is correct because it is the only choice that is grammatically correct. The sentence is not past tense, so "verified" is not grammatically correct. Both "be verified" and "had been verifying" are not grammatically correct.

30. D

Choice (D) is correct because the correct spelling of the word is "effective."

31. A

Choice (A) is correct because "their" correctly indicates possession. The sentence describes who owns the "word." It does not describe the distance from the speaker, nor is it a contraction of "they" and "are."

32. C

Choice (C) is correct because the correct spelling of the word is "eliminated."

33. D

Choice (D) is correct because "filing" is the correct form of "file" and is spelled correctly.

34. B

Choice (B) is correct because "site" describes a location and is spelled correctly.

35. C

Choice (C) is correct because "frightened" is the only answer that is a participle, which is what should be inserted based on the context of the sentence.

36. D

Choice (D) is correct because it best presents the information completely, clearly, and accurately, without redundant, unclear, or missing information. Choice (A) assumes Terrence Edwards is guilty. Choice (B) omits the address and is a bit awkward. Choice (C) omits Terrence Edwards completely. Further, none of these state who reported the incident to police.

37. A

Choice (A) is correct because it best presents the information completely, clearly, and accurately, without redundant, unclear, or missing information. Choice (B) omits the time of the incident. Choice (C) gets Joseph Bandy's name wrong. Choice (D) omits the time of the incident.

38. B

Choice (B) is correct because it best presents the information completely, clearly, and accurately, without redundant, unclear, or missing information. Choice (A) omits the location of the incident. Choice (C) omits the time and is cumbersome to read. Choice (D) omits the time and is awkward to read.

39. A

Choice (A) is correct because it best presents the information completely, clearly, and accurately, without redundant, unclear, or missing information. Choice (B) is repetitive. Choice (C) omits the victim, Michael O'Dell. Choice (D) is awkwardly constructed. Further, none of these state who reported the incident to police.

40. D

Choice (D) is correct because it best presents the information completely, clearly, and accurately, without redundant, unclear, or missing information. Choice (A) omits the time of the incident. Choice (B) omits the road conditions that caused the collision. Choice (C) omits the location of the collision.

41. D

Choice (D) is correct because it best presents the information completely, clearly, and accurately, without redundant, unclear, or missing information. Choice (A) misspells Mr. Grey's name as "Gray," omits the time of the incident, and omits who reported the incident. Choice (B) omits the action taken (the women's arrest). Choice (C) confuses p.m. for a.m.

42. A

Choice (A) is correct because it best presents the information completely, clearly, and accurately, without redundant, unclear, or missing information. Choice (B) omits the fact that no one was hurt. Choice (C) omits the time of the incident. Choice (D) omits the location.

43. C

Choice (C) is correct because it best presents the information completely, clearly, and accurately, without redundant, unclear, or missing information. Choice (A) omits the time of the incident. Choice (B) incorrectly states that Stephanie Fulton was issued a traffic ticket when she received a warning. Choice (D) states the incident happened at two different times, 11 a.m. and 12 p.m.

44. A

Choice (A) is correct because Ellie was riding her bike on the street and hit the open passenger door of the Lexus, which was parked on the left side of Woodward, a northbound one-way street.

45. C

Choice (C) is correct because the passage describes the silver Lexus as having minor damage to the inside of the passenger door and the blue bicycle as having damage to the front tire and handles. The other choices do not correctly describe the state of the vehicles when the officers arrive.

46. B

Choice (B) is correct because the passage states that Jonah and Lloyd both called 911 on their cell phones to report the accident. The other choices do not correctly identify the persons involved.

47. D

Choice (D) is correct because Cassie Ballard is the one who called the authorities to inform them of the domestic dispute.

48. C

Choice (C) is correct because it is the address of the residence of Janelle Fisher, where the domestic dispute took place.

49. C

Choice (C) is correct because it is the only choice that describes an arrestable offense. The other choices describe behavior that is potentially troublesome but not illegal.

50. B

Choice (B) is correct because it is the only shape found in the design.

51. A

Choice (A) is correct because it is the only shape found in the design.

52. D

Choice (D) is correct because it is the only shape found in the design.

53. C

Choice (C) is correct because it is the only shape found in the design.

54. A

Choice (A) is correct because it is the only shape found in the design.

55. C

Choice (C) is correct because it is the only shape found in the design.

56. B

Choice (B) is correct because it is the quickest route of the choices given between the officer's current location and the north side of Brooker Middle School.

57. A

Choice (A) is correct because it is the quickest route between the detective's current location and the location of the accident. Choice (D) is of equal distance but is a more complex route than necessary.

58. B

Choice (B) is correct because it is the quickest route between the officer's current location and the location of the larceny incident.

59. C

Choice (C) is correct because it is the quickest route between the detective's current location and the location of the armed robbery incident.

60. C

Choice (C) is correct because the directions lead the reader to the south end of Grant Avenue, which dead-ends just south of Point 2. The other points are farther away.

61. D

Choice (D) is correct because the directions lead the reader directly to the intersection of Hall Avenue and Martinson Street, which is located at Point 7. The other points are farther away.

62. A

Choice (A) is correct because it is the only situation in which someone "intentionally or recklessly engages in conduct that creates a substantial risk of physical injury" to another person. Though white-water rafting, hiking, and smoking could be considered dangerous (at times), only a drinking contest could be considered intentionally reckless.

63. A

Choice (A) is correct because it is the only one in which someone does not intentionally cause or aid "another person to attempt suicide." Scott could not have known that his uncle would use the gun to shoot himself instead of shooting nuisance birds on his property. In each of the three other situations, the individual has reason to believe that the person he or she is helping or providing guidance to commit suicide.

64. C

Choice (C) is correct because it is the only example of a person appearing in a "public place under the influence of narcotics or a drug other than alcohol" who endangers or annoys anyone. Martha and Lottie have been drinking, so they do not violate the defined law. Gregory is at home, so he also does not violate the law.

65. C

Choice (C) is correct because Terry was alone, and the definition indicates that a person must loiter or remain in any place "with one or more persons" for the purpose of using drugs in order for that person to be guilty.

66. A

Choice (A) is correct because Juliet is the only one who meets the criteria outlined in the statute. Johnny and Mariclaire are too old and not absent due to suspicious circumstances, while Bob is also not absent under suspicious circumstances. None are likely to commit suicide, disabled, or victims of drowning.

67. B

Choice (B) is correct because it is the only face that exactly matches the original face. Choice (A) has no arch in her eyebrows. Choice (C) has a wider mouth. Choice (D) has a smaller, upturned nose.

68. C

Choice (C) is correct because it is the only face that exactly matches the original face. Choice (A) has a smaller nose. Choice (B) has shaggier hair. Choice (D) has paler, smaller eyebrows.

69. A

Choice (A) is correct because it is the only face that exactly matches the original face, aside from the facial hair. Choice (B) has thinner, more angled eyebrows. Choice (C) has a shorter nose. Choice (D) has thinner lips.

70. A

Choice (A) is correct because it is the only face that exactly matches the original face, aside from the different hairstyle. Choice (B) has smaller nostrils. Choice (C) has dark eyes. Choice (D) has thinner, more arched eyebrows.

71. A

Choice (A) is correct because it is the only one that exactly matches the original. Choice (B) replaces the comma with a period. Choice (C) replaces the "0" with an "O." Choice (D) replaces the second semicolon with a colon.

72. C

Choice (C) is correct because it is the only one that exactly matches the original. Choice (A) replaces the quotation marks with an apostrophe. Choice (B) replaces the first asterisk with a dot. Choice (D) inverts the question mark.

73. B

Choice (B) is correct because is the only one that exactly matches the original. Choice (A) replaces the "}" with a "]." Choice (C) replaces the "é" with an "e." Choice (D) replaces the last underscore with a hyphen.

74. A

Choice (A) is correct because it is the only one that exactly matches the original. Choice (B) replaces the vertical line with a "1." Choice (C) replaces the semicolon with a comma. Choice (D) replaces the "§" with an "S."

75. A

Choice (A) is correct because it is the only choice in which the information is presented in a logical order. The other choices begin with a statement that cannot logically be at the beginning because she could not have gone outside without knowing why (1), nor would a stylist call 911 without knowing why she was calling (4).

76. C

Choice (C) is correct because it is the only choice in which the information is presented in a logical order. Choices (A) and (B) begin with information about what happened during the attack itself (1), not what preceded it, while Choice (D) begins with the victim arriving at the car (4) before explaining why she was there.

77. B

Choice (B) is correct because it is the only choice in which the information is presented in a logical order. Choices (C) and (D) begin with information about what happened during and after (1) the attack itself, not what preceded it, while Choice (A) begins with the witness arriving at the store before explaining why he was there (1).

78. D

Choice (D) is correct because it describes a hazardous area on the road that could affect motorists. Choices (A) and (B) are not specific hazards, and a sharp turn, Choice (C), is not a hazard on its own.

79. A

Choice (A) is correct because a gas leak is an imminently dangerous situation. A crowded bar, a school conducting a tornado drill, and a parking garage with a stalled vehicle are not dangerous situations.

80. B

Choice (B) is correct because it describes a situation that is posing an immediate threat to himself and other drivers. The sneezing driver, the driver who fails to turn on windshield wipers, and the driver who fails to dim car lights could potentially lead to dangerous situations, but are not directly threatening.

81. B

Choice (B) is correct because surveillance footage would show when the room was entered and what the burglar looked like. This is the best response of the four choices because no clothing was indicated as being stolen, there is nothing to indicate that the key card was used to enter the room, and there is nothing to indicate that it is the same laptop.

82. D

Choice (D) is correct because it is not directly related to the crime described in the passage. The fact that the defendant was seen carrying what could be the stolen purse, was selling what could be the stolen earrings, and matched the description of the witness could be used to convince a jury to convict.

83. A

Choice (A) is correct because there is nothing to indicate that the intruder put the crack in the corner of the window, intentionally broke the water glass, or wanted to steal the victim's identity. The correct choice explains why the intruder may have broken the lock on the bedroom.

84. A

Choice (A) is correct because the suspect first ran south, then east, then north.

85. C

Choice (C) is correct because the suspect first traveled west, then north, then east.

86. B

Choice (B) is correct because only Line II has an error. The text reads "to young" but should be "too young."

87. D

Choice (D) is correct because only Line IV has an error. There should be a double closing quotation mark at the end of the quote, not a single quote mark.

88. C

Choice (C) is correct because only Line III has an error. The text reads "is stolen" but should be "was stolen."

89. A

Choice (A) is correct because it depicts the driver's statement. Vehicle #2 is traveling west on Palace Avenue, Vehicle #3 is traveling north on 47th Street, and Vehicle #1 is traveling south on 47th Street. Choices (B) and (D) depict Vehicle #2 traveling east on Palace Avenue. Choice (C) depicts Vehicle #3 sitting at the stop sign rather than running through it.

90. C

Choice (C) is correct because it depicts the driver's statement with the correct directions, car position, and streets involved. Choice (A) depicts Vehicles #1 and #2 traveling north on Sabine instead of south. Choice (B) depicts Vehicle #2 in front of Vehicle #1. Choice (D) depicts Vehicle #2 rear-ending Vehicle #3 instead of Vehicle #1.

91. B

Choice (B) is correct because there are two crimes that saw an increase: drug offenses and theft.

92. C

Choice (C) is correct because vandalism went down two percentage points between 2014 and 2016. If the trend holds, vandalism would decrease by two more percentage points.

93. C

Choice (C) is correct because theft increased by 4%. Vandalism, robbery, and arson all saw decreases.

94. B

Choice (B) is correct because it best lines up with where and when the larcenies occur. The other choices are aligned with other crime patterns monitored by Vandy.

95. D

Choice (D) is correct because it best lines up with where and when the larcenies occur. The other choices are aligned with other crime patterns monitored by Vandy.

96. B

Choice (B) is correct because it is the most distinguishing characteristic; the other choices could easily apply to other suspects and/or be altered easily.

97. C

Choice (C) is correct because a missing finger is the most distinguishing characteristic. The other choices could easily apply to other suspects or be altered.

98. A

Choice (A) is correct because a noticeable scar is the most distinguishing characteristic. The other choices could easily apply to other suspects or be altered.

99. D

Choice (D) is correct because Officer Martinez's actions were improper. The fact that the suspect killed himself is not a factor. The officer should never give information from an investigation to the media without the permission of a supervisor.

100. B

Choice (B) is correct because Officer Sterling acted properly in asking for identification, which would be true no matter if the young woman complied with the officer's request or not. The other choices are illogical because the officer would not have questioned the store clerk unless the young woman had been unable to provide identification or if her identification had shown she was too young to purchase alcoholic beverages.

Practice Exam 4

POLICE EXAM
Time—2 hours
Number of questions—100

A CALCULATOR MAY NOT BE USED ON THIS EXAM.

Directions: Choose the ONE best answer for each question.

Questions 1–10

Study the photograph very carefully for five minutes. You will be asked 10 detailed questions about this image. Once you have finished looking at this photograph, you will not be able to look back at it again.

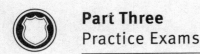
1. Which of the following does the visible signage indicate about the Centralia Community Swimming Pool?

   (A) It is located to the right.

   (B) It is located to the left.

   (C) It is located straight ahead.

   (D) It is closed for the season.

2. What speed limit is shown on the visible speed limit sign?

   (A) 25 mph

   (B) 30 mph

   (C) 35 mph

   (D) 40 mph

3. What is the name of the small cross street located before the gas station?

   (A) Kerr

   (B) Elm

   (C) Lake

   (D) View

4. What additional words appear on the sign for Subway?

   (A) Open Late

   (B) Turn Right

   (C) Your Way

   (D) Eat Fresh

5. Which business is advertised on the sign immediately below Subway?

   (A) Sprint

   (B) Centralia Physical Therapy

   (C) Jack in the Box

   (D) Great Clips Haircuts

6. At the gas station, what is the price difference between a regular cash purchase and a regular credit/debit card purchase?

    (A) 5 cents per gallon

    (B) 10 cents per gallon

    (C) 12 cents per gallon

    (D) 20 cents per gallon

7. Which of the following words does NOT appear on the lower sign for Jack in the Box?

    (A) Tastiest

    (B) Juiciest

    (C) Craviest

    (D) Butteriest

8. Which position on the visible traffic signal is illuminated?

    (A) Top (red light)

    (B) Middle (yellow light)

    (C) Bottom (green light)

    (D) Left turn only arrow

9. Which of the following is NOT visible in the photo?

    (A) A street light

    (B) A fire hydrant

    (C) A pedestrian

    (D) Oncoming traffic

10. What text appears above "GAS Food Mart" on the gas station sign?

    (A) 24-7

    (B) 24 Hr

    (C) All Nite

    (D) Diesel

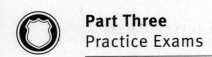
Questions 11–19

Read the short scenarios, and then select the best answer to the following questions.

According to department statistics from the previous year, approximately 2.5% of all drivers stopped at New Year's Eve sobriety checkpoints exceeded the legal limits of intoxication. Officials expect the same rate to hold true for this year.

11. If Officer Evans stops 600 vehicles at his team's sobriety checkpoint this New Year's Eve, about how many drivers should he expect to find who exceed the legal limits of intoxication?

   (A) 10 drivers

   (B) 15 drivers

   (C) 20 drivers

   (D) 24 drivers

Officer Mudgett responds to a reported theft from an electronics store. The store manager lists the following items as stolen:

   - 4 televisions worth $850 each

   - 10 Blu-ray players worth $120 each

   - 1 stereo system worth $250

   - 2 digital cameras worth $375 each

   - 3 smart watches worth $180 each

12. What is the total value of the stolen items?

   (A) $5,220

   (B) $5,780

   (C) $6,020

   (D) $6,140

Officer Bream responds to a reported theft of a beverage delivery vehicle. The driver was delivering cases of canned soda to a number of corporate client offices when the vehicle was stolen. The driver stated that the truck had been filled with $6,000 worth of soda at the start of his rounds and that he had completed one-fifth of his total deliveries when the truck was stolen.

13. Based on the driver's statement, what is the approximate value of the stolen soda?

   (A) $4,200

   (B) $4,500

   (C) $4,800

   (D) $5,400

Officer Mayer responds to a reported theft from a grocery warehouse. The warehouse manager lists the following items as stolen:

- 4 cases of dried noodles worth $65 each
- 28 cases of beer worth $20 each
- 1 case of light mayonnaise worth $35
- 5 cases of tortilla chips worth $15 each
- 7 cases of muffins worth $35 each

The manager later amended the list to include two additional cases of beer and to remove the case of light mayonnaise, which had been misplaced in the warehouse.

14. What is the total value of the stolen items?

    (A) $1,180

    (B) $1,260

    (C) $1,345

    (D) $1,425

According to department statistics, about 1.5 robberies occur for every 1,000 people in the city each year. The newest population data for this year indicates that the population has increased by 6,000 over the previous year.

15. About how many additional robberies should the department estimate will occur this year?

    (A) 6 robberies

    (B) 9 robberies

    (C) 12 robberies

    (D) 15 robberies

Captain Stollberg must place officers along a highly popular parade route, which involves shutting down a major street and its cross streets. He would like to place three officers at each intersection along the route. The parade route consists of 34 intersections.

16. How many officers does Captain Stollberg need to cover all the intersections?

    (A) 78

    (B) 96

    (C) 102

    (D) 112

In one jurisdiction, speeding fines are assessed based on the speed of the offending driver. Drivers are fined $80 for violating the speed limit, as well as an additional $15 for each mile per hour above the speed limit.

17. If a driver is caught traveling 73 mph in a zone with a 55 mph speed limit, what amount would the driver be required to pay?

(A) $95

(B) $170

(C) $270

(D) $350

The department is setting up a holiday security checkpoint along a busy street. Based on past statistics, the department expects about 320 cars per hour to pass the checkpoint that night. From past experience, the department estimates that each officer can clear 1 car every 45 seconds.

18. How many officers would be needed to keep up with the flow of traffic?

(A) 3 officers

(B) 4 officers

(C) 5 officers

(D) 6 officers

Officer Gripp responds to a reported theft from a gift shop. The store manager lists the following items as stolen:

- 26 souvenir plates worth $12 each
- 41 T-shirts worth $11 each
- 24 mugs worth $10 each
- 14 snowglobes worth $5 each

The manager later amended the report to include an additional four souvenir plates and six T-shirts.

19. What is the total value of the stolen items?

(A) $869

(B) $942

(C) $1,073

(D) $1,187

Questions 20–27

In each of the following sentences, choose the word or phrase that most nearly has the same meaning as the underlined word.

20. The prosecutor engaged in an <u>ingenious</u> line of questioning.

    (A) clever

    (B) obvious

    (C) incriminating

    (D) minor

21. The suspect <u>altered</u> the amount on the check.

    (A) warned about

    (B) changed

    (C) erased

    (D) questioned

22. The passenger was injured when the car came to an <u>abrupt</u> stop.

    (A) sudden

    (B) rolling

    (C) dangerous

    (D) explosive

23. The defendant was ordered to <u>desist</u> all harassment of the plaintiff.

    (A) oppose

    (B) apologize for

    (C) stop

    (D) deny

24. The officer attempted to <u>induce</u> vomiting in the overdose victim.

    (A) prevent

    (B) prove

    (C) lessen

    (D) cause

25. Seeing the witness <u>aggravated</u> the suspect's anger.

    (A) calmed

    (B) revealed

    (C) worsened

    (D) disguised

26. The independent report found <u>rampant</u> drug use throughout the city.

    (A) moderate

    (B) widespread

    (C) exaggerated

    (D) unexpected

27. A tree <u>obscured</u> the witness's view of the accident.

    (A) confused

    (B) framed

    (C) swayed

    (D) blocked

Questions 28–35

In the following sentences, choose the correct option to fill in the blank for each sentence.

28. Because of her age, the victim was more _____ to cold exposure.

    (A) susceptable

    (B) sussseptible

    (C) susceptible

    (D) suspectible

29. The suspect _____ denied that he was involved in the attack.

    (A) vehemently

    (B) vehamently

    (C) vehmentally

    (D) veheemently

30. The judge questioned the expert witness's _____.

    (A) competance

    (B) competence

    (C) competents

    (D) competense

31. The officer tracked down the _____ of the stolen goods.

    (A) recipeint

    (B) reciepent

    (C) recipient

    (D) recipiant

32. There _____ three different vehicles stolen on the same night.

    (A) were

    (B) where

    (C) we're

    (D) was

33. The suspects _____ hiding in a drainage pipe.

    (A) founded

    (B) are finding

    (C) was found

    (D) were found

34. The suspect was arrested in the _____ clothing department.

    (A) womans

    (B) womens

    (C) womens'

    (D) women's

35. The protest was well-attended _____ the heat.

    (A) however

    (B) despite

    (C) but

    (D) although

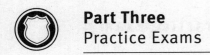
Questions 36–43

Read the short scenarios, and then select the best answer to the following questions.

Officer Little responds to a report of a robbery and gathers the following information:

Location:	9292 Sixth Street
Time:	8:20 p.m.
Victim:	Mrs. Hendricks
Weapon:	knife
Injury:	none (victim was threatened with the knife, but not hurt)
Item Missing:	jewelry box
Suspect:	Joe Hicks
Status of Suspect:	arrested

36. Officer Little is writing a report on the incident. Which of the following expresses the information most clearly and accurately?

(A) Mrs. Hendricks reported that at 8:20 p.m. at 9292 Sixth Street, Joe Hicks threatened her with a knife and stole her jewelry box. Joe Hicks was arrested. Mrs. Hendricks was uninjured.

(B) Joe Hicks was arrested after threatening and stealing with a knife the jewelry box belonging to Mrs. Hendricks from 9292 Sixth Street at 8:20 p.m. She was not hurt.

(C) Mrs. Hendricks was uninjured after being threatened with a knife by Joe Hicks who stole her jewelry box at 9292 Sixth Street. After that, which happened at 8:20 p.m., John Hicks was arrested.

(D) Joe Hicks did not hurt Mrs. Hendricks when he threatened her with a knife and stole her jewelry box but was arrested after the robbery at 8:20 p.m. at 9292 Sixth Street.

Officer Anthony responds to a call from a man who was blocked into a parking space by another vehicle and gathers the following information:

Location:	Merry Hill Courthouse
Time:	3:00 p.m.
Incident:	man blocked into parking space by illegally parked car
Victim:	Joe Bond
Illegally Parked Car:	black Monte Carlo, tag JWQ 577
Action Taken:	In accordance with posted courthouse policy, the illegally parked car was impounded.

37. Officer Anthony has to write her report on the events. Which of the following expresses the information most clearly and accurately?

(A) Joe Bond parked at the Merry Hill Courthouse and then emerged at 3:00 p.m. to find that his car was blocked into a space by an illegally parked car. The car that blocked him in was a black Monte Carlo, tag number JWQ 577.

(B) At the Merry Hill Courthouse at 3:00 p.m., Joe Bond's car was blocked into a space by an illegally parked black Monte Carlo. The Monte Carlo, tag number JWQ 577, was impounded. This impounding was done in accordance with posted courthouse policy.

(C) After being illegally parked at the Merry Hill Courthouse in a manner that blocked in the car of Joe Bond at 3:00 p.m., a black Monte Carlo, tag number JWQ 577, was impounded, in accordance with posted courthouse policy.

(D) At 3:00 p.m., Joe Bond reported that his car was blocked into a space at the Merry Hill Courthouse by an illegally parked black Monte Carlo, tag number JWQ 577. In accordance with posted courthouse policy, the Monte Carlo was impounded.

Officer Grand responds to a call from a man who reports that he has found a wallet. Officer Grand gathers the following information:

Location:	the curb in front of Slippery Water Park
Time:	1:00 p.m.
Person Finding the Wallet:	Ronnie Sawyer
Wallet Description:	black leather wallet with $400 in cash inside
Action Taken:	Wallet matched the description of one that had been reported missing; wallet returned to its owner.

38. Officer Grand is writing a report. Which of the following expresses the information most clearly and accurately?

    (A) At 1:00 p.m., a brown leather wallet was found to contain $400 by Ronnie Sawyer, who called the police, who were able to match the wallet to one that had been reported missing and return the wallet to its owner.

    (B) At 1:00 p.m., Ronnie Sawyer found a black leather wallet containing $400 in cash on the curb in front of Slippery Water Park. Mr. Sawyer notified the police. The wallet matched the description of a wallet that had been reported missing and was returned to its owner.

    (C) An owner got their wallet containing $400 in cash back after Ronnie Sawyer found it at 1:00 p.m. on the curb in front of Slippery Water Park and called the police. The wallet had been reported missing.

    (D) Ronnie Sawyer reported that he found a wallet containing $400 in cash on the curb in front of Slippery Water Park at 1:00 a.m., and the wallet matched the description of one that had been reported missing, and it was returned to the owner.

Officer Patrick responds to a report of an assault and gathers the following information:

Location:	Ben's Lounge
Time:	10:15 p.m.
Victim:	Ben Howard, the owner
Weapon:	box cutter
Injury:	cut arm required 40 stitches
Suspect:	Jane Howard, Mr. Howard's ex-wife
Action Taken:	Ms. Howard was arrested.

39. Officer Patrick is writing his report. Which of the following expresses the information most clearly and accurately?

    (A) Jane Howard assaulted her ex-husband, Ben Howard, at the place he owns, Ben's Lounge, at 10:15 p.m. with a box cutter, and she was arrested.

    (B) At 10:15, Jane Howard assaulted her ex-husband at Ben's Lounge, which he, Ben Howard, owns. She cut his arm with a box cutter, and he needed 40 stitches. She was arrested.

    (C) After reportedly assaulting her ex-husband at 10:15 p.m., Jane Howard was arrested. Ben Howard, the victim, needed 40 stitches for his arm, which she cut with a box cutter.

    (D) Ben Howard reported that at 10:15 p.m. at Ben's Lounge, which he owns, his ex-wife, Jane Howard, assaulted him with a box cutter. The resulting cut on his arm required 40 stitches. Ms. Howard was arrested.

Officer Blum is dispatched to a home where a larceny has been reported. There, Officer Blum gathers the following information:

Location:	80 Cane Street
Time:	around 11:00 p.m.
Crime:	larceny
Victim:	Hobart Austin
Item Missing:	table saw
Suspect:	no description; no witnesses

40. Officer Blum is writing a report on the incident. Which of the following expresses the information most clearly and accurately?

    (A) At around 11:00 p.m., at 80 Cane Street, an unknown suspect allegedly stole a table saw. The owner of the saw, who called the police, was Herbert Austin.

    (B) At around 11:00 p.m., a table saw belonging to Hobart Austin was stolen. There is no description of the suspect because there were no witnesses.

    (C) Hobart Austin reported that around 11:00 p.m., his table saw was stolen from 80 Cane Street. There were no witnesses, so no description of the suspect is available.

    (D) At 80 Cane Street, a man or woman stole a table saw belonging to Hobart Austin at 11:00 p.m. There were no witnesses, so no description is available of the suspect.

Officer Pierre arrives at the scene of a collision between two bicycles and gathers the following information:

Location:	intersection of Second Street and University Drive
Time:	2:15 p.m.
Incident:	bicycle collision
Riders:	Sam Collins and Steve Black
Action Taken:	Both riders were taken by ambulance to the hospital.

41. Officer Pierre is writing her report. Which of the following expresses the information most clearly and accurately?

    (A) Sam Collins and Steve Black were both taken by ambulance to the hospital after colliding with each other on bicycles at the intersection of Second Street and University Drive.

    (B) At the intersection of Second Street and University Drive, two bikers, riding bicycles, Sam Collins and Steve Black, collided and were taken to the hospital in ambulances shortly after the collision occurred at 2:15 p.m.

    (C) At 2:15 p.m. at the intersection of Second Street and University Drive, two bicycles collided. The riders, Sam Collins and Steve Black, were both taken by ambulance to the hospital.

    (D) Ambulances took both riders, Sam Collins and Steve Black, to the hospital after they collided on their bikes at 2:15 p.m.

Officer Marino responds to a call from a stranded motorist and gathers the following information:

Location:	intersection of Juno and Hidalgo Streets
Time:	7:15 a.m.
Incident:	stranded motorist
Problem:	Car stalled and would not restart.
Motorist:	Greta Bailey
Action Taken:	drove Ms. Bailey to her husband's office

42. Officer Marino must write a report on the incident. Which of the following expresses the information most clearly and accurately?

(A) At 7:15 a.m., Greta Bailey was stranded at the intersection of Juno and Hidalgo Streets when her car stalled and would not restart. She was driven to her husband's office by Officer Marino.

(B) At 7:15 a.m., a woman became stranded in her car when it would not start after stalling. Her name is Greta Bailey, and she was driven to her husband's office.

(C) At the intersection of Juno and Hidalgo Streets, Greta Bailey's car stalled and would not restart. She was driven to her husband's office shortly after her car problems began at 7:15 a.m.

(D) The best idea was to drive Greta Bailey to her husband's office after her car stalled and would not restart at 7:15 a.m. at the intersection of Juno and Hidalgo Streets, so that was the plan Officer Marino executed.

Officer Evans responds to a call from a woman who complains about the noise her neighbor is making. He gathers the following information:

Location:	775 Bucket Street
Time:	2:30 a.m.
Complaint:	Late-night lawn-mowing is creating too much noise.
Person Making Complaint:	Ruby Fields
Person Mowing Lawn:	Hiram Stanley, Mrs. Fields's neighbor
Action Taken:	Mr. Stanley was asked to mow his lawn during daylight hours; he complied.

43. Officer Evans must write a report on the incident. Which of the following expresses the information most clearly and accurately?

    (A) Mr. Hiram Stanley decided to mow his lawn at 2:30 a.m., disturbing his neighbor, Mrs. Ruby Fields, who called the police to complain about the noise coming from the mower. Mr. Stanley will now mow his lawn during daylight hours, as he was instructed by police.

    (B) At 2:30 a.m., Mrs. Ruby Fields of 775 Bucket Street reported that her neighbor, Mr. Hiram Stanley, was mowing his lawn, which created too much noise. Mr. Stanley was asked to mow his lawn during daylight hours, and he complied.

    (C) At 775 Bucket Street, Mrs. Ruby Fields was kept awake by too much noise from Mr. Hiram Stanley's lawnmower, which he was using at 2:30 a.m. He was instructed to mow during daylight hours.

    (D) Mrs. Ruby Fields stated that her neighbor, Mr. Hiram Stanley, was mowing his lawn at 2:30 a.m. and was making too much noise. Mr. Stanley was asked to mow during daylight hours and complied.

Questions 44–46

Use the passage below to answer questions 44–46.

While on foot patrol early one weekday morning, Officers Fulton and Watkins are walking through Hilltop Park when they hear shouting, followed by a woman's screams. They run to the site of the incident, at the western edge of the park along Addison Avenue at Pine Street. (The park is bordered by Addison Avenue on the west, Oak Street on the north, Beverly Avenue on the east, and Ash Street on the south. Pine Street dead-ends at the western edge of the park.) Two women are standing on the sidewalk just outside the park gate. One of the women is holding the side of her neck, which is bleeding profusely. Both women are screaming. A bystander has taken off his shirt and is pressing it against the bleeding woman's neck. Another bystander tells the officers that she's called an ambulance on her cell phone.

Officer Fulton reports the incident, while Officer Watkins tends to the woman's injury. She's been cut on the right side of the neck. The cut is approximately 6 inches long but fortunately has missed the major blood vessels. The ambulance arrives, and as the paramedics tend to the victim, the officers interview the two bystanders and the victim's friend.

The friend is Maureen McGowan. She tells the officers that the victim is her roommate, Kelley Masters. They live at 475 Oak Street, two blocks east of the park; they usually leave for work together and walk through the park to the bus stop at the corner of Addison Avenue and Ash Street. This morning, they'd followed their usual routine. As they reached the gate at Pine Street, they saw a man who often loitered on their block. Ms. McGowan said they know him only as Chill. She isn't sure where he lives; a neighbor told her Chill had recently been released from prison and moved in with his grandmother somewhere nearby. Chill had a large male dog that he walked without a leash. Ms. Masters also has a dog, a medium-sized female. Over the past several months, Ms. Masters has had many arguments with Chill. His dog regularly snarled and lunged at her dog and once had torn her dog's ear. He refused to leash the dog or keep it off hers. Ms. McGowan said the most recent argument had occurred early this morning. Ms. Masters had taken her dog out for a walk and had returned very angry. She had seen Chill, who immediately started yelling at her. He said his dog had been taken away by Animal Control, and he blamed Ms. Masters for calling the city. Ms. Masters denied it, but he continued shouting at her, following her to the door of her building. Ms. Masters and Ms. McGowan discussed what to do. Ms. Masters said she would call the precinct house when she arrived at work.

Ms. McGowan said Chill had been waiting for them behind the bushes near the Pine Street gate. "He just jumped out and grabbed Kelley's arm and started yelling at her," she said. Both Ms. McGowan and Ms. Masters shouted at him to leave them alone. Ms. McGowan said she saw Chill step back and thought he was leaving until he lunged forward with the knife. After slashing Ms. Masters's neck, he ran away. Ms. McGowan did not see which direction he took.

The male witness, Clancy Washington, said he'd just returned from buying a newspaper and some juice at the deli across Addison Avenue when he saw the man and two women shouting. "I thought it was some kind of boyfriend/girlfriend thing at first," he said. "Then when he stepped back and pulled out the knife, I thought, 'Oh, man, this is serious.'" He said he began running toward the man, but before he could reach him, the man slashed Ms. Masters and ran away. Mr. Washington said he'd run north, toward Oak Street. He wasn't sure if the man had turned at Oak or continued north. By then, he was trying to help Ms. Masters stanch the blood from her cut.

The female witness, Marisol Alvarez, did not see the slashing incident. She was walking south along the park on the eastern edge of Addison Avenue, heading for the bus stop at Addison and Ash. She heard shouting, then screaming, and a man came running toward her. "He almost knocked me down," she said. "He smelled bad, too, like he hadn't bathed in days. And his eyes were all red and crazy. He was scary." Ms. Alvarez said she turned and watched him run north then cut through the northwest corner of the park, heading east on Oak Street. The screaming continued, and when she got past the bushes near the Pine Street gate, she saw that a woman had been injured, so she called for an ambulance on her cell phone.

Ms. Alvarez, Mr. Washington, and Ms. McGowan gave the officers a description of Chill: white male, late 20s, approximately 5 feet 8 inches and 160 lb, shaved head, multiple ear piercings, and several large tattoos on his forearms, including an eagle clutching a swastika on his left forearm.

44. Who notified the precinct house of the slashing incident?

    (A) Marison Alvarez

    (B) Clancy Washington

    (C) Maureen McGowan

    (D) Officer Fulton

45. Who witnessed the attack on Kelley Masters?

    (A) Clancy Washington and Marisol Alvarez

    (B) Clancy Washington and Maureen McGowan

    (C) Marisol Alvarez and Maureen McGowan

    (D) Clancy Washington, Marisol Alvarez, and Maureen McGowan

46. Why didn't the two women avoid Chill that morning?

    (A) Ms. McGowan had once dated him, and they didn't think he'd really hurt them.

    (B) They felt that avoiding him would encourage him to escalate his behavior.

    (C) They didn't see him until he had already grabbed Ms. Masters.

    (D) They were so frightened at the sight of him that they couldn't move.

Questions 47–49

Use the passage below to answer questions 47–49.

Officers Travis and Benson responded to a 911 call about a man standing in the middle of a residential street, waving a gun and threatening passersby. The officers located the man on Polk Avenue, between First and Second Streets. As they approached in their vehicle, the man, who was dressed only in a pair of underwear and rain boots, warned them to stay back. However, he did not point the weapon at the officers or their vehicle.

While still inside the vehicle, Officer Travis directed the suspect over the car's PA system to set down his weapon. The suspect rambled incoherently for about 30 seconds as Officer Travis continued to order the suspect to drop the weapon. Eventually, the suspect laid the gun on the pavement and stepped away. Both officers then approached the suspect and ordered him to lie down on the pavement, which he did. The suspect was then handcuffed and placed in the patrol vehicle.

The suspect was identified as Thomas Wayne, who lived at 312 Polk Avenue. The officers then obtained statements from witnesses at the scene.

Gayle Staubach, Thomas Wayne's next-door neighbor, stated that she had heard both male and female voices yelling from inside the Wayne house. She then saw a black SUV, which she described as belonging to the suspect's wife, Virginia Wayne, pull out of their garage and travel west down Polk Avenue at a high rate of speed. Less than a minute later, she saw Thomas Wayne walk into the street, carrying a gun and screaming that he was going to shoot himself. She immediately phoned the police and remained inside, but continued to observe Wayne through her upstairs bedroom window until officers arrived on the scene.

Kenneth Randowski, who lives directly across the street from the Waynes, stated that he was returning home from walking his dog around the block when he first saw Thomas Wayne in the street. As Randowski walked along the sidewalk, Thomas Wayne turned toward him and shouted, "Don't try to stop me, or I'll shoot you, too!" Wayne then waved the gun in Randowski's direction. Randowski hurriedly cut through his neighbor's yard and went inside his own house, locking the door behind him. He then called the police.

Jacob Page was staying as a guest at another neighbor's house, two doors down from Thomas Wayne's residence. Page was smoking on the front porch of the house when he saw Thomas Wayne walk out into the street with a gun. Page could hear that Wayne was shouting, but could not make out what he was saying. Page then went back inside.

Virginia Wayne was later located, staying at a friend's house. She stated that Thomas had become upset over texts she had received from a male coworker. After the two argued for several minutes, Virginia decided to leave the house in an attempt to defuse the situation.

47. Which of the following people does NOT live on Polk Avenue?

(A) Thomas Wayne

(B) Gayle Staubach

(C) Kenneth Randowski

(D) Jacob Page

48. Who did Thomas Wayne threaten to shoot?

(A) Himself and Virginia Wayne

(B) Himself and Kenneth Randowski

(C) Kenneth Randowski and Jacob Page

(D) Gayle Staubach and Virginia Wayne

49. Which of the following CANNOT be determined from the passage?

(A) Kenneth Randowski has a dog.

(B) Virginia Wayne drives a black SUV.

(C) Jacob Page uses a vape pen.

(D) Gayle Staubach lives in a multi-story house.

Questions 50–52

For questions 50–52, select the object that is included in the figure below. Only ONE of the answer choices for each question is included in the figure. Objects may be larger, smaller, mirrored, or rotated in the picture, but the proportions will be identical.

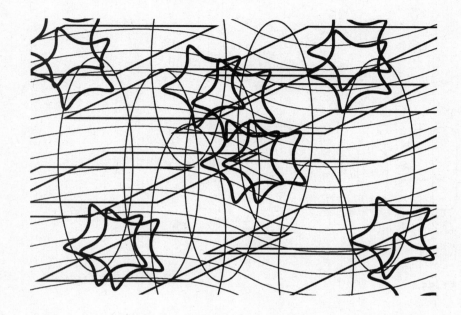

50.

(A)   (B)   (C)   (D)

51.

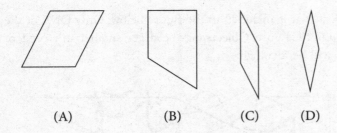

   (A)   (B)   (C)   (D)

52.

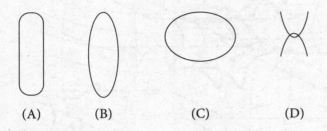

   (A)   (B)   (C)   (D)

Questions 53–55

For questions 53–55, select the object that is included in the figure below. Only ONE of the answer choices for each question is included in the figure. Objects may be larger, smaller, mirrored, or rotated in the picture, but the proportions will be identical.

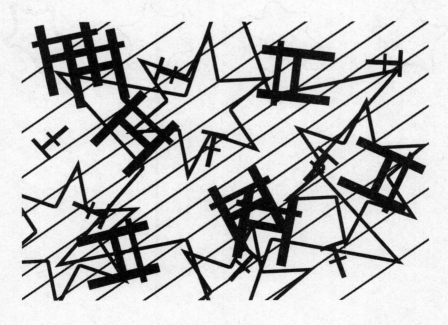

53.

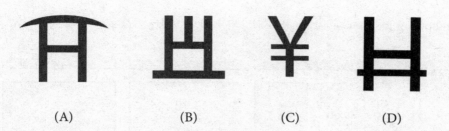

(A)   (B)   (C)   (D)

54.

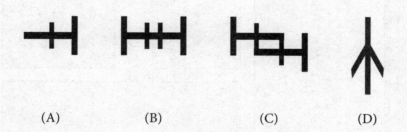

(A)   (B)   (C)   (D)

55.

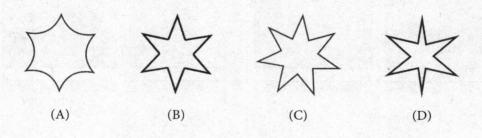

(A)   (B)   (C)   (D)

Questions 56–57

Please use the following map for questions 56–57.

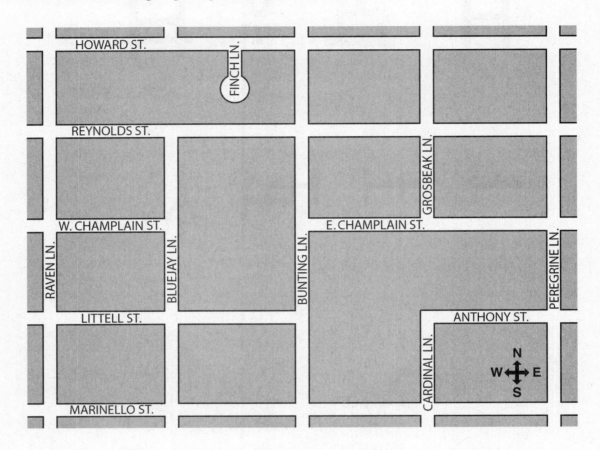

Officer DeKnight has been dispatched to a home at the intersection of Anthony Street and Cardinal Lane. She is currently located at the intersection of West Champlain Street and Raven Lane.

56. Which of the following would be the shortest (least distance) route for Officer DeKnight to take to the incident scene?

(A) North on Raven, east on Reynolds, south on Bunting, east on Marinello, north on Cardinal

(B) East on W. Champlain, south on Bluejay, east on Littell, north on Bunting, east on E. Champlain, south on Peregrine, west on Anthony

(C) South on Raven, east on Marinello, north on Peregrine, west on Anthony

(D) South on Raven, east on Marinello, north on Cardinal

Officer Costa has been dispatched to a home at the end of Finch Lane, which is a cul-de-sac. He is currently located at the intersection of Marinello Street and Bluejay Lane.

57. Which of the following would be the shortest (least distance) route for Officer Costa to take to the incident scene?

    (A) West on Marinello, north on Raven, east on Howard, south on Finch

    (B) North on Bluejay, west on Reynolds, north on Raven, east on Howard, south on Finch

    (C) North on Bluejay, east on Reynolds, north on Bunting, west on Howard, south on Finch

    (D) East on Marinello, north on Peregrine, west on Howard, south on Finch

Questions 58–59

Please use the following map for questions 58–59.

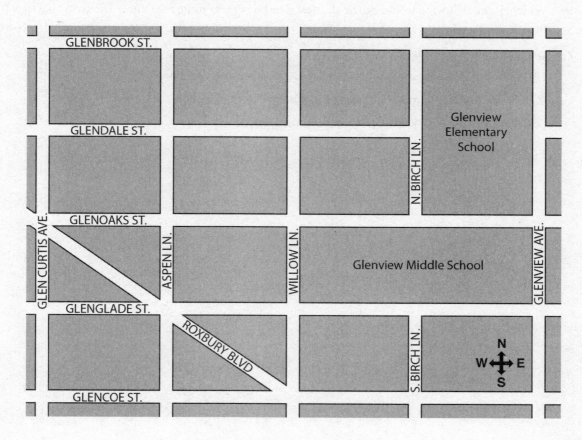

Officer Blake has been dispatched to the west side of Glenview Elementary School. He is currently located at the intersection of Glencoe Street and South Birch Lane.

58. Which of the following would be the shortest (least distance) route for Officer Blake to take to the incident scene?

    (A) West on Glencoe, north on Willow, east on Glenoaks, north on N. Birch

    (B) East on Glencoe, north on Glenview, west on Glenbrook, south on N. Birch

    (C) North on S. Birch, east on Glenglade, north on Glenview

    (D) West on Glencoe, north on Glen Curtis, east on Glendale

Officer Dante has been dispatched to the intersection of Glencoe Street and Glenview Avenue. She is currently located at the intersection of Glendale Street and Glen Curtis Avenue.

59. Which of the following would be the shortest (least distance) route for Officer Dante to take to the incident scene?

    (A) South on Glen Curtis, east on Glencoe

    (B) East on Glendale, south on N. Birch, east on Glenoaks, south on Glenview

    (C) South on Glen Curtis, southeast on Roxbury, east on Glencoe

    (D) East on Glendale, south on Aspen, east on Glencoe

Questions 60–61

Please use the following map for questions 60–61. NOTE: Direction arrows indicate the flow of traffic.

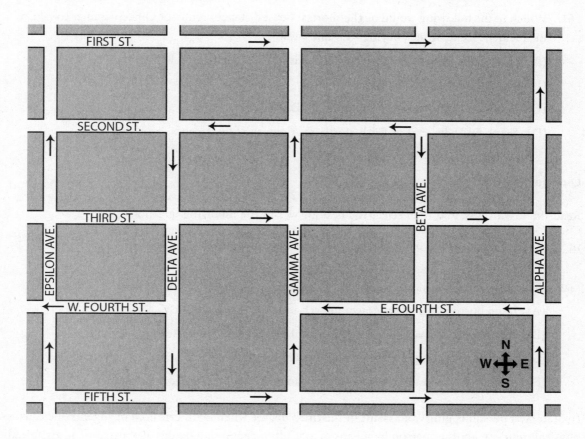

Officer Blandino has been dispatched to the intersection of East Fourth Street and Gamma Avenue. She is currently located at the intersection of Second Street and Epsilon Avenue.

60. Which of the following would be the shortest (least distance) route for Officer Blandino to take to the incident scene, while obeying all traffic laws?

   (A) South on Epsilon, east on Third, south on Gamma

   (B) North on Epsilon, east on First, south on Delta, east on Fifth, north on Gamma

   (C) North on Epsilon, east on First, south on Delta, east on Third, south on Gamma

   (D) North on Epsilon, east on First, south on Delta, east on Third, south on Beta, west on Fifth, north on Gamma

Officer Kramer has been dispatched to the intersection of Second Street and Beta Avenue. He is currently located at the intersection of West Fourth Street and Delta Avenue.

61. Which of the following would be the shortest (least distance) route for Officer Kramer to take to the incident scene, while obeying all traffic laws?

    (A) West on W. Fourth, north on Epsilon, east on Third, north on Beta

    (B) North on Delta, east on Second

    (C) South on Delta, east on Fifth, north on Delta

    (D) South on Delta, east on Fifth, north on Alpha, west on Second

Questions 62–66

Read the definitions, and then select the best answer to the following questions.

In State X, a person is guilty of petit larceny when he intentionally steals property.

62. Given this definition alone, which of the following is the best example of petit larceny?

    (A) Jason borrows his father's lawn mower and forgets to return it.

    (B) At a coworker's party, Fred slips a crystal ashtray into his pocket and takes it home.

    (C) Leaving a meeting, Alejandro mistakes another man's briefcase for his own and takes it.

    (D) Merle uses the last of the lipstick in a sample tube at her local drugstore.

In State X, a person is guilty of assault in the third degree when, with criminal negligence, he causes physical injury to another person by means of a deadly weapon or a dangerous instrument. Criminal negligence is defined as the failure to perceive a substantial risk of such nature that failure to perceive it is a gross deviation from the care that a reasonable person would observe.

63. Based solely upon these definitions, which of the following is NOT an example of assault in the third degree?

    (A) Mrs. Isher fires pellets at birds nesting in the eaves of her house. A dead bird falls from the eaves onto the shoulder of a pedestrian, whose jacket is ruined by the bird's blood.

    (B) Happy to have driven in the last of the stakes needed for his garden, Kenny throws his sledgehammer over his head into his neighbor's yard. The sledgehammer strikes his neighbor in the head and cracks the neighbor's skull.

    (C) During recess at an elementary school near his house, Hank practices throwing his javelin. He misjudges the distance on one of his throws and impales a child with the javelin, severely injuring the child.

    (D) Attempting to catch an elusive fish in a rocky, shallow stream crowded by fishermen, Dack pulls his pistol from its holster and begins shooting at the fish. A bullet ricochets off a rock and pierces the thigh of one of the other fishermen.

In State X, a person is guilty of resisting arrest when he intentionally prevents or attempts to prevent a police officer or peace officer from effecting an authorized arrest of himself or another person.

64. Based solely on this definition, which of the following is the best example of resisting arrest?

(A) In order to alert the officer to an assault occurring across the street, Sinead attempts to flag down a police officer as he is in the process of arresting someone.

(B) After being chased from court by her screaming ex-husband, Theodosia refuses to accompany the bailiff back into the courtroom to proceed with a custody hearing.

(C) Wally yells at and grabs at a police officer who is attempting to arrest his friend, Sam, for public drunkenness.

(D) Colin, in shock after being attacked on a train, runs from the police, who want to get him to a hospital.

In State X, a person is guilty of escape in the third degree when she escapes from custody. "Custody" is defined as restraint by a public servant pursuant to an authorized arrest or an order of a court.

65. Based solely on this definition, which of the following is the best example of escape in the third degree?

(A) Joanie, who has been arrested by a police officer after he saw her steal a skirt from a department store, runs away when the officer is distracted by her belligerent boyfriend.

(B) While his supervisor is not looking, Jason Cunningham, a janitor at the sheriff's office, leaves work 30 minutes before the end of his shift.

(C) After answering several questions at the police precinct about an ongoing investigation, Jesus is thanked for his time and told he is free to go. Being late for a softball game, he runs out of the precinct.

(D) Harrison becomes physically ill during a scheduled visit to his parole officer and asks to be excused before the visit is over.

In State X, a person is guilty of computer tampering in the fourth degree when he uses a computer and, having no right to do so, intentionally alters or destroys another person's computer data.

66. Given this definition alone, which of the following is the best example of computer tampering in the fourth degree?

(A) After Ralph makes up an exam that he had previously failed, Mr. Petrovich, Ralph's teacher, changes Ralph's grade in the school's grading and scoring database.

(B) Sarah Billings uses her roommate's computer without permission to check her own email.

(C) Louise George, a restaurant supervisor, uses her computer password to enter the payroll system and manually correct the number of hours entered for an employee with a malfunctioning time card.

(D) Jacob Johns, a brilliant designer for a private Internet company, gains access to his bank's computer system and adds $100 to his checking account.

Questions 67–70

Look at the provided image, and then select the best corresponding image to answer each question.

67. Which face below is an exact representation of the face above?

  (A)   (B)   (C)   (D)

The woman shown here has since changed her hairstyle.

68. Which face below represents the same woman with a different hairstyle?

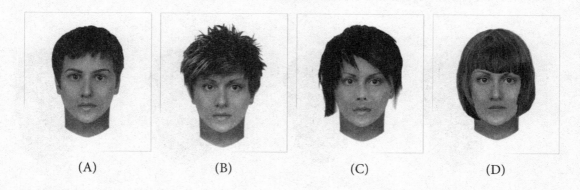

(A)   (B)   (C)   (D)

Use the below image for question 69.

69. Which face below is an exact representation of the face above?

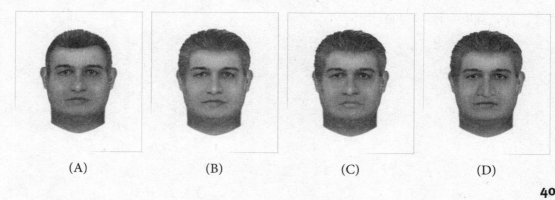

(A)   (B)   (C)   (D)

The man shown here has since grown facial hair.

70. Which face below represents the same man with facial hair?

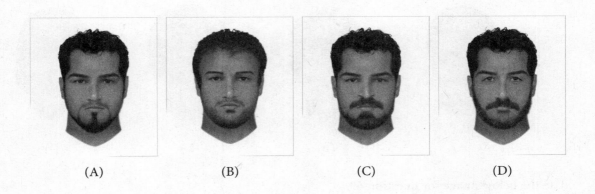

(A)   (B)   (C)   (D)

Questions 71–74

Questions 71–74 each contain a set of letters, symbols, and numbers. Please choose only ONE option for each that contains the exact same pattern of letters, symbols, and numbers.

71. ggjrnm$=sae_pqq'pthyio69

   (A) ggjrnmS=sae_pqq'pthyio69

   (B) ggjrnm$=sae_pqq"pthyio69

   (C) ggjrnm$=sae_pqp'qthyio69

   (D) ggjrnm$=sae_pqq'pthyio69

72. 8BP7A;zzZ7vWbdd,cO0oacun

   (A) 8BP7A;zzZ7wVbdd,cO0oacun

   (B) 8BP7A;zzZ7vWbdd,cO0oacun

   (C) 8BP7A;zzZ7vWbdb,cO0oacun

   (D) 8BP7A;zzZ7vWbdd,c0Ooacun

73. MwvNMWnrm[5SE3]_xX%unr8B

   (A) MwvNMWmrn[5SE3]_xX%unr8B

   (B) MwvNMWnrm(5SE3)_xX%unr8B

   (C) MwvNMWnrm[5SE3]_xX%unr8B

   (D) MwvNMWnrm[S5E3]_xX%unr8B

74. i!lOopqpbdp2S5_7/Zkhhkbc

   (A) i!lOopqpbdp2S5_7/Zkhhkbc

   (B) il!Oopqpbdp2S5_7/Zkhhkbc

   (C) i!lOopqqbdp2S5_7/Zkhhkbc

   (D) i!lOopqpbdp2S5_7/Zkhkhbc

Questions 75–77

Read the short scenarios, and then place the statements in the most logical order.

Officer Grimm is interviewing the victim of an assault. The following six statements appeared in the victim's account of the incident.

1. He told me not to worry about it, but I called for an employee and pointed out the line-cutter.

2. I was waiting in line to get a coffee at the coffee place I visit every morning.

3. I told him it was 8:45, and he thanked me and turned away, remaining in line in front of me.

4. When the employee asked him to move back, he shoved me as he walked past, knocking me into a table and cutting open the back of my head.

5. A guy about 6 feet tall and 200 pounds stepped in front of me and asked me what time it was.

6. I tapped the man on the shoulder and told him that he needed to go to the back of the line.

75. What is the most logical order of these statements?

   (A) 2, 5, 6, 1, 3, 4

   (B) 5, 3, 2, 1, 6, 4

   (C) 2, 5, 3, 6, 1, 4

   (D) 5, 4, 2, 6, 1, 3

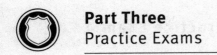
Officer Calderon is interviewing the victim of a theft. The following six statements appeared in the victim's account of the incident.

1. When I left the store, I saw that my bike was gone, and so was the bike chain.

2. The bookstore manager told me she has complained to the police before about the broken bike rack, but they haven't done anything about it.

3. I stopped at the bookstore and chained my bike up to the rack on the sidewalk out front.

4. Upon further inspection, I noticed that the bolt securing the bike rack to the sidewalk was gone, so the rack could be lifted and a bike chain removed without unlocking it.

5. While I was shopping, I saw a guy, about five and a half feet tall with short dark hair, standing near the bike rack, but I didn't pay too much attention.

6. I went back into the bookstore and asked the manager if she could call the police and report my bike stolen.

76. What is the most logical order of these statements?

(A) 3, 5, 1, 4, 6, 2

(B) 1, 3, 4, 5, 2, 6

(C) 3, 1, 2, 5, 4, 6

(D) 5, 3, 4, 1, 6, 2

Officer Reuss is interviewing the victim of an attempted kidnapping. The following six statements appeared in the victim's account of the incident.

1. It was just before midnight, and I drove to the local drug store to drop off a movie rental at the kiosk out in front of the store.

2. I returned my movie rental, and as I walked back toward my car, I heard a man call for help. He was kneeling next to a van farther back in the lot, where the lights were not as bright.

3. The parking spots nearest the rental kiosk are for handicapped customers, and even though the store was closed, I parked a bit farther away along the side of the building.

4. I drove my knee into the second man's groin area, causing him to let go of my wrists. I ran back to my car and locked the doors as the men got into the van and left.

5. I took a few steps toward him and asked what he needed. He said he fell and hurt his leg.

6. I told the man I would call 911 for him, and turned back toward my car, but another man was standing behind me and grabbed my wrists. He began pushing me toward the van.

77. What is the most logical order of these statements?

   (A) 1, 2, 3, 4, 5, 6

   (B) 1, 5, 4, 3, 2, 6

   (C) 1, 3, 2, 5, 6, 4

   (D) 1, 2, 5, 3, 4, 6

Questions 78–80

Use the following charts to answer questions 78–80.

Most Common Robbery Locations, 2010

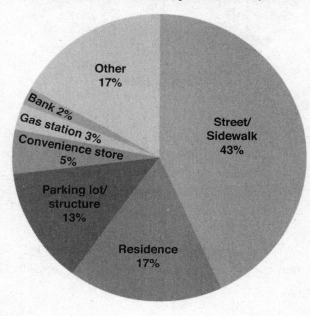

Other 17%

Bank 2%

Gas station 3%

Convenience store 5%

Parking lot/ structure 13%

Street/ Sidewalk 43%

Residence 17%

Most Common Robbery Locations, 2016

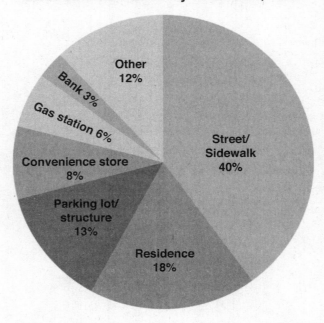

78. Which robbery location did not see a change from 2010 to 2016?

    (A) Bank

    (B) Parking lot/structure

    (C) Gas station

    (D) Convenience store

79. Which robbery location saw the greatest proportional increase from 2010 to 2016?

    (A) Convenience store

    (B) Gas station

    (C) Residence

    (D) Bank

80. Which of the following best describes the data trends from 2010 to 2016?

    (A) Street robberies continued to grow, while other locations stayed about the same.

    (B) Robberies in residences and parking lots grew to be equal to the number of street robberies.

    (C) More robberies are occurring in unusual locations.

    (D) Robberies in store locations went up, but street robberies remained the most common.

Questions 81–83

Read the descriptions of a duty an officer may be called upon to perform, and then select the best answer to the following questions.

A police officer may have to enforce a citywide curfew for everyone under the age of 18.

81. Which of the following should an officer focus on most closely when enforcing such a curfew?

   (A) A movie theater running midnight shows

   (B) A quiet all-night coffee shop frequented by college students

   (C) A neighborhood 21-and-over bar with a strict policy of checking IDs at the door

   (D) A bank with an external 24-hour teller machine

A police officer may have to call for assistance from a supervisor, rather than relying strictly on his or her own experience and instincts.

82. Which of the following circumstances represents an immediate danger to the public requiring an officer to call for assistance from a supervisor?

   (A) A water main breaks, spilling water into the street.

   (B) A suspicious package has been located in a location where a bomb threat was recently called in.

   (C) There is an accident on a busy downtown street, and traffic has to be rerouted.

   (D) A terrible storm causes a tree to fall into a hospital parking lot, blocking the emergency room entrance and exit.

A police officer may be required to remove his or her weapon from its holster in a dangerous situation.

83. In which of the following situations would it be LEAST appropriate for an officer to remove his or her weapon from its holster?

   (A) A driver is speeding down a busy road, firing shots from his pistol in a random fashion.

   (B) Three women fight over a lunch bill. One of the women pulls a knife from her purse, holds the arm of one of the other women against the table top, and threatens to slice her wrist open.

   (C) A college professor is demonstrating the evolution of the firearm when a student pulls his gun from his pants to show it to the class.

   (D) A bank robber appears to have a gun in his pocket, which he points at the teller as he demands money.

Questions 84–86

Use the following passage to answer questions 84–86.

On November 10, Ronald Whitcombe reported a burglary of his residence at 992 West Baron Drive. Whitcombe reported that when he returned home from volunteering at a local nursing home, he found the rear door of his house kicked in. The drawers in the bathroom had been removed and their contents scattered across the floor, and his wife's jewelry box had been taken from the bedroom dresser. Whitcombe estimated that the jewelry was worth about $4,000. Also missing were several bottles of prescription drugs from the bathroom, a laptop computer from the home office, a smart-phone from the bedroom nightstand, and a cordless drill from the garage. Whitcombe also stated that two bicycles were missing from the garage, which was closed, but noted that a burglar could open the automatic garage door from the inside and press the button to close it before departing under the slowly closing door.

84. Which of the following is MOST likely to be true?

   (A) The burglar was someone familiar with the Whitcombe house.

   (B) The burglary was a cover-up for a kidnapping plot gone awry.

   (C) The garage was the first room to be searched.

   (D) There were at least two perpetrators involved in the burglary.

85. Which of the following would be LEAST likely to suggest a suspect was involved in the burglary?

   (A) The suspect was seen pawning a laptop, two bicycles, and a cordless drill at the pawn shop.

   (B) The suspect is a known prescription drug user who has previously stolen drugs like those from the Whitcombe residence.

   (C) The suspect owns boots of the same size and brand that left a boot print on the back door of the Whitcombe residence.

   (D) The suspect matched a description from a neighbor who witnessed strange activity at the Whitcombe residence at the time of the burglary.

86. Which of the following pieces of evidence would MOST likely incriminate the burglar?

   (A) A comparison to a similar burglary in the same neighborhood with a known perpetrator

   (B) A report of a suspect riding a bicycle similar to one of the bicycles stolen from the Whitcombe residence

   (C) A witness description from a neighbor that is consistent with a known suspect

   (D) A prescription pill bottle belonging to Ronald Whitcombe found in a suspect's possession

Questions 87–88

Read the short scenarios, and then select the best answer to the following questions.

A robbery suspect was seen running south on DePaul Street, turned right on Otis Avenue, and then turned left onto Paige Street.

87. According to this information, the suspect was last seen heading:

   (A) South

   (B) West

   (C) North

   (D) East

An assault suspect was pursued by a witness, who said the suspect ran west for one block, turned right and ran for two blocks, turned right again and ran for one block, then turned left and disappeared.

88. According to the witness statement, the suspect was last seen heading:

   (A) West

   (B) South

   (C) North

   (D) East

Questions 89–91

For each question below, please choose the line that contains the misspelled word, grammatical error, or punctuation error by choosing the correct Roman numeral line number. Only one of the lines will contain an error.

89. I.   Officers responded to a nightclub located on Fifth Street,

   II.   where two women had enguaged in a fight that resulted in

   III.   a broken nose for one and two broken fingers for the other.

   IV.   Officers arrested both women and took five witness statements.

   (A) Line I

   (B) Line II

   (C) Line III

   (D) Line IV

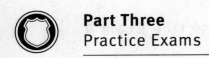

90.   I.   After finishing his shift. Officer Malik stopped at Abe's

      II.   Coffee Shop for breakfast. While there, Officer Malik

      III. witnessed an assault by a male patron against his female

      IV.   companion. Officer Malik arrested the perpetrator.

      (A)   Line I
      (B)   Line II
      (C)   Line III
      (D)   Line IV

91.   I.   Officer Walton responded to a report of a collision between a

      II.   cyclist and an animal. He found that the cyclist had run over a stray

      III. cat and had broken it's leg. Officer Walton called Animal Control to

      IV.   take the cat for treatment and took a statement from the cyclist.

      (A)   Line I
      (B)   Line II
      (C)   Line III
      (D)   Line IV

Questions 92–93

Read the short traffic accident scenarios, and then choose the diagram that best answers the question.

Officer Anthony responded to a traffic accident. According to a witness, the driver of a sedan (Vehicle 1) was traveling westbound on Louise Street when he entered a roundabout intersection at Ball Lane. The driver of Vehicle 1 did not yield to oncoming traffic in the roundabout, and a station wagon (Vehicle 2) struck Vehicle 1.

92. Which of the following diagrams accurately depicts the witness statement?

(A)
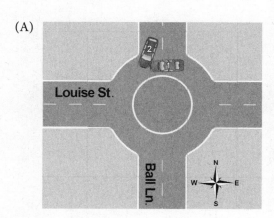

(C)
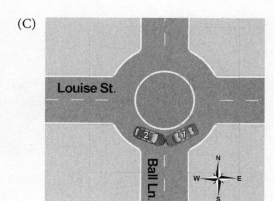

(B)
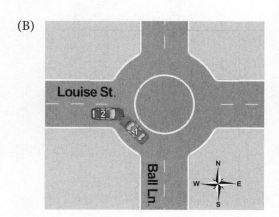

(D)
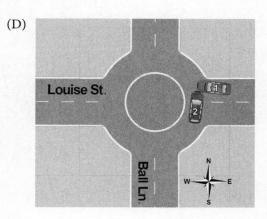

Officer Phan responded to a traffic accident. According to a witness, a sedan (Vehicle 1) was entering Highway 29 northbound via an on-ramp. An SUV (Vehicle 2) was traveling northbound on Highway 29 at a high rate of speed in the right-hand lane. As Vehicle 1 merged onto the highway at a slower speed, Vehicle 2 swerved into the left-hand lane to avoid striking Vehicle 1. Instead, Vehicle 2 struck a van in the left-hand lane (Vehicle 3).

93. Which of the following diagrams accurately depicts the witness statement?

(A)

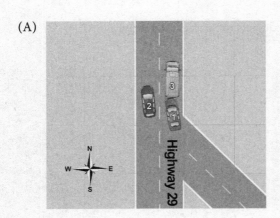

(C)

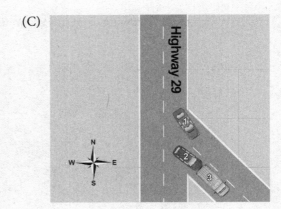

(B)

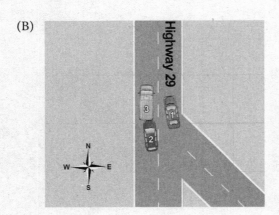

(D)

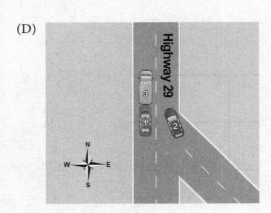

Questions 94–95

Use the following information to answer questions 94–95.

Officer Wang has observed that a chain of restaurants called Sugar's, with several locations in Officer Wang's patrol area, has become a gathering place for certain types of criminals. At Sugar's East, violent gang members gather. At Sugar's West, robbers gather. And at Sugar's Underground, prostitutes gather. Officer Wang has observed that the gang members tend to get together from 10:00 p.m. to 1:00 a.m., robbers from 5:30 p.m. to 11:00 p.m., and prostitutes from 11:00 a.m. to 5:30 p.m. The get-togethers at Sugar's East tend to occur on Fridays. Those at Sugar's West take place on Mondays, Tuesdays, and Thursdays, and those at Sugar's Underground tend to happen on Saturdays and Sundays.

94. Which of the following patrol schedules would enable Officer Wang to MOST effectively observe the prostitutes?

    (A) The area near Sugar's Underground, weekdays, 11:00 a.m. to 6:00 p.m.

    (B) The area near Sugar's West, Saturdays and Sundays, noon to 7:00 p.m.

    (C) The area near Sugar's Underground, weekends, 9:00 a.m. to 6:00 p.m.

    (D) The area near Sugar's West, weekdays, 11:00 p.m. to 7:00 a.m.

95. Which of the following patrol schedules would be LEAST likely to allow Officer Wang to observe the violent gang members?

    (A) The area near Sugar's East, weekdays, 9:00 a.m. to 2:00 p.m.

    (B) The area near Sugar's East, weekdays, 9:00 p.m. to 2:00 a.m.

    (C) The area near Sugar's East, Fridays, 10:00 p.m. to 3:00 a.m.

    (D) The area near Sugar's East, Fridays, 6:00 p.m. to 6:00 a.m.

Questions 96–100

Read the short scenarios, and then select the best answer to the following questions.

Several burglaries were committed in the same four-block area over the course of a month. Based on descriptions of eyewitnesses, it is believed that the same person committed all of the burglaries. Officers are provided with the following description: approximately 25-year-old male with medium-length black hair, approximately 6 feet tall and 400 lb, wearing a black beanie and baggy jeans.

96. Officer Perez stops four males for questioning. Which one of the items of information provided by witnesses should Officer Perez consider the most helpful in identifying the suspect?

    (A) The suspect is approximately 25 years old.

    (B) The suspect has medium-length black hair.

    (C) The suspect weighs approximately 400 lb.

    (D) The suspect is wearing a black beanie.

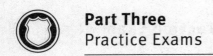

Several assaults were committed around town over the course of a month. Based on descriptions of eyewitnesses, it is believed that the same person committed all of the assaults. Officers are provided with the following description: Caucasian male with very short blond hair, approximately 5 feet 10 inches tall and 175 lb, a tattoo of a cross on his neck below his left ear, wearing wraparound mirror-lensed sunglasses.

97. Officer Lundberg stops four Caucasian males for questioning. Which one of the items of information provided by witnesses should Officer Lundberg consider the most helpful in identifying the suspect?

    (A) The suspect has very short blond hair.

    (B) The suspect has a cross tattoo on his neck below his left ear.

    (C) The suspect wears wraparound mirror-lensed sunglasses.

    (D) The suspect is approximately 5 feet 10 inches tall and weighs 175 lb.

Several car thefts were committed around town over the course of a week. Based on descriptions of eyewitnesses, it is believed that the same person committed all of the thefts. Officers are provided with the following description: male, early 20s in age, approximately 5 feet 7 inches tall and 150 lb, with medium-length hair dyed dark purple, wearing a black zip-up hooded sweatshirt and black jeans.

98. Officer Duke stops four males for questioning. Which one of the items of information provided by witnesses should Officer Duke consider the most helpful in identifying the suspect?

    (A) The suspect is in his early 20s.

    (B) The suspect is wearing a black zip-up hooded sweatshirt and black jeans.

    (C) The suspect is approximately 5 feet 7 inches tall and 150 lb.

    (D) The suspect's hair is medium length and dyed dark purple.

While patrolling an industrial section of town on a Saturday afternoon, Officers Sloan and Dividny observe five teenagers skateboarding in an empty concrete reservoir. The area is marked "PRIVATE PROPERTY: NO TRESPASSING" by a sign that hangs on only one side of the adjacent building, which might not be visible to those approaching from the other sides.

Officers Sloan and Dividny escort the teenagers home and explain to their parents that the teens were breaking the law, although they may not have realized it, and endangering their lives. The officers then call the owners of the property and advise them to construct a fence and post more signage around the reservoir to prevent this from happening again. Further, the officers resolve to keep a watch out for other teenagers who try to skateboard there in the future.

99. The officers' actions were

    (A) proper, because they removed the teenagers from a potentially dangerous situation and advised the property owners on how to make the area safer.

    (B) improper, because they have no jurisdiction over what happens on private property.

    (C) improper, because they should have arrested the parents for neglecting to closely supervise their children.

    (D) proper, because they removed potentially dangerous teenagers from the street and thereby protected the public.

Smoke is billowing from a window many floors above the street in a high-rise apartment building. Officer Chin sees the smoke from his patrol car and immediately calls the fire department.

100. Officer Chin's actions were

    (A) proper, because the fire department needs to be alerted as soon as possible so they can contain what is probably a fire.

    (B) improper, because he should have gotten a closer look at the type of smoke before calling the fire department.

    (C) improper, because he should have called his own precinct first for instructions from a supervisor.

    (D) proper, because fires are not the responsibility of the police department, and he should not have to deal with it.

STOP

END OF EXAM

ANSWER KEY

1.	B	26.	B	51.	C	76.	A
2.	B	27.	D	52.	B	77.	C
3.	D	28.	C	53.	D	78.	B
4.	A	29.	A	54.	A	79.	B
5.	D	30.	B	55.	B	80.	D
6.	B	31.	C	56.	D	81.	A
7.	A	32.	A	57.	C	82.	B
8.	B	33.	D	58.	A	83.	C
9.	C	34.	D	59.	C	84.	D
10.	A	35.	B	60.	B	85.	B
11.	B	36.	A	61.	D	86.	D
12.	D	37.	D	62.	B	87.	A
13.	C	38.	B	63.	A	88.	C
14.	A	39.	D	64.	C	89.	B
15.	B	40.	C	65.	A	90.	A
16.	C	41.	C	66.	D	91.	C
17.	D	42.	A	67.	C	92.	D
18.	B	43.	B	68.	B	93.	B
19.	D	44.	D	69.	B	94.	C
20.	A	45.	B	70.	A	95.	A
21.	B	46.	C	71.	D	96.	C
22.	A	47.	D	72.	B	97.	B
23.	C	48.	B	73.	C	98.	D
24.	D	49.	C	74.	A	99.	A
25.	C	50.	A	75.	C	100.	A

ANSWERS AND EXPLANATIONS

1. B

Choice (B) is correct because the sign indicates that the Centralia Community Swimming Pool is located to the left.

2. B

Choice (B) is correct because the speed limit sign reads 30 mph.

3. D

Choice (D) is correct because the name of the cross street is View Avenue.

4. A

Choice (A) is correct because the sign reads "Open Late."

5. D

Choice (D) is correct because Great Clips Haircuts is advertised immediately below Subway.

6. B

Choice (B) is correct because the cash price is $2.69 per gallon, while the credit/debit price is $2.79 per gallon.

7. A

Choice (A) is correct because the sign reads "Juiciest. Butteriest. Craviest."

8. B

Choice (B) is correct because the middle position is illuminated on the traffic signal.

9. C

Choice (C) is correct because a pedestrian is not visible in the photo.

10. A

Choice (A) is correct because the sign reads "24-7."

11. B

Choice (B) is correct because 2.5% can be written as .025, and $600 \times .025 = 15$ drivers.

12. D

Choice (D) is correct because $(4 \times 850) + (10 \times 120) + 250 + (2 \times 375) + (3 \times 180) = 6,140$.

13. C

Choice (C) is correct because one-fifth of the soda was delivered before the theft. One-fifth of $6,000 is $1,200, so $6,000 - 1,200 = \$4,800$.

14. A

Choice (A) is correct because $(4 \times 65) + (30 \times 20) + (5 \times 15) + (7 \times 35) + (2 \times 20) = 1,180$. Remember to do the math *after* adding in the extra beer cases and removing the mayonnaise from the equation.

15. B

Choice (B) is correct because $1.5 \times 6 = 9$.

16. C

Choice (C) is correct because $3 \times 34 = 102$.

17. D

Choice (D) is correct because the driver was traveling 18 mph over the speed limit, so $80 + (18 \times 15) = 350$.

18. B

Choice (B) is correct because each officer can clear about 80 cars per hour (3,600 seconds in an hour ÷ 45 seconds per car), so it would take four officers to clear 320 cars each hour.

19. D

Choice (D) is correct because $(30 \times 12) + (47 \times 11) + (24 \times 10) + (14 \times 5) = 1,187$.

20. A

Choice (A) is correct because in this sentence, "clever" is closest in meaning to "ingenious." "Obvious" describes something easily discovered or understood. To "incriminate" is "to charge someone" or "show evidence of involvement" in a crime. "Minor" describes something inferior or comparatively unimportant.

21. B

Choice (B) is correct because both "alter" and "change" mean "to make different." To "warn" means "to give notice." To "erase" means to "delete." To "question" means to "ask."

22. A

Choice (A) is correct because both "abrupt" and "sudden" mean "unexpected." In this sentence, "rolling" means the car never fully stopped. Finally, a passenger could be injured in a dangerous or explosive stop, but neither of those words are synonyms for "abrupt."

23. C

Choice (C) is correct because both "desist" and "stop" mean "to cease to proceed or act." To "oppose" means "to disagree." To "apologize" is to express regret. To "deny" is to refuse.

24. D

Choice (D) is correct because in this sentence, "induce" is closest in meaning to "cause." To "prevent" means to "stop." To "prove" means to "establish truth." To "lessen" means to "reduce."

25. C

Choice (C) is correct because "aggravate" and "worsen" both mean "to make more severe." To "calm" means to "soothe." To "reveal" means to "show." To "disguise" means to "obscure or conceal."

26. B

Choice (B) is correct because in this sentence, "rampant" is closest in meaning to "widespread." "Moderate" means "reasonable." "Exaggerate" means "enlarge beyond the truth." "Unexpected" means "unforeseen."

27. D

Choice (D) is correct because in this sentence, "obscured" is closest in meaning to "blocked," both meaning "hid." To "confuse" means to "disturb or blur." To "frame," in this sentence, could mean to "enclose or surround." To "sway" means to "influence for change," as in someone's opinion.

28. C

Choice (C) is correct because "susceptible" is the correctly spelled option.

29. A

Choice (A) is correct because "vehemently" is the correctly spelled option.

30. B

Choice (B) is correct because "competence" is the correctly spelled option.

31. C

Choice (C) is correct because "recipient" is the correctly spelled option.

32. A

Choice (A) is correct because "were" is the correctly spelled option.

33. D

Choice (D) is correct because "were found" matches the plural subject "suspects."

34. D

Choice (D) is correct because "women" is already plural, so the apostrophe should be placed before the "s."

35. B

Choice (B) is correct because "despite" is the grammatically correct word to fill in the blank.

36. A

Choice (A) is correct because it best presents the information completely, clearly, and accurately, without redundant, unclear, or missing information. Choice (B) implies Joe Hicks threatened the jewelry box. Choice (C) mistakes the suspect's name, Joe, for John. Choices (B), (C), and (D) do not indicate that Mrs. Hendricks reported the crime.

37. D

Choice (D) is correct because it best presents the information completely, clearly, and accurately, without redundant, unclear, or missing information. Choice (A) omits the action taken. Choices (B) and (C) are both awkwardly written and fail to mention who reported the incident.

38. B

Choice (B) is correct because it best presents the information completely, clearly, and accurately, without redundant, unclear, or missing information. Choice (A) misstates the wallet as brown, not black. Choice (C) retells the events in reverse. Choice (D) is awkwardly written and confuses p.m. with a.m.

39. D

Choice (D) is correct because it best presents the information completely, clearly, and accurately, without redundant, unclear, or missing information. Choice (A) omits Ben Howard's injury. Choice (B) is repetitive. Choice (C) omits the location of the incident.

40. C

Choice (C) is correct because it best presents the information completely, clearly, and accurately, without redundant, unclear, or missing information. Choice (A) misstates the victim's name as "Herbert." Choice (B) omits the location of the incident. Choice (D) omits Hobart Austin's reporting of the incident.

41. C

Choice (C) is correct because it best presents the information completely, clearly, and accurately, without redundant, unclear, or missing information. Choice (A) omits the time of the incident. Choice (B) is repetitive, mentioning the bikes and the collision twice. Choice (D) omits the location of the incident and does not mention who reported the incident to police.

42. A

Choice (A) is correct because it best presents the information completely, clearly, and accurately, without redundant, unclear, or missing information. Choice (B) omits the location of the incident. Choice (C) doesn't state who drove Greta Bailey to her husband's office. Choice (D) is too conversational for a formal report.

43. B

Choice (B) is correct because it best presents the information completely, clearly, and accurately, without redundant, unclear, or missing information. Choices (A) and (D) omit the location of the incident. Choice (C) omits Mrs. Fields's reporting of the incident.

44. D

Choice (D) is correct because the passage states that "Officer Fulton reports the incident."

45. B

Choice (B) is correct because the passage states that Marisol Alvarez "did not see the slashing incident."

46. C

Choice (C) is correct because the passage states he was waiting in the bushes.

47. D

Choice (D) is correct because the passage states that Jacob Page was staying as a guest at a neighbor's house.

48. B

Choice (B) is correct because Wayne threatened to shoot himself and threatened to shoot Randowski if he tried to stop Wayne.

49. C

Choice (C) is correct because all the other options can be confirmed from the information in the passage. Jacob Page stated that he was outside for a smoke, but says nothing about using a vape pen.

50. A

Choice (A) is correct because it is the only shape found in the design.

51. C

Choice (C) is correct because it is the only shape found in the design.

52. B

Choice (B) is correct because it is the only shape found in the design.

53. D

Choice (D) is correct because it is the only shape found in the design.

54. A

Choice (A) is correct because it is the only shape found in the design.

55. B

Choice (B) is correct because it is the only shape found in the design.

56. D

Choice (D) is correct because it provides the shortest route to the incident scene.

57. C

Choice (C) is correct because it provides the shortest route to the incident scene.

58. A

Choice (A) is correct because it provides the shortest route to the incident scene.

59. C

Choice (C) is correct because it provides the shortest route to the incident scene.

60. B

Choice (B) is correct because it provides the shortest route to the incident scene while obeying all traffic laws.

61. D

Choice (D) is correct because it provides the shortest route to the incident scene while obeying all traffic laws.

62. B

Choice (B) is correct because it is the only one in which the person intentionally steals property.

63. A

Choice (A) is correct because it does not meet the parameters of the crime since the pedestrian was not injured.

64. C

Choice (C) is correct because Wally is directly trying to interfere with the officer's arrest of his friend. Choice (A) features an unintentional interference, and Choices (B) and (D) do not involve an arrest in progress.

65. A

Choice (A) is correct because Joanie is in custody when she escapes. The people in Choices (B) and (C) are not in custody, and Harrison in Choice (D) asks to be excused.

66. D

Choice (D) is correct because Jacob Johns both accesses the bank's system without authorization and changes his data. Both people in Choices (A) and (C) are authorized users, and although Sarah in Choice (B) uses her roommate's computer without permission, she does not alter or destroy data.

67. C

Choice (C) is correct because it is the only face that exactly matches the original face. Choice (A) has a fuller mouth. Choice (B) has a narrower mouth and bigger nose. Choice (D) has darker, more defined eyebrows and a narrower mouth.

68. B

Choice (B) is correct because it is the only face that exactly matches the original face, aside from the hairstyle. Choice (A) has thicker eyebrows and wider eyes. Choice (C) has a less prominent nose. Choice (D) has thinner lips.

69. B

Choice (B) is correct because it is the only face that exactly matches the original face. Choice (A) has a different hairline and style. Choice (C) has fuller lips, and Choice (D) has a broader nose.

70. A

Choice (A) is correct because it is the only face that exactly matches the original face, aside from the facial hair. Choice (B) has thinner eyebrows and a different hairline. Choice (C) has a longer, more pointed nose. Choice (D) has heavier eyelids and a bigger nose.

71. D

Choice (D) is correct because it is the only option that exactly matches the original. Choice (A) replaces the dollar sign with an "S." Choice (B) replaces the apostrophe with quotation marks. Choice (C) replaces the second "q" with a "p."

72. B

Choice (B) is correct because it is the only option that exactly matches the original. Choice (A) swaps the "v" and "W" and changes them from lowercase to uppercase. Choice (C) replaces the second "d" with a "b." Choice (D) transposes the "O" and "0."

73. C

Choice (C) is correct because it is the only option that exactly matches the original. Choice (A) replaces the first "n" with an "m." Choice (B) replaces the first bracket with a parenthesis. Choice (D) transposes the "5" and "S."

74. A

Choice (A) is correct because it is the only option that exactly matches the original. Choice (B) swaps the "!" and the "1." Choice (C) replaces the second "p" with a "q." Choice (D) transposes the "hk" to "kh."

75. C

Choice (C) is correct because it places the statements in the most coherent and logical order. Choices (B) and (D) start mid-incident (5), before we know where the victim is or why he or she is there (2). Choice (A) explains where the victim is and why (2), but has the victim telling the line-cutter the time (3) after their interaction has already turned confrontational (6, 1).

76. A

Choice (A) is correct because it places the statements in the most coherent and logical order. Choice (B) starts with the victim finding his or her bike is stolen out of context to the story (1). Choice (D) depicts the victim noticing the bike rack is not secure (4), but leaving it there anyway (1), which is less likely to have happened. Choice (C) depicts the victim discussing the broken bike back with the bookstore manager (2) before going back into the bookstore to have her call the police (6).

77. C

Choice (C) is correct because it places the statements in the most coherent and logical order. Choices (A) and (D) depict the victim returning the movie rental (1, 2) before finding a parking spot (3). Choice (B) depicts the victim approaching the kidnapper (5) before parking (3) or hearing the kidnapper cry for help (2).

78. B

Choice (B) is correct because the percentage of robberies in parking lots/structures was 13% on both charts.

79. B

Choice (B) is correct because while both the gas station and convenience store showed a 3% increase, the 3% increase in gas station robberies represented a doubling of the previous rate.

80. D

Choice (D) is correct because it is the only statement that is accurate based on the data. Street robberies and robberies in "other" locations decreased, and residential robberies and parking lot robberies do not equal street robberies combined, let alone separate robberies.

81. A

Choice (A) is correct because teenagers attempting to stay out later than allowed under the curfew would be most likely to go to the movie theater, where they might not be questioned about their age and where large numbers of them could get together.

82. B

Choice (B) is correct because a potential bomb threat would be the most dangerous situation to require assistance.

83. C

Choice (C) is correct because it does not present an immediately dangerous situation.

84. D

Choice (D) is correct because the theft of two bicycles, as well as several additional items, would be nearly impossible for a lone burglar to carry off.

85. B

Choice (B) is correct because it does not link a suspect to the specific crime.

86. D

Choice (D) is correct because it would provide the most compelling link between the suspect and the specific crime.

87. A

Choice (A) is correct because the suspect was originally traveling south, then turned right to travel west, and then turned left to travel south once more.

88. C

Choice (C) is correct because the suspect was originally traveling west, then turned right to travel north, turned right again to travel east, and then turned left to travel north again.

89. B

Choice (B) is correct because in Line II, the word "engaged" is misspelled.

90. A

Choice (A) is correct because Line I contains an incomplete sentence; rather than a period after the word "shift," a comma should be used.

91. C

Choice (C) is correct because in Line III, the word "it's" contains an unnecessary apostrophe.

92. D

Choice (D) is correct because it accurately illustrates the witness statement. Choice (A) shows Vehicle #1 striking Vehicle #2, and Choices (B) and (C) show Vehicle #1 traveling the wrong way in the roundabout.

93. B

Choice (B) is correct because it accurately illustrates the witness statement. Choice (A) shows Vehicle #1 instead of Vehicle #2 striking Vehicle #3. Choice (C) shows all three cars exiting the highway. Choice (D) shows Vehicle #2 entering the highway instead of Vehicle #1.

94. C

Choice (C) is correct because prostitutes gather at Sugar's Underground on Saturdays and Sundays between 11:00 a.m. and 5:30 p.m., and the patrol schedule given in (C) is the only one of the four that provides coverage of that location on those days of the week at that time.

95. A

Choice (A) is correct because violent gang members gather at Sugar's East on Fridays between 10:00 p.m. and 1:00 a.m., and the patrol schedule in (A) is the only one of the four that does not provide coverage at that time.

96. C

Choice (C) is correct because a weight of 400 lb is unusual and would be the hardest detail to hide or change.

97. B

Choice (B) is correct because a neck tattoo is unusual and would be a difficult detail to hide or change.

98. D

Choice (D) is correct because dark purple hair is unusual, and although it could be changed by the suspect, it is the most distinctive detail provided by the witnesses.

99. A

Choice (A) is correct because it provides the most logical response to the situation and includes an effort to prevent similar situations in the future.

100. A

Choice (A) is correct because it provides the most logical response and reasoning to the situation.